60°

40°

A S I A

TURKEY

EAN SEA

C H I N A

20°

ARABIA   INDIA

MAGELLAN *IS*
KILLED IN THE
PHILIPPINES, 1521

PACIFIC
OCEAN

CEYLON

PHILIPPINES

SPICE
ISLANDS

0°

DA GAMA
REACHES
INDIA, 1498

A

C A

MAGELLAN'S
CREW SAILS BACK
TO PORTUGAL,
1521 - 1522

20°

AUSTRALIA

INDIAN

OCEAN

40°

VOYAGES OF DISCOVERY
1000 - 1522

40°   60°   80°   100°   120°   140°   160°   180°

ILLUSTRATED
WORLD
ENCYCLOPEDIA

ILLUSTRATED
WORLD
ENCYCLOPEDIA

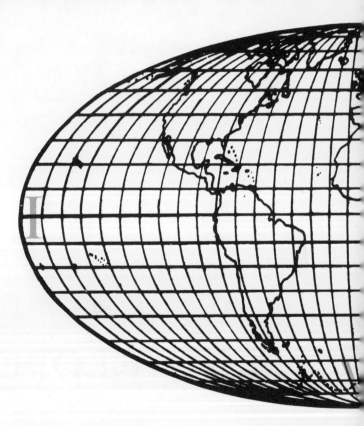

BOBLEY PUBLISHING CORP.

VOLUME **14** VOLUME
Man–Mot

Manitoba

Manitoba is one of the provinces of Canada. It is in the central part of the country and is one of the three important Prairie Provinces. The rich black soil of Manitoba is so fertile that farmers there raise the finest wheat in the world. Manitoba ranks sixth in size among the Canadian provinces, with 246,512 square miles, which makes it almost as big as Texas. In population also Manitoba ranks sixth in Canada, with more than 700,000 people living there. The name Manitoba comes from an Indian word meaning "strait of the spirit." It became a province in 1870. The capital is Winnipeg.

THE PEOPLE OF MANITOBA

The earliest white settlers in Manitoba were British and French fur-traders. They found many Indian tribes living there. Later people came from Scotland, England, the United States, and other parts of Canada.

Most of the people of Manitoba are of English descent. About 15,000 Indians live on reservations.

More than half the people of Manitoba are farmers. They raise large crops of wheat and other grains, and also pota-

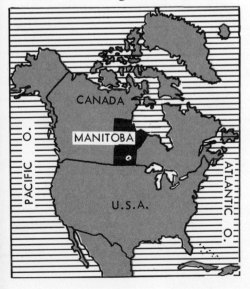

Canadian National Railways

About 35,000,000 pounds of fish are caught in Manitoba's lakes every year. The fisherman is preparing his boat before setting out on one of the northern lakes.

toes, beets, and soybeans. Many farmers raise beef and dairy cattle, and some keep bees for their honey.

Many people live in the cities and work in dairy plants, meat-packing plants, and flour mills. Others work in large factories that make railroad cars, lumber and wood products, and paper.

People also work in rich mines that produce gold, copper, zinc, and other valuable minerals. Others are fishermen who catch whitefish, pickerel, pike, and the Winnipeg goldeye. Still others work in the spruce forests, cutting down the timber that is used to make lumber products and paper. One of the important jobs in Manitoba is fur-trapping. Men catch muskrats and other fur-bearing animals in the forests, while some raise minks on farms.

Most of the people of Manitoba are Protestants, but there are also many Roman Catholics.

Nat'l Film Board

Manitoba is a great wheat-growing area. In the world's wheat markets, "Manitoba No. 1 Hard" is the name given to the finest wheat. Here a threshing machine builds hills of wheat straw and chaff.

WHAT MANITOBA IS LIKE

The northeastern part of Manitoba, along Hudson Bay, is a cold, rocky region where the soil is not very good for farming. Few people live there. The central part of Manitoba is a large plateau, a high, level place, covered with forests. The important minerals are in this region.

The southern part of Manitoba is a rich prairie region. It is part of the very fertile Red River Valley that extends down into North Dakota in the United States. This region is fertile because millions of years ago it was the bottom of a large lake called Lake Agassiz. When

the water drained off it left a rich black soil. The grass makes excellent grazing pasture for cattle. Persons traveling through this part of Manitoba will see great fields of grain like those in the Middle West of the United States. Most Manitoba people live in this part of the province. The important cities are there.

There are three lakes in the prairie region, filled with fresh-water fish. They are Lake Winnipeg, Lake Winnipegosis, and Lake Manitoba, and they are so large that they are called "Manitoba's Great Lakes."

The winters in Manitoba are long and the temperature often drops far below zero. The summers are short and warm, and there is much rain during the growing season.

The rivers and lakes are important for transportation in Manitoba, but railroads reach many parts of the province. Most of the highways are in the southern region, and there are airports in the important cities. Airplanes carry supplies to the northern mining and lumbering camps.

THE GOVERNMENT OF MANITOBA

The head of the government of Manitoba is a lieutenant governor, who is appointed by the British queen on the recommendation of the Canadian government. The province is actually run by a Premier. He is appointed by a legislature,

Manitoba produces many of Canada's iron and steel products. The workman is welding parts to the base of a boiler in a Winnipeg plant.

Nat'l Film Board

Copper was discovered in northern Manitoba in 1915, and since then mining and smelting copper has become a chief industry of the province.

Canadian National Railways

Manitoba links east and west Canada. In the south are farms and cities; in the cold north are mines, timber, and fisheries.

Nat'l Film Board

Can. Nat'l Railway Photos

1. The great city of Winnipeg is the industrial and commercial heart of Manitoba.

2. Most of the fish caught in Manitoba's lakes is processed and shipped to the United States.

3. The fur trade was Manitoba's chief industry when Fort Garry, now in Winnipeg, was built.

4. The cold makes fast play necessary during lunch time at a school in the north.

5. Much of the northern part of Manitoba is flat, frozen land, where life is lonely and hard.

Editorial Assn. Photos

which is elected by the people. The Premier has a cabinet, just as the President of the United States has. He stays in office as long as he can keep the confidence of the majority of the legislature. The legislature is elected for a five-year term. Judges are appointed by the Canadian government in Ottawa, and hold office permanently. The provincial government is in the capital, Winnipeg.

Everyone has to go to school between the ages of 7 and 14, and there are grammar schools and high schools throughout the province. The University of Manitoba, at Winnipeg, had 4,490 students in 1953.

CHIEF CITIES OF MANITOBA

The leading cities of Manitoba, with populations from the 1951 census, are:

Winnipeg, population 235,710, the capital and largest city. There is a separate article about WINNIPEG.

Saint Boniface, population 26,342, the second-largest city, a meat-packing and grain center, in the southern part of the province.

Winnipeg, largest city of Manitoba, is one of the world's great wheat markets. Because many rail lines meet there, Winnipeg is called the "Canadian Chicago."

Brandon, population 20,598, the third-largest city, a railroad divisional point, in the southwestern part of the province.

Portage la Prairie, population 6,700, fourth-largest city, a railroad center and grain market, in the southern part of the province.

MANITOBA IN THE PAST

The first white man to visit the region of Manitoba, more than three hundred years ago, was the English explorer Sir Thomas Button. British fur-traders of the Hudson's Bay Company followed him and began trading with the Indians. Later, French-Canadian fur-trappers from the North-West Company established trade with the Indians, and there was bitter rivalry between the two companies.

Almost 150 years ago, the Red River Valley Colony was settled by Scottish Highlanders, who had been driven off their land. Sir Thomas Douglas (Lord Selkirk) felt sorry for them and induced the Hudson's Bay Company to give them land along the Red River where they could live. The farmers had a very difficult time because the North-West Company objected strongly and tried to drive them off the land. The company burned the houses and destroyed the crops, and finally the colony was disbanded. In 1817 it was reëstablished, again with the help of Sir Thomas Douglas.

Manitoba became a province of Canada in 1870. After a railroad was built, extending from the United States, the province grew more rapidly.

PLACES TO SEE IN MANITOBA

Riding Mountain National Park, 1,148 square miles, 50 miles north of Brandon, in the southwest, on Highway 10. Beautiful scenery; bird and wildlife sanctuary; a popular vacation spot.

International Peace Garden, partly in North Dakota, on the southern border, on Highway 10. Beautiful garden commemorates the lasting peace between Canada and the United States.

Duck Mountain Provincial Park, 1,246

square miles, 70 miles northwest of Dauphin, in the west, on Highway 31. Vacation spot; excellent boating, fishing, hiking, and camping.

Baldy Mountain, 2,727 feet high, 40 miles northwest of Dauphin, in the west, west of Highway 10. The highest point in Manitoba; beautiful view.

Old Trading Post, 43 miles west of Brandon, in the southwest, on Highway 1. One of the old fur trading stations of the North-West Company.

MANITOBA. Area, 246, 512 square miles. Population (1951) 776,541. Capital, Winnipeg. Coat of arms, a buffalo standing on a rock; above it is the Cross of Saint George. Flower, prairie crocus. Admitted to Dominion in 1870. Official abbreviation, Man.

Mann, Horace

Horace Mann was an American who did a great deal to improve schools and ways of teaching in the United States. He lived more than a hundred years ago. He was born in Franklin, Massachusetts, in 1796. When he was 23, he was graduated from Brown  University, in Providence, Rhode Island, with the highest honors possible. Afterward he studied law and became a lawyer.

All his life, Horace Mann worked to improve conditions everywhere he possibly could. He was especially interested in making the schools better. Once he traveled to Europe at his own expense to find out if anything in the European school system might be used to improve schools in the United States. He was often called upon to give legal advice to schools, and he never charged them a fee. He was strongly opposed to slavery, and both wrote and lectured on the evils of such a condition.

For many years Horace Mann served in the Massachusetts State Legislature, and was responsible for the founding of many teachers' colleges, which at that time were called "normal schools." In 1837 he became secretary of the Massachusetts State Board of Education. As secretary he was responsible for improving public schools in that state to such an extent that he has since been considered the father of the American public school. He served also in the House of Representatives in Washington.

Horace Mann's last years were spent as president of Antioch College in Yellow Springs, Ohio. He died in 1859 at the age of 63.

Mann, Thomas

Thomas Mann is the name of a German writer who is considered by many to be the greatest novelist of this century. He was born in 1875. As a young man he worked for a time as a clerk until his first great writing success came with the novel *Buddenbrooks,* a story about a family of merchants. It was published in 1900 when Mann was only 25. Mann's stories and books were widely read from then on. In 1924 he published *The Magic Mountain,* which had taken ten years to write. Four years later he received the Nobel Prize for literature, largely because of this book. Next he started on a four-volume work about the Biblical story of Joseph. The four books together are called *Joseph and His Brothers,* and Mann spent sixteen years on them. The first one was published in 1934.

When Adolf Hitler became dictator of Germany in 1933, Mann left his homeland and later was deprived of his citizenship by Hitler's Nazi government. He lived in Switzerland for five years, and then settled in the United States and became a citizen.  He has since written many other important books. During World War II Mann made many radio speeches to his former countrymen in Germany, urging them to

The "praying" mantis might better be called the "preying" mantis, as it is a fierce fighter and preys on other insects.

help the Allies free Germany from the Nazis. He died in 1955.

manslaughter is the illegal but accidental killing of a human being: see the article on HOMICIDE.

mantis

The mantis is a strange insect that comes from China. About fifty years ago people brought the mantis to the United States because the mantis consumes many insect pests. Unfortunately, people discovered that the mantis also eats bees and other useful insects. Most American mantises live in the southern part of the United States.

Many people call this insect the "praying mantis," because it holds its long, thin front legs together and looks as if it were holding a prayer book. Some mantises are green, but in places where the climate is very warm and there are many bright tropical flowers, the mantis may be brightly colored too. This helps the mantis to hide from its enemies.

The mantis is a savage fighter, and two mantises will fight terrible battles, until one of them is killed. The female mantis lays about two hundred eggs in the autumn. The eggs stick together and harden in a case about the size of a large grape. The babies hatch in the spring.

They must leave the case quickly or they will be eaten by other young mantises. Mantises are good flyers and are sometimes found on the window sills of high office buildings in large cities. Some people catch the mantis and keep it for a pet.

manufacturing, the making of useful products: see MASS PRODUCTION.

Manx cat, a tail-less cat bred on the Isle of Man: see MAN.

Maori

The Maoris are the natives of New Zealand, a group of islands in the South Pacific that form an independent nation in the British Commonwealth of Nations. The Maoris belong to the Polynesian race, which also includes the natives of Hawaii and Samoa. Most Maoris are tall and strong. Their skin color may be anything from a dark white to a dark brown, but light brown is the usual color. Their hair is black, and may be straight or wavy.

Maoris have always been daring and skillful sailors. In dugout boats and canoes they used to sail hundreds of miles out to sea. After white men settled in New Zealand more than two hundred years ago, the number of Maoris declined for many years, but recently it has increased again. In 1951 there were more than 100,000 Maoris in New Zealand. They enjoy full political rights as citizens, and four Maoris are members of the New Zealand parliament. Maori music and customs are taught in the public schools. Read also the article on NEW ZEALAND.

Mao Tse-tung

Mao Tse-tung led the Communist revolution in China and became the most important government official there in 1949. He was born November 19, 1893, in the south of China. His father was a poor peasant, and Mao had to do farm work before he was seven. Later he studied to be a teacher, but while he was at a university in Peiping he became a Communist. He helped form the Communist Party of China in 1921, and soon he became one of its top men. He quarreled with other top men over how to take over China, but went ahead with his plans and became so powerful that in 1934 all the other Communists in China agreed that he should be their leader. Mao fought the national government of China, which was headed by Chiang Kai-shek. Mao set up a Communist government in North China, and after a few years he had a strong army there and controlled much territory.

Then, in 1937, Japan made war on China. Mao did not help the Chinese government, but he had his soldiers make raids on the Japanese troops and trap them in ambushes whenever they could. Many Chinese people joined Mao's army because it fought the Japanese very cleverly. In 1945 the Japanese had to leave China because they lost World War II, and Mao again began to fight the regular government of China. He got modern weapons from Russia for his soldiers. By 1949, Mao's armies controlled all of China and he was head of the government that ruled "Red China." His government was very unfriendly to the United States and fought against the United Nations in Korea.

map

A map is a picture of some part of the earth, drawn on a flat surface. There are many kinds of map. Some show geographical features of a country or region, such as mountains, rivers, and valleys. Some show cities, roads, and railways. Others show what the earth is like at the bottom of the ocean, or how the ocean currents flow. Still others show the positions of the stars and planets in the sky. No matter what kind of map it is, its purpose is to show certain things about an area too large to be seen at one time by the human eye.

Maps are made by surveyors, who determine the size and shape of areas by actual measurement and by mathematics. A great deal of this work is now done by aerial photography. The science of map-making is called *cartography*.

Since the earth is shaped like a ball, the only accurate map of the world or any part of it is the GLOBE, about which there is a separate article. But globes cannot always show the world or small areas of it in sufficient detail, and the globe is not very handy for many uses to which maps are put. Therefore some way had to be found to show on a flat surface the same relation of sizes and distances that the globe can give.

MAP

3276

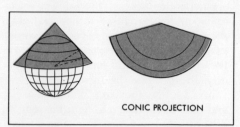

CONIC PROJECTION

In making a conic-projection map, a cone of paper is placed over a globe so that it touches one of the lines of latitude on the globe. The lines of latitude are then projected on the paper in the form of circular arcs. Such a projection gives the least distortion, and shapes are almost the same as on the globe.

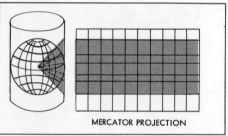

MERCATOR PROJECTION

The Mercator projection, as explained in the article, is used mainly by air and marine navigators for plotting courses.

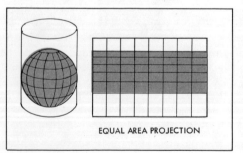

EQUAL AREA PROJECTION

In an equal-area projection, the map is made by drawing lines straight out on paper rolled into a cylinder around a globe. Lines going straight across the map are projections of lines of latitude. Distances between them get smaller as they get farther from the equator. But the areas in each of the boxes on the map are the same as they were on the globe.

PROJECTIONS

Suppose you peel an orange, taking all the skin off but keeping it in one piece. Next you try to lay the skin out so that it is perfectly flat. You will have to stretch the skin quite a bit to flatten it. Wherever you stretch it, different points on the skin will become farther apart than they actually are when they lie on the surface of the orange. The smaller the piece of skin, the less you will have to stretch it to make it lie flat.

Every map shown on a sheet of paper represents some sort of stretching of the surface of the earth. This stretching, or flattening out, of the earth's surface onto a flat map is called a projection. There are many kinds of projection. Some are useful for some purposes, some for other purposes. None is entirely accurate, but it is possible to read them with great accuracy because of the lines you can see crossing each other on every map. These lines are called *parallels* and *meridians*.

PARALLELS AND MERIDIANS

For making a projection, the globe is divided up by a series of horizontal and vertical lines that form what is called a geographic grid. Starting with the equator, which is an imaginary line that circles the earth about halfway between the North Pole and the South Pole, we draw a series of circles above and below the equator until we reach the smallest circle at each of the poles. These lines are called parallels of latitude, so that latitude tells how far north or south of the equator any given spot is. Then a set of lines is drawn from pole to pole, making a division of the earth somewhat like the segments in an orange. Each of these lines is called a meridian of longitude. These meridians are numbered to the east and to the west of the zero meridian.

Every circle, no matter how large or small, is measured in degrees, from zero to 360 degrees. The parallels are numbered from zero at the equator to 90 de-

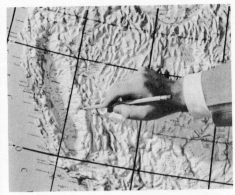

A relief map of the western United States shows the different levels of land. The black horizontal lines are lines of latitude; the black vertical ones are lines of longitude. The pencil is at 119 degrees longitude and 37 degrees latitude.

grees at each pole. The meridians are measured from the zero meridian to 180 degrees going east and 180 degrees going west.

The zero meridian, called the prime meridian, can be placed wherever people want to place it. In modern times, most nations of the world have accepted the Greenwich meridian, which puts zero meridian in a part of London, England, called Greenwich. You can read more about this in the article on NAVIGATION.

If a place lies at the spot where a certain parallel crosses a certain meridian, we can know exactly where that spot is because two lines can cross at only one point.

CONIC PROJECTIONS

When you see a map of the United States, or a single state, or a continent such as Europe, it is usually a conic projection. For a small part of the earth's surface, it shows territories just about as big and places just about as far apart as they actually are.

MERCATOR'S PROJECTION

For a larger area, and especially for the entire surface of the earth, "the skin of the orange" would have to be stretched much farther than is possible in a conic projection. The usual method of showing the entire surface of the earth on a flat map is technically called a *cylindrical projection,* and one kind of it is called the *Mercator projection.*

Mercator was a Flemish map-maker who lived about four hundred years ago. His projection was the first important change in map-making for 1,400 years, and he was the first to use the name atlas for a book of maps. Mercator's real name was Gerhard Kremer. It was the fashion in his day to translate one's name into Latin; *Kremer* means "trader," and so does *Mercator* in Latin.

CYLINDRICAL PROJECTIONS

A cylindrical projection is made by taking a cylinder, or straight-sided tube, of paper, and laying it around the globe with the paper touching the equator. At the equator and for a tiny distance north and south of it, the map will be accurate. However, on the globe the meridians are farthest apart at the equator and they meet at the two poles. On the cylinder they could not be made to meet because the tube of paper was as big at the top and bottom as in the middle. But the parallels were still equally distant from one another. Mercator decided that for every bit that the meridians were farther apart than they had been on the globe, he would make the parallels that much farther apart. That meant that a place on the map near either the North or South Pole would look much larger than a place of the same size near the equator.

You might think this would make the map useless, because there would be no way of telling what size a place really was. That is where the parallels and meridians become important. No matter what size the place may look, the parallels and meridians measure it exactly. The Mercator projection is used chiefly for navigation charts for sailors.

MAP

3278

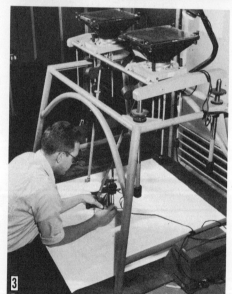

U.S. Coast & Geod. Survey
Aero Service Photos

Map-making is a difficult job that takes a lot of patient and accurate work.

1. The area to be mapped is photographed from an airplane. Many shots are taken.

2. Survey measurements of location and height above sea level are made.

3. The aerial photos and survey information are used in a stereoscopic machine to produce the "manuscript" map.

4. Flat areas are carefully surveyed.

5. The manuscript map is checked in the field. Roads and buildings are located.

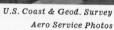

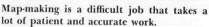

The manuscript is photographed on glass instead of film to keep the scale exact.

Before the map is printed, the work is again carefully and completely checked.

HOW TO READ A MAP

To read a map accurately, one must know scale and direction. Direction is indicated by an arrow pointing north. Scale is always given in a corner of the map. The scale is the size of a place represented on the map in relation to its true size. The scale may be 1 inch = 10 miles, which is a fairly large-scale map, or it may be 1 inch = 100 miles, which is a smaller scale. Large-scale maps are easier to read, and are used mostly in road maps and maps of small areas.

Each map has also a legend, which tells what signs and symbols it uses for different things on the map. A map of the United States will have certain symbols to represent the cities of various sizes. A road map will have special symbols to indicate highways, paved roads, and other things that will help travelers.

A map of a large part of the earth, such as a map of Europe and Asia, will be divided into countries. This is called a political map. Each country will be printed in a certain color, and the terri-tories or possessions of that country will be printed in that color too.

A relief map shows natural features of the earth, such as mountains and rivers. It uses various colors and shadings to show the height of mountains and the steepness of their slopes.

There are many other kinds of map for different purposes, such as weather maps, navigation charts, political maps that show voting trends, business maps that show buying habits in different places, and any number of maps for other special purposes.

maple

The maple is a fine large tree that grows in the midwestern and eastern parts of the United States and in some parts of Canada. There are more than seventy-five different kinds of maple. Those that are best known are the sugar maple and the black, silver and red maples. Many maples grow to be more than a hundred feet high. The maple is a deciduous tree, which means that it loses all of its leaves in the fall. The leaves be-

U.S. Forest Service

The maple is a handsome tree, especially in autumn, when its deeply indented leaves (*see inset*) take on beautiful colors.

ern parts of the United States the sap of the sugar maple tree is used to make maple syrup and maple sugar.

In early spring, when the days are warm and the nights are cool, the sap begins to flow. Men cut the bark of the sugar maple trees about 4½ feet from the ground. (This is called "tapping" the trees.) They attach buckets to the trees and the sap flows out of the bark into the buckets. The sap is then treated in machines that turn it into maple syrup and maple sugar. A single machine can make about four hundred gallons of maple syrup in one hour.

The Indians had no machines. They dropped hot stones into the containers filled with sap. This made the sap boil. Then they froze the sap and it turned to sugar. The early settlers in America cooled the sap by dropping it in the snow. They then poured the sugar into molds and let it harden. Though people now make maple sugar in machines, the method is very much the same.

One maple tree produces about one gallon of maple syrup, or up to eight pounds of sugar. A maple tree lives to be about three hundred years old, and it can produce a great deal of sugar in that time.

When people began to use cane and beet sugar, maple sugar became less important. It is still eaten as a candy, and the maple syrup made from it is used on waffles and pancakes and in many other ways. Most of the maple sugar in the United States comes from the states of Vermont and New York.

marabou

The marabou is a bird that is a member of the stork family. It makes its home in Africa. The marabou is a strange-looking white bird. It has greenish-gray wings and long, thin legs. The marabou has a pouch that hangs from its neck that it can fill with air, like a balloon. The marabou eats tortoises, lizards, and other small animals. It is easily tamed, but it can be a great nuisance because it is fond

gin to come out in early spring, along with tiny, bell-shaped, pale green flowers. In the fall the maple leaves turn beautiful shades of red. The seeds of the maple tree have little wings that are easily blown by the wind to new places where other maple trees begin to grow.

The maple is a very useful tree. Maple sugar comes from the sugar maple tree. The wood of the maple is hard and strong and takes a polish well. It is used to build floors that must be very strong, such as dance floors and bowling alleys, and for furniture, musical instruments, boxes, spools, and automobile parts. Maple wood is also used to make charcoal, wood alcohol, and paper.

maple sugar

Maple sugar is a delicious brown sugar that comes from the sugar maple tree. The Indians were the first people to discover that the sap of the sugar maple was sweet and good to eat. In the north-of chickens and turkeys. The beautiful white feathers of the marabou are used to make scarves and shawls, and people decorate hats with marabou feathers. The marabou is related to the ADJUTANT BIRD, about which there is a separate article.

Marat, Jean Paul

Jean Paul Marat was a leader in the French Revolution, the time when the French people overthrew their king and noblemen and set up a republic, more than 150 years ago. Marat was a "terrorist." He had hundreds of people put to death, often for no good reason.

Marat was born in France in the year 1744, and started out in life as a physician. He did not get along well with other people, and became bitter and cruel, perhaps because of his unhappy experiences. When the French Revolution started in 1789, he joined in with wild enthusiasm, and was one of the most bloodthirsty of the revolutionist mob. He wrote pamphlets and articles that demanded the execution of thousands of people. He had great power in France, but many people hated him for the things he had done. He was assassinated by a young woman named Charlotte Corday on July 13, 1793. Many people thought that she did France a great service, but Marat's powerful political supporters condemned her to death on the guillotine.

marathon

The Battle of Marathon was fought in ancient Greece, almost 2,500 years ago. The Greeks were fighting the Persians on the plain of Marathon, about twenty-five miles from Athens. The Greeks won the battle and a Greek athlete named Pheidippides ran twenty-five miles to Athens to carry the good news. He arrived and proclaimed the victory in the market place, and then fell dead.

In the first modern Olympic games in 1896, there was a "marathon" race of about 25 miles. It was won by a Greek

in 2 hours, 55 minutes and 20 seconds. In 1908 the Olympic games were held in London and the course for the marathon was laid out over 26 miles of roads. At the last minute it was decided that the finish line should be in front of the royal box, where the king was to sit, and this added 385 yards to the course. The distance of that race, 26 miles and 385 yards, was then set as the standard marathon course. In 1952 the marathon was won by the Czech athlete Emil Zatopek, who ran the course in 2 hours, 23 minutes and 3 seconds.

In the United States a marathon race is held every year in Boston, on Patriots' Day, April 19, the date of the first battles of the Revolutionary War. The Boston course is the same distance, and it is run through the city streets, which are lined with thousands of watchers as the runners go by.

The word *marathon* also was given in the 1920s to a succession of endurance fads in the United States, such as the "dance marathon" in which couples danced continuously, with only brief intervals of rest, until they were exhausted. In the 1950s a new kind of marathon was devised, the "telethon," which was a continuous television program put on for the purpose of getting contributions to charity.

marble

Marble is a kind of rock that is used for decorating buildings and for statues. It is used for these two purposes because it is tough and wears well, because it can be given a high polish, and because its many different colors are in beautiful swirls, waves, layers, and other pleasing designs. When marble is pure, it is snow white, but it may be pink, yellow, brown, gray, blue, black, or mixtures of two or three of these colors. You have seen marble lining the walls and floors of banks, office buildings, libraries, museums, city halls, and other public buildings. Marble statues should be protected from rain because water will wear away their high polish. Marble statues that the ancient Greeks and Romans placed outdoors were badly crumbled by rainwater after many centuries.

Sometimes from deep down in the earth, a large amount of rock so hot that it is melted to a liquid is pushed up into the earth's crust. If the melted rock happens to push up into beds of limestone rock or dolomite rock, the great heat and pressure that are created change these two kinds of rock into marble.

The name *marble* comes from the ancient Greek word meaning "sparkle." If you look closely at marble, you will see right below its polished surface many sparkles. Some may be as big as an inch across and some may be so small that you cannot see each one separately. The sparkle comes from the many crystals that marble is made of.

Very beautiful marble comes from Vermont and Georgia. The finest marble comes from Carrara in Italy. The wonderful statues carved by the ancient Greeks were made of an especially fine marble from the Isle of Paros in the Aegean Sea.

Marble used to be carved into little balls that children played games with. The marbles you play with now are made of glass that looks like real marble.

Georgia State Chamber of Commerce

A large slab of marble is polished on round rubbing beds. The beds are revolving steel discs on which water and sand or crushed steel are poured.

marbles

Marbles is a game popular with boys and girls the world over. It is played with small, shiny balls called marbles, although they are no longer made of marble. The best marbles are made of the fine stone called agate. Most marbles today are made of glass and are called aggies, immies, or nibs. They are made to look like marble. Marbles have also been made of stone and clay.

Marbles can be played in several ways, but there is only one form of the game that is played in tournaments according to regular rules. This is called *ringer*. Ringer is played in a ring 10 feet across. Thirteen marbles are arranged in the center in the form of a cross. The object of the game is to shoot these marbles out of the ring. A player scores one point every time he shoots a marble out of the ring. From two to six may play.

Straight lines are drawn to touch the circle on opposite sides. One line is called the *lag line,* the other the *pitch line.* To decide the order in which the players shoot, they lag. This means that they stand at the pitch line and shoot their shooting marbles, called *shooters,* toward the lag line. The one whose shooter is closest to the lag line goes first, the next-closest, second, and so forth.

The play of the game is made from the pitch line. To shoot, the players must knuckle down; that is, shoot with at least one knuckle of the shooting hand on the ground. A player knuckles down at any point on the pitch line and shoots into the ring to knock one or more marbles out of the ring.

A player continues to shoot when he knocks one or more marbles out of the ring, provided his shooter remains inside the ring. When his shooter goes outside the ring, he has to stop and the next player shoots.

If a player misses, he picks up his shooter and the next player shoots. When his turn comes again, he takes *rounders;*

that is, he shoots from any point on the ring line.

The game ends when one player has knocked seven marbles from the ring. If no player has scored seven points when all the marbles have been knocked out of the ring, the player having the largest number of points wins.

march

A march is a musical composition that is written to be played while soldiers are marching, so that they can keep time to the music. Usually a march is played by a military BAND, about which there is a separate article. A *military march* is played in quick time. It usually has three parts. John Philip Sousa's march, *The Stars and Stripes Forever,* is a popular military march. A much slower march is a *funeral march,* or *dead march,* which used to be played in funeral processions. There are also *wedding marches,* played while the bride and her attendants walk to the altar during a wedding. One of the most popular of these is popularly called "Here Comes the Bride."

March

March is the third month of the year. It has thirty-one days. In ancient Roman times the year began with the month of March. About two thousand years ago the Romans began to use the calendar we know now, and March became the third month. In the Latin language the month was called *Martius,* after Mars, the Roman god of war. People who were born in March have the aquamarine, a bluish-green stone, as their birthstone. Another birthstone for March is the bloodstone, a green stone with small red spots on it. The flower of March is the daffodil, because it is one of the first flowers to bloom in the spring.

March, Peyton C.

Peyton Conway March was a general in the United States Army. He was chief of staff in the last year of World War I. He was born in 1864 in Easton, Pennsylvania, and was graduated from Lafayette College and the United States Military Academy at West Point. In 1917, when the United States entered World War I, March commanded the artillery forces of the American Expeditionary Forces. In May, 1918, he was recalled to the United States to be chief of staff. In this post he was successful in improving the Army's efficiency and bringing about a quick victory.

March retired from active service in 1921. In 1932 he wrote a book, *The Nation at War,* which caused a great deal of discussion because it criticized General John J. Pershing, the commander of the American Expeditionary Forces, who had been the chief American war hero.

Marconi, Guglielmo

Guglielmo Marconi was an Italian scientist who invented the wireless telegraph. From this grew both radio and television. Marconi was born in 1874 and began his experiments with electrical waves while still studying at the University of Bologna. In 1895, when he was only 21 years  old, he succeeded in sending signals more than a mile. The next year he patented his system in England and organized a wireless telegraph company. In 1899 he set up a wireless telegraph system to cross the English Channel, and in 1901 he sent the first message across the Atlantic Ocean.

The use of wireless telegraph quickly spread around the world. In 1909 Marconi was awarded the Nobel Prize in physics for his achievement, and he received high honors from many countries. During World War I, he demonstrated the value of wireless telegraphy in warfare. Marconi died in 1937, at the age of 63.

Marcus Aurelius

Marcus Aurelius Antoninus was a Roman emperor and a great philosopher. He was born about the year 120 and died about 180. He was adopted by his uncle, the Emperor Antoninus Pius, and took the name Antoninus from him. Marcus Aurelius studied philosophy and became a Stoic. There is a separate article about the STOICS.

While Marcus Aurelius was emperor he did many things to improve the life of the people. He established funds for orphans, reduced taxes for poor people, and eliminated much of the brutality of gladiator contests. In one way he was not kindly at all. He persecuted Christians. He thought that Christians were dangerous to the empire because they believed in a God more important than the state.

He wrote a famous book called *Meditations* that is still read. In this book he wrote many proverbs, or brief sentences giving good advice. Among them are:

"Nothing is made better or worse by being praised."

"What is not good for the swarm is not good for the bee."

"Do everything as though it were your last act."

Mardi Gras

Mardi Gras is a day of fun and merrymaking just before the period in spring called Lent. Lent is the forty days before Easter, when many people are very serious and give up many things they like. Mardi Gras is the last day of carnival week, which is a whole week. In England Mardi Gras is called Shrove Tuesday. In French the name Mardi Gras means "fat Tuesday." The day after Mardi Gras is called Ash Wednesday, and it is the first day of Lent. There are separate articles about LENT and about CARNIVAL.

margarine

Margarine is an artificial butter. The first margarine was made in 1870 by a French chemist named Mège-Mouries. He made it from oleo oil, which comes from beef fat, and from this oil it got the name *oleomargarine*. Later, vegetable oils were added. Now, in the United States, margarine is made from vegetable oils only.

Margarine is very much like butter; it gives the same amount of nourishment and body heat, and it is easily digested. It can be spread on bread or used in cooking, just as butter can.

To make margarine, cottonseed and soybean oils, along with smaller amounts of peanut, corn, or seed oils, are refined and have their odors removed. Then hydrogen gas is added. It combines with the oils and makes them solid fats. After this, the fats are churned or homogenized with skim milk. This makes a smooth, butterlike material. It is chilled, salt is added, and it is churned again to remove some of the water that was in the skim milk. After the second churning, the margarine looks like white butter. A harmless yellow coloring matter is added to make the margarine look like butter, and Vitamin A is usually added.

In some "dairy" states, where much butter is made, there are laws against putting artificial coloring in margarine, and there are special taxes on it.

Marianas

The Marianas are a group of islands in the western Pacific Ocean about six thousand miles from the west coast of the United States. There are fifteen islands in the group, of which the best known is the island of Guam. Guam and several of the other islands were the scene of much fighting during World War II.

Until 1899 the Marianas were ruled by Spain. Then Guam came under the control of the United States and the rest of the islands under the control of Germany. In 1919, after World War I, the German islands came under the control of the Japanese, who had fought on the side of the Allies in that war. In December, 1941, at the beginning of World War II, the Japanese seized the island of Guam, which they used for a naval and air base. The Marianas Islands were captured by the American forces between June and August of 1944. In 1947 the United Nations placed the Marianas under the protection of the United States.

Maria Theresa

Maria Theresa was an important queen in Europe about two hundred years ago. She was arch-duchess (queen) of Austria and queen of Hungary and Bohemia. She was born in Vienna in 1717. Her father, Charles VI, belonged to the Hapsburg family and was the Holy Roman Em-  peror. Because he had no sons to whom he could pass on his vast lands, he arranged with the various kings of Europe for Maria Theresa to inherit these lands.

When Charles died in 1740, most of the countries lived up to this agreement, and Maria became ruler of Austria, Hungary, and Bohemia. But Frederick the Great, king of Prussia, refused to recognize the agreement and seized the part of Austrian lands called Silesia. This started a great war, called the War of the Austrian Succession, that involved many of the countries of Europe. When the war ended in 1748, Maria Theresa agreed to let Frederick the Great keep Silesia, but in return it was agreed that her husband, Francis I, would be elected Holy Roman Emperor.

One daughter of Maria Theresa and Francis was Marie Antoinette, who became the wife of Louis XVI and queen of France. Maria Theresa died in Vienna in 1780, at the age of 63.

Marie Antoinette

Marie Antoinette was a queen of France who was put to death by revolu-tionaries. She was born an Austrian princess, the daughter of Maria Theresa, the Austrian empress and queen of Hungary.

Marie Antoinette was born about two hundred years ago, in the year 1755. When she was 14, she was married to Louis XVI, who became king of France in 1774. As queen, she was gay and lighthearted, frivolous and extravagant. Marie Antoinette was beautiful, blonde, slender, and graceful, and set the fashion for all of France for many years. At a time when the people of France were grumbling about their poverty and misery, the French court was a place of gaiety, rich parties, and great luxury. At the royal palace of Versailles Marie Antoinette had some farmers' cottages built, where she could play at being a milkmaid.

When one of her advisers tried to explain that the people were dissatisfied because they had no bread, she is supposed to have remarked, "Let them eat cake." She probably did not actually say this, but the story was told to show how little she understood the misery of the people.

The French Revolution started in 1789, and the revolutionists won complete power. They executed first Louis XVI, and then, a few months later, Marie Antoinette, on the guillotine, a machine that cuts off the head. She died in 1793.

marigold

The marigold is a bright yellow or orange flower that first grew in Mexico and South America and is now found in many parts of Europe and the United States. The marigold is an annual plant, which means that it must be planted every year. It blooms in late summer and early fall. The marigold is a hardy plant and grows best in a soil that is not too rich.

There are several different kinds of marigold. The Aztec or African marigold

U.S.M.C. Photo

The flag-raising at Iwo Jima during World War II has become a symbol of the courage of the United States Marines.

is two to three feet high. It is often used to make a border in flower gardens. The French marigold is a little smaller. It has a small yellow flower. The marsh marigold, which belongs to the buttercup family, grows wild near ponds. Several small yellow flowers bloom on one stalk in the spring. Sometimes people eat the leaves of the marsh marigold.

marihuana is a drug that is made from the dried flowers of the hemp plant and is smoked in cigarettes. In Arabia it is called hashish. See NARCOTICS.

Marine Corps, United States

The Marine Corps is one of the four armed services of the United States. It is that nation's force-in-readiness—ready to fight, anywhere, on short notice. Marines also are trained for special duties in almost any part of the world. They fight on land, like the soldiers of the Army; at sea, like the sailors of the Navy; and in the air, like the Air Force men. Before air-fighting was added to their duties,

Marines were called "soldiers of the sea." They are nicknamed "Leathernecks."

The first Marines were formed by a resolution of the Continental Congress on November 10, 1775. These first American Marines were required to have a "knowledge of the sea," and Marines ever since have had that knowledge. The first Marine group numbered only 300. They wore green coats, green shirts, and breeches of light-colored cloth. The Continental Marines of 1775 were replaced by the Marine Corps as it exists today on July 11, 1798, by an Act of Congress.

The Marine Corps expands quickly when war seems near, and shrinks in peacetime. In World War I there were 75,101 officers and enlisted men, including nearly 300 women, in the Marine Corps. In World War II the Corps grew from 70,425 at the beginning of the fighting to a peak of 485,052, including 18,224 women. By 1950 it had been reduced again, to only 74,279 officers and men. It rose during the Korean fighting to 261,343, including 2,787 women. In 1954 it numbered about 230,000, including some 2,500 women. A law passed by Congress in 1947 requires the Corps to maintain always three combat divisions and three air wings. A division ranges from 17,000 to 22,000 men. There are about 12,000 men in a Marine air wing.

WHAT THE MARINES DO

Marines are called on to do many different jobs in many parts of the world, both in war and in peace. Their most important wartime duty is to capture, from the sea or the air or both, shores occupied and fortified by enemy troops. They drive out the enemy and establish *beachheads* there. These are strong points that soldiers of the Army can occupy later and from which they can join the advance against the enemy. This kind of fighting, largely done by Marines, is called AMPHIBIOUS WARFARE, and there is a separate article about it.

Marines have other regular duties.

They guard naval bases in the United States and abroad. Also, they guard United States property all over the world. In peacetime they often are sent to far places to keep order, especially when American people and property need protection. They parade on special occasions, and they furnish escorts, as when important visitors come to the United States. The President may call on the Marines at any time for almost any kind of duty.

Here are some examples of the different kinds of job the Marines have done in their 180 years of existence. Marines fought with General George Washington on land, and with Captain John Paul Jones at sea, in the Revolutionary War. They have made nearly three hundred landings on foreign soil. They fought Barbary pirates in the Mediterranean Sea in 1803. They stopped a Massachusetts State Prison riot in 1824. They battled Indians in Florida in 1836. They helped stop the reckless and illegal killing of seals in the Bering Sea in 1891. They rode camels in the country of Ethiopia, in Africa, while guarding American diplomats in 1903. They protected San Francisco from looting after its great earthquake and fire in 1906. They guarded the United States mail all over the country against robbery in 1921 and 1926.

HOW THE CORPS IS ORGANIZED

The Marine Corps is a part of the Department of the Navy, which is one of the three branches of the Department of De-

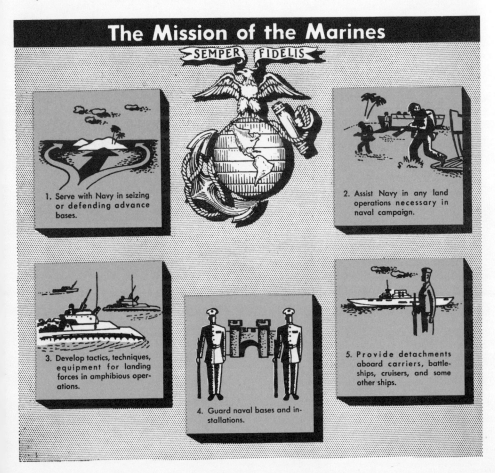

The Mission of the Marines
SEMPER FIDELIS

1. Serve with Navy in seizing or defending advance bases.

2. Assist Navy in any land operations necessary in naval campaign.

3. Develop tactics, techniques, equipment for landing forces in amphibious operations.

4. Guard naval bases and installations.

5. Provide detachments aboard carriers, battleships, cruisers, and some other ships.

Training to be a Marine is rugged work, but it is worth while, because it teaches discipline and teamwork and prepares a man to serve his country.

U.S.M.C. Photos

1. A noncommissioned officer studies map-reading in the library at his base.

2. Recruits march toward the rifle range for their first try at actually firing their rifles.

3. For hand-to-hand combat, they study judo under the guidance of an expert instructor.

4. Student officers attend classes in military science and tactics. Long study and training are needed before they can become lieutenants.

5. Ready, aim, click! Many hours of "dry runs" come before real bullets may be used.

The Marines are proud of their tradition of being prepared at any time to defend their country. They have fought for the United States in every war.

U.S.M.C. Photos

I. The hand grenade is an important weapon in moving in on an enemy strong point.

2. Firing from a concealed position is one of the skills learned during basic training.

3. Dress uniforms are worn during sunset ceremonies at Marine Barracks in Washington, D.C.

4. The Marines pioneered in the use of helicopters. The helicopter can move the domelike plastic shelter and set it down where it is needed.

5. Marinettes do office work and free their Marine brothers for duty in combat zones.

fense. The Marine Corps and the Navy are considered "partners" in the Department of the Navy, working together. For example, the Navy lets the Marines use its dentists, doctors, and chaplains, and the Marines guard Navy bases. The Marines capture places on land that the Navy wants, using special landing ships furnished by the Navy.

The Marine Corps is divided into operating or fighting forces, and supporting forces. The supporting forces include men who furnish ammunition and supplies, and who work to keep the operating forces ready for action. In the operating forces are two Fleet Marine Forces, one for the Atlantic Ocean, the other for the Pacific.

Marines in both these Forces are trained for land-sea-air action. More than half of the men of the entire Corps are in the Fleet Marine Forces.

MARINE AVIATION

The squadron is the basic Marine aviation unit. It is made up of planes, men who fly them, and others who service the planes and keep them ready for flying. Some Marine planes are the same as those used by the Navy. Marines fly the latest jets, such as the *Banshee,* the *Skynight* and the *Fury.* They also fly the giant Skymaster transport, the *Flying Boxcar,* and helicopters.

The Marines are proud of their progress with helicopters. The Corps sent the first transport helicopter squadron in history to Korea in 1951. In October of that year the squadron, in "Operation Bumblebee," lifted an entire battalion of 958 troops and their equipment and carried them fifteen miles into battle. The squadron used twelve Sikorsky HRS helicopters, each carrying six Marine riflemen. These helicopters also performed wonders in picking up wounded men and flying them to hospitals. A new Sikorsky, the XHR 2S, carries twenty-six fully equipped Marines. It opens at the front, permitting a jeep to be driven in.

RANKS AND PAY

Although the Marine Corps is a part of the Navy, its rank and pay scales follow those of the Army. When a man enlists in the Marines he is a private and gets $75 a month. After four months this is raised to $78. It is raised to $99.37 when he becomes a private first class. He can rise to corporal and sergeant and, becoming an officer, to lieutenant, captain, and so on, as in the Army. Each grade draws higher pay than the one below.

The head of the Marine Corps, called the Commandant, is a general who wears four stars. That is the highest rank a Marine may attain. In the article about the U.S. ARMY, there is a chart listing ranks and pay.

TRAINING AND CAREERS

Marines must undergo long and exacting training. For enlisted men there are two Marine Corps Recruit Depots, at Parris Island, South Carolina, and at San Diego, California. These are called "boot camps," probably from the first article of clothing issued to recruits years ago—boots. The course at boot camp lasts ten weeks.

Recruits first get tests to find out where they will best fit in and what schools they will later attend. They learn about military courtesy and discipline. (These are described in the article about the U.S. ARMY.) They practice amphibious warfare under conditions like those in actual battle. At boot camp there is recreation as well as hard work. Marines have thirty days of vacation each year. From boot camp Marines go to special schools.

Young men in the Marine Corps, as in other service branches, may learn how to do many special jobs and work at special trades. The Corps lists 43 occupational specialties, or major job fields, with 470 specialist jobs. There are 140 specialist schools that Marines may attend. A Marine may become an expert in electronics, utilities, photography, motor transport, radar, surveying, engineering, hydraulics, and many other fields. But always, basically, he is a rifleman. He may retire with an income for life after twenty or more years of service.

Many Marines, after completing boot camp, go to the Marine Corps schools at Quantico, Virginia, or to Camp Lejeune, North Carolina. There they take advanced training.

At Quantico there is an Officer Candidate School Course (OCC), which trains promising enlisted men for commissioned rank, and a Platoon Leaders' Course (PLC), which instructs college students during their vacation months. At both Quantico and Lejeune enlisted men study and practice for the infantry, artillery, ordnance, and so on.

WOMEN IN THE MARINES

Women who are between 18 and 30 years of age, are single, and have a high-school education or its equivalent, may enlist in the Marine Corps. They first undergo eight weeks of training at Parris Island. Here they are instructed in military customs and courtesies, administration, drill, Marine Corps history, and other subjects. There are 26 occupation fields and 87 specialties for women in the Marines. Among them are: secretary, typist, job analyst, bookkeeper, draftsman, teletype operator, cryptographer, and others.

MARINE CORPS RESERVE

The Marine Corps Reserve was formed to help expand the service rapidly in time of war. It was created by law in 1914, but little was done about it until the United States entered World War I in 1917. In late 1918 it had 463 officers and 6,773 enlisted men, including 250 women.

The Reserve was reorganized in 1925. There were in 1954 about 91,000 in the Reserve.

In 1953 the Reserve was classified into three branches: Ready (organized); Stand-

The Marine Corps developed the "Mighty Mite" for water-land operations. The men drive down the beach and into the water without a moment's hesitation.

Held up by the four air-filled tubes, the "Mite" is propelled and steered by its wheels. Special tires with deep treads move the vehicle through the water.

U.S.M.C. Photo

Back on dry land. Next the 1,500-pound "Mite" can drive to an airport where a Marine helicopter will airlift it to a mountain top that other vehicles could not reach.

by (volunteer); and Retired. In an emergency the Ready would be called first, then the Standby, then the Retired.

Ground Reserves train at local centers, and take two weeks of active duty each year at a regular Marine Corps base. Marine Air Reserve members are trained in forty-two fighter squadrons and Marine ground control intercept (radar) squadrons at twenty-five Marine and Navy air stations. Volunteers are mostly specialists and technicians.

HISTORY OF THE MARINES

The history of the Marine Corps follows closely the military history of the United States, or the history of the Navy and the Army. (See the separate article on the U.S. NAVY.)

Some of the jobs done by the Marines through history have already been mentioned. Their first amphibious landing was made in the Bahamas in the Revolutionary War, when the men rowed ashore in whaleboats. Marines have fought both at sea and on land in every war since.

Some major Marine actions include the Naval War with France, 1798–1801; the war against Tripoli, 1801–05; the War of 1812 against England; the Florida Indian War, 1835–42; the Mexican War, 1846–48; the Civil War, 1861–65, where the Marines fought at Bull Run; the Spanish-American War, 1898; the Philippine Insurrection, 1898–1902; the Boxer Rebellion in China, 1900; the two World Wars; and the United Nations action in Korea.

In World War I, Marines gained glory at Belleau Wood and other places. France renamed Belleau Wood the *Bois de la Brigade de Marines.* In World War II the Marines, after heroic stands at Wake, Bataan, Corregidor, and Midway, started the first American offensive against the Japanese at Guadalcanal. They followed this with island warfare right up to Iwo Jima and Okinawa. In Korea, they were prominent in the Inchon landing operation of September, 1950.

MARINE CORPS TRADITIONS

Marines are very proud of their traditions and their heritage of two centuries of service. They are usually the first ashore on hostile territory, whether in the hot tropics or the cold Arctic. There is an old saying of which they are especially proud: "The Marines have landed and the situation is well in hand." It is believed to have been coined by Richard Harding Davis, a journalist-author. Marines have fought almost everywhere, from the "Halls of Montezuma" in Mexico, to "the shores of Tripoli" on the Barbary coast, as sung in the *Marines' Hymn.* The first verse of this is:

> From the Halls of Montezuma
> To the shores of Tripoli,
> We fight our country's battles
> In the air, on land and sea;
> First to fight for right and freedom
> And to keep our honor clean;
> We are proud to claim the title of
> United States Marines.

The tune of the *Marines' Hymn,* first sung after the Mexican War in 1847, occurs in an old Spanish folk song and in the French comic opera *Geneviève de Brabant,* by Jacques Offenbach.

The Marine colors are red and gold. The Marine insigne, adopted in 1858, is a globe showing the Western Hemisphere, an eagle, and an anchor, with a motto at the top, *Semper Fidelis,* Latin words meaning "Always Faithful." The 1st Marine Regiment and a British regiment, the Royal Welsh Fusiliers, served together in China in 1900, so each year on March 16 the Marine Corps sends greetings to the British outfit.

MARINE BAND

When Congress authorized the Marine Corps on July 11, 1798, at the same time it voted enough money for "musick" by thirty-two drummers and fifers, with a drum major. There has been a Marine Band ever since. It is said to be the oldest band in the United States. Today it is a

A big helicopter can carry a jeep or eighteen fully equipped Marines to the front.

Helicopters carrying troops and equipment prepare to take off from a carrier.

Marine pilots come in to strafe and bomb enemy positions as leathernecks hit the beach during amphibious operations.

With his white silk parachute like a giant mushroom above him, a Paramarine drops to earth during jump practice.

A file of Marines moves through the snow during cold-weather maneuvers. In case of attack they can take cover in seconds.

full concert band, with about eighty-five members and with every band instrument.

The Marine Band has been called "the President's Own." It has entertained every President of the United States since George Washington. It has always played for many public affairs. President John Tyler in 1845 started the custom of Saturday afternoon Marine Band concerts on the White House grounds. President Andrew Johnson, in 1865, had the Marine Band play for the first egg-rolling at the White House on Easter morning.

The most famous Marine Band leader was the "March King," John Philip SOUSA, about whom there is a separate article. Sousa became leader in 1880. He took the band on nationwide tours, as far as San Francisco. William H. Santelmann, who took Sousa's place as leader in 1898, organized the Marine Band Symphony Orchestra. Many of the players in the orchestra are also players in the band.

Band members do not undergo the regular Marine recruit training, but they must pass the standard physical examination. Each must be able to play at least two instruments. Band members receive the same pay and benefits as other Marines. The leader in 1954 was William F. Santelmann (son of William H. Santelmann), with the rank of lieutenant colonel.

The Marine Corps library of music and arrangements is valued at more than two million dollars.

Marion, Francis

Francis Marion was an American patriot who led a band of South Carolina colonists against the British during the Revolutionary War. Marion had only sixteen men in his band when he first formed it, but later he received the rank of brigadier general from the gov-

ernor of South Carolina and formed a larger force, called a brigade. Marion's brigade was poorly clothed and underfed, but it was very successful in fighting the British in South Carolina. At one time, the brigade was the only force fighting the British in the South. Marion's brigade made many daring raids against the British. William Cullen Bryant, an American poet, wrote a well-known poem called "Song of Marion's Men," which describes these raids. Francis Marion was born in 1732 and died in 1793.

Maritime Provinces

The Maritime Provinces are the three eastern provinces of Canada. They are NOVA SCOTIA, NEW BRUNSWICK, and PRINCE EDWARD ISLAND. There is a separate article about each. Most of the people living there are fishermen or farmers. The beautiful scenery along the Atlantic coast has made these regions popular vacation spots.

Mark, Saint

St. Mark was an early Christian who wrote the second Gospel of the New Testament. His full name was Mark John. He was a friend of St. Peter, one of Jesus' beloved Apostles. St. Mark probably wrote his Gospel from things told to him by St. Peter. He tells the life of Jesus in a very moving way. The story is fast-moving and the reader sees Jesus as a great preacher and man of action.

St. Mark's mother was named Mary. She let St. Peter come to her house after he had been released from prison. St. Mark went with St. Paul to Antioch and Cyprus, where they converted many people to Christianity. Later he did missionary work in Rome, where he saw St. Peter, who was a prisoner there. A very old tradition says that St. Mark died after starting the Christian Church in Alexandria, Egypt. He is the patron saint of the Italian city of Venice, where there is a beautiful cathedral named for him. Artists often use a lion to stand for St. Mark because of the strong picture St. Mark gives of Jesus in the second Gospel. His feast day is April 25.

Markham, Edwin

Edwin Markham was an American poet. His most famous poem was "The Man with the Hoe." He was born in Oregon City, Oregon, in 1852. When he was only 5 years old his father died and he was taken to California, where he grew up working on cattle ranches and studying in country schools. He became a teacher and superintendent of schools, and wrote verse for California newspapers. In 1899 the San Francisco *Examiner* published "The Man with the Hoe," and Markham was famous almost overnight. The poem tells how working people were badly used by rich and powerful rulers for thousands of years. Markham was inspired by a famous painting by the French painter Jean Millet. After this success Markham moved to New York City. One of his best-known later poems is "Lincoln, the Man of the People." Markham died in 1940, at the age of 88.

Mark Twain, a name under which Samuel Clemens wrote. See CLEMENS.

Marlborough, Duke of

John Churchill, Duke of Marlborough, was one of England's greatest military commanders. He was born more than three hundred years ago, in the year 1650. When he was 16 years old he became an officer in the guards of the Duke of York (who later became King James II). The British Prime Minister and World War II commander, Winston Churchill, was descended from the Duke of Marlborough.

John Churchill was not born a duke, or any kind of nobleman. He rose to the rank of general in the British Army, and became first a baron, then an earl, and finally a duke. During his military career,

he fought under four different British rulers. The first was Charles II, when England and France were at war against Holland. Then came James II, and then William and Mary. It was William who made him an earl.

Churchill's greatest military successes came during the reign of Queen Anne, who became queen in 1702. At that time the British were fighting against France in the War of the Spanish Succession. Marlborough and his ally, the Austrian Prince Eugene, won important victories, including a famous one at Blenheim, in Bavaria. Queen Anne made Marlborough a duke and had the finest private palace in England built for him. It is called Blenheim Palace in honor of his victory, and the Dukes of Marlborough, descendants of John Churchill, still live there.

Churchill's wife, the Duchess of Marlborough, was Sarah Jennings Churchill, a woman of unusual talent and intelligence. For many years she was Queen Anne's dearest friend, and this had a great deal to do with the Duke's success, as you can read in the article about Queen ANNE. Later Anne and Sarah stopped being friends, and Marlborough lost his power, but when George I became king after the death of Queen Anne, the Duke recovered his influence. He remained active in Parliament and public life until his death in 1722.

marlin

The marlin is one of the most beautiful and most powerful of all fishes. It lives in the warmer oceans of the world. The marlin got its name because of a long pointed "sword" that extends from its upper jaw. This sword looks like a tool called a marlin-spike that sailors use to separate strands of rope. The blue marlin is found in the Atlantic Ocean from the coast of Florida to New York. It is dark blue in color, with a silver underside. It is about twelve feet long and usually weighs about two hundred pounds, although some marlins weigh much more. The marlin is a fierce fighter. Marlin fishing is a popular sport requiring skill and strength. Marlins sometimes travel in large groups, but often they are found alone or in pairs. The marlin eats other fish.

Several kinds of marlin live in the Pacific Ocean. The black marlin is about fifteen feet long and often weighs more than a thousand pounds.

Marlowe, Christopher

Christopher Marlowe was one of the greatest English playwrights of the Elizabethan period, nearly four hundred years ago, when Shakespeare was also writing plays. Marlowe was born in 1564, and attended Cambridge University. His writings caused a great deal of comment and much criticism, because of the bold way in which he wrote. Christopher Marlowe is the only Elizabethan playwright, other than Shakespeare and Ben Jonson, whose plays are still performed today. *Tamburlaine* and *Dr. Faustus* are two of Marlowe's plays that are still performed. Some people have believed that Christopher Marlowe wrote some things that Shakespeare is supposed to have written, but it is impossible to prove or disprove this. Marlowe died in 1593, as the result of a wound received in a violent quarrel.

Marmara, Sea of

The Sea of Marmara (or Marmora) is part of the important water route that connects the Black Sea and the Mediterranean Sea. It lies between Europe and the westernmost part of Asia, called Asia Minor. The Sea of Marmara is connected to the Black Sea on the north by the Bosporus, and with the Aegean Sea on the south by the Dardanelles. Both of these are narrow straits, passages of water only a few miles wide. The Sea of Marmara is 4,500 square miles in area and more than

4,000 feet deep at its deepest point. The city of Istanbul, in Turkey, is its most important seaport. There are several islands in the Sea of Marmara. The most important is the island of Marmara, which is famous for its marble quarries.

marmot

The marmot is a little animal that lives in the Alps mountains and in other parts of Europe where the climate is cool. It is about as large as a rabbit, with short legs and a long tail. Its fur is gray. Marmots live in burrows, holes that they dig in the sides of hills. Sometimes a burrow has several rooms and two entrances and a large group of marmots lives together in it. When the weather grows chilly in autumn, the marmots retire to their burrows and sleep through the long winter months. They do not come out again until the spring. Marmots eat grass, roots, and insects. The marmots that live in the United States are called *woodchucks*.

Marne

The Marne is a river in northeastern France. It is about 325 miles long and flows into the River Seine near Paris, the chief city and capital of France. The Marne River is not an important river and is remembered mostly because it was the scene of two battles during World War I. Some experts think that these two battles were the most important of the war, because if the Germans had won

The marmot lives in a deep burrow with two entrances. If danger approaches, it lets out a sharp squeal and dives for the safety of its underground home.

them they could have occupied the city of Paris.

The first battle of the Marne took place in September, 1914, a month after the beginning of World War I. The Germans crossed the Marne, and the French were so sure that Paris would be defeated that they moved the government to Bordeaux, a city farther south. The Germans were turned back at the Marne because of the courage and determination of the soldiers fighting under the British commander, Field Marshal Sir John French, and the French commander, General Joseph Joffre. They were told that they must not retreat, and they did not. Help for these soldiers at the front came from the soldiers stationed in the city of Paris, who were moved to the front lines by the French General Joseph Gallieni. He seized every taxicab, private car, bus, and any other kind of transportation in Paris and sent his soldiers to the front, leaving Paris undefended. Finally the Germans retreated, and Paris was saved. This broke the first German offensive of the war.

The second battle of the Marne took place in 1918 near the end of the war. The Germans realized that they were losing the war and decided to try one last major attack on Paris. This time, too, the French thought the Germans might take the city, and had even prepared a public statement titled "When Paris Falls." But Paris did not fall because the Germans were weaker than the French had expected.

In this second battle troops from the the United States under the command of General John J. Pershing drove back the Germans when they crossed the Marne at Chateau-Thierry. Two days later Allied forces, commanded by the French commander, Marshal Foch, attacked the German armies along the Marne. The Germans were driven back, and about 100,000 German soldiers were killed or wounded. The German army's failure at the second battle of the Marne was actually the end of the war for Germany.

Marquesas Islands

The Marquesas Islands are a group of nine islands in Oceania in the south Pacific Ocean. They belong to France. Altogether they are 492 square miles in size, and their population is 2,988. The islands were originally volcanoes that rose all the way from the floor of the Pacific. The largest island is Nuku Hiva. The capital, Atuona, is a tiny town on Hiva Oa, the second-largest island. The Marquesas Islands are fertile. Fruits grow wild on them, and the people grow copra and vanilla.

Marquette, Jacques

Jacques Marquette was a French priest who came to the New World about two hundred years ago to teach Christianity to the Indians and to explore the new country. He and a French trader named Louis Joliet were the first men to explore the Mississippi River. In 1763 they led a small party of men from Mackinaw, Canada, down the Mississippi as far as the mouth of the Arkansas River. Marquette wrote an account of this journey for France. This was a journey of more than 2,500 miles, and the men traveled in open canoes.

Marquette was born in France in 1637. He became a Jesuit, or a member of a special order of teachers in the Roman Catholic Church. He sailed to Canada when he was 29 years old. For almost ten years he worked with the Indians there, learning their languages and setting up missions. He explored much of the region around the Great Lakes at the same time. He died in Canada in 1675.

marriage

When a man and a woman agree to live together, to become husband and wife and have a family, their agreement is called a marriage. In law marriage is an act, or ceremony, in which the bride and groom agree to do certain things. They agree to stay together and to love each other. If they cannot live up to this agreement, in many countries they are allowed to be divorced. (There is a separate article on DIVORCE.) In most religions, marriage is also a religious ceremony and the marriage is performed by a minister and takes place in a church or other place of worship. Roman Catholics consider marriage one of the seven sacraments, and do not allow divorce. Christians consider marriage holy because St. Paul compared the relationship between a husband and wife to the relation between Jesus and the Church.

The marriage of one man to one woman is called *monogamy*. If a man marries more than one woman, or a woman marries more than one man, it is a *polygamous* marriage. Most people think that men have been monogamous since the earliest times, but many ancient civilizations permitted polygamy. It was recognized by the Jewish religion and is still recognized by followers of Mohammed. In the United States, the Mormons under Brigham Young permitted polygamy about a hundred years ago, and many people persecuted them because of it. Polygamy has never been very widespread because, beside the religious and social customs forbidding it, few men have enough money to support several wives and few people can love more than one wife at a time.

An important purpose of marriage is to enable the husband and wife to have children whom they can love, shelter, and educate in the proper way. This means that the family is the foundation of society. Because of this, governments make regulations concerning marriage. For example, some states do not permit first cousins to marry.

MARRIAGE LAWS AND CUSTOMS

In the United States, no one may be married against his will. Usually a girl has to be 18 years old and a man 21 years old before they may marry. If they are younger, they must have the consent of their parents before they may marry.

In many countries, marriages are arranged by the couple's parents. In some the bride has to bring a dowry, or sum of money, and in others the groom has to "pay" for his bride. Most people who get married in the United States decide for themselves whether they will marry, without any dowry or payment. Each state has its own marriage laws, but most of them contain the same basic features. There must be one or more witnesses to the marriage ceremony, the couple must have a license to marry, and they must pass a blood test that shows they have no dangerous disease.

About seven out of every ten people in the United States 14 years of age or over are married. Only five out of every 100 people have been divorced. Most people get married between the ages of 20 and 24. Because men do not usually live as long as women, and usually marry women younger than themselves, there are about 7,500,000 widows (women whose husbands have died) and only 2,500,000 widowers (men whose wives have died) in the United States.

Marriage of Figaro

The Marriage of Figaro is an opera by the Austrian composer Mozart. An opera is a play in which all the words are sung instead of spoken. The story of *The Marriage of Figaro* is based on a play of the same name by the French playwright Beaumarchais, and the words for the opera were written by Lorenzo Da Ponte. This was Beaumarchais' second play about the character Figaro. The first was called *The Barber of Seville,* and the Italian composer Rossini later made an opera of it. *The Marriage of Figaro* was first presented in 1786.

The story of the opera is gay and very complicated. It concerns the Count Almaviva, who is bored with his wife Rosina and has fallen a little bit in love with Susanna, who is engaged to marry Figaro, the barber of Seville. Figaro suspects

Susanna of flirting with the count, and the count suspects his wife Rosina of flirting with a handsome young page named Cherubino. After many intrigues and mix-ups in which even the characters hardly know what is happening, the countess wins back the love of the count and Figaro is again happy with his Susanna.

Mars

Mars was the god of war in the religion of the ancient Romans, more than two thousand years ago.

The Romans built many temples to Mars. They thought he would help them to win their battles if his temples were beautiful and imposing. Next to Jupiter, whom the Romans regarded as king of the gods, Mars was the most important Roman God.

In Greece, the god of war was called Ares. He was supposed to be the same god, but the Greek Ares was much more savage than the Roman Mars. Ares was supposed to delight in the horror and bloodshed of battle, while Mars was supposed to stand for the triumph of victory rather than the killing and cruelty of war itself.

The month of March is named for Mars. So is the planet MARS, about which there is a separate article.

Mars

Mars is one of the nine big planets that rotate about the sun. (The Earth on which we live, is one of them.) Next to the planet Mercury, Mars is the lightest planet in the heavens. It is also one of the smallest, 4,220 miles in diameter, about half the size of the earth.

Mars is usually more than 140,000,000 miles from the sun, but the distance varies greatly throughout the year. The Earth is not much more than 90,000,000 miles from the sun. It takes Mars about 690 days to make one complete revolution around the sun, compared to 365 days

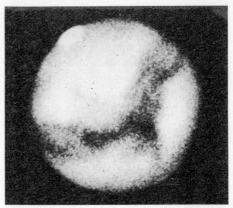

Yerkes Observatory

Mars is farther from the earth than the sun is. Scientists think that the round spot at the top of the picture is a white polar icecap like those found on earth.

for the Earth. A day on Mars lasts about as long as a day on the Earth.

The distance between Mars and the Earth varies from 34,000,000 to 250,-000,000 miles. Except for the moon, Mars is the only object in the sky that we can clearly observe.

Mars has a reddish color. There are places on Mars where the color is green, so there may be plant life on Mars. The white at its North and South Poles indicates that it is covered with snow there.

The temperature on Mars is believed to be about 50 degrees (by the Fahrenheit scale) at its equator during the daytime, only about half what it is at our equator. At night, the temperature goes below freezing. It also is believed that Mars has spring, summer, fall, and winter, just like the seasons on the earth. The seasons on Mars are almost twice as long as those on the earth.

The air around Mars is believed to contain very little oxygen, so that animal life as we know it could hardly exist there.

There are two moons that travel around Mars. The inner moon, named Phobos, goes around Mars three times a day. The outer moon, called Deimos, goes around once in about every thirty hours.

Marseillaise

The *Marseillaise* is a lively, stirring song that is the national anthem of the French people. The song was written in 1792 by Claude Joseph Rouget de Lisle, a French officer, during the French Revolution. The mayor of the town of Strasbourg gave a banquet for a brave group of volunteers who were about to leave for battle. The mayor asked de Lisle to write a song for the occasion. He wrote the words and selected an old tune as the music. The song was first called *Battle Song of the Army of the Rhine.* People in Paris did not hear the song until a few months later. Then a group of soldiers from the town of Marseilles, in southern France, sang it in Paris. The people were thrilled by its music and words and they called it the *Song of the Marseillais,* that is, the song of the men of Marseilles.

Marseilles

Marseilles is the second-largest city in France. It is in the south, an important port on the Mediterranean Sea. The harbor is a colorful and busy place because ships from every part of the world dock there. More than 600,000 people live in Marseilles. They work on the docks and also in many factories that make steam engines, automobiles, soap, oil, and other products.

The original harbor at Marseilles is called the Old Port. A new, bigger and deeper harbor was built more than a hundred years ago. More than four thousand ocean vessels go in and out of the harbor every year.

The old part of the city was noted for its narrow, winding streets. This old part of the city was destroyed by the Germans during World War II. The modern city of Marseilles is built around the old district. It is surrounded by hills covered with vineyards. The Church of Notre Dame de la Garde is one of the most famous buildings in the city. It is on a high hill, and a huge statue of the Virgin Mary stands on top of its steeple. It can be seen far out at sea and serves as a land-

French Gov't Tourist Office

Marseilles is the chief French port on the Mediterranean. One of the most colorful sights of Marseilles is the fishing fleet anchored in the Old Port.

mark for sailors. It is also considered a shrine by the seamen of Marseilles.

The city of Marseilles was founded by Greeks more than two thousand years ago.

MARSEILLES, FRANCE. Population (1954 census) 661,492. In the department of Bouches-du-Rhône. On the Mediterranean Sea.

marshal

Marshal is the title given to the highest-ranking military officers in many countries in which there is or has been royalty. A marshal ranks as though he were a prince of the royal house of the country. He is called "Your Excellency." The only other nonroyal title that ranks as high as marshal is cardinal. A cardinal also ranks with princes of the royal family and is called "Your Eminence." Princes are addressed as "Your Highness." Until about 75 years ago, the English simply gave their highest-ranking military officers titles of nobility; for example, the Duke of Marlborough and the Duke of Wellington. In modern times they have adopted the rank field marshal. Napoleon I, the French emperor, gave many of his officers the title of marshal. Germany's leading officers in World War II held the rank of field marshal. The United States never had any regular rank higher than general until 1945, when it created the rank General of the Army, which is usually known as "five-star general." A United States General of the Army ranks as high as a marshal from any other country. A marshal carries a baton (a small, short wand) as a sign of his high rank, but a General of the Army does not.

Certain law-enforcement officers of the United States government are also called marshals. It is a position like that of a sheriff.

Marshall, George C.

George Catlett Marshall is the name of the United States Army officer who

was chief of staff of the United States Army during World War II. After the war he became even more noted as a statesman, especially as Secretary of State. He was appointed chief of staff in 1939 over the heads of thirty-four higher-ranking generals. In 1944 he was the first man to be given the new rank of General of the Army, or "five-star general." As Secretary of State, Marshall proposed the MARSHALL PLAN (about which there is a separate article) to help the countries of Europe.

Marshall was born in 1880 in Uniontown, Pennsylvania. From early boyhood he had planned to be a soldier, and in 1897 he entered Virginia Military Institute. When he was 22 he was commissioned a second lieutenant in the United States Army. In those days it was a handicap for an officer not to be a West Point graduate, and for this reason promotions came slowly to Marshall. He served in various posts in the United States and the Philippines until World War I, during which he served in France. Under General John J. Pershing, Marshall was assigned to move 500,000 troops and 2,700 guns within two weeks and secretly. Pershing later had high praise for Marshall's successful plan. Marshall was aide-de-camp to Pershing from 1919 to 1924, and the two worked together to convince Congress that the country must be prepared for war at any time. By this time Marshall had moved up to the rank of lieutenant colonel.

From 1924 to 1938 Marshall served in China and in various posts in the United States, and rose to the rank of brigadier general. In 1939, when he became Chief of Staff with the rank of general, he began a difficult campaign of building up American armed forces. He was a member of the policy committee that guided development of the atomic bomb. Marshall took part in most of the important diplomatic conferences of the war years, attending the Atlantic Charter conference, and the meetings of Presidents F. D. Roosevelt and Harry S. Truman with foreign leaders abroad.

In 1945, Marshall resigned as chief of staff and was immediately appointed special representative of President Truman to China. In 1947 he was recalled to become Secretary of State. He was responsible for the United States plan of aid to Greece and Turkey to forestall Communist Russia's moves to take over those countries, and he then proposed the Marshall Plan to head off Russian aims in other countries. Marshall resigned as Secretary of State in 1949. The following year he was appointed Secretary of Defense and held that post for exactly a year, resigning in 1951.

Marshall, John

John Marshall was the fourth Chief Justice of the United States Supreme Court. He was probably the most important Chief Justice in American history. He made the Court a strong branch of the government and made decisions about the meaning of the Constitution that have been followed ever since. When the United States was first made a country, many people thought that each state should have a great deal of power to decide its own affairs and that the central government should not be very strong. Marshall believed that the power of the Federal government should be much stronger in some matters than that of the states, and many of the decisions he made while he served as Chief Justice helped establish that power.

John Marshall was one of the most important of the early Americans who helped form the United States. During his lifetime he served in many positions. He was a lieutenant during the Revolutionary War and was Washington's aide, was one of the men who supported the

new Constitution, was a special envoy to France for President John Adams, and served as Secretary of State and Secretary of War as well as a member of Congress.

John Marshall was born at Germantown, Virginia, in 1755. After serving in the army he practiced law and quickly became well known. George Washington offered him the position of Attorney-General in his first Cabinet, but Marshall refused. President John Adams appointed Marshall Chief Justice in 1801, and he served for 34 years, until his death in 1835. He wrote a biography of Washington and a history of the colonies, but his best writings are the legal opinions that he handed down while he served on the Supreme Court.

Marshall, Thomas

Thomas Riley Marshall was an American lawyer who became Vice President of the United States when Woodrow Wilson was President. Marshall was born in North Manchester, Indiana, and was a descendant of the famous Marshall family of Virginia to which John Marshall, Chief Justice of the Supreme Court, belonged.

Thomas Marshall practiced law for 33 years in Columbia City, Indiana. He became known as an orator who spoke with a great deal of humor. In 1908 he was elected governor of Indiana, and in 1913 and 1917 was elected Vice President.

Marshall is especially remembered for a remark he made while he was presiding at a dull session of the House of Representatives: "What this country needs is a good five-cent cigar." Marshall died in 1925.

Marshall Islands

The Marshall Islands are a group of thirty-two islands in the western Pacific Ocean, about five thousand miles from the west coast of the United States. They were the scene of heavy fighting during World War II. Before World War I the islands belonged to Germany. At the end of the war, they were given to the Japanese, who had fought on the side of the Allies. During World War II the United States forces carried out the war in the Pacific by a policy that is known as "island hopping." They attacked and captured one group of Japanese islands after another, each time coming nearer and nearer Japan itself. Early in 1944 they attacked one of the Marshall Islands, Kwajalein, which they captured after fierce fighting. The rest of the Marshall Islands were taken from the Japanese very shortly after this. After the war was over, the United States kept control of the Marshall Islands.

The most famous of the Marshall Islands today is Eniwetok, where the United States tested the hydrogen bomb. The force of the bomb was so great that it destroyed the island and made the waters around it radioactive and extremely dangerous.

Marshall Plan

The Marshall Plan was the popular name of an offer made by the United States to help other countries become prosperous again after they had spent most of their money fighting World War II. The plan was named for General George C. Marshall, who was the highest-ranking army general in the United States Army during the war, and who was appointed Secretary of State in 1947. In a speech at Harvard University that year, Marshall suggested that the United States would be willing to help the countries of Europe return to good financial condition and rebuild their business and industry. Many European countries immediately accepted this offer, and the United States set up the Economic Recovery Program to work out the details of how the help was to be given. In 1948 President Harry S. Truman signed an act setting up the Economic Coöperation Administration to put the program into effect.

The United States did not actually give money to the people of these countries. The people bought and paid for many things made in the United States that were not available in their countries, such as tractors, machinery, food, drugs, and chemicals. They paid in their own money, but the United States made available to their governments enough United States dollars to pay American manufacturers for these products. The whole idea was that the United States would help them to buy American goods if the countries would help themselves by putting people to work using these goods.

Only the democratic countries of Europe benefited by the Marshall Plan. Czechoslovakia and some other countries under the control of Communist Russia wanted to join the Marshall Plan, but Russia immediately forbade them to take any part in it.

marsh hawk

The marsh hawk is a bird that lives in many parts of the United States. It has a white patch on its lower back that makes it easy to recognize. The wings and tail are long and narrow. The male marsh hawk is pale gray in color, and the female is dull brown. The marsh hawk builds a nest on the ground and carefully hides it in tall marsh grass or under low bushes. The female lays four or five white eggs. The marsh hawk flies close to the ground in order to spot the frogs and mice that it eats. During the mating season, the male marsh hawk flies in graceful circles and power dives to attract the attention of the female marsh hawk.

marsh mallow

The marsh mallow is a plant that grows in Europe and the eastern parts of the United States. The marsh mallow is a perennial, which means that it grows up from the same roots every year. The plant grows best in wet swampy places. It grows to be about three feet high. It has large pink flowers, and its stems and leaves are soft and fuzzy. The roots of the marsh mallow contain a valuable sticky substance. The roots are collected in the fall and dried. Then people scrape the roots to collect the sticky substance, which is used in cough drops and in candy marshmallows, though people have discovered other and better ways to make the candy.

marsupial

A marsupial is an animal that carries its young in a pouch, a fold of skin that is attached to the mother's abdomen. Long ago, these animals lived all over the world. Gradually they died out, and now almost all of the marsupials make their home in Australia. The only marsupial that does not live in Australia is the opossum. It is found mostly in Central and South America, but one variety of opossum lives in the forests of the southeastern part of the United States.

The kangaroo is the best-known marsupial. Its young are carried in a deep pouch until they can care for themselves.

The best-known marsupial is the kangaroo. It grows to be about seven feet high and weighs more than two hundred pounds. The wallaby is a smaller kangaroo. Other marsupials, such as the marsupial mice and moles of Australia, are tiny creatures less than a foot long. There are marsupials that live in trees and others that live on the ground. The marsupial wolf is a fierce animal that eats meat. The wombat, which looks like a small, fat bear, is a shy animal that hides during the day and comes out at night to search for grass and leaves to eat. One marsupial that lives in the jungles of Australia flies through the air; it is called a flying phalanger and it looks like a flying squirrel. Another marsupial swims in the rivers of South America; it is called a yapok and is a member of the opossum family.

The marsupials are very helpless when they are born. All a tiny marsupial is able to do is to crawl into its mother's warm pouch. There it nurses and quickly grows big and strong. When the babies grow too large for the cozy pouch, they climb out. Often they spend some time after that clinging to their mother's back. In case of danger the young marsupial will return to the pouch for safety.

Marsupials are not intelligent animals and they have many enemies. Man hunts some marsupials, and dogs and cats and owls and other creatures often attack them. Some people believe that these animals may slowly die out altogether.

marten

The marten is a small animal about the size of a cat. It lives in the forests of Europe, Asia, and the United States. The marten has a soft, golden-brown fur, with a patch of cream color at its throat. It has a long, bushy tail. The marten is prized for its beautiful fur, and coats made from it are very expensive.

The marten is a member of the weasel family, and like most weasels, it is a fierce and brave little animal that will attack animals many times its size. The marten is such a savage fighter that few animals other than man can kill it. It is very swift and can run up a tree more quickly than the fastest squirrel. Martens eat squirrels, rabbits, and mice. They also eat fruit and berries. The marten usually builds its nest in a hollow tree. Sometimes it builds a burrow in the side of a hill. The marten lines the nest with moss and soft grass. The female marten has four babies at a time.

Martens are not very sociable animals, and they usually live alone. The marten is very curious, and when it sees a trap that hunters have set, its curiosity leads it to investigate, so that it is easily captured.

So many people have hunted the marten because of its valuable fur that now there are not very many martens left.

martial law

The word *martial* is connected with "war." The word comes from Mars, the name given by ancient Romans to the god of war. When a place is under martial law, it is no longer controlled by the usual peacetime government but by the army or some other military group. Martial law is often declared during a war, but it is also put into effect when there is a riot or a disaster, such as a flood or an earthquake. Martial law is necessary for the protection of life and property during a period of disaster and conflict. It is also needed when the usual police force cannot deal with the situation.

In the United States the President or the Governor of a state announces martial law at such a time, and the highest-ranking army officer in the area takes complete control.

martin

The martin is a friendly, sociable bird that lives in almost every part of Europe and the United States. It is a member of the swallow family. It is a grace-

Martins often will build their nest in a birdhouse put up in a garden, and may return to it summer after summer.

ful flyer and is well-known for its lovely song. The purple martin is a handsome, dark purple bird that is about 8 inches long. In the autumn, when the first signs of winter appear, the martins begin their journey south. People build large houses where many families of martins live together and they wait for the martins to return in the spring. Martins will return to the same house for many years. Martins eat flies and other insects. They have large mouths, and as they fly they keep their mouths open so that they can catch insects. The female martin lays about eight shiny white eggs.

The martins that live in England are called house martins. They build their nests on the sides of houses. The nests are made of mud and twigs, with an opening in the side of the nest so that the martins can fly in and out. The house martin is a black bird with white underfeathers.

The sand martin is smaller than other members of the martin family. It gets its name because it hollows out long tunnels in sandbanks to build its nest. At the end of the long tunnel it makes a nest of soft grass and leaves lined with feathers.

Clipper Line

Most of Martinique is rugged and mountainous. Streams from the interior run through cities and farms along the coast.

Martinique

Martinique is one of the Windward Islands in the West Indies. It belongs to France. It is 425 square miles in size, which is less than one-half the size of Rhode Island, and 276,000 people live there, which is about one-third the population of Rhode Island. Its capital city is Fort-de-France, a city of about 75,000, which is also its chief port.

The island is really the top of a volcanic mountain that reaches all the way down to the bottom of the ocean. Martinique itself has several mountain peaks. Between them are fertile valleys where the people grow great quantities of sugar cane. Sugar and rum produced on the island are sent to other countries.

The people are often troubled by hurricanes, earthquakes, and volcanic eruptions. In 1902, Mont Pelée, a volcano about 4,500 feet high, erupted violently and destroyed Saint-Pierre, a town that was then Martinique's leading city.

Martinique is an Overseas Department of France, which means that it can send two senators and three men to represent it in the French National Assembly in Paris. French is the official language, but most of the people speak a "creole" language that mixes French and other languages.

MARTINIQUE. Island in the West Indies. Area, 425 square miles. Population (in 1951), 276,000. Overseas Department of French Union. Chief city and capital, Fort-de-France.

martyr

A martyr is a person who gives his life for what he believes in. Most often the word applies to someone who suffers or dies rather than give up his religion. The spirit of martyrdom pervades the book of Daniel, written at a time when the Jewish religion was being persecuted, in the second century before Christ.

The first Christian martyr was St. Stephen, who was stoned to death for defending his Christian belief. (This is described in the Bible, in the Acts of the Apostles, Chapter 7.) St. Paul, who was then persecuting the Christians, was present and the event probably helped him become a Christian.

The Romans demanded that everyone participate in the state religion. This meant worshiping the emperor. One could worship as many other gods as one chose. Christians could not join in em-

Clipper Line

On market day, many farmers of Martinique go to Fort-de-France, the capital, to sell tropical fruits raised on their farms.

peror worship. They could only worship one Lord, Jesus Christ. In the eyes of the Roman authorities all such people were disloyal and deserved death. When they were brought to the attention of the police they were given a chance to do what was required. If they bore witness that Christ was the only one whom they would worship they were sentenced to die. The word *martyr* is Greek and means "a witness." Some were taken into a crowded arena to be killed and eaten by lions; others were burned to death. Later many martyrs were recognized as saints, and received a day in the calendar. The stories of their martyrdom were then considered good reading for their particular days. There is a great collection of these stories in many volumes.

Men who have died for other beliefs are also called martyrs. Very often they become symbols of that belief, and their courage inspires others to risk their lives in order to make the belief known and accepted by others. Real and supposed martyrs have played an important part in politics. Often a government will refuse to punish a criminal for fear he will be treated as a martyr and in this way awaken revolt.

Marx, Karl

Karl Marx was a German writer and thinker who lived about a hundred years ago and who had many original ideas about how people should live and how they should be governed. The ideas of Karl Marx, which are now called Marxism, led to the development of the system of government that is now called communism, so it may be said that very few men have had a greater influence on today's world than Karl Marx.

Because communism is an enemy of liberty and religion, and most of the people of the world value their liberty and their religious freedom higher than anything else, it is usual in free (democratic) countries today to disapprove of everything Karl Marx said. This is not a very

scientific way to look at it. Karl Marx did not suggest the cruel kind of government that Communists have today. Much of what he taught was wrong, but in some ways he was a brilliant thinker.

Karl Marx was born in Prussia, the largest German kingdom, in the year 1818. As a young man he published a magazine that criticized the government of Prussia. In  those days most countries were governed in about the same way, so Marx was actually criticizing nearly all governments. Countries were run by the "upper classes," who were rich and who lived on the work of the "lower classes," who were very poor. Karl Marx wrote that this was wrong. Most people today agree with him, but strangely enough it is the democratic countries, which do not follow Marx's teachings, that have corrected it, and the Communist countries, which say they follow Marx's teachings, that have not corrected it.

The Prussian government made Marx stop printing his magazine and made him leave the country. He went to Paris, France, but after 1849 he was not allowed to live there either. So Marx went to England, where (as in other English-speaking countries) everyone has freedom of speech. Though Marx attacked the British government as much as he did other governments, he was permitted to live and write in London the rest of his life.

In London Marx was very poor. He was married and had several children, and they had to live in the slums. Here Karl Marx wrote his most famous works. The ideas of Karl Marx are explained in the article on COMMUNISM. With another German writer, Friedrich Engels, he had already published a brief document called the *Communist Manifesto,* in 1848, and in England Engels helped him to write his longest book, *Das Kapital* (which in the German language means "capital" and is about the systems known as CAPITALISM and SOCIALISM, both of which are explained in separate articles).

During Marx's lifetime, an International Workingmen's Association was formed (in 1866) to follow Marx's teachings. Marx died in 1883, at the age of 65, with *Das Kapital* not quite finished, but Engels finished it for him.

Mary, the Virgin

The Virgin Mary was the mother of Jesus. Her story, as told in the Gospels, the first four books of the New Testament, is:

Mary was a young girl of Nazareth, a town in Palestine, the land of the Jewish people. She was engaged to marry a carpenter, Joseph. Before they were married, the archangel Gabriel came to her and told her that she would be the mother of Jesus. This was the *Annunciation*, which

N.Y. Public Library

The Virgin Mary spins thread and St. Joseph works as a carpenter during their stay in Egypt after fleeing from Herod, who sought to kill the infant Jesus.

means "announcing." When Jesus was conceived (began to grow) in Mary, she was still a virgin, which means that she had not known or been married to a man.

Mary then went to see her cousin, Elisabeth, who was also expecting a child (who grew up to be John the Baptist). This is called the *Visitation*. Mary visited her cousin Elisabeth for three months, then returned to Nazareth. Some months after that, she went with Joseph to the city of Bethlehem, where the law required them to go to pay their taxes. There was no room in the inn, so they put up for the night in a stable, and there Mary gave birth to Jesus.

After the birth of Jesus, Joseph, Mary, and Jesus had to flee to Egypt to escape Herod, the king in Palestine; for Herod had heard the prophecy that Jesus would be king, and he was seeking to kill Jesus. When Herod died, they returned to Nazareth. Jesus grew up in the home of Mary and Joseph. He performed his first miracle (changing water into wine) because Mary asked him to; this was at a wedding in the nearby village of Cana, when there was not enough wine for all the guests.

Mary was present at the Crucifixion of Jesus. He told the Apostle John to take care of her, and from then on she lived in John's house. Mary was with the disciples when they were waiting, after Jesus was risen, for the Holy Spirit to come and give them the wisdom and courage to preach the Christian faith; this is told in the first chapter of the Book of Acts of the Apostles.

BELIEFS ABOUT MARY

There are many accepted traditions about the Virgin Mary, and some or all of them are taught in the churches of the various Christian denominations.

Almost all Christians believe that Mary was a virgin, and for that reason she is often called merely the Virgin or the Blessed Virgin. The article on the IMMACULATE CONCEPTION describes the belief that she was conceived without original sin (the sin inherited from Adam's fall). Another belief, called the *Assumption,* is that she was taken up to heaven, body and soul, by God. Another is that Mary was the daughter of Saints Anne and Joachim.

Many people, especially Roman Catholics, pray asking Mary to seek graces for them from God. There are separate articles about the AVE MARIA and the ROSARY. There is a beautiful litany, the Litany of Loreto, that describes her.

There are famous shrines to Mary at Lourdes, in France, and Fátima in Portugal. A new Roman Catholic cathedral in Washington, D.C., is dedicated to Mary, who is the Catholic patron saint of the United States.

Among the hymns to Mary are *Stabat Mater Dolorosa,* telling of her sorrow as she stands near Jesus during his Crucifixion, and the *Salve Regina,* which addresses her as the queen of heaven.

There are many feasts celebrated in honor of Mary. They are celebrated by Catholics and in many cases by Protestants. December 8 is the feast of the Immaculate Conception; February 2, of the Purification of Our Lady; May 31, the Queenship of Mary; July 2, the Visitation; August 15, the Assumption; September 8, the Birthday of Our Lady; November 21, the Presentation of Our Lady in the Temple.

Mary Magdalene

Mary Magdalene was a saint who lived in the time of Jesus. Her story is told in the New Testament. She was a bad woman until she met Jesus. Then she repented and became one of his followers. She was present at the Crucifixion and the Resurrection of Jesus (about which you can read in the article on JESUS). Her name means that she came from the town of Magdala, in Palestine.

Mary, Queens of England

There have been two queens of England named Mary who were rulers in their own right. Others have become queen by being married to a king. The first to become queen by inheritance rather than by marriage was Mary I, or Mary Tudor, the daughter of Henry VIII and Catherine of Aragon. She was born in 1515 and was trained to be a queen from her early

childhood. Her father had his marriage to Catherine of Aragon anulled and married Anne Boleyn, who was the mother of Elizabeth I, Mary's sister. Later he married Jane Seymour, who was the mother of Henry's only son, Edward VI.

While Henry VIII was alive, Mary's life was very sad. Her father favored her sister Elizabeth. He treated Mary cruelly and did not want her ever to become queen. After the death of Henry VIII, Mary's brother Edward VI became king; but Edward died while he was still a boy, and Mary was next in line. Though she had many enemies, she became queen. This was in 1553. She was 37 years old.

When Mary I became queen, some of the people of England were Catholics and some were Protestants, and they were very unfriendly toward one another. Mary was a Catholic, as her mother had been. Her father, Henry VIII, had been a Protestant.

Both Catholics and Protestants suffered persecution during that period. Sometimes Protestants were in power and persecuted Catholics. Sometimes Catholics were in power and persecuted Protestants. There was no such thing as religious freedom. Many people were executed for their religious beliefs. Because of the things that happened during her reign, she was nicknamed "Bloody Mary."

Mary I married Philip, a Spanish prince, but they had no children. This disappointment, and the fact that she was sick much of the time, made her a very unpleasant person. She died in 1558, when she was 43, and her sister Elizabeth became queen.

MARY II

The second queen of England named Mary was born in 1662, about 150 years after the first Mary. The father of Mary II was James II, who was king of both England and Scotland.

When Mary was only 15 years old, she married William, Prince of Orange, who was a Dutch prince. In 1688, when Mary was 26, revolution forced her father to give up the throne and William and Mary became king and queen together. They were crowned in 1689.

This was the only time two persons of equal rank ever shared the British crown. William was often away at wars, and while he was gone Mary II was a wise and popular queen. She died of smallpox in 1694, when she was 32, and her husband continued to reign as William III until he died in 1702. William and Mary College in Virginia was named for them.

MARY OF TECK

The best-known Queen Mary of modern times was the wife of King George V of Great Britain. Her full name was Victoria Mary. Her father, the Duke of Teck, was a German, and her mother was a British princess, Mary Adelaide.

Mary of Teck was born in 1867, and in 1893, when she was 25 years old, she married the man who was then the Duke of York. In 1910 he became King George V of England and Mary became his queen.

Queen Mary always put her duty as queen before her own desires. She felt very strongly that kings and queens are different from other people and should always be very formal and dignified. Queen Mary never used a telephone, because she felt it was not dignified.

King George V and Queen Mary had four sons and one daughter. Two of them became kings—Edward VIII and George VI. Mary had tried to give her children the same strong sense of duty that she had, but her eldest son, Edward VIII, gave up the throne so that he could marry as he wished; he became the Duke of Windsor. Queen Mary lived to see her granddaughter, Elizabeth II, become the reigning queen in 1952. In 1953, two months before Elizabeth was crowned, Queen Mary died at the age of 85.

Mary, Queen of Scots

Mary Stuart, who was Queen of Scotland about four hundred years ago, was one of the most tragic queens in British history. She was born in 1542. Her father died when she was a baby, and she was crowned queen of Scotland when she was less than a year old. When she was 16 she married Francis, son of Henry II, king of France. After about a year, Henry II died, and for nearly two years Francis and Mary were king and queen of both Scotland and France, but Francis died in 1560.

Mary returned to Scotland and immediately encountered difficulties because she was a Catholic and the people of Scotland were mainly Protestant.

Five years after the death of Francis, Mary married Henry Stuart, Lord Darnley, a Scottish nobleman. They had one son, who was later to become James VI of Scotland and James I of England. Later, Darnley was killed when a house in which he was visiting was blown up. Many people suspected that Mary had known about the plot to kill Darnley and had done nothing about it. Another Scottish nobleman, the Earl of Bothwell, was suspected of causing the explosion, and when Mary married him the people became very angry and turned against her. She fled to England, where she hoped that Queen Elizabeth I would help her. Instead, Elizabeth threw her into prison. Elizabeth thought Mary had ambitions to become Queen of England.

For the next eighteen years, Mary plotted to escape from prison. Finally, she was charged with being part of a plot to kill Elizabeth. Tried, convicted, and sentenced to death, she was beheaded at Fotheringay Castle, in February 1587, at 44.

Maryland

Maryland

Maryland is one of the South Atlantic states of the United States. It was one of the thirteen original colonies. Its nickname is the "Old Line State" because Maryland soldiers showed great bravery fighting in the front lines during the Revolutionary War, and received special praise from General George Washington. Maryland is named after Queen Henrietta Maria, the wife of King Charles I of England.

Maryland ranks 42nd in size among the states, with 10,577 square miles. In population it ranks 22nd, with nearly three million people living there. It was the seventh of the thirteen colonies to become a state, in 1788. The capital is Annapolis.

THE PEOPLE OF MARYLAND

The English were the earliest and largest group of Maryland settlers. Most of them were Roman Catholics. They went to Maryland about three hundred years ago because their religion was not the official English religion. Later, many French, German and other European people went for the same reason, religious freedom. Most of these people started farms on the rich Maryland soil, and they brought in Negro slaves to work the plantations. As factories were built in the cities, other immigrants settled in Maryland from Russia, Poland, Italy, and other European countries. Today, most of the people in Maryland are American-born.

Many people in Maryland are still farmers, but even more now work in the large cities, especially in Baltimore, where almost half the people of Maryland live.

The early settlers in Maryland were determined that it should be a place where people of all religions could worship as they pleased, without fear of persecution. They passed such a law more than three hundred years ago. Today, the largest religious group is the Methodists.

WHAT MARYLAND IS LIKE

Maryland is divided into two parts by the Chesapeake Bay. The region around the bay is called the coastal plain, and it is very flat. There are many fine harbors along the jagged coastline. There is fishing for bluefish, oysters, bass, and many other fish, both in Chesapeake Bay and in the Atlantic Ocean. The soil of the coastal plain is very fertile.

In the north central part of the state is the Piedmont Plateau, a high, level region. It is one of the best dairy-farming regions in the country.

The western part of Maryland is the Appalachian Plateau. Here are high mountain ridges of the Allegheny and Appalachian mountains, with narrow, fertile valleys in between. The Potomac River runs through this part of the state, and it has cut many deep gorges in the mountains.

The climate of Maryland is varied. In the eastern and southern parts of the state the winters are mild and the summers hot. In the mountains the summers are cool and the winters very cold. The average temperature in winter is 34 degrees, and in summer about 75 degrees.

Hunting is a favorite sport with people in Maryland. There are many small fur-bearing animals such as the squirrel, rac-coon, and fox. There are also bears and deer in the woods.

Because so much of Maryland faces the water, transportation by boat has always been important to the people. Shipbuilding became an important industry in colonial days, and ships built in Baltimore became famous all over the world. Today, Baltimore is one of the great ports for world trade, and the Chesapeake and Delaware Canal was built to provide a short cut for ocean vessels. It connects an arm of Chesapeake Bay with the Delaware River. Railroads were built to reach parts of the state where there were few rivers, and now Maryland has about 1,500 miles of railroad. The state is crossed by many roads and highways, and many of the old roads in Maryland are historic. The famous Cumberland Road, which today is a big highway, was the route many pioneers took as they went west. Maryland also has many airports, including the Friendship International Airport, which covers 3,200 acres in Baltimore.

THE GOVERNMENT OF MARYLAND

Maryland, like most other states, has a Governor and a Legislature. The Governor is elected for a four-year term. The Legislature is composed of a Senate and a House of Representatives. The members of both houses are elected for a four-year term. Judges are elected for a fifteen-year term. The capital is Annapolis. There are 23 counties.

Everyone has to go to school between the ages of 7 and 16. There are about 818 public schools, including 219 high schools, and 34 colleges, universities and other schools of higher learning. Among the principal colleges and universities are:

University of Maryland, at College Park. Enrollment, 12,414 in 1953 (9,361 men, 3,053 women).

Johns Hopkins University, at Baltimore. Enrollment, 6,089 in 1953 (4,989 men, 1,100 women).

Johns Hopkins University

Beautiful Johns Hopkins University is one of the best-known schools, not only in Maryland but in the entire country.

Maryland is a beautiful state with a rugged coast-line on Chesapeake Bay, which cuts the state in two, and green farm lands in the Piedmont Plateau region. Its flower is the black-eyed Susan.

Maryland Dept. of Inform.

1. Maryland's Colonial State House in Annapolis, built in 1772, is the oldest in America still in use. Here, in 1783, George Washington resigned as commander-in-chief of the colonial army.

2. The Chesapeake Bay Bridge is about seven miles long and extends four miles over water.

3. The successful defense of Fort McHenry against a British naval attack in 1814 assisted in the defense of Baltimore and inspired Francis Scott Key to write "The Star-Spangled Banner."

4. A monument to George Washington at the head of a square in Baltimore.

5. From Louden Heights in Maryland one gets a fine view of Harper's Ferry, West Virginia, where John Brown tried to free the slaves in 1859.

Bethlehem Steel Co.

Baltimore Tour. Devel. Bureau Photos

Baltimore & Ohio Railroad

Morgan State College, at Baltimore. Enrollment, 1,676 in 1953 (826 men, 850 women).

United States Naval Academy, at Annapolis. Enrollment, 3,610 men in 1953.

CHIEF CITIES IN MARYLAND

The leading cities of Maryland, with populations from the 1950 census, are:

Baltimore, population 949,708, the largest city in the state. There is a separate article about BALTIMORE.

Cumberland, population 37,679, the second-largest city, a railroad and industrial center, in the northwestern part of the state.

Hagerstown, population 36,260, the third-largest city, manufacturing center, in the northern part of the state.

Annapolis, population 10,047, the state capital and seventh-largest city. There is a separate article about ANNAPOLIS.

MARYLAND IN THE PAST

The first permanent settlement in Maryland was made by the English, who set up trading posts on Kent Island more than three hundred years ago. In 1632, King Charles I of England gave the Earl of Baltimore a large grant of American land that included Maryland, and in the following years many English colonists settled in the region. These colonists were gentlemen who were used to living comfortably, and they built beautiful houses and had slaves to serve them. They also brought many English customs with them, and one could often see Maryland gentlemen going fox-hunting in their scarlet costumes and celebrating Christmas with large parties, much as they had done in England.

About two hundred years ago Maryland had a disagreement with Pennsylvania, its neighbor to the north, about its boundary. The disagreement was finally settled by the famous Mason and Dixon's Line, which came to be considered the dividing line between the North and the South.

Maryland soldiers fought bravely in the Revolutionary War and the War of 1812 against the British. It was while watching the attack on Fort McHenry near Baltimore, during the War of 1812, that Francis Scott Key was inspired to write "The Star-Spangled Banner," the national anthem of the United States.

At the time of the Civil War, Maryland was in an important position because it lay on the boundary between the North and the South. The Maryland plantation-owners owned slaves, but Maryland, unlike other slaveholding states, did not secede from the Union, though many of its people wanted to.

After the Civil War, Maryland expanded rapidly. Its cities grew and big

Midshipmen of the United States Naval Academy get their sea legs sailing in Chesapeake Bay near Annapolis, capital and site of the Academy.

Maryland Dept. of Inform.

The rugged grandeur of the Great Falls of the Potomac recalls the days when pioneers had to steer their craft through these dangerous waters.

Maryland Dept. of Inform.

Maryland is a state where industry and farming are of equal importance. To visitors it offers good hunting and fishing.

1. Unloading iron ore from a freighter at a large Maryland steel mill.

2. Baltimore, one of the largest shipbuilding and repair centers in the East.

3. Pouring molten steel into ingots.

4. Gathering ripe Maryland tobacco.

5. No need to "stretch" the size of this rockfish taken from Chesapeake Bay!

6. Dusting cabbages on a coastal farm.

Bethlehem Steel Co.

The Havre de Grace Bridge over the Susquehanna is part of the chief highway route between north and south Maryland.

factories were built. Baltimore became one of the large industrial centers in the country. In both World War I and II, Maryland contributed to the war effort with large supplies from its farms and factories.

PLACES TO SEE IN MARYLAND

Fort McHenry National Monument and Historic Shrine, in Baltimore, on U.S. Routes 1 and 40. The successful defense of this fort in 1814 inspired the writing of "The Star-Spangled Banner."

Antietam Battlefield, near Sharpsburg, in the northwest, west of U.S. Route 40. The scene of one of the bloodiest battles during the Civil War, in 1862.

Maryland has many dairy farms, which supply milk and other dairy products to the great metropolitan areas of Baltimore, Philadelphia, and New York City.

Standard Oil Co.

Annapolis National Cemetery, at Annapolis, in the central part of the state.

The United States Naval Academy, at Annapolis. Visitors are usually permitted to enter the grounds and buildings.

Great Falls of the Potomac, north of Bethesda, on U.S. Route 240. Spectacular cataracts made by the Potomac River.

The State House in Annapolis, completed in 1774 and the oldest capitol in the United States that is still in daily use.

MARYLAND. Area, 10,577 square miles. Population (1957 estimate) 2,895,000. Capital, Annapolis. Nickname, the Old Line State. Motto, *Scuto Bonae Voluntatis Tuae Coronasti Nos* (With the Shield of Thy Goodwill Thou Hast Covered Us). Flower, black-eyed Susan. Bird, Baltimore oriole. Song, "Maryland, My Maryland." Admitted to Union, April 28, 1788. Official abbreviation, Md.

Masaryk

Masaryk was the name of two Czechoslovakian statesmen, father and son.

Thomas Garrigue Masaryk is called the "father of Czecho-  slovakia" and is considered its greatest statesman. In 1850, when he was born, Austria-Hungary controlled the territories that later became the nation of Czechoslovakia. Thomas Masaryk was born in Moravia, one of these territories. The Moravians are a Slavic people. Along with the Czechs, Slovaks, and other Slavs, they had tried for years to become independent of their Austrian and Hungarian rulers.

Masaryk became a professor at the University of Prague. He was interested in politics and was elected to the Austrian parliament, which governed Moravia and the other territories. He headed a party that wanted complete independence from Austria. In 1914, when World

War I broke out, Masaryk fled to Paris to avoid being on Austria's side. There he formed an organization called the Czech National Council to work for Czech independence. During the war Masaryk went to the United States to raise money for his organization. When the Allies won World War I, in 1918, they made Czechoslovakia an independent nation. Masaryk's organization became the new Czech government and Masaryk became its first president. He served from 1918 until 1935. When he was 85 years old, he resigned because of his age, and he died two years later, in 1937. He was greatly loved by the people of his country.

Jan Masaryk, his son, was born in 1886. He served as his country's minister to Great Britain from 1925 to 1938. Germany took over Czechoslovakia in 1939 and during World War II Czechoslovakia set up a government-in-exile. Jan Masaryk was the foreign minister of this government. In 1945, when the Allies won World War II, he returned with the government to his country, but then in 1948 the Communists took over Czechoslovakia. Masaryk remained in the cabinet, even though he was not a Communist. A few days later, in the spring of 1948, he died as a result of a fall from a window. It was announced that he had committed suicide, but some believe he was murdered by being forced out of the window.

Masefield, John

John Masefield is the name of an English poet who became poet laureate of his country. The poet laureate is appointed by the king or queen to write poems for special occasions and to commemorate great events. Masefield was born in 1874. His father was a lawyer, but John was too restless for an office career. At the age of 14 he went to sea, and later he worked for a few years in New York City. In 1897 he returned to England and became a newspaperman,

German Tourist Inform. Office

Masks first were used in religious ceremonies, and then by actors in plays. Today, they are most commonly worn at festivals when people are making merry.

writing poetry at the same time. His first books of poems showed the influence of his experiences at sea. One of these was *Salt-Water Ballads,* which contained a famous poem named "Sea Fever."

In 1911 Masefield had published a long story-poem, *The Everlasting Mercy.* This was compared with Chaucer's *Canterbury Tales,* and it was said to bring back to poetry a life and strength that had been missing for hundreds of years. It was followed by three other narrative poems, *The Widow in the Bye Street, Dauber,* and *The Daffodil Fields.* Masefield also wrote adventure stories for boys, and various other books. He was appointed poet laureate in 1930.

masks

Masks are made of cloth, paper, rubber, wood, or some other material and are worn over the face or head. In primitive religions, witch-doctors or "medicine men" have worn masks to make themselves look like gods or spirits. They believe that if they have the appearance of gods they will also have the powers of gods and will be able to cure diseases, protect their people, and punish their enemies. Children often wear masks, particularly on Hallowe'en, for amusement. The catcher on a baseball team wears a mask to protect his face, and people who work in certain industries also wear masks for protection. In wartime soldiers and sometimes civilians wear gas masks for protection against poison gas. Sometimes criminals wear masks so that they cannot easily be recognized.

Another kind of mask is a death mask. For many hundreds of years death masks were made whenever a famous person died. The face of the dead person was covered with wax or plaster that hardened into a mask that looked like the person. This practice was carried on at least two thousand years ago, and because of it we know what many famous people of the past looked like. Masks have also been worn by actors in certain kinds of dramas. You can read more about these masks in the article on MASQUE.

Mason and Dixon's Line

Mason and Dixon's Line, or "the Mason and Dixon Line," is the name given to the boundary between Pennsylvania on the north and Maryland and West Virginia on the south. Before the Civil War, when slavery was allowed in the United States, the Mason and Dixon Line was the boundary between the free states in the north and the slave states in the south. Long before this time, when the United States belonged to Great Britain, the colonies of Pennsylvania, Maryland, and Virginia had argued about the exact boundaries separating them. Two English surveyors named Charles Mason and Jeremiah Dixon had settled the dispute. Both before and during the Civil War, "below the Mason and Dixon Line" was used to mean the southern, or slave holding, states of the United States. We use this term today to refer to the South in general.

masque

A masque is a kind of dramatic entertainment that was popular in England about four hundred years ago and is seen occasionally in modern theaters. The masque is a play in which there is a great deal of music and dancing. Often the characters in the masque are allegorical, that is, they represent thoughts or emotions rather than human beings. The masque gets its name from the word "mask." At first all actors who appeared in this kind of play wore masks. The actors did this because it was the custom in the early Greek theater to have the actors wear masks representing the emotions of the characters in the drama, and the first masques were presented by the Greeks. In England the masques were private entertainments put on at court or at the homes of noblemen. They were in imitation of masques performed in the Italian and French theatres. The best-known writer of masques in English literature is Ben Jonson, but the best-known masque is *Comus,* written by John Milton, one of England's greatest poets.

masquerade

A masquerade is a fancy-dress party or dance at which people wear masks in order to disguise themselves. Masquerade balls have been popular for hundreds of years, but especially in France and England about three hundred years ago. Before that time, masquerades were often part of religious festivals, but many such masquerades were later forbidden by the Church. In the United States masquerade parties are popular, especially around Hallowe'en. The Mardi Gras, a celebration held each year in New Orleans on Shrove Tuesday, the day before Lent begins, is a religious festival that has a masquerade connected with it. At most masquerade parties, people remove their disguises at midnight.

Mass

The Mass, in the Roman Catholic and Eastern Orthodox Churches, is a public religious ceremony. This means that it is a way of praying in public together with other people. The prayer is always performed in a certain way. Many people compare the Mass to a play or drama, because it combines words and actions, and reaches a high point or climax. It is called a sacrifice, because it is recognized as a way of praising God and asking Him for His blessing by offering Him the body and blood of Jesus.

The Roman Catholic and Eastern Orthodox religions consider the Mass as the unbloody sacrifice of the body and blood of Jesus, a representation of his bloody sacrifice on the cross. They recognize the Mass as coming from the Last Supper, when Jesus said to his followers, "This is my body," when he gave them bread, and "This is my blood," when he gave them wine. (This is the way it is described in the Gospel of Luke, Chapter 22). They believe in the doctrine of transubstantiation, which says that when a priest repeats these words over the bread and wine used at the Mass, the bread and wine actually become the body and blood of Jesus (though retaining the appearance of bread and wine). The Mass is the most important way in which people of these Churches worship God.

Most people who go to Mass in the United States would go to one in a Catholic church. The Mass is considered very beautiful. The language used in the Mass is Latin. A person who does not know Latin can follow the Mass in a MISSAL, about which there is a separate article. In a few places Catholics do not use Latin.

HOW THE MASS IS SAID

Only a priest ordained by a bishop can say Mass. He is usually helped by altar boys, who say the responses to prayers. When there is a high Mass, there may be a deacon and subdeacon. Usually they are also priests. A high Mass is one in which many of the prayers are sung or chanted. Most Masses are low Masses, in which the prayers are spoken.

The Mass is divided into two parts: the Mass of the Catechumens, and the Mass of the Faithful. In early Christian times no one who had not been baptized could attend the second and more important part of the Mass. People who had not yet been baptized, but were studying for baptism, were called catechumens. The part of the Mass they were allowed to attend was named for them.

The Mass of the Catechumens is also divided into two parts: the introductory prayers, when the priest and people speak to God, and the instructions, when God speaks to them. The instructions include the epistle, gradual, gospel, and creed. The introit states the main idea of the Mass for the day, and the epistle and gospel are taken from the New Testament. These instructions change every day, and are included in the movable parts of the Mass.

MASS OF THE FAITHFUL

The Mass of the Faithful is also divided into two parts. In one part the priest and people make their offering to God through Jesus. This includes the offertory and the canon of the Mass. In the second part God's love descends through Jesus. This is the communion. In the offertory, the priest offers up bread and wine.

An altar boy rings bells at the end of the offertory. This begins the canon of the Mass. It opens with prayers for all the members of the church. Then the altar boy rings the bell once as the priest spreads his hand over the bread and wine. The priest takes the bread and wine and repeats the words of the Last Supper. This is called the consecration. After consecrating the bread, he raises it for all to see. He does the same with the wine in the chalice. The consecration is the most important part of the Mass, because it is the part recognized as changing bread and wine into the body and blood of Jesus.

The next important part of the Mass is the communion, when the priest consumes the consecrated bread and wine. Consecrated hosts are distributed to any of the people who also wish to receive communion. The Mass ends with prayers of thanksgiving.

Massachusetts

Massachusetts

Massachusetts is one of the New England states in the United States. It was one of the thirteen original colonies, and the place where the Pilgrims landed more than three hundred years ago. The nickname of Massachusetts is the "Bay State" because the early settlers lived along Massachusetts Bay. The people of Massachusetts played important parts in the founding of the United States. You can see some of the most important historical landmarks in American history in

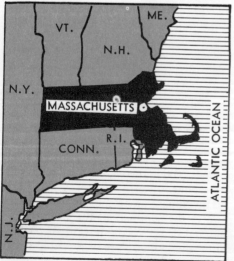

Massachusetts. Today, Massachusetts is one of the great manufacturing states and is also a favorite vacation place. It takes its name from the Indian tribe that lived there before the Pilgrims arrived.

Massachusetts ranks 45th in size among the states, with 8,257 square miles. In population it ranks 9th, with more than four and a half million people living there. It joined the Union in 1788, the sixth of the original colonies to become a state. The capital is Boston.

THE PEOPLE OF MASSACHUSETTS

The first settlers in Massachusetts were English. They were the Pilgrims, who sailed from England in the *Mayflower* and landed at Plymouth Rock in 1620. (You can read about the PILGRIMS in a separate article.) The Pilgrims and later English settlers became farmers and fishermen like the Indians who had lived there before them. It was difficult for farmers to earn a living from much of the rocky New England soil, so many of them turned to manufacturing and started small factories.

As the state grew, immigrants arrived from Ireland, France, and Germany, and later many Italians, Russians, and people from other European countries came

Boston Chamber of Commerce Photos

Above: **The capitol building in Boston.**
Left: **The Mayflower, state flower of Massachusetts.** *Right:* **Trinity Episcopal Church, a Boston landmark.**

to work in the growing factories and mills.

Most of the people of Massachusetts live in the large manufacturing cities and work in factories making shoes, cotton and woolen goods, rugs, electronic equipment, twine, and many other products. Others work in the large fisheries for which Massachusetts is famous. It leads all other states in the value of the fish caught by its fishermen.

Massachusetts farmers produce dairy products, corn, onions, and poultry. They also grow a large part of the country's cranberries, and delicious apples and strawberries. Some of the people work in granite, marble and sandstone quarries.

The largest number of people today are Roman Catholic, but Massachusetts is the original home of the Congregational, Unitarian, Christian Science and other Churches.

WHAT MASSACHUSETTS IS LIKE

The eastern part of Massachusetts, on the Atlantic Ocean, is low and sandy, with several large bays, including Boston Bay and Cape Cod Bay. Cape Cod, which juts out into the ocean like a big hook, is a famous vacation place, with summer

theaters and artists' colonies. In this section most of the Massachusetts cranberries are grown. Off the sandy coast are popular vacation islands, including Martha's Vineyard and Nantucket.

From this low region, Massachusetts rises to a plateau, or high, level region, in the central part of the state. Here the factories are supplied with water power from the swift streams and rivers.

Farther west is the very fertile Connecticut Valley, where most of the farming is done. The Connecticut River runs through this section. The western part of the state is another popular place for vacations, with the Berkshire Hills rising to their highest point at Mt. Greylock, 3,497 feet high. Thousands of people every summer attend the musical festival at Tanglewood. In this part of the state there are also many summer camps for boys and girls.

When the early settlers lived in Massachusetts, it was filled with many wild animals. Today there are only foxes, deer, and rabbits.

The climate along the eastern coast is mild in the summer. In the winter it is cold and damp. In the hills of the Berkshires the winters are very cold, with heavy snow, but in summer it is pleasantly

New buildings of Harvard University stand on the Cambridge side of the Charles River. Harvard, founded in 1636, is the oldest college in the United States and is famous throughout the world.

Harvard University

M.I.T., Cambridge

Mass. Dept. of Comm.

Left: Modern dormitories of M.I.T., famous engineering school, in Cambridge.

Below: Winter in Massachusetts.

Springfield Chamber of Commerce

Left: The men of Gloucester have been fishermen for generations.

Below: The lighthouse serves them as a beacon on stormy nights.

Standard Oil Co.

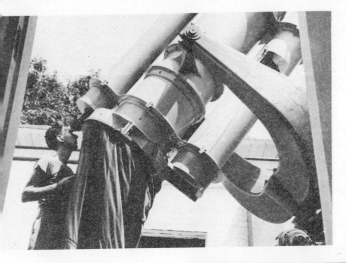

In the 19th century, Massachusetts became the center of American writing and art. Today, its many famous colleges and universities have also made it a great center of the sciences.

Harvard University

Right: Cape Cod grows many strawberries.

Below: Massachusetts leads in growing (and eating) cranberries.

Standard Oil Co.

Cape Cod Ch. of Comm.   *Mass. Dept. of Commerce*

Right: The valley of the Connecticut River has many farms.

Below: Textile mills are an important industry of Massachusetts.

Pepperell Mfg. Co.

cool. The state's average temperature in summer is 69 degrees. In winter it is about 23 degrees.

Massachusetts has many railroads and highways reaching all parts of the state and there are airports in all the important cities.

THE GOVERNMENT OF MASSACHUSETTS

Massachusetts calls itself a "Commonwealth" and not a state, but like the other states, it is governed by a governor and a legislature. The governor is elected for a two-year term. The legislature is called the General Court, and is composed of two houses, a Senate and a House of Representatives. The members of both houses are elected for a two-year term. Judges are appointed for life or until they retire. The capital is Boston. There are fourteen counties.

Everybody has to go to school between the age of 7 and 16. Some of the oldest schools in the country are in Massachusetts, and it has always been a leader in education. It has about 1,688 public

Mass. Dept. of Commerce

Paul Revere's home was already a hundred years old when the famous patriot and silversmith lived there. It is kept just the way it was when he was alive.

schools including 336 high schools, and 70 colleges, universities, and other schools of higher learning, some of which are among the most famous in the world.

There are separate articles about HARVARD, RADCLIFFE, MOUNT HOLYOKE, SMITH, AMHERST, HOLY CROSS, WELLESLEY, and the MASSACHUSETTS INSTITUTE OF TECHNOLOGY. See the article on BOSTON for Boston College and Boston University. Other important colleges include the following:

University of Massachusetts, at Amherst. Enrollment, 3,814 in 1953 (2,528 men, 1,286 women).

Northeastern University, at Boston. Enrollment, 11,135 in 1953 (10,630 men, 505 women).

Clark University, at Worcester. Enrollment, 741 in 1953 (516 men, 225 women).

Wheaton College, at Norton. Enrollment in 1953, 537 women.

CHIEF CITIES OF MASSACHUSETTS

The leading cities of Massachusetts, with populations from the 1950 census, are:

Boston, population 801,444, the state capital and largest city in the state. There is a separate article about BOSTON.

Worcester, population 203,486, the second-largest city. There is a separate article about WORCESTER.

Springfield, population 162,399, the third-largest city, manufacturing center for machinery, in the southwestern part of the state.

Cambridge, population 120,740, fourth-largest city, educational and industrial center, in the eastern part of the state.

MASSACHUSETTS IN THE PAST

More than nine hundred years ago, it is believed Norsemen visited the shores of Massachusetts. Later it was explored by John Cabot and John Smith. The first settlers did not arrive until 1620, one of the important dates in American history, when the Pilgrims landed at Plymouth Rock. Many others later joined these settlers at Plymouth Colony, which grew into a prosperous community. A group

Standard Oil Co. Photos

Mass. Dept. of Commerce

No state has an older American tradition than Massachusetts, where the fight for American independence began.

1. Visitors to Old Sturbridge must leave cars behind. The village is just as it was in early American times.

2. Longfellow wrote of the Wayside Inn in his *Tales of a Wayside Inn*. Washington and Lafayette were among its guests.

3. Narrow streets in Marblehead remain as they were when America was young.

4. The homes and churches of beautiful Cape Cod are historic landmarks.

Cape Cod Chamber of Commerce

of Puritans from England started the Massachusetts Bay Colony farther north. The Puritans were a strict people, and dealt harshly with those who did not agree with them. You can read about the PURITANS in a separate article.

The Massachusetts Bay Colony and the Plymouth Colony were finally joined and given a charter by the English king. The colony prospered but as more and more taxes were placed on them by England, the people protested, and finally they became leaders in the struggle for freedom and independence. John Adams, Samuel Adams and John Hancock were the Massachusetts leaders. The Boston Massacre and the famous Boston Tea Party were two of the important events that led to the Revolutionary War. The first battles of the Revolutionary War were fought at Lexington and Concord in Massachusetts, in 1775.

Massachusetts continued to grow as a manufacturing state and also as a cultural center. Some of the great American writers and thinkers lived in the state about a hundred years ago. They included Emerson, Longfellow, Hawthorne, and many others. The Massachusetts people were also very much against slavery. The ABOLITION (anti-slavery) movement, about which there is a separate article, was most important in Massachusetts.

In the Civil War, Massachusetts sent more than 150,000 men to fight in the Union Army. In World Wars I and II, it contributed many men and important supplies to the armed forces.

PLACES TO SEE IN MASSACHUSETTS

Adams Mansion National Historic Site, at Quincy, in the east, on State Highway 135. The home of Presidents John Adams and John Quincy Adams.

Salem Maritime National Historic Site, at Salem, in the northeast, on State Highway 114. Contains the Old Custom House where Nathaniel Hawthorne worked, and other places associated with New England's history.

Plymouth Rock, at Plymouth, in the east, on U.S. Route 44. The place where the Pilgrims probably landed in the *Mayflower* in 1620.

Minuteman Statue, at Lexington, in the northeast, on State Highway 25. A statue dedicated to the Minutemen who fought in the Battle of Lexington, the first battle in the Revolutionary War.

Old North Church, in Boston, in the east, on U.S. Route 20. The famous church from which Paul Revere received the signal that the British soldiers were going to attack Lexington. The tower from which the signal was given was blown off by a hurricane in 1954.

Bunker Hill Monument, in Boston, in honor of the men who fought so bravely at the Battle of Bunker Hill in the Revolutionary War.

Charleston Navy Yard, in Boston. The famous warships *Constitution* and *Constellation* can be seen here.

Sleepy Hollow Cemetery, at Concord, in the northeast, on State Highway 126. Some of the most famous American writers are buried here: Emerson, Thoreau, Hawthorne, and the Alcotts.

Standard Oil Co.

Massachusetts is the center for the New England style of architecture. The interior of Christ Church in Cambridge is a fine example of its simple elegance.

MASSACHUSETTS. Area, 8,257 square miles. Population (1957 estimate) 4,866,-000. Capital, Boston. Nickname, the Bay State. Motto, *Ense Petit Placidam Sub Libertate Quietem* (By the Sword We Seek Peace, but Peace Only Under Liberty). Flower, Mayflower. Bird, chickadee. Song, "Massachusetts." Admitted to Union, February 6, 1788. Official abbreviation, Mass.

Massachusetts Institute of Technology

Massachusetts Institute of Technology is one of the most important universities in the United States. It is located in Cambridge, Massachusetts, and was founded in 1865. Many of the leading engineers, architects, and scientists in the United States and other countries have been graduated from M.I.T. This school also has done outstanding research in many branches of science. Much work on the development of the electronic brain was carried on here. The students at M.I.T. are mostly men, but some women attend the advanced schools. In 1958 6,179 students were enrolled at the school, nearly all of them men. There were 1,049 teachers on the faculty.

massage

Massage is a method of rubbing or kneading (pinching) the body. This makes blood and lymph (another fluid in the body) flow more freely. Certain pains in the muscles, such as backache, are relieved when the circulation of the blood is greater. Heat also increases the circulation of the blood and other body fluids, and rubbing always produces greater heat in the muscles. Massage is good for certain diseases, such as infantile paralysis (poliomyelitis) and cerebral palsy. A man skilled at giving massages is called a *masseur,* and a woman is called a *masseuse.* A machine such as an electric vibrator can produce some effects that are the same as a massage by hand. Massage cannot remove fat from overweight persons.

News Service, M.I.T.

The Massachusetts Institute of Technology is one of the greatest engineering schools in the world. The massive dome is the Institute's main architectural feature.

Massasoit

Massasoit was the sachem, or king, of the Wampanoag Indians who were living in the lands around Plymouth, Massachusetts, when the Pilgrims landed there in 1620. Massasoit had once been a very powerful sachem, with more than thirty thousand Indians in his tribe. Shortly before the Pilgrims came, all except three hundred of the tribe had died from a terrible disease. Massasoit and the Pilgrims signed a peace treaty in 1621 that was not broken by either the Indians or the Pilgrims during Massasoit's lifetime. The settlers helped Massasoit when he was sick and hungry, and he was so grateful that he warned them of a plot that unfriendly Indians had made to destroy them. Massasoit gave up many of his lands to the new settlers, and went to live in what is now the town of Warren, Rhode Island. He died in 1661, when he was about eighty years old.

Massey, Vincent

Vincent Massey is a Canadian statesman and the first native-born Canadian to become Governor-General of Canada. In Canada the Governor-General acts in place of the British queen, who is also Queen of Canada. Massey was born in 1887. He was graduated from the University of Toronto in Canada and from Oxford University in England. He taught history at the University of Toronto from 1913 to 1915, and served as chancellor of the university from 1947 to 1953. Massey served on the military staff of Canada during World War I, was the Canadian minister to the United States from 1926 to 1930, and served as a delegate to the United Nations Assembly in 1946. He was appointed Governor-General in 1952. Vincent Massey was married in 1915. He has two sons. His brother, Raymond Massey, is a well-known actor in motion pictures and the theater.

mass production

Mass production is the making of many manufactured products of the same kind at the same time. For thousands of years, such products were made one at a time, by hand, and no two were exactly alike. In mass production they are all exactly alike.

The two most important things in mass production are *interchangeable parts* and the *assembly line*.

Eli Whitney, the American inventor who is best remembered because he invented the cotton gin, also was the first man to use interchangeable parts. This was more than 150 years ago. In the year 1798, the United States gave Whitney a contract to manufacture some muskets for the army. He took so long to deliver the muskets that the government was going to cancel the contract. But in the meantime Whitney had made tools that could turn out the separate parts of a musket very rapidly. When all his tools were completed, a worker could take one of each part and put a musket together a hundred times as fast as it had ever been done before. In modern mass-production manufacturing, "tooling up" to make the separate parts may take many months, but once the tools are finished the parts can be made and put together so rapidly that each worker can make thousands of finished products in the

time that a worker once would have needed to make one.

The assembly line is a moving belt or chain that carries an unfinished product from one worker to another. Each worker puts on one part or does one particular job on the product, such as polishing or painting it. The worker stays in one place, which saves time. He has only one part to reach for and only one operation to learn. After the moving belt has passed all the workers, the product is completed and drops off the line, ready to be shipped to the user.

Assembly-line production was tried in France and other countries nearly a hundred years ago, but most of the credit for it is given to Henry Ford. By using the assembly line to make automobiles, beginning in 1913, Ford was able to make several thousand cars a day and sell them at very low prices. Other manufacturers learned from him and soon the assembly line was being used in nearly all modern factories.

AUTOMATIC MACHINERY

Mass production depends also on automatic machinery that does many jobs that once were done by hand. Many automatic machines are actually assembly lines in which the work is done mechanically instead of by hand.

For example, in a plant that makes soft drinks there are machines that mix the drink in big vats, automatically pour exactly the right quantity into each bottle, put a cap on the bottle, pack the bottles into cartons or boxes, and deliver them to a loading platform where a truck is waiting for them. A chewing-gum machine automatically mixes the gum, chops it into sticks of the right length, wraps it, counts out the right number of wrapped sticks and wraps them together as a package, counts the right number of packages and puts them in a carton, packs the cartons in a box for shipment and even addresses the box. Such machines take in rolls of paper, print it, cut it

MINERALS

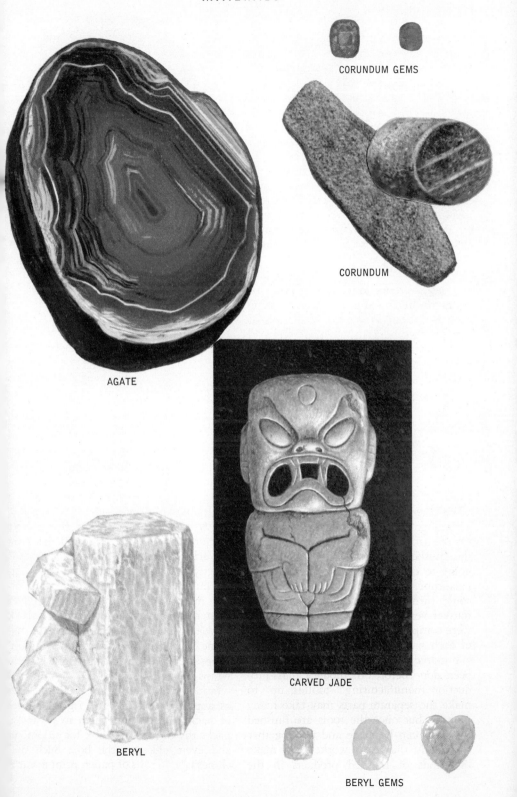

CORUNDUM GEMS

CORUNDUM

AGATE

CARVED JADE

BERYL

BERYL GEMS

MINERALS

ASBESTOS

GOLD

OPEN-PIT IRON MINE

SILVER

COPPER

into the right lengths, and deliver it to the place where the gum is to be wrapped. At another place in the machine, rolls of cardboard go in and printed cartons come out at the right spot.

The first automatic machines were mostly made for the textile industry (the industry that makes cloth and other fabrics). A knitting machine was invented more than 350 years ago. Machines to spin thread and to weave cloth automatically were invented almost two hundred years ago. The first machines of this kind were invented in England and the textile industry that grew out of them made England the richest country on earth. During the 1800s, dozens of automatic machines were invented, and in the 1900s there have been many more. Mass production is practiced more in the United States than in any other country. In some countries, manufactured products are made cheaply because of "cheap labor": The workers are paid so little that they cannot live comfortable lives. In the United States, manufactured products are made cheaply because of mass production, and the workers are paid more instead of less. This has given the United States the highest living standard in the world. It is the same in Canada. Several European countries are almost as far advanced in mass production, but most countries of the world are far behind.

Masters, Edgar Lee

Edgar Lee Masters was an American poet who became famous for one book of poems, *Spoon River Anthology*. He was born in 1869 in Kansas, but he grew up in Illinois in a town on the Spoon River. He became a successful lawyer in Chicago, and wrote poetry under an assumed name for fear that being known as a poet would hurt his law practice.

Spoon River Anthology was published anonymously (that is, without any name signed to it), but Masters became known and famous as the author. The book is a collection of epitaphs for the grave-stones of a small-town cemetery. The 250 epitaphs are supposed to have been written by the dead persons whose graves they mark, and each one reveals his secret hopes and fears, good and bad deeds, joys and sorrows. The book was a sensation when it was published in 1915. Masters also wrote novels, a biography of Abraham Lincoln, and the story of his own life, *Across Spoon River*. Masters died in 1950, at the age of 81.

mastiff

The mastiff is a giant of a dog. It has been known for two thousand years in England, and there were mastiffs in ancient Egypt as long ago as 3000 B.C. They are heavy, powerful dogs, and long ago they were used as fighting dogs in competition with bulls and other animals. They are kept today mainly as watchdogs and pets, but they are so large they are seldom seen in the city. A mastiff usually has a gentle, friendly disposition, but if anyone threatens a member of the family it will quickly become angry. It is strong enough to knock down a man with a single leap.

The mastiff is about 30 inches high at the shoulder and about 33 inches long from the chest to the base of the tail. It may weigh as much as 150 or 160 pounds. It has strong, straight legs, a

The mastiff is a fine pet because it has a kind and gentle disposition, but is also a strong and courageous watchdog.

square muzzle, and a long, straight-hanging tail. Its coat is short and thick, with the hair lying flat against the skin. It is usually light in color, either tan or golden brown, and sometimes it has dark stripes over the entire body. The nose and head are usually quite dark, almost black.

The *bull mastiff* is another kind of dog, bred from the mastiff and the bulldog. It was originally intended to be a game-warden's assistant and its job was to keep off poachers (hunters who were after animals belonging to the landowner). It is slightly smaller than a mastiff, and its muzzle is like that of a bulldog.

mastodon

The mastodon was an animal that lived in many parts of the world thousands of years ago. The mastodon looked very much like an elephant, but there were some important differences between the mastodon and the elephant that we know. The mastodon had a much flatter head, and its jaws were longer. The mastodon was about 10 feet tall, and it had long shaggy hair to keep it warm. It ate leaves and roots and branches. The teeth of the mastodon were not as complicated as the teeth that elephants have now.

People in the United States have discovered the bones of many mastodons, especially in New York State. Scientists believed that when the first men lived in North America, mastodons roamed the

Before men came to North America, the mastodon roamed the forests. Though it looked like an elephant, it was only between four and five feet high.

country. Now people who visit large museums can see the bones of these animals.

Matanuska Valley

The Matanuska Valley is a fertile region in south central Alaska. It is about one thousand square miles in size, and only about three thousand people live there. In 1935 the United States government sent 208 families from Michigan, Minnesota, and Wisconsin to start a farming project there. These people were farmers who were suffering from the depression and droughts and had to give up their farms in the United States. The government gave them loans and sent men to help them clear the land and build houses. Many of these families left, but still the community grew. The farmers raise grains, vegetables, berries, poultry, and dairy products. They ship their products by the Alaska Railroad and by a highway that runs through the valley.

match

Matches are sticks of wood or cardboard tipped with a chemical that bursts into flame when rubbed against a rough surface. The most important chemical used in matches is phosphorus, which bursts into flame very easily.

Three main kinds of match are made today. The wooden, "strike-anywhere" match ignites (begins to burn) when it is rubbed against any rough surface. Wooden matches used to cause fires because rats used to nibble at them until they ignited. They are now made with a substance that is distasteful to rats.

A second kind of match is the wooden *safety match*. This is ignited by striking it on a special strip on the side of the box in which the matches are packed. Some of the chemicals needed to create fire are in the head of the match and some in the striking strip on the box.

The third kind of match is the *book match*. Book matches are similar in principle to the wooden safety match, but they are made of cardboard. In the Unit-

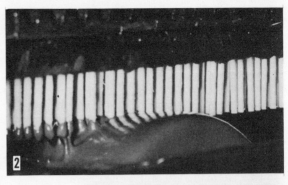

1. Chemicals used in the composition of match heads are prepared and poured.
2. The wood splints pass over a grooved roller and get their first chemical coating.
3. They look like an endless parade of soldiers as they move toward the last dip.
4. Then they are boxed, with half pointing one way and half the other for flat packing.

ed States book matches are the ones most used. About 250 billion of them are made each year. Few people pay for book matches, for they are given away with cigarettes and cigars and are used as souvenirs by hotels, restaurants, and other companies. The United States is the only country in which most matches are free. Most match books contain advertising, and the advertiser pays the cost of the matches.

HOW MATCHES ARE MADE

Matches are made in huge machines, 60 feet long and as high as a two-story house. A machine changes a small stick of wood or cardboard into packaged matches in sixty minutes, and turns out 1,125,000 matches an hour.

The machines that make wooden matches begin the process by taking blocks of pine wood and cutting them into *splints* (little sticks). These splints are held in a chain of metal plates, each with twelve rows of holes. The splints then ride through a series of five dips and baths in chemicals that treat the wood to prevent afterglow, provide a collar of paraffin to speed burning, put on the heads, or tips, and finally dip the heads into a chemical that protects them from changes in the weather. Thirty-two different chemicals are used. The matches are then dried and pour down a trough to drop into endless chains of boxes waiting for them.

THE STORY OF MATCHES

Matches are so much a part of our everyday lives that it is hard to believe that the match as we know it is little more than a hundred years old.

The story of matches begins in 1668, when a German alchemist named Hennig Brandt discovered phosphorus. A few years later a British scientist, Robert Boyle, coated paper with phosphorus and splinters of wood with sulfur. When the splinter was drawn through the paper, it burst into flame. But in those days phosphorus cost about $250 an ounce, so not many of these early matches were sold.

Beginning about 1781, a number of more practical matches were invented. They bore such odd names as the phosphoric candle or ethereal match, the pocket luminary, and the instantaneous light box. The phosphoric candle consisted of paper tipped with phosphorus and sealed in a glass tube. When the glass was broken, air rushed in and set the paper flaming.

The first true match was invented in 1827 when an English druggist, John Walker, tipped small sticks of wood with chemicals that ignited when they were drawn over sandpaper. An improvement was made a few years later when Charles Sauria of France first used phosphorus as an ingredient for match heads. But phosphorus was a dangerous chemical for match workers to handle, for it attacked their bones and gave them a deadly disease known as *necrosis*, or "phossy jaw." Matchmaking was not made safe until 1911 when William A. Fairburn found a way of making phosphorus harmless by mixing it with another chemical.

Wooden safety matches were invented in Sweden in the middle of the 19th century. In 1892 the book match was invented by an American lawyer, Joseph Pusey. Since then the chief improvements in the match have been the invention of matches without an afterglow and matches that have no disagreeable smell.

During World War II, a waterproof match was invented that will light after it has been in water for eight hours.

The United States leads the world in the production of matches. Other large manufacturers are Great Britain, Russia, and Sweden.

mathematics

Mathematics is most familiar to us as the study of numbers. We use numbers every day of our lives, in counting, measuring, and computing. But there is much more to mathematics than that. It is the study of relations, or proportions—how different things compare with one another. Every natural science has a mathematical side, which tries to discover general "laws," or truths, with which we can discover new facts, predict future events, and make useful inventions.

The mathematics taught in elementary schools and high schools deals with operations that are useful in every field, including everyday life.

In *arithmetic* we study the operations of addition, subtraction, multiplication, and division as applied to the simplest numbers. We have to understand arithmetic to buy and sell goods, invest money, read clocks or thermometers, measure land, lumber, cloth, gasoline, groceries and other things, make plans for houses, bridges, airplanes, and so on.

Algebra includes more complicated numbers. It introduces letter symbols such as x, a, p, to stand for these numbers. It studies the relations that hold true whatever the numbers may be. It uses such symbols as $=$ (equals), $<$ (is less than), and many others. The field of algebra is so large that it is divided into at least two parts: elementary algebra, taught in high schools, and advanced algebra, taught in college.

Mathematics is the "mother of sciences" because every science has its mathematical side. But it is just as important in such everyday affairs as buying a pound of potatoes.

Geometry deals with measurements and relations in space, with distances, sizes and shapes. *Trigonometry* deals with the properties of triangles and provides important methods of measurement used in surveying, engineering, astronomy, and many other fields.

Calculus is the "arithmetic of higher mathematics." It deals with quantities that change continually, such as the speed of a bomb falling to earth from an airplane. It is the basis of much of the mathematics dealing with the physical world—light, heat, sound, gravity, electricity, magnetism, and other things.

Knowledge of arithmetic is necessary in our everyday life. High-school students are required to study also elementary algebra and geometry. They may not need to use this knowledge in later life, but it teaches them the mathematical way of thinking. Anyone who intends to make a career in a science such as physics, astronomy, chemistry, electricity, or electronics, or in engineering, must continue the study of mathematics in college.

There are separate articles on the different branches of mathematics.

Mather

Increase Mather and his son Cotton Mather were two important American clergymen in Massachusetts in colonial times. In those days, clergymen had a great deal to say in the governing of Massachusetts. Both Increase and Cotton Mather were PURITANS, about which there is a separate article.

Increase Mather was born in 1639 and at the age of 17 was graduated from Harvard College. He was pastor of the North Church in Boston for 62 years, and for a time was also president of Harvard College. He went to England and from King Charles II obtained a charter that joined the Plymouth Colony with the Massachusetts Bay Colony. He died in 1723, at the age of 84.

Cotton Mather was born in Massachusetts in 1663 and entered Harvard when he was only 12 years old. At the age of 17 he became his father's assistant at the North Church, and four years later was ordained a minister. Cotton Mather is best remembered for his activities in the witchcraft trials in Salem. He believed there were evil spirits that made people act strangely, against the forces of good, and he wrote several books on the subject. (See the article on WITCHCRAFT.) Cotton Mather helped to found Yale University. His ideas about witches seem strange to us today, but in some ways he was a forward-looking man and was one of the first people to approve of inoculation against smallpox.

Cotton Mather died in 1728, at the age of 65.

Mathewson, Christy

Christy Mathewson was a pitcher in professional baseball. Some experts have considered him the greatest pitcher of all time. His full name was Christopher Mathewson, and he was born in Factoryville, Pennsylvania, in 1880. He was graduated from Bucknell University in 1902 and became a member of the New York Giants, at a time when it was very unusual for a college graduate to be a professional baseball player. During his career, which lasted until 1918, he won 373 games. He joined the United States Army in 1918 and fought in France, where he was injured by poison gas. He died in 1925.

Matisse, Henri

Henri Matisse is the name of a great French painter and sculptor. He was one of a group who called themselves Fauvists, from the French word for "wild beast." They used this name because their painting was so new and violent, full of strange shapes and strong colors. Matisse was born in 1869. While he was still studying painting in Paris he was such a fine artist that he got a job copying the paintings of old masters for the French government to sell. He painted in the classic style until about 1900, when he began to develop his new method. Many of his paintings can now be seen in museums in the United States. One of Matisse's greatest achievements was the designing of the chapel Ste. Marie du Rosaire at Vence, France.

Matisse died in 1954.

matter

Matter is anything that takes up space and has weight. The air around you is matter; so is the water in the ocean and the ground under your feet. In fact, you cannot go anyplace on the earth without coming upon some sort of matter.

Of course, there are places where there is hardly any matter at all. Hundreds of miles above the earth, the air becomes very thin, much too thin to breathe. But there is some matter even there, even though it is a very small amount.

There are three different kinds or states of matter: liquid, solid, and gas. Water is a liquid form of matter. Air is a gaseous form of matter. The ground under your feet is a solid form of matter. (There are separate articles on LIQUID, SOLID, and GAS.)

Liquids and gases are often called *fluids* because their parts can flow or move and can be separated from one another. Solids cannot flow and must be heated or struck hard to split them up into separate parts. Solids always have a definite shape. Liquids and gases change their shape whenever their parts move from one space to another.

When people speak of empty space, they usually mean a space that does not contain either a liquid or a solid. However, the space usually does contain air or some other gases. Most of the time, these gases cannot be seen. That is why the space is often said to be empty. But to be truly empty, the space must contain no matter at all, not even a gas. A space that contains no matter whatsoever is called a *vacuum*.

Volume is the amount of space filled by matter. Volume is measured in cubic inches and cubic feet. (You can read more about cubic measurements in the article on CUBE.)

Mass is the amount of matter filling a space. Mass is measured in several different units, such as ounces, pounds, and tons. In most cases the mass of an object is measured by weighing it. Therefore most people confuse the mass of an object with its weight. But the mass and weight of an object are not always the same. The weight of an object is the amount of force with which it is being pulled or attracted to the earth by gravity. Matter has mass even when it is not being pulled to earth by gravity.

Since all matter has volume and mass, we say that all matter also has *density*.

The three different kinds or states of matter are: liquid (1), solid (2), and gas (3). Liquid and gas are called fluids because their parts can flow or move.

The density of matter is found by dividing the mass by the volume. This gives the amount of mass that is contained in a particular space. Density is measured in pounds per cubic foot, as well as in several other units of measurement.

All matter is made up of very tiny particles called *molecules*. Different substances have different kinds of molecule. These molecules are made up of even smaller particles called *atoms*. A substances have different kinds of molecule. without changing into a different substance. When the molecules are broken up into atoms, the substance is changed.

Substances contain millions of molecules. In a solid, these molecules are packed tightly together. They are more loosely packed in a liquid. The molecules of a gas are so loosely packed that they can easily separate from one another so that a gas will always fill any size space into which it may be put.

See also ATOM and MOLECULE.

Matthew, Saint

St. Matthew was one of the twelve Apostles sent out by Jesus to preach the Christian faith. In the Bible, the first book of the New Testament, which is a Gospel or story of Jesus' life on earth, is titled "the Gospel according to St. Matthew."

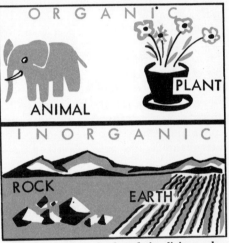

Organic matter is found in living substances, such as animals and plants. But the rocks and minerals of the earth are described as inorganic matter.

The Gospel of Matthew gives a beautiful picture of Jesus as a teacher.

Matthew, who was also called Levi, was a publican. A publican was a man who collected taxes for the Roman emperor. The people in Palestine at the time of Jesus hated publicans. Many of the people were shocked when Jesus made Matthew his friend. But others, who had faith in Christ, saw in this a lesson: That a man's past is not the important thing. The New Testament tells us very little about Matthew. We do know that he probably was richer than the other Apostles. He had enough money to give a big dinner for Jesus at his house. The last time the New Testament speaks about him is when the Holy Spirit comes to the Apostles, as told in chapter 13 of the Acts of the Apostles. There is a very old story that Matthew was killed while preaching in Ethiopia. Artists often use a young man or angel to picture St. Matthew. His feast day is September 21.

Maugham, W. Somerset

William Somerset Maugham is the name of an English writer of plays, novels, and short stories. He was born in 1874 in Paris, France, where his father was a member of the British Embassy. Maugham studied medicine and spent a year as an intern at a hospital in London. From this experience he wrote his first novel, *Liza of Lambeth*. His most famous novel, *Of Human Bondage,* is partly the story of his own early life. One of his short stories, "Miss Thompson," was made into a play and later into motion pictures under the titles *Rain* and *Sadie Thompson*. Several other of his books became successful motion pictures, including *The Razor's Edge* and *The Moon and Sixpence*. His successful plays include *The Constant Wife* and *The Letter*. Groups of his short stories also were made into films, called *Quartet* and *Trio*, with Maugham himself introducing them on the screen.

Mauldin, William

William H. Mauldin is an American author and cartoonist who became well known during World War II for his cartoons of the American soldier. He signed these "Bill Mauldin." In 1944 he won a Pulitzer Prize for these cartoons. Mauldin was born in New Mexico in 1921. He served in the United States Army during World War II in Italy, in France, and in Germany. He received the Purple Heart and the Legion of Merit. During that time many of his cartoons were published in the Army newspaper *Stars and Stripes,* for which he also wrote

many articles. Mauldin wrote several books, of which the most famous are *Up Front* and *Back Home*. After World War II Mauldin acted in two motion pictures and wrote a number of magazine articles.

Mau Mau

The Mau Mau is the native name for a secret society formed in the Kenya colony, in northeast Africa, early in the 1950s. Kenya is a British possession, and most of the good land is owned by British people, while the native people work for them. Most of the natives are members of the Kikuyu tribe. The Mau Mau swore to drive all foreigners out of Kenya, by murdering the white people whenever they could and by destroying their possessions. The Mau Mau not only murdered the white settlers but also killed or tortured Kikuyus who refused to join the Mau Mau. British troops, helped by Kikuyu soldiers who were loyal to them, began in 1952 to fight against the Mau Mau and killed several thousands of them but did not break up the society. Every white man and woman in Kenya made it a rule always to have a pistol or rifle within reach, day and night.

Mauna Loa is a large volcano on the island of Hawaii. See the articles on HAWAII and VOLCANO.

Maupassant, Guy de

Guy de Maupassant was a French writer, considered by many to be the greatest writer of short stories. He was born in 1850, served in the French Army for a time, and then studied literature with another great French writer, Gustave Flaubert. De Maupassant's style of writing has been imitated by thousands of writers since his death. His stories have been translated into many different languages, and are still read throughout the world. Toward the end of his life he suffered from a mental illness. He died in 1893, at the age of 43.

Mauritius

Mauritius is an island in the Indian Ocean. It belongs to Great Britain. It is 720 square miles in area, and more than four hundred thousand people live there. It is one of the most densely populated islands in the world. Many of the people are Indians, and many are Creoles, whose descendants were Europeans and Africans. A number of British and French also live on the islands. Most of the people are farmers, who raise sugar cane in the fertile central plateau. In the cities people make rum, perfume, and drugs. Port Louis is the capital. Mauritius has a warm climate, and in summer the temperature around Port Louis can go up to 95 degrees. The island was first settled by the Dutch more than three hundred years ago, and was named for Maurice of Nassau. It came under British control in 1810. Slavery was abolished more than one hundred years ago.

MAURITIUS. Area, 720 square miles. Population (1944 estimate) 432,648. Capital, Port Louis. Colony of Great Britain.

Maury, Matthew Fontaine

Matthew Fontaine Maury was an American naval officer and scientist who lived more than a hundred years ago. He was an oceanographer, which is a scientist who studies tides and currents and winds and other things that affect the ocean.

Maury was born in Fredericksburg, Virginia, in 1806. He went to sea when he was only 19 years old, but fourteen years later he was in a bad accident that left him lame. He was then put in charge of the Navy's Depot of Charts and Instruments, and later of the Naval Observatory. He made studies of the winds and currents of the Atlantic Ocean that proved to be very valuable to seamen.

When the Civil War broke out, in 1860, Maury resigned from the United States Navy and helped the Confederates, first in the United States and later in England. After the war he became a professor

of meteorology (the study of weather) at the Virginia Military Institute, where he remained until his death in 1873. A building at the United States Naval Academy at Annapolis is named in his honor, and his birthday, January 14, is a school holiday in his native state of Virginia.

Maxim

Maxim is the name of an American family of inventors. The most famous member of the family was Sir Hiram Stevens Maxim, the inventor of the Maxim machine gun, about which you can read in the article on MACHINE GUN. Hiram was born in 1840 in Sangerville, Maine. He worked in machine shops and iron works in New England and New York. At the age of 27, he invented a device for making cheap gas with which to light homes. In 1877, he invented an electric light bulb. This was two years before Thomas A. Edison invented his light bulb, but Maxim's proved too expensive to manufacture.

Maxim soon directed all his attention to the making of guns, and in 1884 he invented the first fully automatic machine gun. He then went to England, where he formed a company to manufacture his new invention. He remained in England until his death in 1916, working on such inventions as a smokeless powder and an airplane powered by steam engines. He was knighted by the King of England in 1901. This made him Sir Hiram Maxim.

Hudson Maxim, the brother of Sir Hiram, was a chemist who developed the first smokeless powder used in the United States. He also developed an explosive called *maximite* that could smash the strongest armor plate. The explosive *motorite,* later developed by him, was used to shoot torpedoes through the water. Hudson Maxim was born in Orneville, Maine, in 1853, and died in 1927.

Hiram Percy Maxim, the son of Sir Hiram, was a mechanical engineer. He was born in Brooklyn, New York, in 1869. He is best known for his invention of the Maxim silencer. This is a device used on guns, in automobile exhausts, and in ventilating machines, to reduce noise. You can read more about the silencer, or *muffler,* in the article on INTERNAL COMBUSTION ENGINE. Hiram Percy Maxim died in 1936.

Maximilian

In the early 1860s, the United States was so occupied with the Civil War that

it could not pay much attention to other American affairs. The French emperor, Napoleon III, was a very ambitious man and he thought this would be a good time for him to seize control of Mexico. He decided to do this by putting in a Mexican king, or emperor, that he could control. For this purpose he chose a young Austrian archduke (prince) named Ferdinand Maximilian Joseph, and made him the Emperor Maximilian of Mexico.

Maximilian was born in Vienna, the capital of Austria. In 1857 he married Princess Charlotte of Belgium, who was afterward known as Carlotta (the Austrian spelling of her name). Maximilian and Carlotta set sail for Mexico in 1864.

Part of Mexico was then under the control of France, and part was independent, with its own government under President JUAREZ, about whom there is a separate article. From the start, Maximilian had an impossibly difficult time. Juarez and his supporters were violently opposed to the idea of having a foreign ruler. As soon as the Civil War was over, in 1865, the government of the United States told Napoleon III that it was opposed to the presence of a foreign emperor in Mexico—and that there were two million United States soldiers to back this up. Napoleon III quickly decided to

inform Maximilian that he must abdicate —give up his crown.

The Empress Carlotta went to France in an attempt to persuade Napoleon to help her husband, but she was unsuccessful. The worry and disappointment affected her mind, and she became insane.

Maximilian refused to give up, and attempted to fight it out with Juarez. He was badly defeated, was captured, and was sentenced to death. He was shot in Querétaro, Mexico, in 1867, when he was only 35 years old. Carlotta remained insane, but lived for sixty years more. She died in Belgium in 1927. Maximilian's brother, the Austrian emperor Francis Joseph, had his body buried in the imperial vault in Vienna.

Maxwell, James Clerk

James Clerk Maxwell was a Scottish scientist who lived about a hundred years ago. He was a physicist, which means that he studied matter (anything that has weight and takes up space). He is best known for his idea that light is a form of electricity and magnetism. This is called the electromagnetic theory of light.

Maxwell was born in Edinburgh, Scotland, in 1831, and attended the University of Edinburgh and Cambridge University in England. After graduating, he set out to investigate many of the things that interested him. He examined the planets in the sky and was the first to explain the rings around the planet Saturn. He showed that almost all colors can be made by combining three primary colors: red, blue, and yellow. Before he was 35, he had developed the electromagnetic theory of light

He was asked to set up an experimental physics laboratory at Cambridge University. He did and was head of the laboratory until his death in 1879. See also the article on INDUCTION.

May

May is the fifth month of the year. It has thirty-one days. In ancient Roman times the year began with March, and May was the third month of the year. It was called *Maius*. It is believed that the month was named after Maia, the Roman goddess of earth and growth, since May is the time when things begin to grow. About two thousand years ago the Romans began to use the calendar we know now, and May became the fifth month.

People who were born in May have the emerald, a very valuable green stone, as their birthstone. The flower of the month of May is the lily of the valley.

Maya

The Mayas were American Indians who lived thousands of years ago in parts of the present countries of Mexico, Guatemala, and Honduras, in Central America. They lived on the Yucatan peninsula (a piece of land surrounded on three sides by water). There the Mayas built a great civilization that lasted for thousands of years. At one time it had a population of several million.

Scientists have spent much time studying the civilization of the Mayas, but no one knows very much about their early history. Some believe that their history goes back more than two thousand years before the time of Christ. Usually the Maya civilization is divided into two periods that are called the Old Empire and the New Empire. The mighty Mayan civilization died out several hundred years ago. There are different ideas about why this happened. Some think it was caused by wars. Others blame it on disease, or on the fact that the Mayan people could no longer raise crops on the land because the soil became poor.

WHAT THE MAYAS WERE LIKE

The Maya Indians were dark-skinned

Honduras Embassy

Near Copán in Honduras there are ruins of an old Mayan city. The stone carving was made before the birth of Jesus.

people. They were not tall but they were strong. Some of them lived in high mountains where the weather was very cold; others lived in warm valleys. The Mayas were farmers. They raised corn and beans and pepper. They also raised bees.

The Mayas were skillful weavers and made beautiful cloth that they dyed in rich colors and decorated. They were fine artists and carved figures and designs out of wood, stone, and jade. They made jewelry out of gold, silver, and copper. They used copper for money. The Mayas did not know how to make tools out of metal, but made them out of wood and stone.

The Mayas built their houses of mud and branches, and they lived in villages. Each village was ruled by a chief. They also built great ceremonial centers of stone and plaster.

The Mayas achieved three remarkable things. They developed a system of mathematics, a calendar, and a system of

Mexican Gov't Railway System

The ruined Mayan city of Chichén Itzá in southern Mexico contains many examples of handsome Mayan-style building.

writing. They knew much about astronomy, the study of the stars. They made their hieroglyphics (written symbols and pictures that stand for things) on the walls of temples and palaces, and they wrote on sheets of paper that were folded and looked very much like the books we have now. When the Spaniards came to the cities of the Mayas, about four hundred years ago, they destroyed many of the books. Fortunately several books remained and these have been studied and translated. From these writings we have learned many important things about the Mayan religion and way of life.

The Mayas were great builders. They used limestone and mortar to make temples and flat-topped pyramids. Their buildings were grouped around a plaza (an open place) and the temples were built on terraced hills that they made. The Mayas put carvings and decorations on the walls of their buildings. The ruins of some of these buildings still stand in Mexico and Central America.

In war, the Mayas used bows and arrows, stone-edged wooden swords and spears, slings, and armor of thick cotton. They tried to capture enemy prisoners, to use as slaves. The Mayas worshiped four gods whom they called "Lords of the Forest." They also believed the sun and the moon were gods.

By the time the Spaniards landed in Central America the great Maya civilization had almost died out and the people were scattered all through the jungles.

May apple

The May apple is a plant that grows in many parts of the United States where the climate is not too hot or too cold. It grows best in shady woods. The plant is about one foot high and has large flat green leaves. Many May apple plants grow together, so that their leaves make a kind of awning that covers the ground. The plant bears one white waxy flower, shaped like a cup. In late summer, after the white flower dies, an egg-shaped yellow fruit appears. The fruit has many seeds. It does not taste sweet, and most people do not eat it, but some people make jelly from it. The May apple is sometimes incorrectly called the mandrake.

Mayflower

The *Mayflower* was a ship that carried the Pilgrims to America in the year 1620. The Pilgrims were the first English settlers of what is now Massachusetts and some other parts of New England. They left England because their religion was

In 1620, the tiny *Mayflower* brought 102 English Pilgrims to New England.

not the same as the official English religion, and they hoped to find religious freedom in the New World. There is a separate article about the PILGRIMS.

The *Mayflower* actually sailed from Leyden, a city in Holland (The Netherlands). The Pilgrims had gone there first from England. They had planned to use two ships for their trip to America but one of the ships, the *Speedwell,* was not in good condition and had to be left behind. Altogether, 102 Pilgrims were on the *Mayflower.* It was a three-masted wooden ship, driven by sails as all seagoing ships were in those days, and displacing 180 tons. The Atlantic crossing took it sixty-three days. First it anchored in Cape Cod Bay, on November 21, 1620. Then it sailed again and anchored in Plymouth Harbor on December 21, 1620. During the first winter it served as headquarters for the Pilgrims while they were building houses on land. The following spring the *Mayflower* sailed back to England.

In 1894 the Society of Mayflower Descendants was founded in the United States. Any person who is 18 years of age or older and a descendant of one of the signers of the Mayflower Compact may belong to this society. The Society was formed to honor the memory of the Pilgrim Fathers, to preserve things and places connected with the Pilgrims, and to defend the freedoms for which the Pilgrims founded the Plymouth Colony. In 1954 the Society had more than seven thousand members.

May fly

The May fly is an insect that makes its home near fresh-water lakes in many parts of Europe and the United States where the climate is not too cold. There are many May flies, especially around the Great Lakes in the United States. The May fly has two sets of delicate wings that you can see through. The back wings are much smaller than the front wings. There are two or three long feelers that

are attached to the end of the May fly's body. As the insect flies, these feelers stream out behind it.

The May fly has an unusual life. In the spring the female drops clusters of thousands of eggs into the lake. These eggs hatch, and little brown creatures called *naiads* begin their underwater life. It may take as long as three years for a naiad to become full-grown. Then it rises to the surface of the lake, sheds its skin, and flies to a place nearby where it again sheds its skin and emerges as a beautiful May fly.

The fully grown May fly lives only a few hours or a few days. The May fly is useful to man because it is one of the most important foods of fish.

Mayo

Mayo is the name of a family of American doctors and surgeons. They

William Worrall Mayo (*top*) opened a small clinic in Rochester, Minnesota, in 1889. His sons, William (*middle*) and Charles (*bottom*), developed it into the Mayo Clinic, one of America's greatest institutions for medical education and research.

are remembered for having founded a great clinic and center for medical research, the Mayo Clinic in Rochester, Minnesota.

William James Mayo was born in Le Sueur, Minnesota, in 1861; his brother Charles Horace Mayo was born in Rochester, Minnesota, in 1865. Both studied medicine and entered practice with their father, William W. Mayo, who was a pioneer doctor. The two young surgeons were constantly searching for new methods of curing disease. Around 1900 they founded the Mayo Clinic.

The Mayo Clinic grew and expanded, and today it consists of several buildings for research and for diagnosis (finding out what illness a person has). Each year some 140,000 patients visit the Mayo Clinic, which has a staff of more than 300 doctors and scientists. In 1915 the Mayo Foundation for Medical Education and Research was endowed by the Mayo brothers as a branch of the University of Minnesota.

Mazarin, Cardinal

Jules Mazarin was an Italian cardinal of the Roman Catholic Church who became Prime Minister of France, about three hundred years ago. He was born near Naples, Italy, in 1602. His family name was originally Mazarini; his first name in Italian was Giulio. He went to France when Cardinal Richelieu was Prime Minister, during the reign of Louis XIII. At that time he changed his name to its French form, Mazarin. When Richelieu died, Mazarin became Prime Minister.

At the death of Louis XIII, the young king, Louis XIV, was only 5 years old. Mazarin practically ruled the country, and Louis XIV's mother was completely under his control. The people of France resented him, because he was an Italian. A civil war broke out in 1648, and Mazarin was banished to Germany for a while. In 1654 he returned to France and took control again. He died in Paris in 1661, at the age of 58.

Mazzini, Giuseppe

Giuseppe Mazzini was an Italian patriot who worked for years to make Italy a united nation and a republic. He was born in Genoa in 1805. Italy had been divided into small kingdoms for hundreds of years. The American and French revolutions, which had been successful a few years before, inspired him. He came from a rich family but believed in the ideals of democracy. His efforts attracted many enthusiastic supporters, some of whom were imprisoned for their violent revolutionary efforts. The unification of Italy as a single kingdom under the first King Victor Emmanuel encouraged him somewhat, but he still worked to have the kingdom become a republic. He was imprisoned for his opposition to the king's government, but was soon released. When Mazzini died at Pisa, in 1872, he was so loved that more than fifty thousand people attended his funeral.

Meade, George Gordon

George Gordon Meade was a general in the Union, or northern, army during the Civil War in the United States. He was in command of the northern forces that defeated the forces of the southern General Robert E. Lee at the Battle of Gettysburg, the most important battle of the Civil War. Meade was born in 1815. He was born in Spain but his parents were Americans. He was graduated from the United States Military Academy at West Point and served in the war against the Seminole Indians in Florida and in the Mexican War. He was made a general in command of volunteers in the Union Army when the Civil War broke out in 1861. He was in command of forces at the second Battle of Bull Run and at the Battles of Antietam, Fredericksburg, and Chancellorsville. He was placed in command of the Army of the Potomac, the chief Union army in the east, just three days before the Battle of Gettysburg, and he remained in command of it until the end of the war. He served as commander of various military districts after the war. He died in 1872.

meadowlark

The meadowlark is a pretty bird that lives in many parts of the United States. It got its name because it builds its nest on the ground in meadows and fields. The meadowlark can hide very well in the tall grass because its back feathers are brown and tan. The meadowlark has a bright yellow breast, and the male has a black bib. The short outer tail feathers are white, and when the meadowlark flies they flash in the sun. The female meadowlark is not as brightly colored as the male. The female lays several spotted eggs.

The meadowlark that lives in the western part of the United States is especially noted for its lovely song. It is very useful to farmers because it eats insects that destroy crops and the seeds of weeds.

Am. Mus. of Nat. Hist.

The meadowlark builds its nests on the ground instead of in a tree. Its melodious song is delightful to hear.

measles

Measles is a disease that most children get between the ages of 5 and 10 years. When a very young child or a baby gets measles it is serious, but for most children measles is not a dangerous disease. It is important for a child who has measles to receive very good care, because measles can lead to pneumonia and other serious complications.

If you have been near someone who has measles, and you have never had measles, you are likely to catch it. Measles is a contagious disease; you can catch it very easily from someone who has it. Often in the spring there are epidemics of measles and many children get the disease.

You will not know whether you have been infected with measles for about ten days. The disease begins like an ordinary cold. The person has a fever and a cough and has to blow his nose frequently. His eyes may be red and watery. Peculiar spots appear inside his mouth. About three days later slightly raised red spots appear on the face and neck. The rash spreads to the arms and legs and the rest of the body. The rash itches and is uncomfortable. The person's eyes ache. He should not look into a bright light when he has measles.

After about a week the rash begins to fade, and the person feels better. It is very important to stay in bed and be careful at this time so that there will be no serious complications.

A person who has measles usually develops immunity to it. That is, he cannot get it again.

measurement

Measurement is a way of finding out distances, weights, temperature, time, and other information of the same kind. Accurate measurements are necessary in nearly all branches of manufacturing and building, and in many other kinds of work.

All measurements depend on some standard unit. In the United States and in British countries, the standard unit of length is the *foot,* the unit of time is the *second,* of weight the *pound,* and of temperature the *degree* (on the Fahrenheit

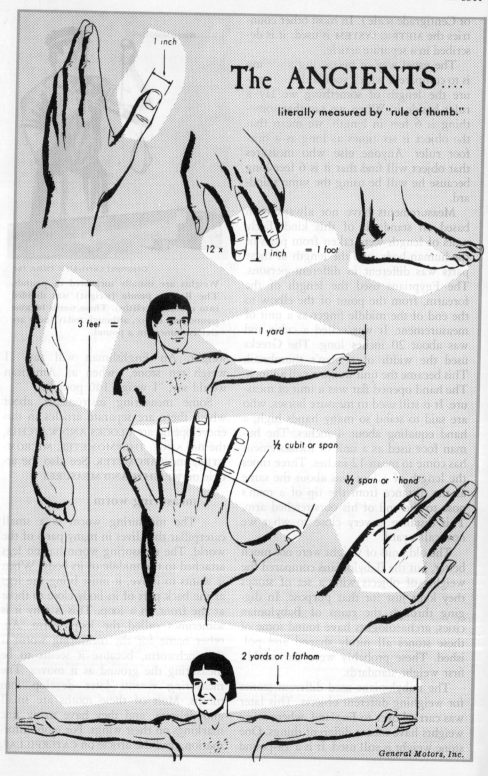

The ANCIENTS....

literally measured by "rule of thumb."

1 inch

12 x 1 inch = 1 foot

3 feet = 1 yard

½ cubit or span

½ span or "hand"

2 yards or 1 fathom

General Motors, Inc.

or Centigrade scale). In most other countries the METRIC SYSTEM is used; it is described in a separate article.

The usual way of measuring anything is to compare it with a standard. To measure the length of something we lay a ruler beside it. When we say that something is 6 feet in length, we mean that the object is six times as long as a one-foot ruler. Anyone else who measures that object will find that it is 6 feet long because he will be using the same standard.

Measurements have not always been based on standards of this kind. Early units of length were taken from parts of the human body, and the length of these parts was different in different persons. The Egyptians used the length of the forearm, from the point of the elbow to the end of the middle finger as a unit of measurement. It was called a cubit and was about 20 inches long. The Greeks used the width of a man's thumbnail. This became the unit we now call an inch. The hand opened flat was a unit of measure. It is still used to measure horses, who are said to stand so many hands high, a hand equaling about 4 inches. The human foot used as a unit of measurement has come to mean 12 inches. Three times the length of a foot was about the same as the distance from the tip of a man's nose to the end of his outstretched arm. This distance is very close to what we now call a yard.

The old units of weight were not much better, but the Babylonians compared the weights of objects with a set of stones they kept just for that purpose. In digging through the ruins of Babylonian cities, archaeologists have found some of these stones all nicely shaped and polished. These probably were the world's first weight standards.

The Babylonians used different stones for weighing different objects. This later was carried over to England, where stone weights have meant different things. One stone weight is still used. It is a 14-pound

Copyright Curriculum Films, Inc.

Weights are usually measured in pounds. The Roman *pondo* (weight) was divided into *unciae* (twelfths). These words became pound and ounce, although today there are sixteen ounces in a pound.

weight. An Englishman will say, "I weigh ten stone," when an American would say, "I weigh 140 pounds."

Some measuring instruments about which there are separate articles in this encyclopedia are CLOCKS AND WATCHES, the BALANCE, THERMOMETER, MICROMETER, and BAROMETER. See also the article on WEIGHTS AND MEASURES.

measuring worm

The measuring worm is a small caterpillar that lives in many parts of the world. The measuring worm has no legs attached to the middle of its body. When it wants to move, it must bring the legs at the back part of its body close to those at the front, in a loop. This is why it is sometimes called the loop worm. Another name for the measuring worm is the inchworm, because it seems to be measuring the ground as it moves. The measuring worms later develop into moths. Most of these moths are small and delicate, and they have many fine markings on their wings. For more information, read the article on CATERPILLAR.

Meat and Meatpacking

meat and meat packing

Meat is the flesh of any animal used for food. In this sense meat includes poultry and fish, but in ordinary use meat is only the flesh of cattle, sheep, and swine, or pigs. That is, beef or veal, lamb or mutton, and pork. Meat was one of the first foods eaten by man in the days before history began, and today it is the most important and widely used food in the world.

The United States and Canada are meat-eating nations. There are few other countries in which the people eat so much meat, though there are some notable exceptions. The principal meat-eating countries are:

1. Uruguay, 248 pounds per person per year
2. Australia, 215 pounds
3. Argentina, 191 pounds
4. New Zealand, 180 pounds
5. Denmark, 175 pounds
6. United States, 154 pounds

Since meat is the most nutritious of all foods, meat-eating habits have contributed greatly to the steady improvement in health and the increase in height of the children of each new generation in the United States and Canada. Once very few people could afford to eat meat daily. Now most American families can.

KINDS OF MEAT

Different parts of meat animals are called by different names when they are used for food. The meat of swine (that is, hogs and pigs) is called *pork.* Among the more important pork products are ham, pork chops, shoulder butts, bacon, and sausage. The meat of steers, or male cattle, is called *beef,* and it provides various cuts of steak and roasts. The meat of calves, called *veal,* is prepared as chops, shoulder of veal, and breast of veal, among other cuts. The meat of sheep is called *mutton.* It is very popular in England and eastern countries, but is little used in the United States. *Lamb,* the meat of young sheep, is more widely used in the United States, in the form of chops, leg of lamb, and breast of lamb. Some of the organs of all these meat animals are used as food, such as the liver, kidney, heart, brains, and pancreas, (called sweetbreads).

From ancient times men have known the importance of careful preparation and storage of meat. Some of the most ancient laws we know are concerned with the handling and eating of meat. The ancient Romans were forbidden to eat goat's meat, but they had a great liking for pork and they knew the importance of cooking it very thoroughly. The Greeks knew how to salt meat to preserve it. The Egyptians and the Hebrews were not permitted to eat pork at all. The Phoenicians did not eat the meat of cows or hogs, but they did eat dog meat. As early as the year

700, Germany had regulations about the use of meat. As civilization progressed and nations and cities grew up, the laws and regulations concerning the preparation of all foods for sale became more strict and more efficient. The United States developed the handling and preparation of animals to be used for food into a science and an industry.

HOW MEAT-PACKING DEVELOPED

In colonial days in America, the settlers had to provide their own meat as they did every other thing they needed for life in the new land. Either they raised their own animals, or they got meat from neighbors who had raised the animals. As the cities of the eastern coast grew larger and busier, it became impossible for the people there to live on what could be raised in their own communities. They began to depend more and more on the western regions for many kinds of food, including meat. Gradually the supplying of food became a problem of large-scale transportation, and companies grew up to handle and transport food products.

As the West opened up, it became a center for the raising of cattle and other livestock. At first the animals had to be driven on foot to the eastern markets. This took weeks, the animals had to be fed on the way, and many of them ran wild. As early as 1820 the first meat-packing plants were established for the handling of pork in places near where the animals had been raised. The hog carcasses were cut into large pieces and packed in barrels of brine (heavily salted water). The barrels then could be shipped east by wagon or by boat. All of this work had to be done in winter, because in warm weather the meat spoiled before the salting could preserve it. Also, transporting the meat by rivers had to be done in spring, when floods made the water high.

In the early days the biggest meat-packing center was Cincinnati, Ohio, which was nicknamed "Porkopolis." In the 1840s other river cities had meat-packing plants. Then, as the railroads moved west, plants sprang up in cities that were rail terminals. In the 1850s the principal center of the industry shifted to Chicago. It is still there, although other midwestern cities such as St. Louis and Kansas City are important meat-packing centers.

The canning of meat began about 1870 with corned beef, and later included other canned-meat products. The original purpose was to preserve the meat.

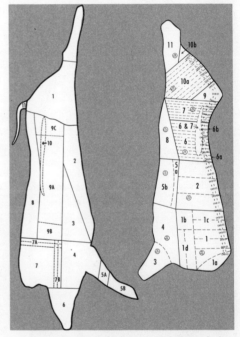

After an animal has been slaughtered, its carcass yields many different cuts. The cuts of pork (*left diagram*) are: 1. Ham. 2. Bacon. 3. Spareribs. 4. Picnic. 5. Hock (A) and foot (B). 6. Boned rolled butt. 7. Boston butt and shoulder steak (A, B). 8. Fat back salt pork. 9. Center loin roast (A), rib chop (B), and loin chop (C). 10. Tenderloin. 11. Tail. The cuts of beef (*right diagram*) are: 1. Neck (a), Boston cut (b), bladebone chuck (c), round-bone chuck (d). 2. Standing or rolled rib roast. 3. Shank. 4. Brisket. 5. Plate. 6 & 7. Tenderloin. 6. Short loin, club steak (a), and porterhouse and T-bone steak (b). 7. Sirloin steak. 8. Flank. 9. Rump. 10. Round steak (a) and heel of round roast (b). 11. Hind shank.

Swift & Co. Photos

1. The story of meat-packing begins when the animals arrive at the slaughterhouse.

2. Whole sides of beef are chilled before being shipped to retail and wholesale butchers.

3. Workmen "roll" beef carcasses and stamp the beef's grade on them with vegetable dye.

4. The hogs have been dehaired. Next they will be butchered into wholesale cuts.

5. Fresh hams are taken into the smoking house. Smoking gives ham a special flavor.

6. Sliced luncheon meats are vacuum-packed in the meat plant's modern sausage kitchen.

Armour & Co. Photos

Armour & Co. Photos

The modern meat-packing plant operates on an assembly-line basis. Cleanliness and efficiency are the watchwords.

1. Frankfurters are peeled of the casings used in processing and dropped onto a belt moving to the packaging section.

2. Sliced bacon moves on stainless steel ribbons to be weighed and packaged.

3. Fresh hams are graded for quality and weight average before they are cured.

4. Refrigerated trucks are loaded with meat. The meat is kept chilled at all times.

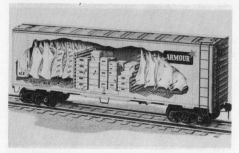

Armour & Co.

The cut-away drawing shows the interior of
a. typical refrigerator car. Whole carcasses
are hung from hooks. The boxes contain
fresh meats.

Later "meal in a can" dishes such as beef
stew, corned-beef hash, chili, and many
others became popular because they were
easy to prepare.

MEAT-PACKING IMPROVEMENTS

The greatest development in meat-
packing was refrigeration. This was
needed in the processing plants so that
work could be carried on in summer as
well as in winter. It was also needed in
transportation so that fresh meats as well
as salted ones could be sent to market.
The first refrigerator railroad cars were
hardly more than iceboxes on wheels.
With the invention of mechanical refrigeration fresh meats could be shipped long
distances with complete protection all the
way.

As improvements were made in refrigeration methods, freezing came into
use. For many years certain cuts of meat
were frozen-in the fall and winter when
supplies were plentiful, and used in the
summer when meat was harder to get.
Shortly before World War II, "quick-
freezing" was invented, and frozen meats
packaged for individual use began to be
sold in stores. Cetrain meats are better
suited to quick-freezing than others. The
most popular are pork chops, veal cut-
lets, cube steaks, and hamburger. The
more expensive cuts such as steaks and
roasts can be frozen, but the cost of the
process makes them more expensive.

HOW MEAT-PACKING IS DONE

The meat-packing industry is one of
the most carefully operated and most
carefully inspected food industries in the
United States. From the raising of the
animals to the labeling of the meat and
its sale in neighborhood stores, every precaution is taken to see that the buyer gets
fresh, pure meat and knows exactly what
quality he is buying. Meat inspection and
grading is handled by the Meat Inspection Division of the Bureau of Animal
Industry, which is part of the Department
of Agriculture.

The inspections begin with the arrival
of the animals at the slaughterhouse, or
abattoir. They are herded into holding
pens while an inspector watches their
movement into the pens and their condition while at rest. Any animal whose
condition seems doubtful is removed and
tagged "U.S. condemned," which means
that the animal cannot be used for food,
or "U.S. suspect," which means that further examination is required.

The animals are slaughtered quickly
and almost painlessly, and the second inspection takes place. This is the examination of certain glands and organs to de-
tect possible disease. The carcass is then
handled in one of several ways, depending on whether or not the hide is to be
used for leather or for its wool. When the
hair or hide has been removed, the carcass
is sent to the chilling room, where it remains for 24 to 48 hours until it is
thoroughly cooled. The meat is then divided into the various cuts that will be
shipped to wholesale or retail markets
throughout the country.

An assembly-line method is used, with
the carcass passing by a succession of
butchers and inspectors. The cuts of pork
that are to be cured and smoked go to
curing cellars. The cuts of beef that are to
become "aged beef" go to special chilling
rooms, where they are kept at even temperatures for two to three weeks. The fat
is trimmed off and processed to make lard
and other shortenings.

Armour & Co.

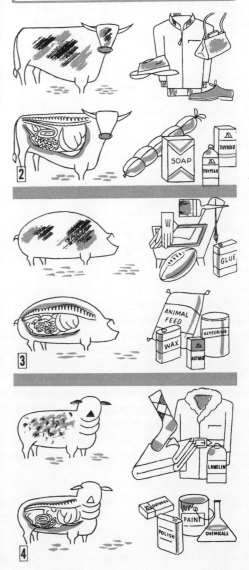

The by-products of meat packing are almost as important as the meat itself.

1. Parts that cannot be used for any other purpose are ground into animal feed.

2. Cattle by-products include leather from the skin, and soap and drugs from the various organs that are not eaten.

3. The swine contributes pigskin and glue, as well as products from internal parts.

4. The sheep provides wool and lanolin, in addition to various chemical products.

BY-PRODUCTS OF MEAT-PACKING

Some of the by-products of the meat-packing industry have become almost as important as the meat itself. The by-products are things made from parts of animals that otherwise would be thrown away. These are some of the principal by-products of the meat-packing industry:

The first by-product of meat was soap. Most of the inedible parts of the meat animals are placed in tanks and put under high steam pressure until the fat comes to the surface. The fat is then drawn off and used to make soap. In the soap-making process, glycerine is obtained. There are more than 1,500 uses for glycerine, from medicines to automobile polish.

One of the newer by-products is drugs. Doctors have found that from some parts of healthy animals they can obtain substances to help human beings who are ill. One of these drugs is a "wonder drug," ACTH, which is used in the treatment of rheumatic heart disease, asthma, burns, and many other ailments. ACTH is made from the pituitary gland found in the heads of all animals. Other medicines obtained from the meat-packing process are insulin, liver extract, and thyroid.

Leather is another major product that is really a by-product of the meat-packing industry. There are all colors, textures and weights of leather, from rough sole leather to fancy kid and pigskin glove leathers. The hair from the hides is processed and used in mattresses and upholstery.

About 15 percent of all the wool produced in the United States is *pulled* wool, that is, wool removed from the sheep carcass instead of being sheared before the animal is sold for slaughter.

Glue is one of the oldest and still one of the most important meat by-products. Different kinds of glue are made from bones, hides, and other inedible portions of animal carcasses. Sheep intestines are used to make the catgut that surgeons use to sew up wounds and surgical incisions. Intestines of other animals form the casings for sausages.

The parts of meat animals that cannot be used for any other purpose are prepared by heat and pressure into *tankage*. Most tankage was once sold as fertilizer, but modern methods have improved the quality and now most tankage is used as livestock and poultry feed.

Mecca

Mecca is the most famous city of Arabia. It is the birthplace of Mohammed, founder of the Mohammedan religion, and to Moslems, those people who believe in the religion of Mohammed, Mecca is a holy city. It is in a rocky valley where few things can grow. Few things are manufactured there. The ninety thousand people who live in Mecca mostly make their living by selling goods to pilgrims who visit the holy city. The temperature of Mecca is often far above 100 degrees. Many pilgrims faint from the heat, and every year some of them die.

Any Moslem who can, makes a pilgrimage to Mecca. There he visits the great mosque. (A mosque is a building in which Moslems pray.) In the middle of the courtyard of the mosque is the Kaaba. This is a block-shaped building. In it is the Black Stone, recognized by Moslems as the most holy object in the world.

The most important part of the pilgrimage to Mecca is when the Moslem kisses the stone. After kissing it, he walks around the Kaaba seven times. About one hundred thousand Moslems make this pilgrimage every year. The pilgrimage is called a *Hajj,* and a person who has made it is addressed with the honorary title *Hajji.*

People who do not belong to the religion of Mohammed are not allowed to visit Mecca. Some men have done it. One of these was Richard Burton, who made the pilgrimage to Mecca about 75 years ago, disguised as a Moslem. He wrote a famous book about his experiences on the way to Mecca, and at the shrine.

mechanics

A mechanic is a man who works on machines, but mechanics is the name of a science. It is the study of how various forces can produce motion or change motion.

There are various branches of mechanics. The study of how forces affect moving objects is called *dynamics.* The study of how forces affect objects that are standing still is called *statics.* Then there are special names that depend on what substance is affected by the forces; the following are some of them:

Aerodynamics is the study of how forces affect the air or other gases. This study is of the utmost importance in aviation.

Hydraulics is the mechanics of liquids that are moving, and *hydrostatics* is the mechanics of liquids that are standing still.

Pneumatics is the mechanics of gases.

Mechanics itself is one of the branches of the science of PHYSICS, about which there is a separate article.

FORCES STUDIED IN MECHANICS

Most of the forces that are studied in mechanics are produced by machines: the lever, the pulley, the inclined plane, the screw, the wheel and axle, and the wedge. Many other forces are produced by our own bodies, as when we dive into a pool of water, or open a door, or even walk along the ground. Mechanics studies how these forces are produced and how they act on different objects.

Another force that is studied in mechanics is the force of gravity. It is the force that pulls things down toward the center of the earth and gives them weight and that causes objects to fall to earth.

Read also the articles CENTRIFUGAL FORCE and FORCE.

Medea

Medea was a woman in Greek mythology, the stories the ancient Greeks told about their gods and goddesses, thousands of years ago. Medea was the daughter of the king of Colchis, and she was supposed to have magic powers. She married Jason, and helped him capture the Golden Fleece. (There are separate articles about JASON and the GOLDEN FLEECE.) Later when Jason left Medea to marry Creusa, Medea killed both Creusa and her own children in order to pay Jason back for the suffering he had caused her. Great playwrights of many countries and ages have written dramas about Medea. They include the Greek playwright Euripides, the Roman playwright Seneca, and the French playwright Corneille. In the 1940s Robinson Jeffers, an American poet, wrote a poetic drama about Medea, based on the drama by Euripides. Judith Anderson played the part of Medea when this drama was produced on Broadway.

Medes

The Medes were an ancient people who lived in the western part of present-day Iran. Their country was called Media.

The name Mede was given them by the Romans; the Medes called themselves Arii, which means noble.

Media was a fertile country. In ancient times it was famous for the wine, figs, oranges, and honey produced there. The people followed the Magi religion, which was the religion of the three Wise Men who journeyed to visit Jesus at his birth.

In the early period of their history, the Medes were greatly feared as fighters. They had developed strong, swift horses, and were fine horsemen. Mede soldiers could shoot arrows very accurately while riding. But a long period of peace, coupled with wealth and luxurious living, left the Medes weak. About 2,500 years ago the great ruler of the Persian Empire, Cyrus the Great, easily conquered the Medes. The Medes were afterwards considered examples of the weakness that follows too much luxury and love of pleasure.

Medici

Medici is the name of a family that was rich and powerful in Italy hundreds of years ago. They lived in Florence, which was then an independent republic.

The first Medici to become well-known was Giovanni de' Medici, who saved a fortress in Florence from attack by soldiers of Milan in the year 1351. Salvestro de' Medici, a few years later, gained popularity with the people by resisting the tyranny of the nobles, and he was chosen chief magistrate of Florence.

The family engaged in commerce and banking, and grew rich. The second Giovanni de' Medici was the most successful of all the Medici. He died in 1429 and left an immense fortune to his sons. The family coat of arms had three balls on it, and this has remained the symbol of a pawnshop because the Medici were bankers and moneylenders.

The Medici were important in the Roman Catholic Church. Two Popes and two cardinals were members of the Medici, but one of the Medici, Lorenzo

I, who lived from 1449 to1492 and was known as Lorenzo the Magnificent because of his hundreds of great public works, was an enemy of Pope Sixtus IV. Lorenzo's troops and the Pope's troops fought several battles.

A great-granddaughter of Lorenzo the Magnificent, Catherine de' Medici, became a powerful queen of France. There is a separate article about CATHERINE.

medicine

Medicine is the science and study of diseases and the ways to treat or cure them. A man trained in this science is called a *physician* or (usually) a "doctor," because he holds the degree M.D., which means "doctor of medicine." Medicine is a profession, which means that it requires knowledge and skill that can result only from training. When a doctor works at his profession he is said to "practice medicine."

Medicine is one of the oldest of the professions. It may be the oldest. More than four thousand years ago, when nearly everyone was superstitious and believed that disease was a punishment from one of the many gods that were worshiped, some men were studying disease in a scientific way and had also learned ways to make splints for broken bones and tourniquets to stop bleeding. About 2,500 years ago, a Greek physician named Hippocrates studied the causes of disease and made records of them for the benefit of other physicians. He also wrote a statement of what a doctor should and should not do, and this statement (called the Hippocratic Oath) is still followed by doctors.

The Greek god of medicine was called Asclepius (the Romans called him Aesculapius), and the "priests" of this god were running hospitals two thousand years ago, treating diseases in ways they had found to be best by actual practice, and keeping records of what happened.

In spite of its early start, the science of medicine advanced very slowly through the centuries. There has been more progress in the last two hundred years than in all the ages before. Great forward steps were made when the English physician William Harvey discovered the circulation of the blood, when the French chemist Louis Pasteur proved that bacteria can cause disease, and when the English physician Edward Jenner discovered the principle of vaccination, the English physician Joseph Lister developed the use of antiseptics, and the German chemist Robert Koch founded the science of bacteriology. Hundreds of other physicians have made important contributions to medicine.

SPECIALIZATION

Today so much is known about different diseases and the working of different parts of the body that many doctors *specialize.* That is, they treat only certain diseases or parts of the body.

A doctor who does not specialize is called a *general practitioner,* or "G.P." Some of the kinds of specialist are:

A *surgeon* operates—cuts into the body to remove diseased parts or to repair damaged ones. Many specialists are surgeons who usually operate only on particular parts of the body.

A *pathologist* studies the causes of disease.

A *diagnostician,* or "internal medicine man," treats diseases that do not require surgery.

Until modern times doctors could not do much more than guess. An Anglo-Saxon manuscript seven hundred years old shows several doctors discussing a case.

There are dozens of other fields of specialization.

THE MEDICAL CAREER

A young man or woman who wants to be a doctor must give up years of study and hard work to the career.

First, it is necessary to take a full four-year college course. This should be a "premed" course, which includes certain subjects important to medicine (such as chemistry, which is later helpful in understanding drugs, and Latin, the language in which much medical information is written). After this, the student attends a medical school for four years. Upon graduating from medical school, the student has his M.D. degree but must still be

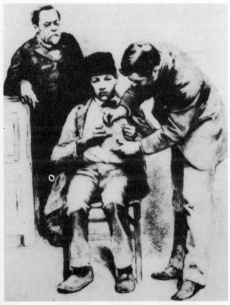

Louis Pasteur (*left*) and Robert Koch (*right*) were pioneers in the use of inoculation. Immunization against many once dangerous diseases is now available to all.

A *pediatrician* treats diseases of children.

An *obstetrician* takes care of childbirth, and a *gynecologist* treats diseases of women. Most often a doctor specializes in both these fields at once.

A *psychiatrist* treats mental diseases.

An *ophthalmologist* treats diseases of the eye.

Reasearch in the last hundred years has shown that many previously mysterious diseases are caused by germs and in most cases has found effective means of cure.

Dermatology, which deals with diseases of the skin, studies its function and its structure.

Urology deals with diseases of the kidneys, bladder and reproductive organs of men and women.

Gynecology deals with diseases of women, including care before, during and after childbirth.

Clinical pathology is the research study of the changes in the body that are caused by disease.

Radiology uses X-ray and radium in diagnosing diseases, and in many cases in treating them.

Geriatrics, which deals with health in old age, is a rapidly growing branch of medicine.

Public health has many branches. It prevents disease by education and by enforcing sanitary laws.

an *intern* for one or two years. An intern lives in a hospital, receives very little pay (seldom enough to live on), and works very hard treating patients in the hospital.

Finally, after these nine or ten years, a person can begin to practice medicine; but it still takes some money to buy the equipment needed in a doctor's office. Some doctors start in salaried jobs, working for hospitals or helping established doctors, until they save enough to "hang out their own shingles" (open their own offices).

Even after he is practicing on his own, a good doctor must continue to study nearly every day, because the science of medicine is moving forward so fast that there is always something new to learn.

Because it takes so long and requires so much hard work, medicine as a career appeals only to those who are so interested in medicine that they do not want to do anything else. Fortunately, there are many of these.

MEDICAL ETHICS

A doctor is not allowed to solicit business. That is, he must not advertise and must not ask anyone to become his patient. When a doctor sends a patient to another doctor (for example, to a specialist), he is not supposed to receive any commission. This would be "fee-splitting," which is considered wrong by the members of the medical profession. A doctor must treat anyone who needs his help, even if the person is poor and cannot afford to pay a satisfactory fee. (See also the articles on HOSPITALS, ANATOMY, DISEASE, and DRUGS.)

AMERICAN MEDICAL ASSOCIATION

The American Medical Association is a national organization of doctors in the United States. It publishes magazines and booklets of interest to doctors, its committees decide on what is ethical or proper for doctors to do, and it helps to spread new information among doctors every-

where. Each state of the United States has a state medical association that is associated with the national organization. Usually the legislature (lawmaking body) of a state consults with the state medical association before making laws that have to do with the practice of medicine.

GROUP MEDICINE

Group medicine is a form of insurance that has become very popular within the last thirty years. A person pays so much per month, and if he or any member of his family gets sick the group organization pays all or part of the expense. One form of group medicine is called "hospitalization." This pays hospital expenses only. The biggest hospitalization group is known as the Blue Cross. Allied to it is the Blue Shield, which pays doctors' bills for its members.

The American Medical Association and most of its members have opposed group medicine plans that pay doctors' bills. They and others have attacked such plans as "socialized medicine." In Great Britain, real socialized medicine was put into effect in the late 1940s. The government paid the cost of all medical care for everyone, including dental care and such things as glasses and hearing aids. The United States administration of President Harry S. Truman proposed in 1948 that the United States adopt a plan that would not go so far as the British plan but would pay most of the people's medical expenses. The Congress did not make such a law.

medicine man

A medicine man, or "witch doctor," is a kind of priest that some primitive or uncivilized tribes have. His job is to treat diseases, but he does not do this scientifically as physicians do. He does it by appealing to the sick person's superstition, which is a kind of belief in things that do not exist. For example, the medicine man wears fierce-looking masks to frighten away "evil spirits" that are causing the

Internal medicine includes diagnosis and treatment of diseases that do not need surgery.

Pediatrics is concerned with the diseases of children, especially those of pre-school age.

Otolaryngology deals with diseases peculiar to the ears, nose, throat, and sinuses.

Surgery treats diseases and injuries by means of internal operations and use of instruments.

Ophthalmology deals with diseases that affect the eyes, including pinkeye and cataracts.

Psychiatry is concerned with illness of the mind, which makes normal behavior impossible.

Neurology deals with diseases of the nervous system, not including mental or neurotic disorders.

disease, and he makes up drugs, or potions, that are based on strange mixtures (of lizards' tails, and frogs' teeth, and such things) instead of on chemistry. Many primitive tribes still believe in medicine men.

Medina

Medina is a city in Saudi Arabia. It is built on an oasis in the middle of the desert. About 12,000 people live there. Medina is important because it is a holy city of the Moslems (followers of the religion of Mohammed). Mohammed is probably buried in the great mosque that is the chief building of Medina. Moslems making the pilgrimage to Mecca, the Moslem holy city, also stop at Medina.

Mediterranean Sea

The Mediterranean Sea is a large body of water lying between Europe, Asia, and Africa. It is the world's largest inland sea and is one of the most important shipping routes in the world. The Mediterranean is about 965,000 square miles in size, or about a third the size of the United States. It is more than 14,000 feet deep at the deepest point. It is connected to the Atlantic Ocean by the Strait of Gibraltar; to the Red Sea by the Suez Canal; and to the Black Sea by the Dardanelles, the Sea of Marmara, and the Bosporus.

The Mediterranean has several "arms" that are small seas in themselves. The

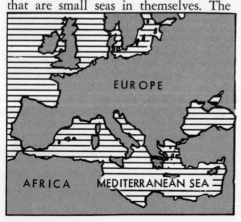

EUROPE

AFRICA   MEDITERRANEAN SEA

Tyrrhenian, Adriatic and Ionian Seas are off the coasts of Italy. The Aegean Sea is off the east coast of Greece. There are several important islands in the Mediterranean, including CORSICA, SARDINIA, SICILY, CRETE, and CYPRUS (about which there are separate articles).

The Mediterranean is filled with hundreds of different kinds of fish, and the finest sponges in the world grow there. Its water is salty. The people who live along the Mediterranean enjoy a warm, sunny climate. Thick evergreens and shrubs grow along the coasts, and farmers grow tropical fruit trees, grapes, and olives. The winters are mild and dry. Sometimes a hot, dry wind filled with dust blows across the region from the Sahara Desert. This is called a sirocco. Along the shores of the Mediterranean and some of the islands are several of the most famous volcanoes in the world, such as Mt. Vesuvius and Mt. Aetna.

THE MEDITERRANEAN IN THE PAST

In ancient times, three thousand years ago and more, the Phoenicians used the Mediterranean as a trade route. Later, Greece, Rome, and Carthage fought for control of it. The Roman Empire, two thousand years ago, called the Mediterranean *mare nostrum,* meaning "our sea." In the Middle Ages, the Mediterranean was the greatest trade route in the world, but it grew less important as shipping on the Atlantic Ocean was opened to ports in Spain, France, and England.

After the Suez Canal was opened in 1869, the Mediterranean again became one of the great shipping routes and a region of great political importance. Many countries have wanted control of it. The British have powerful military bases at Gibraltar, Malta, and Cyprus. Control of the Mediterranean during World War II was so important that the United States sent large armies into North Africa and Italy.

Some of the most important Mediterranean ports today are Barcelona, Spain;

Marseilles, France; Genoa and Naples in Italy, and Algiers in North Africa.

Medusa was one of the three hideous sisters known as the GORGONS, about whom there is a separate article.

meerschaum

Meerschaum is a very light, creamy-white mineral that is highly prized for making the bowls of pipes and the tips of cigarette holders. Some meerschaum has a yellow or red tinge. It is translucent. This means that you can see light through it, but you cannot see things on the other side of it as you do when you look through glass. When meerschaum is mined it is soft and can be easily carved to whatever shape is wanted. The name meerschaum is the German word for "sea foam." It is a good name for this mineral because, besides being white like foam, dry meerschaum is full of tiny bubbles that make it light enough to float on water as sea foam does. Scientists call meerschaum *sepiolite*. This is from a Greek word meaning "stone like cuttlefish bone," and it was given because cuttlefish bone is light and full of pores, too.

When meerschaum pipes and cigarette holders have been used for a while, the tobacco tars enter the pores and color the meerschaum golden brown. Smokers who have colored their meerschaum pipes brown are very proud of them.

The best meerschaum comes from Asia Minor. Meerschaum is also found in Greece, Czechoslovakia, Spain, and Morocco. In the United States it has been found in Pennsylvania, Utah, New Mexico, and California.

Meighen, Arthur

Arthur Meighen is the name of a Canadian political leader who was twice Prime Minister of Canada. He was born in Ontario, in 1874, and attended Toronto University. He became a member of the Canadian House of Commons in 1908, and held several government posts

German Tourist Office

Die Meistersinger **is filled with good humor and pleasant music, qualities that have made it a favorite Wagnerian opera.**

until 1920, when he was chosen Prime Minister. The following year his administration was defeated, and Meighen resigned. In 1926 he was again Prime Minister, but resigned within the year. He was appointed to the Senate in 1932 and remained there for ten years. In 1942 he was defeated in a contest for a seat in the House of Commons, and he retired from public life.

Meistersinger, Die

Die Meistersinger von Nürnberg ("The Mastersingers of Nurenberg") is an opera by the German composer Richard Wagner. An opera is a play in which all the words are sung instead of spoken. Wagner wrote both the libretto (the words) and the music of *Die Meistersinger*. It was first produced in the city of Munich in 1868. It is the only one of Wagner's many operas that is a happy story instead of a tragedy, and also is the only one that is based on actual history instead of on legend.

The Mastersingers were a group of musicians and poets in Germany, four to six hundred years ago. Each person who wanted to become a Mastersinger had to write a song according to very strict rules. One of the best poets among the Mastersingers was a shoemaker named Hans Sachs, and Wagner put this real man into his opera.

The story of *Die Meistersinger* concerns a young man named Walter who is in love with Eva, the daughter of a goldsmith. Eva's father had promised his daughter to the winner of a song contest to be held by the Mastersingers. Although Walter is not a Mastersinger, he composes a song to sing in the contest. The song does not meet all the strict rules of the Mastersingers, but Walter hopes it will win him membership anyway. The "villain" of the opera, Beckmesser, knows every tiny bit of the rules, but still he cannot write a good song and cannot even properly sing Walter's song, which he has stolen. Then Hans Sachs reveals that it is Walter's song and after Walter has sung it, Sachs persuades the Mastersingers that the beauty of the music should outweigh the technical flaws. Although Sachs himself is in love with Eva, he gives up his hopes to help Walter win admittance to the Mastersingers and thus marry Eva.

The most frequently played music of *Die Meistersinger* is the "Prize Song" itself, and also the overture, which contains an orchestral version of this song.

Mekong River

The Mekong River is the largest river in Indo-China and southeast Asia. It is about 2,600 miles long, which is somewhat longer than the Mississippi River in the United States. The Mekong rises in Tibet, flows between Burma and Thailand, crosses Cambodia, and empties into the China Sea. The name of the river changes at various points along its course. At the mouth of the river is the large Mekong delta, a great rice-growing region. Ships cannot go very far up the Mekong because of rapids and sandbars.

Melanesian

Melanesia is the name given to a large division of the islands of the South Pacific Ocean, including New Guinea, the Solomon Islands, New Hebrides, New Caledonia, the Bismarck Archipelago, and the Admiralty and Fiji Islands.

The natives of these islands are called Melanesians. The Melanesians are scattered over so many thousand of miles of ocean that they differ widely in appearance and customs. Most Melanesians are dark-skinned. Many Melanesians are highly skilled in such arts as the making of masks, wood carvings, and shell and stone ornaments. Some early Melanesians were cannibals, but this practice has largely disappeared. Farming, fishing and livestock-raising are the principal ways of life in Melanesia. There are more than a hundred Melanesian languages.

Melbourne

Melbourne is the second-largest city in Australia. It is also the capital of the state of Victoria. It is on the Yarra River and is an important railroad and commercial center. More than 1,500,000 people live in Melbourne. They work in mills, factories, and offices. Many work in the big port at Melbourne. This is more than two miles away but large vessels can go up the Yarra River to the city's center. A large part of Australia's exports is shipped through Melbourne.

Melbourne is a beautiful, modern city, with wide streets, fine parks and gardens, and high buildings. It is noted for its water sports. The University of Melbourne is one of Australia's great universities.

Melbourne was settled in 1835, and was named after Lord Melbourne, the British Prime Minister. The city was scientifically planned, and the streets were named after important people in history.

MELBOURNE, AUSTRALIA. Population (1954 census) 1,522,000. Capital of Victoria. On the Yarra River.

melon

There are several kinds of large, juicy fruit called melons. They are grown in many parts of the world where the climate is warm. Some people who live in places with a cold climate grow delicious melons in greenhouses. The melon

MINERALS

FLINT

QUARTZ

TALC

MICA

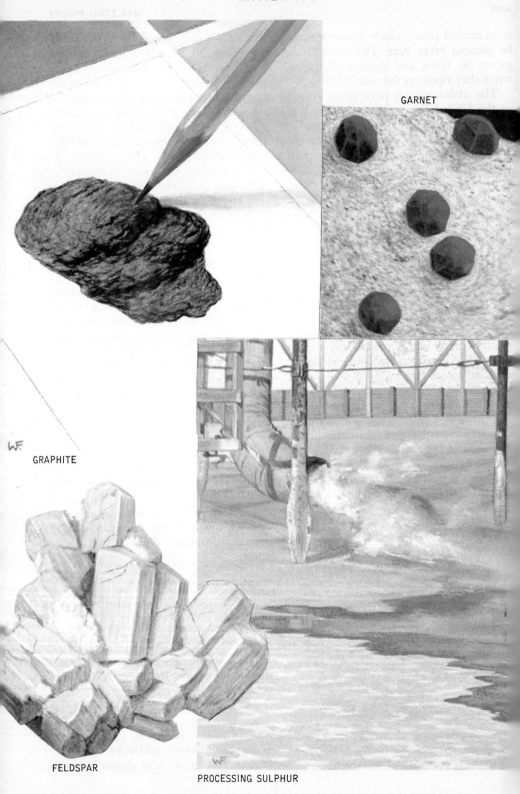

GARNET

GRAPHITE

FELDSPAR

PROCESSING SULPHUR

is an annual plant, which means it must be planted every year. The round fruit grows on vines, and melons taste best when they ripen on the vine.

The melon that is most often grown in the United States is the muskmelon, also called the cantaloupe. The muskmelon is about the size of a grapefruit. It has a grayish skin with pockmarks in its surface. The flesh of the melon is a golden orange color, and it has a sweet smell and taste. Melons in the United States were first grown in Colorado. Now people in many parts of the country raise melons.

The Persian melon and the honeydew melon are two popular melons. Both of them are larger than the cantaloupe. The Persian melon has a rough skin and, like the cantaloupe, has flesh that is golden-orange in color. The honeydew has a smooth green skin, and its flesh is pale green. The Persian melon and the honeydew are winter melons. They take longer to ripen than the other muskmelons and keep very well.

People in Europe grow a cantaloupe that has a harder skin than the muskmelon. The flesh is a dark yellow color. People believe that this melon first grew wild in the southern parts of Asia. The ancient Egyptians and Romans were fond of this fruit.

Watermelon is a melon that grows in Africa, and it is raised in Europe and the United States, in places where the climate is warm. The watermelon is a large juicy

The muskmelon is one of the best-known members of the melon family. It is grown mostly in the South and Southwest.

fruit that is egg-shaped. It often weighs more than 50 pounds. It has a smooth dark green skin. The flesh of the watermelon is a deep pink, and it has oval-shaped slippery black or white seeds. The sweet and juicy fruit of the watermelon is a very refreshing food on a hot day. Some people pickle and candy the skin of the watermelon.

Watermelon was eaten by people in India and in Egypt thousands of years ago. The early Egyptian artists drew pictures of watermelons in their paintings.

melting point

The melting point of a substance is the temperature at which it changes from a solid into a liquid. A substance usually will melt if it is heated to a high enough temperature. Most solid substances have a definite temperature at which they suddenly melt. For example, aluminum melts at 660 degrees on the Centigrade scale (1220 degrees on the Fahrenheit scale). Some substances do not have such a definite melting temperature. Sealing wax and glass are two substances that change gradually from a solid to a liquid. For this reason, glass is easily shaped. It becomes softer and softer as it is heated instead of changing suddenly from a solid to a liquid.

Ice changes to water when its temperature is brought to zero Centigrade, or 32 degrees Fahrenheit. That is its melting point.

WHY SUBSTANCES MELT

When a solid changes into a liquid it is because it has been given more heat and the molecules of the substance move faster. This means that the molecules no longer just vibrate, but must move about in the substance. In this way the substance melts, becoming a liquid.

Most substances increase in volume when they melt, because of the greater activity of the molecules. However, this is not true of water and some other substances. Water at zero degrees on the

Centigrade scale has only about nine-tenths the volume of ice at the same temperature.

The melting point of a substance can be changed by increasing or decreasing the pressure on the substance. For some substances, an increase in pressure lowers the melting point. For others, an increase in pressure raises the melting point.

A combination of two metals usually has a lower melting point than either of the metals heated separately.

Melville, Herman

Herman Melville was one of America's great writers. His best-known novels are about sailing ships and sailors. He was born in New York in 1819 and ran away to sea when he was 18. His first voyage gave him a lasting interest in sailing. In 1841 he shipped aboard a whaler and sailed to the South Pacific. The cruelty of the ship's captain disgusted him so much that he deserted when the ship docked at the island of Nukahiva in the Marquesas. He lost his way and was captured by natives who were cannibals, and they held him for four months until he was rescued by an Australian ship. He returned to the United States on an American naval vessel. The flogging and other harsh treatment of the sailors that he had seen on the sailing ships infuriated Melville, and when he got home he wrote a novel about it, *White Jacket.* This book aroused so much protest that the treatment of the men was improved. Melville became a farmer in Pittsfield, Massachusetts, and divided his time between writing and farming. His most famous book is *Moby Dick,* the story of a sea captain's search for a white whale, Moby Dick, that had bitten off one of his legs. Other stories by Melville describe life aboard ship and among the natives of the South Seas. For more than ten years he lived in Massachusetts and was a friend of Nathaniel Hawthorne and other great New England writers. He died in New York in 1891, at the age of 72.

membrane

A membrane is a tough, skinlike tissue that covers organs or bones inside the body. It may be seen on some of the meat that you eat. Membrane looks somewhat like a thin film, and is translucent (light shines through it) but is not transparent. *Mucous membrane* is membrane from which flows a thick liquid called *mucus,* which keeps it moist. The eyes, stomach and lungs are lined with mucous membrane, as are some other parts of the body.

Memel

Memel is a city in Lithuania. It is a port on the Baltic Sea, and in 1941 there were 41,297 people living there. The Lithuanian name of the city is Klaipeda or Klaypeda. It is a manufacturing city.

Memel was once part of Prussia, but after World War I Germany had to give it up and in 1923 Lithuanian troops seized it. Almost half of the people were Germans, however, and in 1938 Adolf Hitler, the German dictator, threatened war unless Lithuania gave up Memel. In 1939 Lithuania surrendered Memel and the surrounding territory to Germany. At the end of World War II Russia took Memel and made it part of Lithuania.

Memnon

Memnon was a character in Greek mythology, the stories the ancient Greeks told about their gods and goddesses. He was a king of Ethiopia who brought an army to help the Trojans fight the Greeks. Memnon killed the Greek Antilochus but almost immediately afterward was himself slain by Achilles. (See the article on the TROJAN WARS.) A large statue of Memnon, about sixty feet high, was one of a pair in Thebes, Egypt. It was called "the vocal Memnon" for many years, because sounds were reported to come from it at sunrise. Some people thought that the sound was produced by a trick, with someone hidden inside the pedestal, but actually the sound was caused by the expanding of the stones in the heat of the morning sun.

Memorial Day

Memorial Day, sometimes called Decoration Day, is a holiday set aside in honor of United States servicemen who gave their lives for their country. It is usually May 30. It was established in 1868 by General John A. Logan, commander-in-chief of the Grand Army of the Republic (an association of United States veterans), in remembrance of soldiers who died in the Civil War. General Logan set May 30 as Memorial Day, but because there was still great bitterness between the North and the South, the Confederate states refused to recognize this day. The southern states set their own days and these are still observed, although more and more the South is coming to recognize May 30 also. The Confederate Memorial Days are variously set on April 26, May 10, and June 3.

Observances of Memorial Day include military parades and the placing of flowers and wreaths on the graves of soldiers and sometimes civilians. There are special services at the battlefield at Gettysburg, Pennsylvania, and the Arlington · National Cemetery in Washington, D.C.

memory

Memory is the mind's ability to retain past experiences and to recall them (bring them to mind again). The brain retains everything it experiences, but it can recall only certain ones. All memories fade gradually as time passes. Those experiences that have pleased us, or that have had the strongest immediate effect on us, are remembered longest. Some people deliberately forget unpleasant things, though they may not know they are doing so. Psychologists assure us that these memories are retained in the brain and can be recalled under some kinds of treatment for mental disturbances.

Sometimes experiences are recalled wrongly, and there are several reasons for this. Most people have a tendency to exaggerate or improve on an experience in telling about it, to make a good story. Sometimes people remember things not the way they happened, but the way they think the events should have happened. Sometimes a person intends to do a certain thing, and the intention is so strong that the memory takes hold of it and the person "remembers" having done it although he never did. These are only a few ways in which the memory can play tricks on people.

There are some people who have remarkable memories for things they have seen or read only once. You may have heard people say "I never forget a face," and this may be perfectly true. Such people have what is called a "photographic" memory. Ability to remember things is not necessarily a sign of superior intelligence.

Memory is sometimes divided into two kinds, visual and auditory. A person with visual memory is able to remember best things that he has seen. A person with auditory memory remembers best things that he has heard.

People in general remember best the things that interest them, or that have an important part in their lives. For example, a great baseball pitcher such as Bob Feller may remember years later the details of a game. He can remember the order of batters that faced him, each ball he pitched, his reasons for choosing those particular pitches, and what happened to the ball. A good golf player can tell you about every stroke on every hole in a game played years before.

The study of ways to train the memory is called *mnemonics*. Mnemonics teaches ways of training the memory by associating things or events with other things. The verse that begins "Thirty days hath September" is a mnemonic method of aiding the memory.

Loss of memory is called AMNESIA,

Memory (game)

There is a card game called Memory that is popular with children and grown-ups alike. The game is also called *Concentration*. It is one of the few games in which children can often beat grownups. Any number may play.

A full pack of 52 playing cards is laid out on a large table, with their faces down, each one separated from each other. A player turns two cards face up. If they are a pair (both jacks, or both sixes, and so on) the player takes them in and turns up two more cards. Every time he turns up a pair he may take the cards in and turn up two more cards. If at any time the two cards are not a pair, he turns them both face down, making sure to leave them in the same place that they were in when he turned them up. Then the next player turns up two cards.

The object is to take in as many cards as possible. The skill of the game is in remembering where certain cards were turned up before. If a player turns up a

six, and remembers that a card in a certain place was turned up before and was a six, he can turn up that card and make a pair. The player who takes in the most cards wins.

Memphis

Memphis is the largest city in the state of Tennessee. It was named after Memphis, the capital of ancient Egypt, about which you can read in the article on EGYPT. Memphis, Tennessee, is on the Mississippi River, and is one of the greatest cotton markets, hardwood-lumber markets and mule markets in the world. About 400,000 people live in Memphis. They work in the important freight yards and in iron and steel foundries, machine shops, chemical plants, and rubber factories. Memphis is the most important distributing or shipping point on the Mississippi River between St. Louis and New Orleans. Farmers in the fertile region around the city send their cotton, corn, sweet potatoes, tobacco and soybeans to Memphis for shipment.

Memphis has many places of historical interest, as well as museums and universities. Every year thousands of people go

Memphis Chamber of Commerce

Memphis is often called the "cotton capital of the world." Nearly one-third of all the cotton grown in the United States each year is sold in the markets of Memphis.

to Memphis to enjoy the colorful Cotton Carnival. It is a gay celebration that lasts for five days, beginning on the second Tuesday in May. A King and Queen of Cotton are chosen to rule the carnival.

The French and the Spanish were the first white people to come to the place where Memphis now stands. The first permanent settlement was made in 1819, by Andrew Jackson and several other men. It became a city in 1849.

MEMPHIS, TENNESSEE. Population (1950 census) 396,000; (1954 estimate) 440,650. County seat of Shelby County. Founded in 1819.

Mendel, Gregor

Gregor Johann Mendel was an Austrian priest and a student of plant life. He lived about a hundred years ago. His experiments with plants were very important to our knowledge of how different characteristics or traits of plants and other living things are passed on through the seeds to their offspring. The facts he discovered are called Mendel's law.

In one experiment Mendel used two kinds of garden pea. One was very small, the other very tall. He kept these plants covered so that the pollen (the small grains that help make plant seeds) from other plants would not fall on them.

First he put some pollen from the very small plant onto the very tall plant. Then he put some pollen from the very tall plant onto the very small plant. This is called *cross-breeding*.

When the seeds had developed, he planted them in the ground, and expected that the plants grown from them, called the *first generation*, would be of medium height, not too tall or too small. Instead, all of the plants that grew from the seeds were very tall. Because tallness had shown up in all of the plants, Mendel called it the *dominant* trait. Because

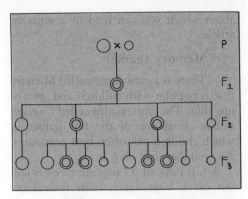

Mendel's experiment with peas led to knowledge of how different traits of plants are passed on through the seeds to their offspring. When he crossed a tall plant with a small one (P), he got all tall plants in the first generation (F_1). But in the F_2 generation, there were three times as many tall plants as small ones. The ratio of three to one remained the same in the F_3 and all following generations.

shortness had receded or withdrawn from all the plants, he called it the *recessive* trait.

Mendel next planted the seeds made by using only the pollen of first generation plants. Some of the plants that grew from these seeds, called the *second generation*, were tall and some were small. About three times as many plants were tall as were small. This showed that the seeds from the first-generation plants had contained both traits, even though all the plants had been tall. Such plants are called *hybrids*.

A hybrid will always breed or produce mixed offspring, some of which will have the dominant trait and some the recessive trait. Plants whose seeds contain only one kind of trait are called pure breeds. They will always breed plants that have the same trait. This is called *breeding true*.

Mendel's ideas have been very important to the science of GENETICS, about which there is a separate article.

Mendelssohn, Felix

Felix Mendelssohn was a German composer, or writer of original music, who lived more than a hundred years ago. Although he lived to be only 38, he wrote a great deal of music. Mendelssohn was born in 1809, in Hamburg, Germany, of a wealthy and cultured family. He is one of the few great composers whose lives were not filled with hardship. As a child, he was composing music almost before he could talk, and at the age of 6 he played the piano well. When he was 9 he gave his first public concert in Berlin. His father was not sure whether to let Mendelssohn devote his life to music, and he took him to Paris to see the composer Cherubini and other musicians. They all predicted a brilliant future for the boy, whose career was then decided. Mendelssohn gave many successful concerts. By the time he was 15 he had  written his first symphony. In 1827, when he was only 18, his *Overture to A Midsummer Night's Dream* was performed and won him tremendous popularity.

Mendelssohn traveled widely and found inspiration for many of his works in foreign lands. Among his most famous works are two great oratorios (musical stories), *St. Paul,* and *Elijah.*

Until 1845, Mendelssohn taught music, conducted orchestras, and gave concerts. Then he resigned all his positions to devote himself to writing music. His favorite sister, Fanny, died in 1847, and Mendelssohn never recovered from his grief. He died less than six months later. His full name was Jakob Ludwig Felix Mendelssohn-Bartholdy.

menhaden

The menhaden is a fish that lives in the Atlantic Ocean, near the eastern coast of the United States. It is a greenish-brown fish that has a black spot on its shoulder and a silver underpart. The menhaden is about a foot long. Although many people have never heard of the menhaden, fishermen catch about a billion of these fish every year in huge nets. People do not eat the menhaden (some people do eat the eggs), but the fish is very useful in other ways. The menhaden is made into feed for hogs, cattle, and chickens. It is also used for fertilizer to make the soil rich so that better crops will grow. The oil of the menhaden is used to make soap, paint, and insecticides (poisons that kill harmful insects).

meningitis

Meningitis is a serious disease in which the membranes (linings) that cover the brain and spinal cord become inflamed. The disease is caused by a germ called *meningococcus.* The germ enters the body through the nose and throat. Meningitis is very infectious, which means that a person can easily catch it from someone else. Sometimes a person is infected with meningococcus germs and although he does not feel ill himself he spreads the disease to other people. Such a person is called a "carrier." Meningitis usually occurs in the winter and early spring. It is most likely to occur in barracks and schools and other places where many people crowd together.

A person who becomes ill with meningitis develops a fever and a severe headache. It often becomes painful to bend the head forward. Sometimes the person develops a skin rash. Until recently people who had meningitis usually died. Now the antibiotics, or "wonder drugs," help cure the disease. A person who gets meningitis should receive treatment from a doctor immediately and should be kept away from other people as much as possible.

Mennonite

Mennonites are Christians who follow the teachings of Menno Simons, a Dutch reformer who lived about four hundred years ago. Menno believed that people should live very strictly, and should follow closely the teachings of the Bible. He recognized two sacraments, baptism (but of adults, not babies) and communion or Lord's Supper. His followers were persecuted for a long time after he died in 1559.

The Mennonites first came to colonial America in 1683. Today many Mennonites live in Pennsylvania, Ohio, Indiana, and Illinois. They refuse to go to war or to take oaths, because of their religion. Most Mennonites are farmers and people enjoy visiting Mennonite communities because of the simple, pious way the Mennonites live. Their cooking is famous. There are several branches of the Mennonite church; a separate article tells about the members of one of these, the AMISH.

Menotti, Gian-Carlo

Gian-Carlo Menotti is an American composer, or writer of music. He is best-known for the operas he has written. Operas are plays in which the words are sung rather than spoken. Menotti writes both the libretto (words) and the music. Menotti was born in Italy in 1911, but became a citizen of the United States. His most successful operas include *The Medium, The Telephone, The Consul,* and *The Saint of Bleecker Street.* In 1951 Menotti wrote an opera, *Amahl and the Night Visitors,* especially to be performed on television at Christmas. It has been performed every Christmas since then.

mental illness

A person is mentally ill when his mind does not work properly. Such a person may imagine that things are so when they are not, or may have impulses (desires to do things) that he cannot control and that cause him to do unnatural things. Mental illness may be caused by damage to the brain, for example by a hemorrhage (bleeding) inside the head or a severe blow on the head; but most often the principal causes of mental illness are disturbing experiences that a person has had

Nat'l Assn. for Mental Health

Children suffering from mental disease are treated in special hospitals. When they are well, they will return home.

during his life. Such a disturbing experience is called a *trauma.* Extreme worry or fear are examples of disturbing experiences, but many people can have such experiences without suffering any permanent effects, while some other people can be made mentally ill by experiences that they seem hardly to notice at the time.

In the 1950s mental illness cost the United States more than a billion dollars a year, and this amount was increasing each year by $100,000,000. A million persons each year were being treated in mental hospitals and 100,000 more were receiving treatment elsewhere for mental illness. About half the hospital beds in use throughout the United States were occupied by mentally ill persons. During World War II four of every ten men discharged for reasons of health were mentally ill.

There was a time when mental illness was considered disgraceful, something to be ashamed of; but modern science has brought most people to realize that a mental disease is simply a matter for medical treatment, just as pneumonia or appendicitis or any other serious disease is.

The serious kind of mental disease is called *psychosis.* A less serious mental illness or disturbance is called *neurosis,* or *psychoneurosis,* and a person who is suffering badly from neurosis is often said to have a "nervous breakdown."

Mental illness is treated by doctors, called *psychiatrists,* who are specialists in mental cases. *Psychologists* who are scientists but are not medical men, also are trained to help in the treatment of people who are suffering from mental troubles.

NAMES OF MENTAL ILLNESSES

One of the words most often heard in connection with serious mental illness is *schizophrenia* (which means "split personality"). Nearly one out of every four persons suffering from psychosis is found to have schizophrenia. A person suffering from another mental disease that is as common as schizophrenia is called a *manic-depressive.* A manic-depressive person will be extremely cheerful and active, and then for no apparent reason he will feel very depressed (unhappy) and may want to kill himself. More depressives commit suicide than any other group of mentally ill persons. There are many other kinds of mental illness and some of these, such as AMNESIA, HYSTERIA, and

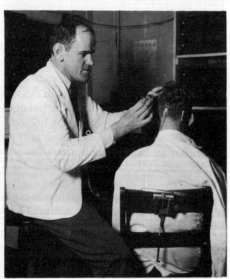

Nat'l Assn. for Mental Health

A doctor uses an electroencephalograph to measure the brain waves of a patient. Variations from normal help him to trace the cause of the patient's mental disease.

PARANOIA, are described in separate articles in this encyclopedia.

A person suffering from a serious mental illness, or psychosis, is said to be "insane," but insanity is not a name for a form of mental illness. Insanity is a term used mostly in courts of law, where a person is said to be insane if his mental condition is such that he cannot tell the difference between right and wrong and is not responsible for his actions. A psychiatrist who specializes on deciding whether or not a person is legally insane is called an *alienist.*

There are other words, such as *madness, lunacy, craziness,* and others, that are often used to describe mental illness, but these are not scientific words and may mean almost any kind of mental illness.

MENTAL DEFICIENCY

Some persons are born without normal intelligence, or lose some or all of their normal intelligence because of an injury or illness that affects the brain. There are special words for deficiency (lack) of intelligence. An *idiot* has only the intelligence of a two- or three-year-old child. He cannot dress himself or carry on a conversation (if he can talk at all). A *cretin* is a special kind of idiot. An *imbecile* is one grade above an idiot. Mentally he is no better off than a little child. A *moron* has a low "I.Q." (about which you can read in the article on INTELLIGENCE TESTS). He is often said to be "dull" or "mentally retarded," but he can learn to read and write (with difficulty) and live a more or less normal life.

TREATMENT OF MENTAL ILLNESS

When mental illness is caused by damage to the brain, it is sometimes possible to cure it by an operation. In other cases in which the brain is damaged, a person may be able to learn again the things that the injury caused him to forget. For example, a person may forget how to write, due to a brain injury, but he can learn again.

Some mental diseases are caused by bacteria that attack the brain and nervous system. These are treated by destroying the bacteria. Penicillin and other antibiotic drugs are effective against most of these bacteria.

When mental illness has psychological causes, the cure is not so easy. The best-known treatment is PSYCHOANALYSIS, about which there is a separate article. In psychoanalysis, the patient is helped to find out what experiences in his previous life were so disturbing that they led to the mental illness. The psychiatrist can usually make the patient feel better by various forms of treatment, such as changing the patient's living habits and actions to reduce the sources of his worry.

Occupational therapy, that is, doing work that is enjoyable and gives a sense of accomplishment, is used to help patients overcome mental disease.

MENTAL HOSPITALS

There are hundreds of public and private hospitals for the care of people who are mentally ill. There was a time when these were called "lunatic asylums" and were classed with prisons, but modern science has progressed and mental hospitals are now like other hospitals.

A person may become a patient in a mental hospital in one of two ways. In many cases the person realizes he is suffering from a mental illness and volunteers to enter a mental hospital for treatment. Once he is in the mental hospital, he may leave whenever he wants to, unless the doctors in charge of the hospital think it would be unsafe to release him.

The other way in which one enters a mental hospital is by *involuntary commitment*. In such a case, the person may not want to go to the mental hospital, but doctors who have examined him certify that he is too ill mentally to know what is good for him and that he requires hospital care. A person cannot be committed to a mental hospital against his will except by a court of law after two psychiatrists have examined him and have certified that he would not be safe outside of a mental hospital.

A mental hospital always has a staff of psychiatrists and trained psychiatric nurses who understand the problems of those who are mentally ill. The mental hospital also has special equipment for the several different methods of treating those who are mentally ill. Because little was known about mental illness until the last fifty years or so, and the building of hospitals is seldom fast enough to keep up with new medical knowledge, there are not enough mental hospitals in any part of the world to take care of all the patients who need treatment. Mental hospitals in the United States are the finest in the world, but even they are often crowded and do not have enough doctors and nurses to take care of all the patients. This has led to many reports of bad conditions in mental hospitals, especially in those that are supported by state governments. Some of these reports have been exaggerated and some have been true, but nearly every state and country is making efforts to improve the treatment of those who are mentally ill.

NATIONAL INSTITUTE OF MENTAL HEALTH

The National Institute of Mental Health was set up by the United States government in 1946 to promote mental health throughout the nation. The Institute awards money to local institutions for training psychiatrists, social workers, nurses, and other staff members. It awards money to students who want to follow careers in mental health and conducts training programs for persons already in that field. It also assists the states in conducting their mental health programs by helping them to establish clinics and programs in the schools, and by other activities. It conducts research in the problems of juvenile delinquency and in the special problems of older people as well as studying the causes and cures of mental diseases. It also helps spread information on mental health throughout the country.

menthol

Menthol is a substance that will give you a cool feeling if you put some of it on your skin or on your tongue. It is very useful in medicine. Menthol not only cools but it also relieves pain in those parts of your body—the skin and mouth and the inside of the nose and throat—where it can touch the endings of nerves. This is why doctors put it on itching and burning skin. If you have a sore throat, the doctor may spray it with menthol dissolved in alcohol, or he may give you cough drops that have menthol in them. Menthol is mixed with wax to rub on chapped lips. Menthol is also a mild germ killer, but it is not much used for this purpose by itself.

Menthol is made by freezing peppermint oil. When the oil becomes cold enough, colorless crystals of menthol separate from it. Menthol is sometimes called peppermint camphor.

Mercator, Gerardus

Gerardus Mercator was a Flemish geographer and mapmaker who lived about four hundred years ago. He is best remembered for a kind of map that he invented, called Mercator's projection. It is explained in the article on MAP. Mercator was born in 1512. His real name was Gerhard Kremer. In those days it was the fashion to use the Latin spelling of one's name. The German name *Kremer* means "trader," and so it became Mercator (Latin for "trader"). Mercator surveyed and made a map of his native country, Flanders. He made maps of the world and of the skies. His first map using Mercator's projection was published in 1569. In 1585 Mercator began to put together a book of maps, which he called an atlas. He was the first to use this term for a collection of maps. In 1594 Mercator died before finishing the atlas. His son completed it and published it that same year.

merchant marine

The merchant marine of a country consists of all its ships that carry goods and passengers over oceans, rivers, and other water routes. In peaceful times a country carries on much of its foreign trade with its merchant marine, and few countries can prosper without foreign trade. When war threatens, all ships in a country's merchant marine are usually taken over by the government and many of them are used for carrying troops, ammunition, equipment, food, and other supplies to the battle area. In war the merchant marine is called a "second line of defense." To keep this line of defense strong, governments encourage and help shipbuilders, and often *subsidize,* or help with money, operators of large ships.

TONNAGE

A country's merchant marine is measured by the number of ships in it, and their total *tonnage.* Tonnage is a ship's carrying capacity, or the weight of the cargo it can transport, expressed in tons. There are several ways to figure tonnage. It is generally estimated that each 100 cubic feet of space inside a ship can carry a *long ton,* which is 2,240 pounds. Figuring this way, the entire space inside the *Queen Mary* of the Cunard White Star Line can carry 80,773 long tons. Its *gross tonnage* is therefore 80,773. *Deadweight*

U.S. Merchant Marine Acad. Photos

The merchant marine needs men with all kinds of skills—from the cook whose meals keep the men contented to the captain who is responsible for the ship and its crew.

1. Sailors practice boat drill. Each must know his part in case of emergency.

2. The crew of a large liner stands inspection during a Coast Guard boat drill to test the liner's safety.

3 and 4. Midshipmen must learn all about the engines that drive merchant ships. Everything must be kept shipshape in the engine room—the heart of the ship.

5. Future officers learn how to climb down ropes into a lifeboat.

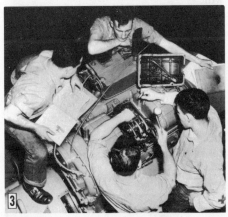

tonnage is the officially estimated weight of the cargo a ship normally carries. Another term is *displacement tonnage,* which is the weight of sea water that a ship displaces when it floats. The *America* of the United States Lines has a displacement of 35,440 tons.

These two ships are passenger vessels, although they usually carry a small amount of goods or cargo. There are also general cargo vessels, or *freighters,* which carry only a few passengers if any. The usual cargo ship has a displacement of about 12,000 tons. Some of these are on regular schedules, going to and from certain seaports at specified times. Others, called *tramp ships* or *tramps,* go to almost any port at which they may pick up a cargo going to almost any destination. These have no definite time of sailing; they simply leave when they are fully loaded. A merchant marine also includes *tankers,* which carry liquids such as oil; and *colliers* or *ore ships,* which take coal, iron ore, and so on. There are also *tugs, icebreakers, fishing trawlers,* and many types of smaller vessels.

Many sailors of the merchant marine risk their lives in time of war. These British sailors survived torpedoing by a German submarine during World War II.

SHIP REGISTRY

Ships must register under the flag of some country. If the United States has helped to build or operate a ship, its owner must register under the United States flag. Some countries, including the United States and Canada, have strict laws regarding taxation, ship insurance, and the health, wages and living conditions of crews. Some shipowners transfer their ships to the flag of a country that does not have such strict laws, such as Panama or Liberia. Many ships owned by United States and Canadian citizens are registered under those flags. Little Panama in 1954 had the fourth-largest merchant marine in the world, largely for that reason.

Through the centuries, various countries have risen to power by the strength of their merchant fleets. For a while Holland ruled the oceans, with 3,000 ships against England's 300, and Dutch was the language of the admirals. Then for more than two hundred years, up to World War II, Britain's merchant marine was the largest. Britain's fleet was badly hurt by German submarines in World War I.

In World War II, the United States built a huge merchant fleet. In 1946 it had more than half of the world's total tonnage, with about 5,500 ships totaling 40,000,000 tons. In 1954, the United Kingdom (the British) again had the world's largest active, privately-owned merchant marine, with 22,626,000 deadweight tons. The United States was second with 14,727,000 tons, but it also had a large government-owned "mothball" or reserve fleet numbering about 2,000 ships, and many troop transports in the Navy. In 1954 Norway was third, Panama fourth, and Greece fifth.

Merchant Marine Academy, United States

The United States operates several academies, or colleges, that teach young men to be officers in its armed forces: at

West Point, New York, for the Army; at Annapolis, Maryland, for the Navy; at New London, Connecticut, for the Coast Guard; at Colorado Springs, Colorado, for the Air Force. There is a similar academy, the United States Merchant Marine Academy, at Kings Point, New York. This trains young men to serve as officers on ships carrying goods and passengers, not warships of the Navy. These ships, which in peacetime are not fitted out with guns but which are useful in wartime for carrying men, food, and other supplies, form what is called the Merchant Marine. When war comes, the Merchant Marine is under orders of the government.

The United States Merchant Marine Cadet Corps was started on March 15, 1938. The Academy was dedicated in 1943. In World War II there were 2,670 men at the Academy; in peacetime about 700 are enrolled, with 200 more in training at sea.

Young men study at the Academy for four years. They are members of the Merchant Marine Cadet Corps, also Mid-

U.S. Merchant Marine Acad.

The United States Merchant Marine Academy trains the young men who will eventually command the ships of the merchant marine.

shipmen of the Naval Reserve, so they are called Cadet-Midshipmen. They study either Nautical Science to become Deck Officers, or Marine Engineering to become Engineering Officers. Men who graduate become Third Mates or Third Assistant Engineers, and earn about $500 a month aboard ship. They become Ensigns in the United States Naval Reserve, and in wartime serve in the Navy. They also receive degrees of B.S., or Bachelor of Science, as do graduates of technical colleges.

The first year at the Academy is for basic training, when the student learns military customs and discipline and also takes study courses. First-year men are officially Fourth Classmen, but are nicknamed "plebes" as at West Point. The entire student body is trained as a regiment, which is divided into battalions and companies. The second year is spent at sea, and the Cadet-Midshipman may sail 40,000 miles on several ships, visiting far-off countries. During this "sea year" men are paid $82.50 a month by the shipowner. In the last two years, special studies are taken, such as electronics, astronomy and engineering, as well as languages, history, economics, and

U.S. Merchant Marine Academy

An officer swears in members of the graduating class at the United States Merchant Marine Academy at Kings Point, N.Y.

other college subjects. The Academy has athletic teams as do most colleges. Its campus, which occupies sixty-five acres facing Long Island Sound, has good equipment for sports.

To enter the Academy, one must be between 16 and 21 years of age, a United States citizen, unmarried, and physically sound. He must have a high school education or its equivalent. He must pass competitive examinations held each April. Students receive tuition, room, board, uniforms like those of Navy men at Annapolis, textbooks, and medical and dental care, at government expense. They have thirty days' leave a year and vacations at Easter and Christmas. Incoming Cadet-Midshipmen have certain expenses, but in later years these are made up to them.

Mercier, Cardinal

Désiré Joseph Mercier was a Roman Catholic priest who became a cardinal, the highest Church office next to that of the Pope. He was born in Belgium in 1851 and was ordained a priest in 1874. Eight years later he became a professor of philosophy at the University of Louvain, in Belgium. In 1906 he was made Archbishop of Malines, and the next year the Pope appointed him to be cardinal. Cardinal Mercier became famous in World I for his bravery in defying the Germans. When the king of the Belgians was separated from his people, Cardinal Mercier became spokesman for the Belgians. His letters to his countrymen did much to help them resist the invaders. He also wrote letters abroad telling the world what the Germans were doing to his country. After the war Cardinal Mercier visited the United States and Canada. He died in 1926.

mercury

Mercury is a silvery metal that is a liquid at ordinary temperatures. Mercury is also called *quicksilver* because it slides very quickly over surfaces. In fact, it got

the name mercury from the Roman god Mercury, who was a very swift runner. Mercury is a chemical element, which means that it is one of the one hundred substances of which the world is made. It is the only element that is usually seen in liquid form.

In a thermometer the silvery line whose height you read to tell the temperature is a thin column of mercury. Mercury is also used in other scientific measuring instruments, such as BAROMETERS and HYGROMETERS, about which there are separate articles. Mercury is very good for this purpose because it does not rise as high up into a tube as water does. A mercury barometer is only 30 inches high, while a water barometer would have to be about 34 feet high.

If you cool mercury to 76½ degrees below zero Fahrenheit, it will freeze solid. Mercury is nearly as heavy as lead. If you filled a quart milk bottle full of mercury it would weigh 28 pounds. Mercury is a very good conductor of electricity, and it is used in many electrical appliances.

Some mercury is found in the ground in tiny droplets, but there is very little of it in this pure form. We get most of our mercury from a red mineral called *cinnabar*. Cinnabar is a combination of mercury and sulfur. To separate these two elements, you heat the cinnabar in a vessel that is open at the top. The sulfur will combine with the oxygen gas of the air to form a gas called *sulfur dioxide.* The sulfur dioxide rises out of the vessel and leaves mercury behind. Cinnabar is mined chiefly in Spain, but also in Austria, Italy, Mexico, Texas, and California. Mercury is sold in iron flasks, each one of which holds 76 pounds. Mercury has been known since ancient times.

USES OF MERCURY

You can combine mercury very easily with other metals, except iron and platinum, to form substances called *amalgams.*

This fact is used to separate gold and silver from the rock of their ores. The ore is crushed with mercury. The grains of silver and gold amalgamate or combine with the mercury, but the other elements in the rock do not. The mercury in amalgam form is poured off, leaving the rock behind. Then the mercury is boiled away and what remains is silver or gold.

MERCURY COMBINATIONS

There are many useful combinations of mercury and other elements. For instance, mercury and chlorine form *mercuric chloride,* also called *bichloride of mercury* or *corrosive sublimate.* It is a very powerful germ killer, but only doctors should use it, for it is also a dangerous poison. If you combine mercury and chlorine in a different way, you get a substance that is called *mercurous chloride* or *calomel.* It is used in medicine as a laxative and as a way of killing worms that live inside the intestines of people with certain diseases. Mercury and oxygen combine to form *mercuric oxide,* a substance used in ointments, and in paint that keeps sea water from eating holes in the hulls of ships. A very pure combination of mercury and sulfur is used to make the artists' paint called vermilion. Mercury combined with nitrogen and oxygen forms a substance called *mercuric nitrate* or *fulminate of mercury.* If you strike it, it will explode. It is used to set off other explosives, such as dynamite and the high explosives packed into bullets, shells, grenades, and torpedoes.

When mercury is placed into a bulb from which the air has been pumped, and an electric current is passed through the bulb, the mercury takes on a glow that gives off the very valuable *ultra-violet rays.* These bulbs are called mercury-arc lamps.

Mercury

Mercury was a god of the ancient Romans, two thousand and more years ago. To the Greeks he was known as

N.Y. Public Library

Mercury, the messenger of the gods, wore a winged cap and sandals. His staff, the *caduceus,* is the symbol of medicine.

Hermes. The Greeks considered him a messenger of the gods, as well as a patron of music, astronomy, military tactics, and gymnastics. The Romans believed that he was the god of trade and profits, and the merchants of Rome celebrated his feast day to insure their own business success. He is supposed to have invented the lyre and the flute. Mercury, or Hermes, is usually shown in statues wearing a cap with wings, with wings on his heels, carrying a winged staff with two snakes winding around it. With these he flew rapidly to carry messages from the gods. The winged sandals are still used as a symbol of speed, and Mercury's staff, called the *caduceus,* is used as a symbol of doctors and the practice of medicine. Ancient Greek and Roman statues of Mercury are still in existence.

Mercury

Mercury is the smallest of the nine planets (which include the Earth) that revolve around the sun. It is the one closest to the sun, about 36,000,000 miles away from it. Mercury is less than half the size of the Earth. The Earth weighs twenty-five times as much as Mercury does. Because Mercury is so much lighter, its force of gravity is much less than the Earth's. A person weighing 100 pounds on the Earth would weigh only 26 pounds on Mercury.

It takes Mercury about 88 days to make one complete turn about the sun, compared to 365 days for the earth. The speed of Mercury as it travels through the skies is about 30 miles a second. Mercury takes about 88 days to make one complete turn on its own axis, compared to 24 hours for the earth. One side of Mercury is always light, while the other side is always dark. Because Mercury is so close to the sun, the light side has a temperature of about 770 degrees on the Fahrenheit thermometer. The dark side is about 500 degrees below zero. Mercury has the hottest and the coldest places of all the planets.

Mercury and the moon are about the same size and seem to have the same appearance when viewed with a telescope. Like the moon, Mercury has very little air surrounding it, so it is unlikely that any plant or animal lives on it.

The surface of Mercury has a reddish-yellow color. Every two months, starting at the beginning of each year, Mercury can be seen in the sky as a morning and evening star. For about two weeks of each of the two months Mercury appears in the morning for about an hour and in the evening for about an hour.

Meredith, George

George Meredith was an English writer. He is best known for his novels, but he also wrote fine poetry. He was born in England in 1828. As a young man he planned to become a lawyer, but found he preferred to be a writer. He wrote many novels. The best known are *Diana of the Crossways, The Egoist,* and *The Ordeal of Richard Feverel.* Meredith died in 1909, at the age of 71. Because he lived in a time when there were many very great poets, he was not given as much credit for his poetry as he might have received if he had lived in another period.

merganser

The merganser is a duck that makes its home in many parts of the United States and Canada where the climate is not too warm. It is also called the *shelldrake.* It dives into deep water to catch the fish it eats. The merganser has a bill with sharp edges that are like teeth, and it can hold a slippery fish very tightly. Its contrasting colors, of black, reddish-brown, and white, make it a beautiful bird. Some mergansers are two feet long.

Mergansers make their nests among grasses and rocks on the ground. Sometimes they build their nests in hollow trees. They line the nests with soft feathers. The female lays several light-colored eggs. Mergansers are strong fliers and they make long journeys to warm climates for the winter. The flesh of the merganser has a fishy taste.

The merganser lives in the sea, except during mating season, when it moves to lakes and ponds. Its hooked and horny bill is useful in catching fish.

The hooded merganser is a handsome black-and-white bird that is about 18 inches long. The red-breasted merganser has a speckled, brownish-red breast. It is not good to eat.

mermaid

A mermaid is an imaginary creature who lives in the sea. Her upper part looks like the body of a beautiful woman, but her body ends in the tail of a fish. There are also stories of *mermen,* but mermen are not heard of so often. The folk tales and legends of many countries tell of mermaids who sit on a sandy shore holding mirrors and combing their long golden hair. In some of the stories mermaids take on completely human shapes, and they often lure mortal men to live in the sea with them, or even stay to live on land. No one is sure where the idea of mermaids and mermen began. It is believed that sailors in ancient times may have seen seals or other sea mammals in the distance and mistaken them for half-human beings.

mesa

In the southwestern desert of the United States, especially in Arizona and New Mexico, there are many flat-topped mountains and hills rising steeply up from the surrounding desert. These are called mesas. *Mesa* is the Spanish word for table. It is used because the tops of mesas are flat, as tables are.

Mesas are the remains of plateaus (high, level regions) that have been worn down by erosion, the destroying action of water and wind. The top of a mesa is usually a kind of rock that is hard and can stand the erosion better than the ground around it.

Most mesas extend for only a few hundred feet, but there are larger ones, such as the Mesa Verde of Colorado, which is fifteen miles long and eight miles wide and rises two thousand feet above the lowland. Very small mesas are called buttes.

Mesabi Range

The Mesabi Range is a chain of high hills in northern Minnesota. Originally it was the most important iron-ore mining region in the United States and in the world. More than half the iron ore used in the United States was dug from the mines in the Mesabi Range. Much of the ore has now been used, but the mines are still very rich. The ore is so near the surface that the miners do not have to go underground, but work out in the open, digging out the ore with steam or electric shovels. This is called open-pit mining. The chief mining centers are at Hibbing and Virginia. The iron ore is shipped by freight cars to ports on Lake Superior, then it is carried in big ships across the Great Lakes to steel-producing cities.

The great iron-ore deposits in the Mesabi Range were first discovered in 1887.

Mesopotamia

Mesopotamia was an ancient country in western Asia. It was in the region between the Tigris and Euphrates rivers, the region of the modern country Iraq. The region is often called "the cradle of civilization" because many of the first known cities of the world were located there. There are separate articles about two of these cities, UR and BABYLON.

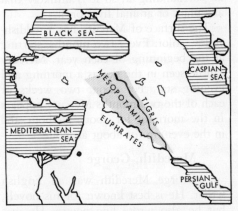

The region of ancient Mesopotamia is often called the "cradle of civilization."

Later, Mesopotamia fell under the Assyrian, Babylonian and Persian empires. The land of Mesopotamia is very dry, and one of the earliest irrigation systems was built there in ancient times. Today this region has many important oil fields, and is also visited by scientists who study ancient peoples.

mesquite

The mesquite is a small tree or shrub that grows in Mexico, in parts of the West Indies and South America, and in the western part of the United States. The mesquite also is one of the most valuable trees on the Hawaiian islands, to which it was taken from America. The mesquite needs very little water and can grow well in deserts. It has a few scrubby leaves, sharp thorns, and pods that contain its seeds. The pods and seeds of the mesquite shrub are sweet and make a good food for cattle. A gum that comes from the mesquite is used to make candy.

When the mesquite shrub grows in a place where it gets plenty of water, it becomes a tall tree. The wood of the mesquite tree is hard and strong. It is used to make fences and railroad ties.

Messiah

In the Old Testament, there are many predictions that God will send a king who will save the Jewish people both from their sins and from those who oppress them. This king is called the Messiah or "anointed one." This refers to the Jewish custom of anointing a king by pouring oil over his head. The Messiah will be anointed, that is, made king, by God. The prophets of the Bible describe the Messiah as a king and ruler. He will be a descendant of King David. He will suffer for the people, but also bring them power and wealth. Pious Jews still wait for the Messiah. Christians recognize Jesus as the Messiah, and give him the title of Christ, which is the Greek word for Messiah.

metabolism

Metabolism is the process by which the body uses food and water and air to make its flesh, bones and other tissues and to stay alive. The body does this by a kind of burning process, and like any burning it produces heat.

Nearly all parts of the body take part in the metabolic process. If some of the parts of the body are not working properly, a person may become too fat or too thin, even though he is eating properly; or he may not have enough energy or strength. Doctors test this by giving a person a BASAL METABOLISM test, about which there is a separate article. See also the article on the HUMAN BODY.

metal and metallurgy

A metal is a substance that is solid, shiny, and hard. It is opaque, which means that you cannot see through it. You can hammer it into whatever shape you want and you can draw it into wire. It conducts heat and electricity very well. It melts at a high temperature, and it is usually quite heavy.

Not all of these things are true of all metals. Mercury is a metal but it is a liquid, not a solid. Sodium and potassium are metals but they are quite soft. Bismuth and vanadium are very brittle, tin, lead and zinc melt at temperatures that are not very high, and there are other exceptions.

Some metals, such as silver, gold, iron, and aluminum, are chemical *elements*. That is, they are among the hundred basic substances of which everything in the world is made. Other metals are *compounds* or *alloys*. That is, they are made by combining two or more elements. Brass, copper and steel are examples of alloys.

PROCESS METALLURGY

The study of metals, how to get them from their ores, and how to use them, is called *metallurgy*, and the people who study metals for these purposes are called *metallurgists* or *metallurgical engineers*.

The first problem in metallurgy is to get metals from their ores. This is usually done by smelting the ores—heating them to a high temperature in a furnace, so that the metal will melt and separate from the rest of the ore. Along with the ore, certain materials called *fluxes* are put into the furnace. The fluxes combine with the nonmetallic part of the ore, leaving the metal free. Iron is smelted.

In other cases an electric current is used to separate the metal from a solution of the ore by means of the process called ELECTROLYSIS, about which there is a separate article. Aluminum is obtained by electrolysis.

Once the metal is free of its ore and melted, it is poured into molds, where it cools into rough, thick bars called *pigs*. The pigs are shipped to the users of the metal.

This work is called *process metallurgy*. There are two main branches of process metallurgy. *Ferrous* process metallurgy deals with the production of iron, steel, and their alloys. *Nonferrous* process metallurgy deals with the production of all other metals (the ones containing little or no iron) and their alloys. Chief among the nonferrous metals are copper, lead, zinc, aluminum, magnesium, chromium, tin, mercury, nickel, platinum, gold, and silver.

PHYSICAL METALLURGY

The user of a metal must know many things about it before he is certain he can use it. He wants to know how pure the metal is, how strong it is, whether it is as hard or soft as he wants it, whether it can be bent and shaped easily, whether it can be forged or machined. A metallurgist makes tests of all these properties of a metal and many others besides. For instance, he might find out how many hundreds or thousands of pounds of power are needed to pull apart a metal bar of a certain thickness. This would be testing

Bureau of Mines

Workmen skim impurities from molten lead that will be used as casing for cables, or as piping for plumbing systems.

the metal for its *tensile strength*. He might test a piece of metal for its hardness. To do this, he puts the metal in a Brinell machine, which presses a very hard steel ball into the metal. Then, with a microscope, he measures how big a dent the ball made in the metal being tested. All of this work is called *physical metallurgy*.

When metals are cast into different forms they sometimes have air bubbles in them. These weaken them. Physical metallurgists called *metallographers* examine castings (metal poured into molds to harden) with X-rays and microscopes to find the bubbles and to learn how to prevent bubbles from forming in castings. Metallographers also examine metals to learn why they crack in places where they get a lot of bending or bumping. Such metal is said to be "fatigued."

TEMPERING AND ANNEALING

Tempering is treatment of metal by heat, to harden it or make it resist corrosion. Metallurgists heat the metal to a temperature they have found best for the hardness they want to get. They control the temperature by watching the changes in color as the metal is heated. First it becomes cherry red. Then, as it becomes hotter, it turns orange, yellow, and finally white. When the metal is the right color, the metallurgist suddenly cools it by plunging it into cold oil or cold salt water. Tempering may make the metal too hard or the sudden cooling may set up strains inside the metal. To avoid this, metallurgists heat the metal slowly to a temperature well below the tempering heat; then they cool it very slowly, sometimes taking days to do so. This process is called *annealing.*

A physical metallurgist also studies ways of putting protective surface coatings on metals by means of plating, galvanizing, or burnishing. *Powder metallurgy* is the making of articles by heating and pressing metal powders to the shape wanted, until the powder grains combine into a single piece of metal. One of the most important tasks of physical metallurgists is the planning, making, and testing of alloys to fit thousands of special requirements.

IF YOU WANT TO BE A METALLURGIST

If you want to become a metallurgist you should study scientific subjects, es-

U.S. Steel

New ways of improving metals and new uses for them are developed through painstaking research by metallurgists.

pecially chemistry, physics, and mathematics.

To qualify as a metallurgist you will need at least a four-year college course leading to a Bachelor of Science (B.S.) degree in metallurgy, metallurgical engineering, or sometimes in chemical engineering. The first job you will get when you are just out of school will probably be that of laboratory assistant in testing or research, or an assistant in the operation of furnaces or electrolysis equipment, or an observer in smelting and refining operations.

metamorphosis

Metamorphosis is a change in the form of certain animals, especially insects and amphibians. It includes changes in habits. Many insects and animals change their habits as they grow older. Dragonflies live in water when they are young, and begin to fly only after they have grown larger. Butterflies and moths change from caterpillars, which eat solid food, into insects that suck juices from plants. The metamorphosis of many insects is very complicated and may have as many as six different stages as they change from eggs into full-grown insects. (Read also the article on BUTTERFLIES AND MOTHS.)

meteor

There are countless little pieces of iron and stone that move in the space between the planets. These pieces are called *meteorites.* Most of them are no bigger than peas.

When one of the meteorites comes close to the earth, it falls to the ground. It comes in at a speed of about 30 or 40 miles a second. This is so fast that friction with the air makes the meteorite so hot that it burns. We see the burning as a *meteor.*

About 25,000,000 of these meteors fall every day, but they burn up while they are still 50 or 60 miles high. Bigger meteorites are closer to the earth when

Yerkes Observatory

Left: The stone meteorite which fell in Arkansas is the largest that scientists have observed while it was falling. It weighs 845 pounds. **Right:** As the meteor enters the atmosphere, it begins to glow. When it reaches the denser atmosphere, friction makes it burn at a white heat. In most cases it breaks and burns up before it reaches the ground.

they burn up. The largest ones burst and drop fragments (little pieces) on the earth, usually in the woods or in a field or in the ocean. If a big piece fell on a person it would kill him, but so far it is not known that any person has been killed by a meteorite.

A meteor is sometimes called a *shooting star* or a *falling star*. Of course, it is not really a star falling. Stars do not fall.

Meteors can be seen on any clear evening. More can be seen on moonless nights, and there are more after midnight than before. Sometimes meteors come in great numbers. People call this a "meteor shower." These showers come every year. Most of them are in the fall, but the best one comes on August 11 each year.

meteorology

Meteorology is the scientific study of how and why the weather changes. People who study the weather are called *meteorologists*. They collect information, such as the changes in atmosphere (air) pressure, temperature, direction and strength of the wind, the amount of mois-

ture in the air, and so on. From this, they sometimes can tell how the weather will change. For this reason, a meteorologist is often called a "weatherman."

methane

Methane is a gas that burns well and for this reason is an important fuel. It is a very important part of the mixture of gases burned in the gas furnaces that heat houses, cook foods on kitchen gas ranges, and make power for industrial plants.

If you stand in a marsh on a warm sunny day, you probably will see bubbles rising through the water from the mud. The bubbles are methane. This explains why methane is sometimes called marsh gas. Methane is being made beneath the mud by the dead plants as they decay and have no contact with air. Plants and trees that died and were buried millions of years ago went on decaying and making methane. They formed pockets of gas that have become gas wells. Pipes are put down to these gas wells, and the gas is brought up to the surface of the ground and stored in tanks for use. When a gusher oil well spouts oil high in the air, the pressure that pushes the oil upward so hard is provided by methane gas that has formed above the underground pool of oil.

Methane is found deep in coal mines. Miners call it *firedamp*. To a miner, "damp" means gas or vapor, so firedamp means a gas that will catch fire. There is a separate article on FIREDAMP.

Methodist

A Methodist is a person who belongs to one of the Protestant Christian churches that grew out of the movement started by John Wesley. John Wesley was a minister in the Church of England about 225 years ago. With his brother, Charles Wesley, and a friend, George Whitefield, he resolved to lead a very strict life and to preach wherever he could find people to listen. All three lived a life of "rule and method." Their followers came to be called Methodists.

The special quality of Methodist preaching was enthusiasm. The Methodists lived strict lives and tried to follow the teaching of Jesus closely. Many of them became missionaries and preached their religion all over the world.

The first Methodists came to the United States before the Revolutionary War. In 1784, the Methodists left the Church of England and formed a separate Church. Francis Asbury was in charge of this Church in the United States. It was called the Methodist Episcopal Church of the United States of America. An episcopal church is one that has bishops. Many Methodists did not want bishops and broke away to form the Methodist Protestant Church. Several other Methodist churches were formed. In 1939, the Methodists decided that they should unite again. They formed the Methodist Church, to which most Methodists now belong. The Methodist Church is the largest Protestant body in the United States, with more than nine million members.

Methodists believe in one God, that Jesus was the son of God and died for men's sins, that each man must be saved by Jesus, and that the basic religious truths are found in the Bible. Methodists have built many hospitals and homes for orphans. They have missions and they publish newspapers and magazines. The Methodist commission on world peace has worked hard to find ways to prevent wars.

Methuselah

Methuselah is the oldest man named in the Bible. He lived to be 969 years of age. His was one of the first names in the recorded history of man. Adam was 930 years old when he died. Noah, who was Methuselah's grandson, was 950 years old when he died. Historians and scholars of modern times have attempted to explain these figures, but do not agree. Today we speak of very old persons as "Methuselahs."

metric system

The metric system is a system of measurement based upon a unit of length called the *meter*. It was adopted by the French government in 1793, and is now used by nearly all scientists throughout the world.

A meter is about 39 inches long (more exactly, 39.37 inches). It was supposed to take ten million meters to cover the distance from the North Pole to the Equator when measured along a line running along the surface of the earth through Paris, France. A standard meter bar made of platinum-iridium alloy is kept under carefully controlled temperatures and pressures in a laboratory in Paris and serves as the standard for the entire world. Accurate copies of this standard meter are kept in other countries for use by scientists.

The metric system is a decimal system, which makes it possible to change one unit into another of the same kind by moving the decimal point a certain number of places. All units can be found by multiplying or dividing by 10. There are ten *decimeters* in a meter, 10 *centimeters* in a decimeter, and 10 *millimeters* in a centimeter. If we wish to change 52,-624 centimeters to meters, we move the decimal point two places to the left, giving 526.24 meters, there being 100 centimeters in a meter.

There are 10 meters in a *dekameter*, 100 meters in a *hectometer,* and 1,000 meters in a *kilometer.*

The metric system also has volume and weight measures. The *liter* is the basic measure of volume. It corresponds roughly to our quart. For weight, the basic unit in the metric system is the *gram.* This is a very small unit, for it takes a thousand grams, called a *kilogram,* to balance with a little less than 2¼ pounds.

At first the metric system proved difficult to adopt. In France, just as in other countries of Europe, people were accustomed to think in terms of yards and inches and pounds and quarts. The metric system did not fit in with the customs of the people. After nineteen years, during which most of the French people still used the old familiar weights and measures, Napoleon, who was then the French emperor, had to give up the metric system.

In 1837 France went back to the meter, this time to stay. Today, much of Europe and South America uses the metric system. The United States, as well as Great Britain, Canada, and Australia, uses the foot and pound system.

metronome

A metronome is a device used by musicians to help them keep time while playing a piece of music. It is a kind of pendulum or swinging clock that can be set in motion at any desired speed. A flat metal rod is held by a spring at the bottom of a wooden box. The spring causes it to move from side to side at a speed that does not change. Each time the rod completes one swing, it makes a clicking noise by which a musician can tell if he is playing too fast or too slow. The speed of the metronome can be changed by sliding a weight up or down on the rod. In an electric metronome, an electromagnet varies the speed. Often a sheet of music may have 100 MM written at the top, indicating that the metronome should be set for 100 clicks a minute.

Metternich, Prince von

Prince Clemens von Metternich was an Austrian statesman who was one of the most important men in Europe for a period of nearly fifty years. His career began about 150 years ago, when the French Revolution had begun a series of changes that were to throw Europe into a turmoil. Metternich was born in 1773  and was made an ambassador before he was 30 years old. Several times he made or kept peace between Austria and the French ruler, Napoleon, but in 1814 he organized the group of European countries that conquered Napoleon. After Napoleon fell, Metternich was one of the statesmen who worked out a settlement of the difference between European countries and, in 1815, fixed national boundaries that lasted with little change for a hundred years, until World War I. Metternich remained powerful in Austria until 1848, called "the year of revolutions" in Europe, when his government fell. He fled to England, where he lived until his death in 1859 at the age of 86.

Mexican War

From 1846 until 1848 the United States and Mexico were at war. The main reason for this war was that part of Texas was claimed by both Mexico and the United States. In 1837 Texas had become independent from Mexico, and in 1845 it had become part of the United

States. The disputed territory was between the Nueces and Rio Grande rivers in what is now southern Texas. When Texas became part of the United States, Mexico announced that it would fight to keep this territory.

President James K. Polk sent United States troops to Texas to defend this territory. General Zachary Taylor, who later became a United States President, was in charge of these troops. Taylor had about 1,500 men under his command. He went first to Corpus Christi and then to the border of the Rio Grande, both places in the disputed territory. The Mexican government said he was in Mexican territory and warned him to leave. Instead Taylor built a fort there, which he called Fort Brown.

The Mexican forces attacked the fort, and in May, 1846, the Congress of the United States declared that a state of war existed between Mexico and the United States. The government called for 50,000 volunteers to fight the war, and raised $10,000,000 to pay for the war.

Mexico was not as strong as the United States and it had fewer good generals. Also it was having trouble with the people in its own country. Two United States armies, led by General Taylor in the north and General Winfield Scott in the south, fought the Mexicans in many battles, most of which the United States won.

In September of 1847 about 13,000 men under General Scott started a march against Mexico City, the capital of Mexico. Several fierce battles were fought before the United States forces finally captured the city. More than 2,000 Americans and about 7,000 Mexicans were killed in these battles. The capture of Mexico City, was the last important battle of the war, but it was not until February of 1848 that Mexico and the United States signed a peace treaty.

RESULTS OF THE WAR

While these battles had been going on, smaller United States forces had marched through other territories belonging to Mexico and had claimed them for the United States, particularly the territory that is now the state of California. The Mexican War was ended by a treaty signed at Guadalupe Hidalgo, a town in Mexico, and by this treaty these territories became the possessions of the United States.

The United States government paid Mexico $15,000,000 for what is today the states of California, Nevada, and Utah, and parts of New Mexico, Arizona, Colorado and Wyoming. The United States also agreed to withdraw its troops from the rest of Mexico's territory and to pay certain debts that Mexico owed to individual United States citizens. The boundary of Texas and Mexico was also decided upon.

The Mexican War was bitterly opposed by many people in the United States. Some people believed that the United States had deliberately gone to war with Mexico in order to win the valuable western territories, and that the United States had been wrong to fight such a weak country and take away so much of its territory.

N.Y. Public Library

The battle of Chapultepec took place two days before the fall of Mexico City, and assured victory for the United States forces under General Winfield Scott.

Mexico

Mexico

Mexico is a country in North America, on the southern border of the United States. It is more than 760,000 square miles in area, almost three times as large as Texas, and more than twenty-seven million people live there, four times as many as live in Texas. Many of the people of Mexico live and work as their ancestors did, in sleepy little villages. Visiting these villages is like going back many centuries in time, but parts of Mexico, for example the capital, Mexico City, are very modern. Many people go to Mexico for vacations because of the beautiful scenery and to see the ancient remains of the highly civilized Maya and Aztec Indians who lived there long before the white men came.

THE PEOPLE WHO LIVE THERE

Almost two-thirds of the Mexican people are a mixed race. They have some ancestors who were American Indians and some who were Europeans from Spain. These people are called *mestizos.* A smaller group are pure-blooded Indians. They have not intermarried with the Spanish and have kept their own customs and ways of living. A still smaller group are those with no Indian blood.

These are members of families that came from Spain, the United States, and Canada.

Most of the Mexican people belong to the Roman Catholic Church. They speak Spanish, but it is mingled with many Indian dialects. Many Mexicans also speak or understand English, especially in northern Mexico.

There is a great difference in the way various groups of Mexicans live. Some of the people are very rich. They live in beautiful Spanish-style houses. Usually such a house has white columns in front, an open balcony on its second story, and an inner courtyard, or *patio,* where flowers and vines grow, and where the family can gather to eat and entertain guests.

Most of the Mexicans are very poor. They earn only about a hundred and fifty dollars a year, which is less than the aver-

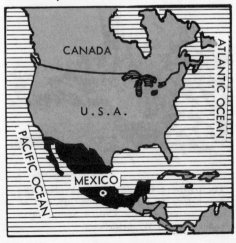

Mexicans are courteous and friendly. Most of them are farmers, and some are very poor.

Ewing Galloway

1. A fisherman of Lake Pátzcuaro. The lake abounds in fish and is a popular summer resort.

2. Indian women doing their washing in a tiny stream.

3. The snow-capped crater of Mt. Popocatepetl. Mountain climbers make regular ascents to its 17,887-foot peak.

4. A farmer standing next to a typical wooden plow.

5. A scene at a bullfight. In Mexico, as in Spain, this is a highly popular sport.

American Airlines Photos

U.S.D.A.

Though Mexico is just across the Rio Grande from the United States, life there is very different.

Ewing Galloway

Ewing Galloway

1. The ancient cathedral of Mexico City, off El Zocalo (the Square), nerve center of the city.

2. The Pyramid of the Sun, a monument of Aztec civilization.

3. The white houses and cobblestone street of a typical small Mexican village.

4. The 57,000-pound stone Aztec calendar in the National Museum. The Aztecs, who were skilled astronomers, made it in 1479.

5. The brilliantly decorated University of Mexico.

Ewing Galloway

Ewing Galloway

age person in the United States makes in a month. The Mexicans live in houses made of sun-dried bricks or of mud and straw, called adobe. These houses usually have no windows and are not very comfortable. The people have little furniture and sleep on the floor or on straw mats.

The Mexican worker most often wears a pair of cotton trousers, a shirt, a wide-brimmed straw hat, and a pair of sandals called *huaraches.* A Mexican woman wears a blouse and a full-length skirt, with a shawl, called a *rebozo,* on her head. She usually goes barefooted.

The Mexicans love highly seasoned food. The most popular food in the country is the *tortilla,* a kind of dumpling made of corn. With it they eat boiled black beans, called *frijoles.* They rarely eat meat, though on holidays they celebrate with turkey, cooked with a highly spiced sauce.

The Mexicans love holidays and celebrations, and there are many festivals, called *fiestas,* during the year. For these celebrations, the people dress in bright-colored costumes, and there are singing, dancing, and fireworks.

Rich and poor Mexicans alike are famous for their *siestas.* The siesta was the afternoon nap that everybody used to take after lunch. Shops were closed and all work was stopped for two or three hours. In recent years, the siesta was done away with and people now have a work-day more like the one in the United States, but many people still take their siesta in the afternoon.

HOW THE PEOPLE LIVE

More than two-thirds of the people in Mexico are farmers. They still use methods and equipment like those of their ancestors. Though much of the land is fertile, the farmers do not raise nearly as much as they would if they used more modern methods. In recent years farmers have improved their land by using irrigation, and they now raise enough corn, sugar, and rice to feed the country. They also raise beans, tomatoes, and coffee, which are important parts of a Mexican's diet. Many of the farmers raise cattle.

Many people work in the valuable Mexican mines, which are among the richest in the world. Mexico produces more silver than any other country, and ranks second in the production of lead. There are also zinc, copper and gold mines. Mexico ranks seventh in the production of petroleum.

Some of the most popular products made by Mexicans are their beautiful silver jewelry, pottery, and leather goods. These are made by hand.

Children have to go to school in Mexico up to the age of 15. Fifty years ago, most of the people could not read or write, but many schools have been built since then and now more than half the people have had some education.

WHAT KIND OF A PLACE IT IS

The northern part of Mexico is mostly a desert. Not many people live there. The central region is a high, level region. It is

Black Star
The most impressive peaks in Mexico are volcanoes. There are so many volcanoes that the Aztecs always drew a glowing volcano to represent a mountain.

Pottery is one of the treasured handcrafts of Mexico. Skilled artists shape and decorate their work with colorful designs. Like many Mexican arts, the pottery combines Spanish and Indian styles in a very distinctive way.

Mexican Gov't Tourist Bureau

surrounded by the Sierra Madre mountain ranges, with their valuable mineral deposits. Most of the people in Mexico live in this region. The soil is fertile and the climate is healthful and cool because it is so high up. Mexico City, the capital of Mexico and one of the biggest cities in the world, is on the highest part of the plateau. It is noted for its beautiful scenery. People visiting Mexico City can see the towering snowcapped peaks of Popocatepetl and Ixtaccihuatl, two famous volcanoes.

The southern part of Mexico consists of low plains that are very hot and damp. Few people live in this region. A great deal of rain falls there and it is swampy and filled with tropical vines and underbrush. This region is infested with mosquitoes.

There are many wild animals in Mexico—wolves, bears, coyotes, and monkeys, as well as many small fur-bearing animals. Mexico is also famous for its many bright-colored birds, many of which fly to Mexico from the north during the winter months.

Mexico has few navigable rivers, but there are many railroads and highways. Also there are many seaports, and steamships travel from Mexico to all the important ports in the world. A great river, the Rio Grande, is a boundary between Mexico and the United States.

THE GOVERNMENT OF MEXICO

Mexico is a republic. It has a President, who is elected for a six-year term. It also has a Legislature (like the United States Congress) composed of two houses, a Senate and a Chamber of Deputies. The Legislature makes the law. Members of the Senate are elected for a six-year term. Members of the Chamber of Deputies are elected for a three-year term. Mexico is divided into twenty-nine states, and each has its own government as do the states in the United States. All married men over 18 and all unmarried men over 21 have the right to vote.

CHIEF CITIES OF MEXICO

The leading cities of Mexico, with 1953 population estimates, are:

Mexico City, population (1950 census), 2,233,709, the capital and largest city in Mex-

The beautiful cathedral in Mexico City is the oldest Christian church in North America. It was built on the foundations of an Aztec temple 400 years ago.

ico. There is a separate article about MEXICO CITY.

Guadalajara, population 399,016, the second-largest city. There is a separate article about GUADALAJARA.

Monterrey, population 352,880, the third-largest city, industrial center, in the northern part of the country.

Puebla, population 233,667, the fourth-largest city, railroad and commercial center, in the central part of the country.

IN THE PAST

When the white men came to Mexico, more than four hundred years ago, Mexico was ruled by the Aztec Indians. Their capital was where Mexico City now stands. The Aztecs had high buildings of beautifully carved stone, and they made beautiful sculpture and pottery. It is believed that about 100,000 Aztecs lived in the capital and more than six million Indians lived in Mexico.

The Spanish conqueror Hernando Cortez landed with his men in Mexico in 1519, and within two years he had conquered the country. He destroyed the Az-

tec temples and brutally put down all resistance. For the next three hundred years Mexico was ruled by the Spanish. Most of the people suffered under this rule because the Spanish were interested only in getting the mineral wealth from the country. The people were heavily taxed and had nothing to say about the making of the laws. The people grew more and more dissatisfied and wanted to be independent. Finally, in 1810, the first attempt to break away from Spain occurred. It was led by Miguel Hidalgo. The uprising was put down, and it was some years before Mexico became an independent country, but Hidalgo is considered the George Washington of his country, and the day of the uprising that he led on September 16 is still celebrated as a national holiday.

Other uprisings followed, and in 1821 Mexico was recognized as an independent country. The people did not know very much about ruling themselves, and there were many revolutions and continual unrest in the country. In 1846 Mexico had further trouble when it became involved in the Mexican War with the United States. As a result of the war, Mexico had to transfer to the United States a large territory, which became the states of California, Nevada, and Utah, and parts of Colorado, Wyoming, and New Mexico.

In 1860, Benito Juarez became the President of Mexico and he tried to improve the country. (There is a separate article about JUAREZ.) For many years afterward, Mexico was ruled by a powerful dictator, Porfirio Diaz. The people suffered under Diaz, though he improved the country in some ways. In 1910, the people overthrew Diaz, but again the country was in great confusion. Leaders rose and fell and no one was able to establish a strong and peaceful government. From 1934 to 1940 Lazaro Cardenas was President. He made many changes in the government and life of the Mexican people. It was the most successful and peaceful time Mexico had known.

During World War II, Mexico fought on the side of the Allies. It joined the United Nations after the war. Mexico is one of the countries toward which the United States is most friendly.

MEXICO. Area, 760,373 square miles. Population (1952 estimate), 27,283,148. Language, Spanish. Religion, chiefly Roman Catholic. Government, republic. Monetary unit, the peso, worth about 12 cents (U.S.). Flag, three vertical bands, green, white, and red; coat of arms on white band.

Mexico, Gulf of

The Gulf of Mexico is a large body of water along the southern coast of the United States and the eastern coast of Mexico. It is an "arm" of the Atlantic Ocean. Its waters are about 9 degrees warmer than those of the Atlantic Ocean because the Gulf Stream enters the Gulf of Mexico by way of the Yucatan Canal and raises the temperature of the water. The Gulf of Mexico is about 700,000 square miles in size, and is more than 12,000 feet deep at the deepest point.

The low, curving coastline of the Gulf of Mexico is smooth and has few good harbors. The most important ports are New Orleans, Mobile, Tampa, Galveston and Houston in the United States, Vera Cruz and Tampico in Mexico, and Havana in Cuba.

Mexico City

Mexico City is the capital and the largest city in Mexico. It is the highway, railroad and airline center of the country, and in recent years it has become an important manufacturing city. More than two million people live in Mexico City. Many of them work in factories that make cigars and cigarettes, jewelry, textiles, and machinery. Many work in the big markets, to which products are shipped from other parts of the country.

Many of the people of Mexico City are Indians and mestizos (people who are of Indian and Spanish blood). They work in the factories and on the farms in the surrounding region. Many people from other countries live in Mexico City, and they manage businesses.

Mexico City is set in a beautiful region. It is built on a plateau, or high, level region, more than 7,000 feet high, surrounded by mountains. Because of this altitude, the climate of Mexico City is extremely pleasant and cool all year round, unlike many other parts of the country, which are very hot. The city is surrounded by fertile farm land and rich mines. In the distance are the famous snow-capped volcanoes of Popocatapetl and Ixtaccihuatl.

The city itself is a mingling of the old and the new. They are beautiful modern buildings and shops, tree-lined avenues, and parks filled with flowers. The most popular entertainment is the bullfights. There are ancient buildings and palaces. Mexican Indians sell their wares in open markets and on the streets as their ancestors did. One of the interesting but confusing things about Mexico City is that the streets change their names at almost every block, according to Spanish custom.

Mexico City is very ancient and is believed to have been settled by the Aztec Indians more than six hundred years ago. It grew into an important Aztec city where many thousands lived. The Spanish, under Hernando Cortez, conquered the city in 1521, after much bitter fighting in which the Spaniards destroyed a large part of the city. Cortez rebuilt it and made it the capital of Mexico. Today Mexico City is the oldest capital in the Western Hemisphere. It is a popular vacation place, and thousands of people visit it every year.

MEXICO CITY, MEXICO. Population (1950 census) 2,233,709. Capital of Mexico. In the Federal District.

Miami and Miami Beach

Miami is the largest city in the state of Florida. It is on Biscayne Bay. It is one of the most popular vacation resorts in the United States. More than a million

Miami's rapid growth, which earned it the name "Magic City," is reflected in its skyline of ultra-modern buildings. This view is across Biscayne Bay from MacArthur Causeway.

visitors go there each year to enjoy the sun, the white beaches, and the many outdoor sports.

More than 200,000 people live in Miami all year around, and many of them take care of the vacationists. Many of the people also work in factories making airplane parts, canned fruits and vegetables, and furniture. Miami is an important railroad and airline center, and the people ship large quantities of oranges, lemons, and other citrus fruits. It is a beautiful modern city, with skyscrapers, luxurious hotels, shops, and theaters. Tall palm trees grow along the wide boulevards. Miami was first settled in 1870, and became a city in 1896.

Miami Beach is an island that lies across Biscayne Bay from Miami. It is connected with Miami by several causeways, or roads across the water. Like Miami, it is a popular resort and has beautiful hotels, shops, and boulevards lined with palm trees. More than 46,000 people live there, but many thousands more go there each year on their vacations. Fifty years ago, Miami Beach was a wilderness with swamps and sand dunes. The swamps were filled in and the land area made larger. In 1917 it became a city, with a tiny population of 300. Today it is the sixth-largest city in Florida.

MIAMI, FLORIDA. Population (1950 census) 249,276; (1955 estimate) 259,035. County seat of Dade County. Founded in 1870.

MIAMI BEACH, FLORIDA. Population (1950 census) 46,282.

mica

Mica is the name for a group of minerals that can be split into thin sheets that you can see through. Before the days of window glass, mica was used for windows. Because it is also fireproof, mica is still used for windows in stove and furnace doors. Valuable papers are covered with thin sheets of mica to protect them from loss by fire. Mica is an insulator; it can stop the passage of electric current better than any other material. It is used in all kinds of electrical, radio, and television apparatus to shield certain parts from the flow of electricity. Small flakes of mica are the "snow" you see under Christmas trees. If you see wallpaper with a sparkly sheen, it probably has powdered mica on its surface. Mica is elastic; you can bend it easily and it will snap back.

About four out of every hundred rocks have mica in them. The different kinds of mica and their colors are: muscovite (colorless), phlogopite (brown), biotite (black), lepidolite (violet), and fuchsite (yellow or green). Only muscovite and phlogopite are of much value. Muscovite is best because it is clear like glass, and it can be split into the largest sheets. Some muscovite sheets are as much as two feet long and two feet wide. Mica is sometimes called *isinglass*.

When mica is taken out of the ground, any rock attached to it is knocked off with a hammer. Then it is split with a hammer into thick slabs called *books*. The books are split into thin sheets with a knife. In the United States, mica is mined in the Appalachian and Rocky Mountains. Two other countries that mine much mica are India and Brazil. In 1950, the United States mined 62,922 tons of mica, and the whole world mined 100,000 tons.

Michael, Saint

St. Michael is an angel described in the Bible as a great fighter. Artists have painted him as a prince with a great sword, with which he fights against and conquers Satan. The French warrior and saint, Joan of Arc, saw a vision of St. Michael. St. Michael's feast day is called Michaelmas in England, and is celebrated on September 29. See the article on ANGELS.

Michael, King of Rumania

Michael is the name of the last king of Rumania, before it was taken over by a Communist government in 1947. In Rumanian, his name is Mihai. Twice Michael was king as a boy. He was born in 1921 and became king at the age of 6 because his father, Carol II, had given up his right to the throne. Three years later, Carol reclaimed the throne, but in 1940 Carol gave up the throne again and Michael became king at the age of 19. It is difficult to say how good a king Michael was, because he did not have much power. From 1940 to 1944, Rumania was controlled by a fascist party allied with Nazi Germany, and after 1944 the Communists of Russia controlled the country. In 1947 the Communists made Michael abdicate (resign as king) and he left the country. In 1948,

In his self-portrait, Michelangelo captured his own deep vision, which enabled him to create many of the most beautiful paintings and statues the world has known.

Michael married Princess Anne, a descendant of a branch of the Bourbon family, which also was a royal family without any country to rule over.

Michelangelo

Michelangelo was an Italian sculptor, painter, poet, and architect who lived more than five hundred years ago. He was the most famous artist of his time, and even today there is no greater figure in the history of art. Popes, kings and princes begged for the honor of having work done by his hand. His poetry, much of which was deeply religious, was greatly admired. Michelangelo felt himself to be first of all a sculptor.

His full name was Michelangelo Buonarotti. He was born in Caprese, a town in Italy, in 1475. He was the son of a public official in Florence. As was the custom in those days, the baby was given to the care of a nurse. This nurse was the wife of a stonemason, and Michelangelo said he drank in his love of sculpture with his milk. At the age of 13 he was apprenticed (sent as a pupil) to the Ghirlandaio brothers, who were noted artists, and in their studio the boy painted his first picture. When he was 15, some of his early sculptures came to the attention of Lorenzo de' Medici, a great patron of art who was practically the ruler of Florence. Lorenzo invited Michelangelo to live in his house, and there the young man became acquainted with most of the leading men of literature and art. He lived there for two years, until the death of Lorenzo. Only two works of these student days survive, but they show his genius.

In 1496 Michelangelo went to Rome, where he stayed five years. During this period he created the *Pietà* in St. Peter's Church, which immediately brought him

On one of the walls of the Sistine Chapel in the Vatican is Michelangelo's conception of the Last Judgment. This detail from the painting gives an idea of the great power of his work.

fame as the greatest sculptor of his day. The *Pietà* is a sculpture of the dead Jesus in the arms of his sorrowful mother Mary at the foot of the cross.

When Michelangelo returned to Florence he was commissioned to carve a huge statue 18 feet high from a single block of marble, to commemorate a military victory of the city. This was a statue of David from the Biblical story in which David slew the giant Goliath. It was the last work of Michelangelo's early style, in which he depicted all his subjects with great realism and naturalism. From that time he drew on his vivid imagination as much as on life.

PAINTING THE SISTINE CHAPEL

In 1508 Michelangelo began what was to be his greatest work of painting. He was ordered by Pope Julius II to decorate the ceiling of the Sistine Chapel in the Vatican. He did the painting almost without help and it took four years. A large part of the time he worked lying on his back on the scaffolding. The great painting is divided into many sections, showing scenes from the Bible such as the creation, the fall of man, the deluge or flood, and many other subjects.

After the death of Julius II, Michelangelo carved a great statue of Moses, perhaps one of his most famous sculptures, for the Pope's tomb.

When he was 60 years old, another Pope, Paul III, commissioned him to paint more frescoes in the Sistine Chapel. The greatest of these was a painting to cover the entire altar wall. It was called *The Last Judgment,* and it contained more than a hundred figures, all larger than life.

The last years of Michelangelo's life were mostly devoted to architecture. In 1546 he was appointed chief architect of St. Peter's Church in Rome. He designed the dome of St. Peter's. He took no pay for this position, believing it his religious duty to devote himself to the Church. Michelangelo died in 1564.

Michigan

Michigan

Michigan is one of the north central states in the United States. Its nickname is the "Wolverine State." The reason for this is not known. Wolverines were never found in this region.

Michigan is a big and busy state on the Great Lakes. Three-fifths of all the automobiles in the world are manufactured in Michigan, and it is the leading state of the United States in furniture-making. Michigan also ranks first in the production of cherries and second in the production of iron ore. The state gets its name from Lake Michigan, which comes from an Indian word meaning "great water."

Michigan ranks 23rd in size among the states, with 57,022 square miles. In population it ranks 7th, with nearly eight million people living there. It became a state in 1837, and was the 26th state admitted to the United States. The capital is Lansing.

THE PEOPLE OF MICHIGAN

The first settlers in Michigan were French fur trappers and traders, who came there almost three hundred years ago. Much later, people from England,

Scotland, and the eastern United States settled in the region. As the lumber and mining industries grew, immigrants from all over Europe came to work there. In the past forty years, many more people from Italy, Russia, Poland, and other European countries, and many Negroes who had been farmers in the South, came to work in the automobile industry and other factories. About half the people in Michigan are American-born.

Almost three-quarters of the people live in big cities and work in huge automobile factories and factories that make iron and steel, machinery, furniture, chemicals, and breakfast foods. Many people are farmers and produce dairy products, cattle, and large crops of cher-

Michigan Tourist Council
Above: The Michigan state capitol in Lansing, built in 1878.
Right: The business district of Detroit, Michigan's chief city.
Left: The apple blossom, state flower.

ries, apples, pears, and grapes. Others work in the rich iron and salt mines, and many earn their living by catching lake trout, whitefish, herring, and many other kinds of fish in the Great Lakes.

The Roman Catholics are the largest religious group in Michigan. There are also many Methodists, Baptists, and Lutherans.

WHAT MICHIGAN IS LIKE

Michigan is divided into two parts by Lake Michigan and Lake Huron, so that it forms two peninsulas (land almost, but not wholly, surrounded by water). The Upper Peninsula is low in the east, but rises to beautiful mountains, covered with pine forests, in the western part. There are many fine lakes and rivers, and valuable iron and copper mines in this part of the state. The Lower Peninsula is where most of the farmers raise their crops. Most of the important industrial cities are in the Lower Peninsula.

More than a hundred years ago, Michigan had many beavers, otters, and muskrats, but they were hunted so greedily for their furs that today hardly any remain.

The climate of Michigan is very pleasant on the whole, since the state is surrounded by four of the Great Lakes.

Many summer resorts have been built along the lakes because of the cool breezes, and in winter the lakes keep the region from getting too cold. In the Upper Peninsula the winters are more severe. The average temperature in Michigan in winter is 20 degrees and in summer is about 69 degrees.

The lakes and many rivers in Michigan have always provided excellent transportation. The Grand River in the Lower Peninsula is the longest in the state. The Great Lakes have long been the great waterway to the west. Railroads and highways reach almost all parts of the state, and there are airports in all the big cities.

THE GOVERNMENT OF MICHIGAN

Michigan, like most other states, is governed by a Governor and a Legislature. The Governor is elected for a two-year term. The Legislature is composed of two houses, a Senate and a House of Representatives. The members of both houses are elected for a two-year term. Judges are elected for an eight-year term. The capital is Lansing. There are 83 counties.

Everyone has to go to school between the ages of 6 and 16. There are about

Though Michigan is far from being the largest of the states, few can equal its great variety of scenery. Forests, lakes rivers, farmlands, towns, and vast industrial cities —all can be found in Michigan. Visitors enjoy the many aspects of this busy state.

Mich. Tour. Council Photos

1. The Detroit skyline. The great industrial city is just across the river from Windsor, Canada.
2. Hartwick Pines State Park. The park has a replica of an early Michigan lumbering camp.
3. The Rackham Memorial Building in Detroit. It is part of the city's Art Center.
4. Cranbrook Academy of Arts, one of the best schools and museums of art in the Midwest.
5. Advertising its own products. Michigan has heavy snows, and is proud to announce that tractors made there remove the snow with ease.

Henry Ford Mus., Dearborn

Detroit Convention and Tour. Bur.

Detroit Convention and Tour. Bur.

In 1899 the first automobile factory in America opened in Detroit. Since then, Michigan has become the world's chief center of automobile production.
1. The Henry Ford Museum in Dearborn, copied from Independence Hall in Philadelphia.
2. The museum's collection of 165 early automobiles. The oldest is a Roper Steam Carriage made in 1865.
3. The Ford Rouge plant, the world's greatest industrial concentration, employing 63,000 people.

Chrysler Corp.

Michigan Tour. Council

4. An iron mine. Michigan is second as an iron-mining state.
5. Conveyors carrying automobile bodies in an assembly plant.

4,800 public schools, including 655 high schools, and 49 colleges, universities and other schools of higher learning. Among the principal colleges and universities are:

University of Michigan, at Ann Arbor. Enrollment, 19,800 in 1953 (12,837 men, 6,963 women).

Michigan State College, at East Lansing. Enrollment, 14,779 in 1953 (9,717 men, 5,062 women).

University of Detroit, at Detroit. Enrollment, 7,668 in 1953 (5,892 men, 1,776 women).

Wayne University, at Detroit. Enrollment, 17,491 in 1953 (9,786 men, 7,705 women).

CHIEF CITIES OF MICHIGAN

The leading cities of Michigan, with populations from the 1950 census, are:

Detroit, population 1,849,568, the largest city in the state. There is a separate article about DETROIT.

Grand Rapids, population 176,515, the second-largest city, manufacturing center known for its furniture, in the southern part of the state.

Flint, population 163,143, the third-largest city, automobile-manufacturing center, in the southern part of the state.

Lansing, population 92,129, the state capital and sixth-largest city. There is a separate article about LANSING.

MICHIGAN IN THE PAST

The first white man to visit the Michigan region was probably Étienne Brulé, a French explorer, who went there more than three hundred years ago. He found vast forests filled with fur-bearing animals, and soon French fur-trappers and traders followed him. The first permanent settlement was made by Father Marquette at Sault Sainte Marie, in 1688. Detroit was founded in 1701 by Antoine Cadillac. Other villages soon grew up.

After the French and Indian Wars, about two hundred years ago, the Michigan territory was given to the British. The Indians living there were not friendly to the British settlers, and they attacked the British forts and often massacred the people.

Michigan was given to the United States after the Revolutionary War, but the Indians continued to attack the settlements until the warlike tribes were defeated by General Anthony Wayne.

For a while Michigan was part of the NORTHWEST TERRITORY, about which there is a separate article. Then it became a separate territory, and in 1837 it finally became a state.

The people of the state discovered the great wealth they had in the woodlands and mountains. They rapidly cut down

Industry and agriculture are both important in Michigan. *Left:* The Blue Water Bridge joining Port Huron in Michigan and Sarnia in Canada is a symbol of a state famous for its steel products. *Right:* The farmer who grows wheat and corn must not be forgotten.

Standard Oil Co.   *Michigan Tourist Council*

Coast Guard Photo

Michigan is bordered by four of the Great Lakes. The lighthouse at Spectacle Reef in Lake Huron warns lake boats of danger.

the valuable forests with no thought to the future, and they mined the copper and iron ores. Industries thrived and the population of Michigan grew enormously, but about forty years ago the state realized it had not been wise to use up its natural resources so thoughtlessly. Forests had been stripped and the wild life had almost entirely disappeared. Now there is a program of conservation to protect Michigan's natural resources.

PLACES TO SEE IN MICHIGAN

Hiawatha National Forest, 882,013 acres, near Shingleton, in the northwest, on U.S. Route 2. Beautiful woods and scenic spots.

Isle Royal National Park, 133,838 acres, a forested island, the largest in Lake Superior; distinguished for its wilderness and great moose herd.

Fort Custer, six miles northeast of Battle Creek, in the south, on State Highway 89. An important military camp.

Automobile plants in Detroit, Dearborn, and other cities. Tours are conducted through these big plants where automobiles are made.

Sparks Illuminated Cascades, at Jackson, in the south, on U.S. Route 12. A group of waterfalls beautifully lighted at night.

Greenfield Village, at Dearborn, in the east, south of U.S. Route 12. An "old American" village, built by Henry Ford, containing many historic buildings, including the laboratory where Thomas A. Edison worked.

Pictured Rocks, about 8 miles northeast of Munising, on State Highway 28. Magnificent cliffs, beautifully colored and in strange shapes.

Dutch settlements, one named Holland, along Lake Michigan. People have continued the Dutch tradition; farming carried on in typical Dutch style; tulip festival held each year.

MICHIGAN. Area, 57,022 square miles. Population (1957 estimate) 7,803,000. Capital, Lansing. Nickname, the Wolverine State. Motto, *Si Quaeris Peninsulam Amoenam Circumspice* (If You Seek a Pleasant Peninsula, Look Around You). Flower, apple blossom. Bird, robin. Song, "Michigan, My Michigan." Admitted to Union, January 26, 1837. Official abbreviation, Mich.

Michigan

Michigan is the name of one of the most popular card games played in the United States. It is played also in many other countries. There are several other names by which the game is known: Stops, Boodle, Newmarket, Saratoga, and Chicago.

The game is played with a standard pack of 52 cards. There is a *layout* on the table, made of four cards taken from another pack of cards: any ace, king, queen and jack, but they must be of different suits. These are called the *boodle* cards. Each player uses chips or matches as counters. Three to eight players may play.

Before the deal, the dealer puts two chips on each boodle card and each other player puts one chip on each boodle card.

The dealer deals the cards one at a time, face down, to each player and to one extra hand called the *widow*. The widow belongs to the dealer. If he does not like his hand (the cards dealt to him) he may throw it away and take the widow instead. If he wants to keep his hand, he may sell the widow to the highest bidder. A player who owns the widow must throw his own hand away before looking at the widow.

The player at the dealer's left then puts down a card from his hand. This is called a *lead*. He must lead the lowest card in the suit he selects, but may select any suit. Any player who holds the next-higher card of the same suit must then play it, and so on. The player must announce the card he plays. For example, the leader puts down the three of spades, saying, "Three of spades." Whoever holds the four of spades must then play it and say, "Four of spades." The same is true for the holder of the five, the six, and so on. When nobody has the next card in order, it means that the missing card is in the widow or dead hand. The player who played the last card then leads.

When a player plays a card that matches one of the boodle cards, he takes all the chips on that boodle card. When a player gets rid of his last card, play ends. Each other player pays him one chip for every card that player has left in his hand.

Michigan, Lake

Lake Michigan is the third-largest of the Great Lakes, which lie between the United States and Canada. It is the only one of these lakes entirely within the United States. It is 22,400 square miles in size, and 923 feet deep at the deepest point. Lake Michigan borders most of the state of Michigan, and part of the states of Wisconsin, Ilinois, and Indiana.

Lake Michigan often has sudden and dangerous storms, but a great deal of shipping is carried on there. Boats bring huge amount of iron ore, coal, grain, and lumber to ports along its shores. The southern ports are open all through the year, but the northern ports are closed with ice for four months in the winter. The most important port on Lake Michigan is Chicago, on the southwest shore. Other important ports are Gary, Indiana, and Milwaukee, Wisconsin. Lake Michigan is part of the vast waterway system in the United States that links the lake with the Atlantic Ocean and the Gulf of Mexico.

microfilm

Microfilming is a way of photographing important papers so that the pictures can be used in place of the originals. A number of photographs are recorded on one long strip of film. The pictures on the film are too small to read, but they are projected onto a screen, or viewed in a special device called a *reader,* and are magnified so that they can be read easily. The film can also be developed as a photograph of the original paper.

Microfilming is used to make a permanent record of many important historical documents. Often these are on paper that is so old it will fall apart if handled. Students look at the microfilm picture instead.

Many business firms save space by microfilming important letters, contracts, checks, and other papers. Hundreds of such papers, which would occupy a whole file drawer, can be microfilmed on a strip of film that takes up only a few inches of a desk drawer. Librarians save a great deal of valuable space by microfilming newspapers.

Engineers microfilm plans to save the space that the bulky original drawings take up. The microfilm can be kept for protection against possible loss of the originals by fire.

micrometer

A micrometer is an instrument for measuring objects as thin as a ten-thousandth of an inch. The word means "measurer of small things."

The idea for the micrometer was first thought of by a French astronomer, William Gascoigne, in 1638. He was interested in measuring the size of the sun, the moon, and various planets. To do this, he placed two metal bars, or indicators, outside the eyepiece of the telescope. By turning a screw connecting them, Gascoigne could move the indicators nearer together or farther apart until they just enclosed the image of the planet he saw in the eyepiece of his telescope. Then he would measure the distance between the indicators, and, using other information, could figure out the width of the planet.

However, to do this properly Gascoigne had to measure the distance between the indicators very accurately. This could not be done by an ordinary ruler. In fact, no ruler could be made with marks fine enough to give him the accurate measurements that he needed.

Gascoigne then came up with the idea that is the basis of the micrometer. He counted the number of times he had to turn the screw to open the indicators from a fully closed position. First he counted the number of threads or cuts in the screw in a distance of one inch. By dividing this number into one inch, he found out the distance between threads. In this way, he knew how far the indicators would move for every complete turn of the screw. If the screw was given only part of a turn, the indicators would move only a fraction of this distance.

Gascoigne's idea was improved upon by another Frenchman, several hundred years later, so that distances could be measured quickly and easily without figuring out the distances between screw threads. The screw has 40 threads to an inch and the barrel that turns the screw has 25 evenly spaced marks around it. Turning the barrel to one of the marks moves the screw one-thousandth of an inch.

The object whose width is to be measured can be clamped in the micrometer as in a vise, and its width can be read directly off the barrel.

When an object (O) is placed in a micrometer and the thimble (T) is twisted so that the object is held between the ends of the spindle (S), the markings on the hub (H) and thimble give the exact thickness of the object. Each small division on the hub represents 25 thousandths of an inch, and each small division around the thimble represents one thousandth.

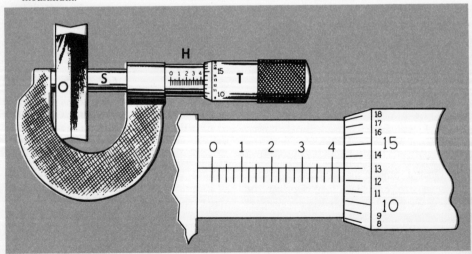

Industrial and Engineering Chem.

Learning to use a microscope looks easy. Actually, the girls had to practice quite a while before they learned to adjust the delicate lenses with accuracy.

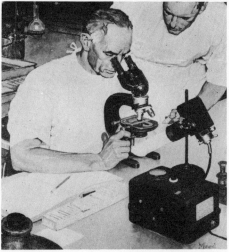

Squibb & Sons

Just as scientists use the telescope to study the great stars of the heavens, so also they use the microscope to study the tiny universe in every bit of matter.

microscope

A microscope is an instrument that is used to help see things that are too small to be seen with the naked eye. With the microscope, scientists can see tiny organisms that cause diseases, examine the structure of metals, observe the behavior of small insects and plants, and so on. This has helped them to make many important discoveries in science.

A simple microscope is a single magnifying glass. The microscopes used by scientists in the laboratory contain two or more magnifying glasses in a tube, and are called *compound microscopes.* They can magnify things (make them appear larger) as much as 1,000 times. The microscope that is bought for use in the home usually can magnify 50 to 100 times.

The glass at the top of the tube into which you look is called the *eyepiece.* The glass at the bottom of the tube, directly above the object to be observed, is called the *objective.* The object is placed on a glass *slide,* which rests on a platform below the objective and above a small movable mirror. The mirror directs light onto the object.

The object is magnified by the objective and then further magnified by the eyepiece. The magnifying power of the microscope is the magnifying power of the objective multiplied by the magnifying power of the eyepiece. If the objective makes an object seem 6 times larger, and the eyepiece makes it seem 3 times larger, the magnifying power of the microscope is said to be 18 diameters, written 18$\times$.

You can make an object appear larger in a microscope by turning the barrel of the eyepiece so that the eyepiece is moved farther away from the objective. The object can be made to appear smaller by bringing the eyepiece closer to the objective.

Sometimes an object is stained with dyes, which helps brighten certain parts of the object and makes them easier to see. Often a drop of oil may be placed on the object, to bring the rays of light closer together so that the object can be seen more clearly. In many cases ultraviolet light is used. Ultraviolet light cannot be seen with the naked eye. In such cases the eyepiece and objective are made of quartz instead of glass, because glass absorbs the ultraviolet light while quartz does not. Ultraviolet light is made up of very short waves and makes it possible

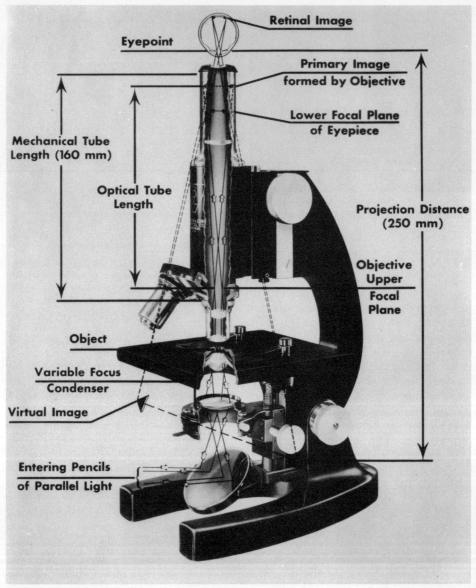

Retinal Image

Eyepoint

Primary Image
formed by Objective

Lower Focal Plane
of Eyepiece

Mechanical Tube
Length (160 mm)

Optical Tube
Length

Projection Distance
(250 mm)

Objective
Upper
Focal
Plane

Object

Variable Focus
Condenser

Virtual Image

Entering Pencils
of Parallel Light

Bausch & Lomb

The diagram shows the path of light from the point where it enters a dynoptic microscope through the eyepoint to the retina, where the mental image of the object is formed.

to see objects too small to be seen in ordinary light.

The *resolving* power of a microscope is its ability to make the fine details of an object show up clearly upon magnification. Occasionally an object may be magnified so much that its details appear fuzzy. This is called *empty magnification* and occurs when the magnification has gone beyond the resolving power of the microscope. The magnification must be reduced until the object is clear (*in focus*). This point is called *useful magnification*.

Sometimes a microscope may have two and even three objectives in the bottom of the tube. These have different magnifying powers and can be swung into position above an object when desired. Only one objective can be used at a time.

A *binocular microscope* has two eyepieces side by side, so that it is possible to look at an object with both eyes. Such microscopes are constructed in much the same way as BINOCULARS, about which there is a separate article.

THE ELECTRON MICROSCOPE

An *electron microscope* is a very highpowered microscope. Instead of glass lenses, it uses magnets. Also, special waves of electrons (particles of negative electricity), called *DeBroglie waves,* are used instead of ordinary light. These waves are focused by the magnets in the same way as light is focused by the objective and eyepiece in the optical microscope. The object then appears on a special screen, or is made to fall on a photographic plate. About 30,000 volts of electricity are required to operate an electron microscope. A modern electron microscope is about the size of a desk and is operated by a control panel set into the top. It can magnify objects as high as 100,-000 times, so it is about 100 times as powerful as most optical microscopes.

The electron microscope is mostly used in medical and biological research. It has been very useful in understanding the causes of many diseases such as influenza and the common cold.

Midas

Midas was a king in the legends, or stories, told by the ancient Greeks thousands of years ago. He was king of a Greek country called Phrygia. In return for a favor to the god Bacchus, or Dionysus, he was told that any wish he made would be granted. Midas asked that everything he touched might turn to gold. He was granted his wish, but found he could no longer eat, because even his food

R.C.A.

The young man at the right is James Hillyer, who did pioneer work in perfecting the very powerful electron microscope.

turned to gold. He almost starved, and begged Bacchus to take back his power. Bacchus instructed him to bathe in the waters of the River Pactolus. This removed the power, and made the sands of the river turn to gold.

In another story, Midas judged a musical contest between the gods Pan and Apollo. Midas decided in favor of Pan. This made Apollo so angry he turned Midas's ears into the ears of an ass (donkey). Midas wore a cap to hide his ears, but the servant who cut his hair saw them. The servant was afraid to tell any one, but he dug a hole in the ground and whispered into it, "King Midas has ass's ears." Reeds grew up there, and legend says that whenever the wind blew over the reeds they whispered those words.

Midas is supposed to have killed himself by drinking the blood of an ox.

Middle Ages

The Middle Ages were a period of about a thousand years in the history of the world. This period began at about the time when the city of Rome, capital of the mighty Roman Empire, fell to Germanic invaders. This was in the year 476. The period ended at about the time that Columbus discovered America, in 1492.

While the Romans ruled most of the civilized part of Europe, laws were enforced and art and literature were active. During the Middle Ages, there was no strong government in many parts of Europe and the strongest fighters could rob or rule their neighbors. People were so busy protecting themselves that few of them had time for learning. For this reason the Middle Ages are often called the Dark Ages. Only the Christian Church, in its abbeys and monasteries, kept learning alive.

The Middle Ages were the time of the CRUSADES, and of FEUDALISM and KNIGHTHOOD, about which there are separate articles.

The Middle Ages ended with a new birth of learning, called the RENAISSANCE, about which there is a separate article.

midnight sun

Near the North Pole, the sun shines all day during the summer. The "land of

Greenland Inform. Dept.

The midnight sun lasts from May to August in places above the Arctic Circle. Here, it seems just about ready to set over the coast of East Greenland.

the midnight sun" is a region in the far northern part of Norway and Sweden, so near to the North Pole that in summer the sun may still be shining at midnight. You can read more about this region in the article on LAPLAND. Because of its pleasant summer climate, the land of the midnight sun attracts many tourists.

Midway

Midway is the name of two tiny islands in the central Pacific Ocean, about four thousand miles from the western coast of the United States. The islands are known mostly because the United States Navy won a great victory in a sea battle off Midway early in World War II. Some experts think this was the most important battle of the war.

The Midway Islands came to belong to the United States after the Spanish-American War in 1898, but were captured early in World War II by the Japanese. In its attack on Pearl Harbor, the Japanese had almost destroyed American naval power in the Pacific, and the American Navy did not have enough strength left there to defend Hawaii or even the Pacific Coast of the United States. Japan sent a large fleet to take advantage of this weakness. What the Japanese did not know was that United States Naval cryptographers had broken the Japanese code and knew exactly what the Japanese were going to do. When the Japanese fleet approached Midway it was heavily bombed by American torpedo bombers. At the same time Japanese aircraft bombed the small American fleet that had been gathered together and sent out to meet the Japanese. For three days this air battle continued, until finally the Japanese fleet was forced to turn back, without having exchanged a single shot with the American fleet. In this battle the Japanese lost four carriers, one cruiser, three destroyers, 275 planes, and about 5,000 men. The Americans lost one carrier, one destroyer, 150 planes, and about 300 men.

mignonette

The mignonette is a plant that first grew in the northern part of Africa. It is now raised in gardens in Europe and the United States. The mignonette is an annual, which means that it must be planted every year. It is a hardy plant and grows best in a cool soil that is not too rich. It grows to be about one foot high. The plant has thick, dark green leaves and lovely sprays of greenish, white, or pale yellow flowers. The flowers have a very sweet smell. The mignonette usually blooms in June. Some people plant seeds again in July and then the mignonette blooms a second time before the first frost in the fall.

migration

Migration is the traveling of a large group of animals from one place to another. In the early times of men's life on earth, thousands of years ago, entire tribes of men would leave the place where they were living and travel to find a new home where it might be easier to raise vegetables for food and kill animals for meat and skins. Such migrations sometimes took many years, in which the people who began the migration would die and their children and grandchildren would be the first to reach the new home. The American Indians probably populated the entire Western Hemisphere by great migrations from Asia. The Germanic peoples spread over Europe by the migrations of their tribes from one part of the continent to another.

Animals of many kinds migrate. Grasshoppers or locusts by the millions leave one place and fly to another. Fish in large numbers leave a river in which they are born, swim hundreds of miles through the ocean to a new home, and later return to the same spot in the same river to lay eggs and produce a new generation of fish that will migrate just as they did. Birds migrate when they change their homes from a northern land to a southern one in the winter and from the south-

Italian State Tourist Office

Milan has many beautiful buildings built hundreds of years ago. The General Hospital, with its arched columns and delicate sculptures, dates back to the Renaissance.

ern one back to the northern one in the summer. Scientists have not found the reason for the migration of many insects and fishes, and not even the migration of the birds can be explained by their change to a warmer climate.

Milan

Milan is the second-largest city in Italy. It is in northern Italy, and is the most important commercial city and the largest railroad and financial center in the country. About 1,300,000 people live in Milan. They work in big factories that make automobiles, furniture, musical instruments, and textiles. Many also work in publishing houses. Like most Italians, the people of Milan love music, and the La Scala Opera House in Milan is the most famous in the world.

Milan has many beautiful buildings and churches, though during World War II many of them were destroyed by bombings. The great cathedral of Milan was only slightly damaged. Milan has wide, modern streets, fine libraries and schools, and valuable collections of paintings and sculpture that attract visitors every year. The most famous work of art is Leonardo da Vinci's *The Last Supper.*

Milan is an ancient city, more than two thousand years old. It became a powerful and wealthy city under the Romans, and in later centuries was ruled by the Huns, Germans, Spaniards, and Austrians. It became part of Italy in 1859. In 1945, during World War II, Benito Mussolini, the dictator of Italy, was executed in Milan.

MILAN, ITALY. Population, 1,272,934 (1951 census). Capital of the province of Milan. On the Olona River.

mildew

Mildew is a fungus, or simple kind of plant, that feeds on dead matter or on other plants. When it eats other plants it causes a disease that often destroys the plants. (You can read more about this in the article on FUNGUS.)

There are two kinds of mildew. Downy mildew feeds on the leaves of grapes, lettuce, onions, and other plants. It forms white patches on the leaves of these plants and they shrivel up and die. Powdery mildew makes a kind of cobweb growth on the leaves and sometimes on the stems of many different flowers and fruit plants. Roses, lilac bushes, and cherry and peach trees are some of the plants that are often attacked by mildew. Tiny rootlike threads pierce the leaves of the plant and gather the food.

Housewives know that mildew also attacks cloth, paper, and foods. Mildew grows best in places where there is very little sunlight and where it is damp. People do not store books and papers and clothes in damp, dark places for this reason. There are many poisonous sprays and powders that people now use to protect plants and kill mildew. The tiny organisms from which mildew grows are carried from place to place by the air.

Military Academy, U.S.

The United States Military Academy is a special college where young men study to become officers in the United States Army. It is located high above the Hudson River at West Point, New York, and is generally referred to simply as "West Point." West Point graduates are commissioned as second lieutenants, and receive a degree of B.S. (bachelor of science). Enrollment in January, 1954, was 2,296, and there were about 320 teachers, most of whom were officers.

Men between 17 and 22 years of age, unmarried, with a good school and character record, of sound body, and between 5 feet 6 inches and 6 feet 4 inches in height, are eligible to enter West Point. The course is four years, and students— who are called *cadets*—do not have the usual college summer vacations. They have occasional "leaves," or short vacations, but are under strict discipline all the time. Entering cadets must deposit $300 to cover uniforms, books, and equipment, and the government adds $600 to that sum. The cadet repays this $600 out of his monthly salary of $81.12, at the rate of $30 per month for twenty months.

To get into West Point, a youth must first receive an *appointment.* These are allotted as follows: eight from each state; four from each Congressional district, from each territory, and from Puerto Rico; six from the District of Columbia; two from the Panama Canal Zone; 172 from the United States at large; and 180 from the regular Army and Army Reserves. Others may be appointed from among sons of men who won the Medal of Honor, and from foreign countries.

HOW APPOINTMENTS ARE MADE

Various officials, governmental bodies and military organizations have the privilege of making appointments, or naming candidates, for West Point. There are also *competitive* nominations, given to those who do best in certain tests. All persons named must pass regular examinations to become cadets. These are mental, medical, and physical.

Noncompetitive nominations are made by: Congressmen, four each; Senators, four each; the Vice President, three; Hawaii and Alaska, four each; District of Columbia, six; Panama Canal Zone, two; and Puerto Rico, four. For each West Point vacancy four men may be named, a *principal*, and a *first, second* and *third alternate*. If the principal fails to qualify, the first alternate tries, followed by the others in order. Young men seeking appointments should apply to their own Senators or Congressmen, or to their territorial government.

The competitive appointments are awarded to youths who make the best scores in the West Point Achievement Tests in Mathematics and English and the West Point Aptitude Test. These tests are held on the first Tuesday in March, when all other West Point examinations begin. Enlisted men in the Army

U.S. Army Photo

Cadets at the United States Military Academy, wearing full-dress uniform, march with sharp precision. The future officers receive very strict training.

The ivy-covered Headquarters Building at West Point is one of the first sights that greets visitors. Its windows overlook the majestic Hudson River.

and Air Force, regular and reserve, may win 180 such appointments. The President makes 89 other appointments from among the sons of military men. For sons of deceased veterans, forty appointments are reserved. Forty others go to Honor military and naval schools. Up to twenty may go to Latin American youths, and one to a Filipino. Information about these may be obtained from The Adjutant General of the United States Army, Washington 25, D.C.

During the first or freshman year, cadets are called *plebes*. Then they become third (sophomore) year, second (junior) year, and first (senior) year men. They live in dormitories, which they must keep clean and neat. They study hard, drill, and also have strenuous gymnastics plus the choice of seventeen sports. In studying, science takes up more than half of the curriculum. West Point uses the "honor system," under which the cadets themselves make sure all rules are obeyed.

U.S. Army Photo
West Point cadets receive instruction on wire splicing. Their training takes in just about every phase of combat.

Small classes at West Point permit individual attention to each student. The courses include economics and government, as well as sciences and engineering.

WEST POINT IN THE PAST

The Academy was officially established on March 16, 1802, at the key military fortress of West Point. It was opened on July 4, 1802. There were two reasons why it was considered necessary. During the Revolutionary War the colonists had depended largely on foreigners to drill and lead many of their soldiers. They had also been obliged to use foreign engineers and artillerymen. President Washington wrote in his 1797 message to Congress: "However pacific (peaceful) the general policy of a nation may be, it ought never to be without a stock of military knowledge for emergencies. . . . The art of war demands much previous study." The second reason was that the foreign situation at that time was threatening, because of the Barbary pirates, frontier battles, and boundary disputes.

The site of West Point had been occupied by the Army since 1778. The first Superintendent was Major Jonathan Williams. He had ten cadets. When the War of 1812 began, the strength of the Corps of Cadets was increased to 250.

From 1817 to 1833 Colonel Sylvanus Thayer was Superintendent. He was called the "Father of the Military Academy." He had one ideal: to produce men who would be trained and worthy leaders. He demanded excellence of both character and knowledge. He increased the study of civil engineering, made every cadet pass his courses or drop out, and permitted no classes larger than 10 to 14 members.

From time to time the Academy has changed its course to keep up with trends in modern warfare. General Douglas MacArthur, who became Superintendent in 1919, emphasized physical fitness, and also taught lessons learned in World War I.

Most of the great United States military leaders have been West Point graduates.

Young men serving in the armed forces who wish to enter West Point may get special instruction at the United States Military Academy Preparatory School at Stewart Air Base, Newburgh, New York. This school is maintained by the Army and is supervised by the West Point Commandant. It helps candidates pass the entrance examinations to West Point. Classes begin in September and last the usual school year.

military police

The military police of an army keep order among the soldiers and arrest sol-

M.P. Corps

Military Police enforce military law on and off Army posts. In combat zones, they also take charge of enemy prisoners.

diers who break the army's rules, just as a police force does in enforcing the laws of a city or state. The United States Army has a branch called the military police, under the command of an officer called the Provost Marshal General. When large numbers of soldiers are in a city, military police patrol the city streets to make sure the soldiers do not get into trouble and that they return to the army post safely, but if soldiers break the laws of the city it is the city police and not the military police who arrest them. Like other police forces, military police are on hand to help the soldiers. Military police also do other kinds of police work, such as directing traffic. The United States Navy has a similar branch called the Shore Patrol.

milk

Milk is a fluid made by the bodies of most female mammals for the feeding of their young. Mammals are animals whose young are born alive and nursed by their mothers. For thousands of years man has used as food the milk of cows, goats, ewes (female sheep), asses, camels, buffaloes, reindeer, and other animals. The word milk, as most often used, means the milk of cows.

Milk is the most nearly perfect of all human foods. Besides its use as a drink it is also the basis for a number of other

foods, such as BUTTER, CHEESE, CREAM, and ICE CREAM, about which there are separate articles. It is important in the preparation of various foods in the home and in factories.

Fluid whole milk supplies almost all the food needs of babies, and it is very valuable in the diet of children and grownups. In the United States, every man, woman and child consumes an average of nearly three quarts of milk a week. Even more is consumed in other forms of milk and milk products.

WHAT MILK IS MADE OF

Milk contains proteins, fats, carbohydrates, and minerals, all of which are necessary for health. The principal milk proteins are *albumin, globulin,* and *casein,* which are made up of amino acids and are substances needed by the human body for the building of muscle tissue and blood.

Of the minerals found in milk, calcium is the most important. It is needed by children to build bones and teeth, and by persons of all ages to keep these parts of the body strong and healthy. Milk also contains phosphorus, iron, potassium, and

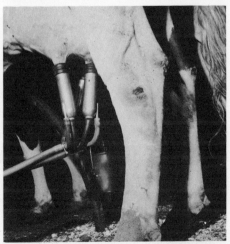

Standard Oil Co.

Mechanical milking takes less than five minutes, compared to the ten or more minutes it takes by hand. The milking machine works on a vacuum principle.

Nat'l Dairy Council

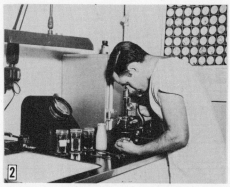

Nat'l Dairy Council

The Borden Company

Nat'l Dairy Council

Margot L. Wolf

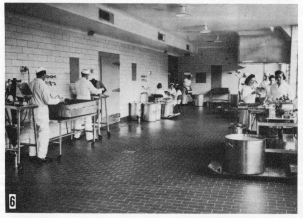

Nat'l Dairy Products Corp.

1. Milk is pasteurized at carefully controlled temperatures to kill disease-causing bacteria.
2. Next, samples are examined in the laboratory to make sure the milk is pure.
3. Wax containers are automatically put into a machine that fills them with milk.
4. Butter, an important milk product, is tested by taste and smell to assure good flavor.
5. Every country makes its own special cheeses from milk. Shown here is Dutch Edam.
6. Strawberries from this crushing room will flavor ice cream, a healthful milk product.

magnesium, all of which the body must have.

The fats in milk are an important source of energy. The milk fats contain substances that give milk its odor and flavor. They also contain the pigments found in the green plants eaten by cattle. These give milk its color. Milk also contains all known vitamins but it is principally a source of Vitamin A and riboflavin.

HOW MILK IS PRODUCED

The production, processing, distribution and marketing of milk has become a huge industry in the United States. The various levels of government, from national down to state, county, and city, have set up many regulations to insure the purity and good quality of the milk supply.

The United States leads the world in the production of milk, with a total of more than 120,000,000,000 pounds every year. About half of this is sold as whole milk and cream. About a quarter is used to make butter, about one-tenth to make cheese. Ice cream and other frozen dairy products take up a small percentage, and the rest goes to make evaporated milk, powdered milk, and other products.

Since fluid milk spoils easily, it must be handled carefully and quickly. The milk is collected from farms and taken to receiving stations where it is inspected, weighed, and chilled. It is then transferred to a pasteurizing plant in special tank trucks or railroad cars. Pasteurizing is required by the United States government for most milk. It kills all dangerous bacteria in milk and makes it safe to drink. The milk is heated to at least 143 degrees Fahrenheit for 30 minutes, or to 161 degrees for 15 seconds. At the pasteurizing plant some of the milk is *homogenized,* which means it is treated to break down the fats so that the cream stays distributed throughout the milk and does not rise to the top. Some of the milk is made more nourishing by adding Vitamin D. It is then cooled quickly, is bottled and capped, and is ready for distribution.

Milk for home use is distributed mainly through retail stores in paper cartons or bottles, or by delivery in bottles to homes.

SPECIAL KINDS OF MILK

Certified milk is a trade name for milk produced under special regulations and guaranteed pure by a medical commission. Certified milk may be sold raw or pasteurized.

Evaporated milk is useful where refrigeration is not available. It is whole milk that has been homogenized, boiled to remove about half of the water, sealed in cans, and sterilized. In this form milk will keep for long periods. Condensed milk is evaporated milk with a certain amount of sugar added to make it keep longer. Condensed milk was invented by Gail BORDEN, about whom there is a separate article.

Skim milk, sometimes called fat-free milk, is milk from which most of the fat has been removed. It retains most of its food value, and is useful in special diets. Dried skim milk is a powder produced by removing nearly all of the water from skim milk. It is used by bakers, candy and ice-cream manufacturers, and other food industries. Recently it has been sold for use in homes.

milkweed

Milkweed is the name of a group of plants that contain a milky juice. Milkweed grows in many parts of the world where the climate is warm. The milkweed is a perennial plant, which means that it grows up from the same roots every year. Milkweed grows best in a damp soil.

There are many different kinds of milkweed. The butterfly milkweed has attractive orange flowers and it is sometimes planted in flower gardens. Other

Standard Oil Co.

Milkweed is sometimes called silkweed because of its silky seed, which is carried by the wind. The plant is found in many parts of the United States.

milkweeds have pale lavender flowers and are not so handsome. Some milkweeds have crimson flowers. There are milkweeds that have a sweet smell and others that have an unpleasant odor.

The milkweed has pods that contain small seeds with soft tufts of hair attached to them. These soft hairs are used to stuff pillows and mattresses. Some milkweed plants that grow in the deserts in the western part of the United States contain latex, a valuable substance that is used in making rubber.

Milky Way

The Milky Way is the name given to the more than one hundred billion stars and cloudlike patches of matter called *nebula,* that can be seen from the earth. Such a collection of stars and nebula is called a *galaxy,* which comes from the Greek word meaning "milk." The Milky Way is just one of a million galaxies that make up the universe. The sun is part of the Milky Way, and so are all the stars and constellations described in other articles in this encyclopedia.

The Milky Way is shaped like a large wheel, and is believed to be about six million million million miles wide, and about six hundred thousand million million miles thick. Traveling at the speed of light, 186,300 miles a second, it would take about 100,000 years to go from one end of the Milky Way to the other.

The center of the Milky Way is near the constellation Sagittarius. The sun is about eighteen thousand million million miles away from it. The entire Milky Way is turning about its center at a speed of 150 miles a second. Because of its tremendous size, it takes the Milky Way two hundred million years to make one complete turn.

The Milky Way was first closely examined by the German-born English astronomer, Sir William Herschel, in 1784. Most of our knowledge of the shape and structure of the Milky Way has come from the work of Harlow Shapley and Bart J. Bok of Harvard University.

Millay, Edna St. Vincent

Edna St. Vincent Millay was an American poet, by many critics considered the greatest of this century. She was born in Rockland, Maine, in 1892, and graduated from Vassar College. Her first long poem, "Renascence," was written when she was only 19. It is so good that at first people could hardly believe anyone so young had written it. It is still among the best she ever wrote. It was published in 1917 as the title poem in her first volume of verse. Two more volumes followed, and then in 1922 came the *Ballad of the Harp-Weaver,* for which Miss Millay won the Pulitzer prize for poetry in 1923. She also wrote three poetic plays, and the libretto (or story) for Deems Taylor's opera *The King's Henchman.* Miss Millay was married in 1923 to Eugen Jan Boissevan. She died in 1950.

millet

Millet is the name of a large group of grasses that have small seeds. The seeds are used as food. Millet grasses are grown in many parts of the world where the climate is not too hot or too cold. Some millet, such as the foxtail millet, grows in about two months. It is an important food for cattle. The foxtail millet is a very old grass that was one of the sacred plants of the Chinese people about three thousand years before Christ.

The people of India, China, and Japan eat millet as a cereal and use it to make bread and cake. People in the United States do not eat millet.

Millet, Jean François

Jean François Millet was a French painter who lived about a hundred years ago. He came of a poor farming family and he gained his fame as the painter of scenes of peasant life. Millet was born in 1814. As a boy he worked in the fields, but he was always sketching and drawing.

Millet's father sent him to Cherbourg to study painting, and later the town of Cherbourg gave Millet an award so that he could study further in Paris. There he painted the pictures that made him famous, among them *The Gleaners, The*

The Angelus is typical of Millet's paintings, in the best of which he portrays the simplicity of French farm life.

Angelus, and *The Man with the Hoe.* This last painting was the inspiration for a poem, "The Man with the Hoe," by the American poet Edwin Markham. Millet never made much money with his painting, and he died a poor man in 1875. Very soon after his death his work became highly prized. Many of his pictures now hang in museums in the United States and Europe.

Millikan, Robert

Robert Andrews Millikan was an American scientist who won the Nobel Prize in Physics in 1923 for finding the amount of electricity in an electron (a small particle found in all atoms of matter) and the amount of energy in a photon (a small bundle of light).

He was born in Morrison, Illinois, in 1868, and attended Oberlin College in Ohio and Columbia University in New York City. He was professor of physics at the University of Chicago for twenty-five years and head of the research laboratory at the California Institute of Technology for thirty years. He died in 1953.

millinery, the business of making hats for women and the materials used in them: see HAT.

Milne, A. A.

Alan Alexander Milne is the name of an English writer who has written famous stories for children. Milne was born in 1882, and he first wrote plays and stories for grownups. When his son Christopher Robin was 3 years old, Milne wrote a book of verses for him and put Christopher Robin himself into most of them. Then followed *Winnie-the-Pooh* and *The House at Pooh Corner,* stories that were peopled with many of the child's stuffed animals. Pooh himself is a "bear of very little brain," and there are Piglet, Kanga and Little Roo, Rabbit and all his relations, and many others. *Now We Are Six* is another book of verse. Milne died in 1956.

Milton, John

John Milton was one of the greatest of all English poets. Some consider him the greatest. He was born in London in 1608, and when he was very young he began to study Latin, Greek, and Hebrew. He also learned to play the organ. He was a handsome slender young man, with gray eyes and light brown hair that fell in curls to his shoulders. He decided early to be a writer.

It is difficult for modern readers to appreciate some of Milton's poems. They are filled with names and statements taken from the ancient Latin, Greek and Hebrew literature. In Milton's time, all educated men studied the Latin and Greek classics, because they were considered a necessary part of a good education.

Among Milton's earliest well-known poems were *L'Allegro, Il Penseroso,* and *Lycidas.* Experts have said that *Lycidas* is the most nearly perfect poem in the English language. Milton wrote it when he was 29 years old, to mourn the death of a man named Edward King who had been his friend at Cambridge University. Milton wrote many sonnets, short poems of fourteen lines each. No one except Shakespeare ever wrote them so well. His most famous sonnet is about his blindness. He became blind when he was 46.

Milton's life was eventful. He lived during a time when England was in the midst of a religious and political revolution. Most of the writing he did for twenty years was of a political nature. He was on the side of the Puritans, the religious group that opposed the English king.

Milton's greatest work was his long poem, *Paradise Lost.* It is about the original sin of Adam and Eve in the Garden of Eden. He started it after he became completely blind, and dictated most of it to his daughters. *Paradise Lost* was finished in 1663. Milton received only twenty-three pounds for it; this was English money worth about $115, though it was actually worth more than $600 is worth today.

Paradise Regained, another long poem, appeared in 1671. It is about the temptation of Christ in the wilderness, as told in the Bible.

Milton wrote constantly for more than fifty years, and never stopped studying. He often declared that he wrote well only from fall till spring. The work he did during the summer months never pleased him.

John Milton died in London in 1674, after a long illness. He was 66 years old.

Milwaukee

Milwaukee is the largest city in Wisconsin. It is on Lake Michigan and has the most beautiful harbor on the lake. It is one of the most important ports in

Milwaukee Assn. of Commerce

The City Hall in Milwaukee, built in 1896, was copied after German buildings because so many of Milwaukee's citizens came from Germany or were of German ancestry.

the Middle West. More than 600,000 people live in Milwaukee. They work in large factories that make hosiery, heavy machinery, automobiles, tractors, and many other things. Milwaukee is famous for its great brewing plants, which are among the largest in the world. Milwaukee ranks tenth in the United States in the value of its products.

Milwaukee has many fine avenues and parks. Lake Park and Juneau Park, along Lake Michigan, are noted for their beauty. There are beautiful beaches along the lake. Milwaukee has many colleges, and it has one of the largest zoos in the world.

Milwaukee was founded by Solomon Juneau in 1818, when he built a trading post where the city now stands. In 1835 the town was laid out. It grew rapidly. It was largely settled by German immigrants. For a long time the people spoke German more than they did English, and more German newspapers were published than English newspapers. There was a theater where plays were given in German. This gradually changed, and today Milwaukee is like any large American city.

MILWAUKEE, WISCONSIN. Population (1950 census) 637,392. County seat, Milwaukee County. On Lake Michigan. Settled, 1818.

mimosa

Mimosa plants grow in parts of the world where the climate is warm. Some mimosa plants grow as tall as trees, while some are small and are grown as ornamentals in greenhouses. The mimosa plants are perennial, which means that they grow from the same roots every year.

One kind of mimosa that is sometimes called the "sensitive plant" is a pretty plant with light purple flowers. It grows to be about two feet high. It gets this name because when a person touches its dark green leaves they close up.

The mimosa is a legume; like the pea and bean plants, it has pods that contain the seeds.

Mindanao

Mindanao is the second-largest island in the Philippine Islands. It is at the southern end of the islands in the Pacific Ocean. It is 36,537 square miles in size, which is about the size of Indiana, and nearly two million people live there. Most of the people are farmers. They grow coconuts, corn, Manila hemp and rice in the fertile Cotabato and Agusan valleys. The Cotabato Valley is the largest farming region in the Philippines. There are iron, coal and gold mines in the mountains, which are the highest in the Philippines. These mountains are covered with dense forests and some of them are active volcanoes. Mount Apo is the highest point in the Philippines. It is 9,690 feet high. The most important rivers in Mindanao are the Rio Grande de Mindanao and the Agusan River. In the central part of the island there are many wild sections where nobody lives. In this region there are forests of valuable woods.

The largest city of Mindanao is Davao, a city of about 110,000. Cagayan and Cotabato are other principal cities.

During World War II, the Japanese occupied Mindanao, and several battles were fought there. See the article on the PHILIPPINES.

mine   (see also MINING)

A mine is a container with a heavy explosive charge in it. Mines are used in warfare. They are like bombs, except that they are not dropped on the enemy. They are put in the sea where enemy ships may come, or on land and bridges over which enemy tanks and troops may pass. When the enemy reaches the mine, it explodes.

NAVAL MINES

The mine used at sea is tub-shaped and large, containing several hundred pounds of an explosive (usually TNT). It is called a submarine (underwater) mine because it remains below the surface of the water so that approaching enemy ships cannot see it. A special ship called a *minelayer* places the mines in the water. Most mines are moored (attached by a cable) to the bottom of the ocean so that they will stay in one place and their location will be known. As it lays the mines, the minelayer makes a chart of where they are. Then the ships of the minelayer's country can steer clear of the mines, while enemy ships, not knowing where they are, may run into them.

During wartime, thousands of mines are laid in this way to protect harbors and trade routes that are much traveled. One purpose of mines is to keep enemy warships, especially submarines, from attacking a country's ships or coasts. Another purpose of mines is to sink the enemy's

Official U.S. Navy Photo

Minesweepers perform valuable service by destroying enemy-planted submarine mines and keeping sea lanes open. The men are lowering an orapesa float. The cable attached to the hook in its nose traps moored mines, which are then drawn into a device that cuts the mooring gear. The mine rises and is exploded by gunfire.

merchant ships. Mines are so powerful that the explosion of a single mine will usually sink a merchant ship or small warship.

MAGNETIC MINES

During World War II, magnetic mines were much used. The mine was magnetized so that it would be attracted to the steel sides of a ship. After magnetic mines were used for a while, ships began to protect themselves by carrying a magnetized metal band, all around the ship, that would repel the magnetic mine instead of attracting it. (The principle of this is explained in the article on MAGNETISM.) This device was called a *paravane,* but actually a paravane is a cutting device used by special ships called *minesweepers.* As the minesweeper moves through the water, the paravanes in front of it cut the cables by which the mines are moored to the bottom. The mines then float, and guns are shot at them to explode them at a safe distance. When a fleet moves through mined waters, minesweepers go ahead to clear out the mines. Then the fleet follows safely.

Mines were once very good protection against submarines, but radar and similar detecting devices have made it easier for submarines (and other warships) to avoid them.

When a war ends, all the warring nations sweep out the mines they have laid, so that the shipping lanes will be safe again. Even so, some mines are overlooked and can cause damage to shipping years later.

LAND MINES

Land mines are usually much smaller than naval mines. They are buried underground, and are built so that when anyone steps on the ground overhead they explode. Ground troops, like minelaying ships, carefully chart the places where they put mines, so that friendly troops can avoid them. A mined place is called a "booby trap" by soldiers.

U.S. Army Photo

An antitank mine is about twelve inches in diameter and three to six inches deep. It is buried in the ground and will explode when a tank or other heavy vehicle passes over it. The officer is probing for hidden wires. Next, he will disarm it by dismantling the detonator.

When an army goes forward through territory that the enemy may have mined, men go first with *mine detectors*. A mine detector has a long handle so that a soldier can hold it out in front of him. When the mine detector passes over a spot where there is metal, it gives an electrical signal. This warns that there may be a mine there, and no one ventures on the spot until the mine has been exploded.

CONTROLLED MINES

Controlled mines are often used to prevent the enemy from passing over a bridge or similar narrow passage. The mines are laid and are connected by wires to a switch at some point at a distance. Stepping on the bridge or on the mined spot will not set off the mine. The mines can be made to explode at a particular moment by use of the switch.

During World War I and other wars in which there was much fighting in trenches, troops called *sappers* would dig long tunnels underground to lay mines under the enemy trenches or near them. These also were usually controlled mines, exploded by a fuse or by an electric current.

mineral

A mineral is a natural substance that is taken out of the earth. Gold, silver, iron, diamond and sulfur are only a few of thousands of minerals. Next to crops, minerals are the things in nature most useful to mankind.

All minerals are taken out of the earth, but not all things in the earth are minerals. Nothing that ever grew—that is, nothing that is animal or vegetable—is a mineral. Bones or tree roots are not minerals even if they are buried in the ground.

HOW TO TELL A MINERAL

People who study minerals are called *mineralogists*. They have made very definite rules as to what a mineral is and how you can tell it from a rock or something buried in the ground.

First, a mineral is a natural substance; this means that it is not made by anyone, but is found in nature.

Second, all of each mineral is composed of the same substance. This means that no matter how many pieces you divide a mineral into, all of them will be made of the same substance.

Third, all pieces of the same kind of mineral are made up of the same chemical elements. For instance, all nuggets of gold that are dug up anywhere in the world are made of the same element— gold. Mineralogists make a distinction between minerals of this kind and rocks. Rocks are mineral matter, but they are composed of pure minerals plus impurities.

Fourth, any piece of the same kind of mineral always is formed in the same way as any other piece of the same mineral.

These four rules make it possible always to tell one mineral from another.

WHERE MINERALS COME FROM

Some minerals are formed when melted rock from deep in the earth pushes up to the surface of the earth, where it cools and hardens. Quartz is a mineral formed this way. Seas drying up leave behind all the minerals that were dissolved in them.

There is a separate article on ROCKS.

mineral water

Mineral water is water that comes from underground springs and has minerals dissolved in it. Ever since ancient times people have drunk it and have bathed in it because they believed it would cure gout, rheumatism, liver trouble, diseases of the blood, and many other kinds of sickness. Some people still use mineral water as a cure, but doctors do not think it will help many diseases. Mineral springs do have their uses. Some mineral springs are hot, and when people with rheumatism bathe in the warm wa-ter they get relief from their pains. Some mineral waters have Epsom salt in them and this makes them very good as laxatives.

SPARKLING WATERS

Certain mineral waters have gas dissolved in them. Like carbonated water, they are full of bubbles. These are the "sparkling waters," that are used in mixing drinks.

Many kinds of mineral water are put in bottles and you can buy them at drugstores.

WHERE THE SPRINGS ARE

Among the most famous American mineral-water springs are those at Saratoga Springs, New York; White Sulphur Springs, West Virginia; Hot Springs, Arkansas; and French Lick, Indiana. Some of the ones in Europe are at Bath, England; Aachen, Germany; and Aix-les-Bains, France.

Some mineral waters have been carefully analyzed by chemists to learn what minerals are in them. Then these waters are made artificially in a factory by putting the same minerals into pure water.

Minerva

Minerva was one of the goddesses who were worshiped by the ancient Romans, thousands of years ago. The ancient Greeks called the same goddess Athena, or Pallas Athena. According to the legend, she was not born in the usual way but sprang full-grown from the forehead of Jupiter (or Zeus), the chief god. She was goddess of heroism among men, and patron of all the womanly arts, such as sewing, weaving, and spinning. In addition, she was the goddess of wisdom and the symbol of thought. The Greeks of Athens built their most beautiful temple to Athena. It was called the Parthenon, and was on the ACROPOLIS, about which there is a separate article.

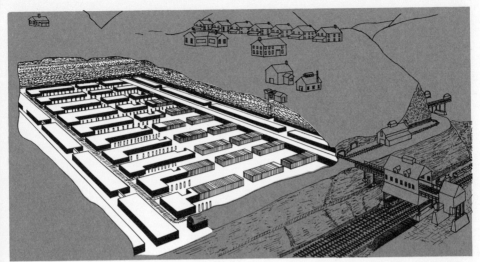

Bureau of Mines

The room-and-pillar mining system is common in the United States. The cut-away diagram shows how pillars of coal are left standing to support the roof. If the vein is especially good, the pillars are mined after all the coal has been taken from a room.

mining

Mining is finding useful minerals, digging them out of the ground, and getting them ready for market. All metals come from minerals that are mined. Many gems, except pearls, are mined. Many other things such as asbestos, marble, granite, gypsum, salt, and sulfur, are mined.

MINERAL DEPOSITS

A quantity of mineral that is underground in one place is called a *deposit.* If the deposit is in thin branching sheets enclosed in rock, it is called a *vein.* When a group of veins are so close together that they and the rock enclosing them can be mined together, the deposit is called a *lode.* Deposits that are hundreds of thousands of feet thick are called *beds.* Thinner beds, especially when they are of coal, are called *seams.* Deposits of sand and gravel that contain valuable minerals are called *placer deposits.* The worthless rock, sand, and earth with which a mineral may be mixed, and which is thrown away, is called *gangue.* This word is pronounced just like "gang."

PROSPECTING

Before you can dig for minerals, you must find them. Searching for the places where minerals are buried is called *prospecting.* In ancient times, chunks of minerals that were found lying on the ground told miners that they might find more if they dug nearby. Miners sometimes found mineral deposits by coming upon breaks in the earth's crust, called *faults,* that exposed the minerals to plain view. In the early days of the United States, especially in the western states, lone prospectors and their burros wandered in the wilderness for months at a time, seeking silver, gold and other minerals.

GEOLOGISTS AND GEOPHYSICISTS

Prospecting is done by two kinds of scientists. They are called *economic geologists* and *geophysicists.* The economic geologists know what kinds of land and what kinds of rock are most likely to contain valuable minerals. This saves a lot of useless searching. Geophysicists locate deeply buried minerals. They fire a charge of explosive on the ground, and then they measure how fast the shock of the explosion travels through the ground. They know that the shocks will move through certain minerals at certain speeds. When they get measurements, they make calculations that tell them at just what place and how far below ground the mineral deposits lie.

SAMPLING AND ASSAYING

After a deposit has been found, mining engineers dig up small pieces of it, called *samples,* from different parts of the deposit. They send these pieces to a chemist who analyzes them in order to tell how much of the deposit is valuable mineral and how much is gangue. The job the chemists do is called *assaying.* When you see the report of the assay, you can tell whether your mineral deposit contains ore.

ORE

Ore is a mineral deposit that contains enough of the valuable part of the min-

eral so that you can sell it at a profit. It is not always easy to say just what is or is not ore. For example, before the first atomic bomb was made, almost the only use for uranium was to make a dark greenish glaze on chinaware. Very little uranium was needed and the price paid for it was low. So, if you had a uranium deposit, it had to be very pure in order to be called an ore deposit. But when the invention of the atomic bomb was followed by so great a need for uranium, deposits containing even very small amounts of uranium along with much gangue became very valuable ores.

If you owned an iron deposit in Minnesota, it need not contain rich samples, because you could easily, quickly, and cheaply send your ore over water to iron foundries and steel mills in Chicago. If you owned an iron deposit in the frozen ground of northern Canada, no matter how rich the deposit, it would not be ore. Even if you could find ways to mine it,

Bituminous Coal Inst.

The largest mines in the world are open-pit mines that take minerals from the surface of the ground, rather than from shafts or pits dug into the ground. This method is both cheaper for the operator and safer for the miner. However, it can make the land useless for farming once the mine is played out.

1. Fields of alfalfa are planted to reclaim land after coal has been removed.

2. Surface mining of bauxite for aluminum has created mountains and valleys.

3. Mines mentioned in the Old Testament are again mined in modern Israel.

Aluminum Assn.

Israeli Inform. Service

without railroads or highways it would cost you so much to ship it that you would lose money.

CLAIMS

Once you have located your mineral deposit and have decided it contains ore, you will probably file a *claim*. In the United States, this means that above the deposit you must measure off a piece of land not more than 1,500 feet long and 500 feet wide, and then you must place at the corners wooden stakes with your name on them. Then you tell the United States government just where your land is, how large it is, and what you want to use it for. This is your claim. You must also advertise your claim in a nearby newspaper. After you have done these things, and if no one has done them before you, you pay the government a small amount of money for each acre of your land. The land now becomes your claim, and is yours as long as you work on it.

When most people think of mining they picture grimy men facing constant danger as they work with their picks in the bowels of the earth. Safety measures and modern machinery have changed the picture in most United States mines.

1. A timbering machine places a "header," or crossbar, in position to support the roof of a mine section. Today, dreaded cave-ins that trap miners seldom occur.

2. An electric drill bores holes for explosives in the "face" of the coal.

3. A mobile drill cuts through soil and rock as a preparation for blasting.

Bituminous Coal Inst.

MINES AND QUARRIES

Once you are ready to dig your ore, you must decide how to do this so that it will cost the least. Suppose you know that you have a seam of coal a thousand feet underground. If you just start to dig a big hole to get at the coal, you will spend so much time and money in removing the earth above it (called the *overburden*) that you will never be able to sell the coal for enough to get back the money you spent digging down to it. Therefore you must dig a narrow hole, or *shaft,* down to the coal. Once you have reached the coal, miners can go down the shaft and start to dig tunnels, or *stopes,* sidewise into the coal. Most mines, not only coal mines, are shaft-and-tunnel mines.

If you have an iron deposit like those of the Mesabi district of northern Minnesota, you could just use steam shovels to dig up the ground and dump it into freight cars, because there is no overburden here—the ore comes right up to

Bureau of Mines

the surface. Mines like this soon become vast holes and are called *open pit mines*.

If you want to mine stone, such as marble or granite, you drill and split the stone in an open pit called a *quarry*.

If you have a placer deposit that contains grains and flakes of gold, you will use powerful hoses, like fire hoses, to wash the gravel into a line of long wooden boxes called sluice-boxes. The gravel will wash away and leave the heavy gold behind in the sluice-boxes. This kind of mining is called *hydraulicking*.

MINING FOR OIL

Getting oil out of the ground is a kind of mining. Of course, you do not dig for it. Instead, you drill a narrow hole down to the pool of oil. If there is natural gas stored above the oil pool, the pressure of the gas will push the oil out in a gusher, and you have to get a pipe over the gushing oil so that you do not lose your oil all over the landscape. If the well is not a gusher, you have to pump the oil out of the well.

ORE CONCENTRATION

People who buy ore from mines pay for it by the ton. So, of course, they want as much useful ore and as little gangue as possible. Getting all the ore together and getting rid of the gangue is called *ore concentration*. This is usually the job of scientists called metallurgists. You can learn about how they do this job by reading the separate article on METALS AND METALLURGY.

MINING LONG AGO

Mining began long before history was first written. It began when first man figured out that he could get more pieces of flint by digging than just by searching on top of the ground. Places have been found where flint was being mined as long ago as 125,000 years. In Egypt and Mesopotamia, 3,500 years ago, men were digging copper and tin out of the ground to make bronze. They were also mining turquoise and other stones they prized for their beauty. When Egyptian miners wanted to get at valuable minerals in rock, they heated the rock with fire and then threw cold water on it to make it crack. They learned how to run water through gravel so as to wash away the lighter material—the stones and sand— and leave the heavy gold.

The Greeks and Romans were very skillful miners. They showed much engineering skill by working large underground mines. They had no machinery; their mines were worked by slaves who were treated very cruelly.

After the end of the Roman Empire, people in Europe forgot how to mine. But mining was one of the first industries to be started up again during the late Middle Ages. In the 16th century in Europe, none of the miners were slaves. They had three shifts a day—early morning, noon, and evening. And they worked only five days a week. They were known by the job they did. They were miners (who used pick, wedge, hammer, and crowbar), shovelers, carriers, and windlass men (who turned a big crank that wound up rope and pulled buckets of minerals up from the mine). They broke rock with fire and water, just as the ancient Egyptians did. They had ventilators to get fresh air into the mines and pumps to remove underground water that seeped into their mine tunnels. Still their job was not easy. Mines were cold, dark, and wet, and like all miners, they had to face the danger of cave-ins.

minister

To minister to someone is to help him or serve him. Many clergymen are called ministers, or ministers of the Gospel, because of their work of caring for the people and trying to save their souls. The period in which Jesus preached to the people and cured or helped them is called the period of his ministry.

Certain government officials are called ministers in many countries. They are the

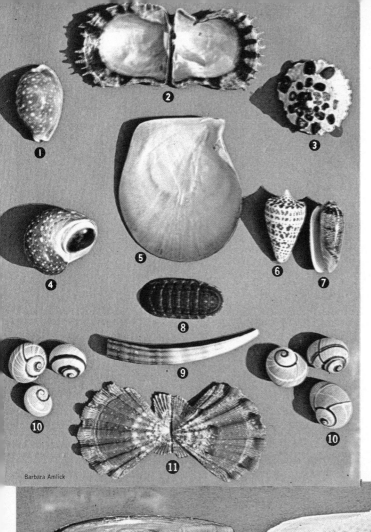

MOLLUSKS

(Left)

1. Cypraea vitellus
2. Pearly oyster
3. Carrier shell
4. Tapestry shell
5. Pearl oyster
6. Chinese alphabet cone
7. Lettered olive
8. West Indian chiton
9. Elephant's tooth
10. Painted snail
11. Lion's paw

(Bottom)

1. Green razor clam
2. Angel wing
3. Little keyhole limpet
4. Dipper shell
5. Surf clam
6. Pecten laqueatus
7. Crown conch
8. False angel wing
9. Stout razor clam
10. West Indian worm shell
11. Spoon shell

Barbara Amlick

Barbara Amlick

MOLLUSKS

(Left)

1. Lettered cone
2. Harp shell
3. Marble cone
4. Star Shell
5. Pyramid shell
6. Pecten laetus
7. Bleeding tooth
8. Turkey wing
9. Top shell

(Bottom)

1. Episcopal miter
2. Flamingo tongue
3. Murex pele
4. Scorpion shell
5. Leafy jewel box
6. Striate cone
7. Conus rubiginosus
8. Pecten nobilis
9. Turret shell
10. Auger shell
11. Cypraea pyrum
12. Pelican's foot

Barbara Amlick

most important assistants to the head of the government and are heads of the chief government departments. In the United States, men holding the same positions are the heads of the government departments and are usually called secretaries, such as the Secretary of State. In other countries the man holding the same position would be called the Minister of Foreign Affairs. Ministers are members of the cabinet, which in most countries is a committee that decides government policies. The head of this committee is called the Prime Minister or Premier, and the other members are called *cabinet ministers* or simply ministers. A member of the cabinet who is not the head of a department of the government is called a *minister without portfolio*.

mink

The mink is a small fur-bearing animal that lives in many parts of Europe, Asia, and the United States. The mink makes its home near marshes and streams, and it is an excellent swimmer. It has a soft, deep brown fur with long black hairs that protect its coat when it is in the water.

The mink is a member of the weasel family. It is only about two feet long, but like most weasels it is a brave fighter and will attack a fox or any other animal that threatens it. The mink has glands in its body that give off a certain odor that keeps some of its enemies away.

The mink usually makes its home in a hollow tree. Sometimes it digs a burrow in the side of a river bank. Here the mink stores fish, muskrats, and other food. The female mink has between four and eight babies in the spring. The mink family stays together during the summer months. Minks are playful and often have wild roughhouse games. When autumn comes the young minks go off to make new homes.

The mink is prized for its beautiful fur and coats made from it are very expensive. People in the United States now raise minks for their fur, but the fur of the mink raised on farms is not considered as fine as that of the wild mink.

For information on how mink is used as a fur, see the article on FUR.

Minneapolis

Minneapolis is the largest city in the state of Minnesota. It is built on both sides of the Mississippi River, near a waterfall called the Falls of St. Anthony. The waterfall supplies the city with power. Minneapolis is so close to the city of St. Paul that the two cities are called the "Twin Cities."

Almost 500,000 people live in Minneapolis. Many of them work in flour and lumber mills. Minneapolis is an important center for both these products. Others make butter. Minneapolis is sometimes called the "Butter Capital of the United States." Some of the people who live in Minneapolis make cloth and jewelry, and work in printing plants. Minneapolis is a railroad center and has a large airport.

Minneapolis is a very attractive city, with wide streets and handsome public buildings. In it are more than twenty lakes and many fine parks. Minnehaha Falls is in one of the parks in Minneapolis. The heroine of Longfellow's poem *Hiawatha* was named Minnehaha. The climate of Minneapolis is clear and cool.

The University of Minnesota is built on a hill that overlooks the Mississippi River. Minneapolis has an art school, a music school, a fine art museum, and the Minneapolis Symphony Orchestra, which is one of the finest in the United States.

The Falls of St. Anthony was discovered by a French explorer, Father Hennepin, almost three hundred years ago. A military fort, Fort Snelling was built there in 1823. (It is now a military training center just outside the city.)

MINNEAPOLIS, MINNESOTA. Population (in 1950) 492,370. County seat, Hennepin County. On Mississippi River. Incorporated 1856.

Minnesota

Minnesota

Minnesota is one of the north central states of the United States, on the Canadian border. Its nickname is the "Gopher State" because of the number of gophers that have been found there. The Minnesota region was the setting of Henry Wadsworth Longfellow's poem *Hiawatha*. Minnesota has rich rolling farm land. Its dairies produce more butter than any other state. It ranks second in the production of milk, eggs, and oats, and leads in the production of wheat flour. The state gets its name from an Indian word meaning "sky-colored water," and Minnesota is sometimes called "the land of the sky-blue water."

Minnesota ranks 12th in size among the states, with 84,068 square miles. In population it ranks 18th, with more than three million people living there. It became a state in 1858, and was the 32nd state admitted to the United States. The capital is St. Paul.

THE PEOPLE OF MINNESOTA

The first settlers in the Minnesota region were English and French, but about a hundred years ago large numbers of people from Norway, Sweden, and Denmark came to Minnesota and settled on the fertile farm land. Later, people from many parts of Europe came to work in the iron mines and factories. Today most Minnesotans are American-born.

More than half the people of Minnesota live in the cities and work in factories that make food products, machinery, and chemicals. Many also work in printing and meat-packing plants. Minneapolis is famous for its flour mills, and Duluth has large iron and steel mills.

Although more people work in cities than on farms, farming is still the largest industry in the state. The farmers living in the fertile Red River Valley in the western part raise large crops of potatoes and wheat. In other sections are big co-operative dairies. Farmers in Minnesota raise the second-largest flax and oat crops

Above: The Minnesota state capitol in St. Paul was built in 1904. *Right:* The beautiful, rugged shores of Lake Superior along which Minnesota's state flower, the moccasin flower (*left*) grows wild.

in the United States, and much corn, hay, barley, and clover.

Many people work in the rich iron mines in the northeastern part of the state. Minnesota leads all other states in the production of iron ore, and furnishes almost three-quarters of the country's supply. A number of people also work in the forests, cutting down the large trees for lumber.

One of the biggest industries of the state is taking care of the many vacationists who come to Minnesota each summer to enjoy the beautiful scenery and outdoor sports. There are many fine resorts along the state's thousands of blue lakes, called "the land of the sky-blue water."

The two largest religious groups in Minnesota are the Roman Catholics and the Lutherans.

WHAT MINNESOTA IS LIKE

Most of Minnesota is a rolling prairie, but in the north there are rocky ridges that are part of an old mountain range. The beautiful pine forests and the valuable iron mines are in this part of the state.

Hunters in Minnesota will find many fur-bearing animals in the woods—mink, muskrat, and red fox, as well as black bear, deer, and moose, and game birds including the duck and pheasant.

Minnesota is very cold in the winter, but the air is very dry. Summers are pleasant, though near Lake Superior it is very hot during the day. The average temperature in summer is 70 degrees and in winter about 10 degrees.

Minnesota has many rivers that have been used for transportation since the time of the Indians. The great Mississippi River starts in this state, as does the Red River of the North. These rivers with their many tributaries also furnish valuable water power. The Minnesota River, the St. Croix, and the Rainy River are among the navigable rivers in the state. Lake Superior carries a large portion of the water traffic. There are railroads and highways that reach almost every part of the state, and airports in all the big cities.

THE GOVERNMENT OF MINNESOTA

Minnesota, like most other states, is governed by a Governor and a Legislature. The Governor is elected for a two-year term. The Legislature is composed of two houses, a Senate and a House of Representatives. Members of the Senate are elected for a four-year term. Members of the House of Representatives are elected for a two-year term. Judges are elected for a six-year term. The capital is St. Paul. There are 87 counties.

Everybody has to go to school between the ages of 8 and 16. There are about 4,650 public schools, including 651 high schools, and 42 colleges, universities and other schools of higher learning. Among the principal colleges and universities are:

University of Minnesota, at Minneapolis. Enrollment, 19,074 in 1953 (13,457 men, 5,617 women).

Hamline University, at St. Paul. Enrollment, 1,153 in 1953 (432 men, 721 women).

St. Olaf College, at Northfield. Enrollment, 1,483 in 1953 (780 men, 703 women).

College of St. Thomas, at St. Paul. Enrollment, 1,316 men in 1953.

CHIEF CITIES OF MINNESOTA

The leading cities of Minnesota, with populations from the 1950 census, are:

Minneapolis, population 521,718, the largest city in the state, and St. Paul, population 311,349, the state capital and second-largest city. These are called the Twin Cities. See the article on MINNEAPOLIS AND ST. PAUL.

Duluth, population 104,511, the third-largest city, iron and steel center, in the northeastern part of the state.

Rochester, population 29,885, the fourth-largest city, seat of the Mayo Clinic, one of

the most famous medical centers in the world, in the southeastern part of the state.

MINNESOTA IN THE PAST

French fur-traders were the first white men to visit the region of Minnesota three hundred years ago. Other French traders came and set up trading posts. The first permanent settlement was made at Grand Portage, in 1731. After the French and Indian Wars, about two hundred years ago, a large region that included Minnesota was given to the British, who set up fur-trading companies. The eastern portion of Minnesota was given to the United States in 1783, and the western part was included in the Louisiana Purchase from France, in 1803.

The Minnesota region grew slowly. For many years it remained a place for fur-trading, and large sections were still held by the Indians. After the Indians finally gave up millions of acres west of the Mississippi River, settlers from the eastern part of the United States moved in. By 1858, Minnesota was large enough to be admitted as a state.

Out of these early pioneering days, grew the famous story of Paul Bunyan and his blue ox, Babe. This mythical figure was made up by boasting lumbermen, who told how there was nothing Paul Bunyan could not do. He was so strong

The skyline of Minneapolis, the largest city in Minnesota, is a welcome sight to vacationers, for the city is the gateway to the lake country of northern Minnesota.

Minn. Div. of Publicity

Duluth is at the west end of Lake Superior and is Minnesota's chief port. It has been an important ore-shipping point since iron was found nearby in the 1890s.

Duluth Chamber of Commerce

U.S. Steel

U.S. Forest Service

Only Iowa has more good farm land than Minnesota, and most of the state's industries process farm products.

1. The open-pit iron mine at Hibbing, largest man-made hole in the world.

2. A pine plantation to replace valuable forests ruined by fire and cutting.

3. Coal being shipped from Duluth.

4. One of the many giant flour mills.

5. Hoeing lima beans. A nearby plant will can the entire crop after picking.

6. Hunting, a favorite Minnesota sport.

Duluth Chamber of Comm.

General Mills

U.S.D.A.

Minn. Div. of Publicity

St. Paul Assn. of Comm.—Riehle Studios

Minn. Div. of Publicity

Minnesota, with more than ten thousand lakes, is a popular vacation land. Tourists also can visit many historic places.

1. The legendary woodsman Paul Bunyan and his blue ox Babe are supposed to have lived in Bemidji. The 18-foot statue is "life size."

2. The tower of Fort Snellin, in St. Paul, protected pioneers against Indian attacks in the early 1800s.

3. Many people believe that Scandinavian explorers visited Minnesota and left a stone carved with runes (early Germanic letters) long before Columbus discovered America.

4. A revolving statue of an Indian god of peace stands in St. Paul's City Hall.

he could uproot trees with his bare hands, and his footprints were said to form Minnesota's many lakes. There is a separate article about Paul BUNYAN and some of the feats he was supposed to have performed.

Minnesota continued to grow into an important industrial and farming state, particularly after the iron mines were opened up about seventy years ago.

PLACES TO SEE IN MINNESOTA

Pipestone National Monument, 115 acres, at Pipestone, in the southwest, on U.S. Route 75. Quarry from which Indians obtained materials for making peace pipes used in ceremonies.

Grand Portage National Historical Site, 660 acres, in the northeast, 5 miles north of Portage, on U.S. Route 61. Nine-mile portage on a principal route of Indians, explorers, missionaries, and fur traders into the Northwest interior.

Itasca State Park, 31,976 acres, 20 miles north of Park Rapids, in the central part of the state, on U.S. Route 71. Beautiful forest area, noted for its wild animals and lakes. Lake Itasca is the source of the Mississippi River.

Misquan Hills, 2,230 feet high, in the northeast, in the Superior National Forest, north of U.S. Route 61. The highest point in Minnesota.

Lake of the Woods, on the Canadian border, in the north. A beautiful boat trip can be taken here in summer; excellent hunting and fishing.

MINNESOTA. Area, 84,068 square miles. Population (1957 estimate) 3,321,000. Capital, St. Paul. Nickname, the Gopher State. Motto, *L'Etoile du Nord* (The Star of the North). Flower, moccasin flower. Bird, American goldfinch. Song, "Hail! Minnesota." Admitted to Union, May 11, 1858. Official abbreviation, Minn.

minnow

Minnows are the largest group of fish that live in the fresh waters of Europe and the United States. People usu-

Minn. Div. of Publicity

Algonquin Indians ruled the region of Minnesota until after the War of 1812.

ally think of minnows as being the tiny brightly colored fish that swim in home aquariums. But there are hundreds of different kinds of minnow; some of them are less than an inch long, while others are several feet long.

There are important differences between minnows and other fish. A minnow does not have teeth in its jaw as most fish do. Instead, a minnow has a few large teeth in its throat. The minnow also has a special network of tiny bones that connects the ear with the air bladder.

Some minnows hollow out places in the sand to lay their eggs. Other minnows do not build any nest at all. Minnows are very useful to man because they eat mosquitoes and other insects. They also eat many water plants. When people want to catch fish they often use minnows as bait, because minnows are one of the most important foods of other fish.

Minoan civilization

The Minoan civilization was a very advanced culture that existed on Crete and other islands of the Aegean Sea and on the shores of Asia Minor almost four thousand years ago. The ruler of the Aegean people was called Minos, a title like that of the pharaoh of the Egyptians. For this reason, their civilization is called

Minoan. No one knew of the existence of the Minoan civilization until 1870, when a German scientist named Heinrich Schliemann began digging first at Troy in Asia Minor and later at other sites. He found whole cities and enough evidence to reconstruct the lives and times of the Minoans. The Minoan people seem to have lived amazingly modern lives. Apparently almost everyone could read. Women had equality with men in everything. Games and sports were popular, and the Minoans were the first to build stone theaters. Their principal deity was a goddess, and there was only one male god. The Minoans had great artists and sculptors. There were factories that turned out pottery, cloth and metal goods. Beginning about 1,600 years before the birth of Jesus, the Minoans and their civilization were wiped out by invasions of Greeks, who were a related people but were still barbarians. By 1200 B.C. the Minoan civilization had vanished.

minor

A minor is a person whom the law does not consider old enough to make decisions for himself. Such a person is said to be in his *minority*. He does not have ful legal rights until he *attains his majority,* or becomes "of age." In the United States, each state decides the age at which a person attains his majority; in some countries, the national government decides. In most states, a person is a minor until he is 21 years old. Until then, the law gives him certain protection. He cannot be forced by law to fulfill an agreement or contract or to pay a debt. In some cases, his parent or guardian is responsible for what he does. Separate laws usually state the age at which a person can get married without his parents' consent. In most states the age is 21 for men and 18 for women.

Minotaur

The Minotaur was a monster told about in Greek mythology, the stories the ancient Greeks told about their gods and goddesses. The Minotaur had the head of a bull and the body of a man. It belonged to Minos, the king of Crete. Each year Minos forced the people of Athens, whom he had conquered, to send him seven young men and seven young girls to be sacrificed to the Minotaur. The Minotaur lived in a labyrinth, a strange and complicated place full of winding paths from which no one ever escaped. At last the Greek hero Theseus entered the labyrinth, killed the Minotaur, and was helped to escape by King Minos' daughter Ariadne. See the article on THESEUS.

minstrel

The minstrel was the musical entertainer of England in the Middle Ages, five to seven hundred years ago. Such entertainers were known in many countries and called by many different names. In Germany they were the minnesingers, in the northern countries they were the skalds, and in Ireland they were the bards.

In the Middle Ages, minstrels traveled from court to court, entertaining the nobility with their songs and stories.

In France, the men who wrote their own verses and songs were usually noblemen and were called troubadours. The men who accompanied them on musical instruments, or sometimes were hired by noblemen to sing and play, were called jongleurs. The French took this idea to England about nine hundred years ago, and the jongleurs provided the principal entertainment of the country. In addition to singing and playing musical instruments, the jongleurs danced, performed acrobatics, and did juggling acts (from which fact we get our word *juggler*). They were mostly people of the poorer classes, and they were considered untrustworthy wanderers.

After several hundred years the jongleurs were taken up by the noblemen of the feudal castles, and they received a new name and a new position. They became minstrels, a name that came from the Latin word for court attendant. They became more highly respected and had an easier life.

It is not known exactly how many of the ballads and songs of the Middle Ages were composed by the minstrels. Many of the most famous ones were, and the minstrels were responsible for keeping alive and passing along others that they did not write themselves. Minstrelsy flourished for a long time, but it began to die out when printing became more and more widespread. When that happened people could read books and no longer had to depend on personal entertainers.

THE MINSTREL SHOW

In the United States in the middle of the 1800s, a kind of musical show called a minstrel show became popular. It did not disappear until early in the 20th century, with the coming of radio and the motion picture.

The minstrel show consisted of three parts. In the first part the company of men called minstrels paraded around the stage in a song-and-dance act, then marched to their places in a semicircle of chairs facing the audience. One was called the interlocutor. He always sat in the center of the semicircle. He would then give the order, "Gentlemen, be seated." After this he would go into an act of funny conversation and jokes with the end men, who sat at the ends of the semicircle. The end men were always in blackface, that is, had their faces blackened with burnt cork to make them resemble Negroes. An end man was usually called Mr. Bones, or Sambo, or Rastus. The end men were the real stars of the show. In the second part, or *olio*, various specialty acts, such as songs and dances, were presented by different members of the company. This was followed by either a burlesque making fun of a popular play or opera, or a singing and dancing number by the whole company.

The first minstrel show was presented in 1843 by a company headed by Daniel D. Emmett, who is best remembered as the writer of the song "Dixie." By the time of the Civil War the popularity of the minstrel show was well established, and companies were appearing in cities all over the country. Some of the famous comedians of the 1900s got their start in minstrel or "blackface" shows, including Al Jolson, Eddie Leonard, George Jessel, Eddie Cantor, and others.

mint

A mint is a place where metal coins are made. The manufacture of coins is known as *minting*.

There are three mints in the United States: in Philadelphia, Pennsylvania, in San Francisco, California, and in Denver, Colorado. They produce all the coins used in the United States. They are controlled by the Bureau of the Mint in Washington, D.C., a part of the Treasury Department.

The Mint of the United States was established by Act of Congress, April 2, 1792. The first mint was set up in Philadelphia and in 1793 produced the first

United States coin, the copper cent or penny. In 1794 the first silver dollars were made, and in 1795 the first gold coins.

There are four separate processes in minting a coin: *assaying* (testing the raw metal for its purity); *refining* (removing the impurities); reducing or changing the metal into ingots or bars; and, finally, *coining*.

After the first three processes, the metal is pressed into thin strips just thick enough for each coin cut from them to have the right weight. The strips are then cut into coin blanks, or *planchets,* which are weighed to see that they are not too light or too heavy. The lightweight planchets are sent back to be remelted, and the overweight ones are filed down to the correct weight.

The blanks of the correct weight are cleaned and sent through a milling machine where they are given a very fine edge. They then are baked, hardened, and cleaned once more. They now are

In former times, each coin was minted by hand. Many coins made then were beautiful enough to be called works of art.

ready to be stamped on both sides by two powerful dies, or metal stampers. These dies press on the coin blanks with a force of as much as 150 tons.

About a hundred coins are produced each minute. When they come from the presses, they are inspected and weighed and then placed in canvas bags to be stored in the vaults of the mint or shipped to the treasury of the Federal Reserve System. From these points, the coins are issued to banks and placed in circulation.

mint

Mint is a plant that grows in almost every part of the world where the climate is not too hot or too cold. Mint is a perennial plant, which means that it grows from the same roots every year. The mint is a hardy plant and can grow in almost any climate, but it grows best in a damp soil. There are many different kinds of mint.

The most useful mints are peppermint and spearmint. They grow to be two or three feet high and have purple flowers. The stems of the plants are square and the leaves are small. The leaves of the mint contain a sweet-smelling oil that has a pleasant flavor. The oil from the mint plant is used in many ways. Ice cream, chewing gum, tobacco, and drinks are flavored with mint. Mint is used in tea and as a seasoning for meat and cake. People make mint jelly and a candy that is flavored with mint. Mint is also used in many medicines and toothpastes, and in soap and perfume.

Minuit, Peter

Peter Minuit was the first governor of the Dutch colony of New Netherland, an area in the New World around the mouth of the Hudson River. In 1626 Minuit bought Manhattan Island from the Manna-hatan Indians for about $24 worth of trinkets, hatchets, and knives. The village founded on this island as a trading post was first called New Amsterdam. It is now New York, the largest city in the world. Peter Minuit was born in 1580 and died at sea while setting out for a new colony in the West Indies in 1638.

minuteman

Minuteman was a name given to many American colonists who were soldiers in the Revolutionary War. These colonists were called minutemen because they declared they were ready to fight for their independence from Great Britain at a minute's notice. Minutemen was a name used particularly to describe the farmers in Massachusetts who fought against the British at the Battles of Lexington and Concord, the first battles of the Revolutionary War. There is a famous statue of a minuteman in the town square at Lexington, Massachusetts.

Mirabeau

Gabriel, Count of Mirabeau, was a French statesman who was one of the leaders in the French  Revolution, when the people threw out their king and noblemen and France became a republic. Mirabeau helped the revolutionists though he was a count, one of the noblemen against whom the people were fighting.

Mirabeau was born in 1749 in Paris, and was an unusually ugly child. One foot was twisted, he was tongue-tied, and smallpox disfigured him with scars. His father was so ashamed of him that he was sent to a school far from home, under a false name. He was a brilliant student, and became extremely popular in spite of his appearance. He spent several years in prison for debt because his rich father refused to help him.

Mirabeau became interested in politics, and when the French Revolution started in 1789 he was one of its eloquent spokesmen. He had mastered his tongue-tied condition and was a superb orator. He fought for the rights of the people,

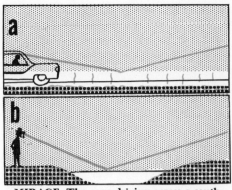

MIRAGE. The man driving across a southwestern desert (*a*) "sees" a pool of water. It is a mirage. The light passing through the cool air has bounced off the warm air near the ground without ever really touching the ground, and looks as if it is reflected by a pool of water. The light reflected in a real pool of water (*b*) looks very much the same.

but he insisted that the royal family also had the right to just treatment. Mirabeau died, after a long illness, in 1791.

miracle

A miracle is something that happens by a special act of deity (God), when it could not possibly happen by the usual processes of nature. The Bible tells of many miracles, including a number of miracles performed by Jesus. The first miracle of Jesus was at a marriage at Cana, a town in Palestine, when he turned water into wine; later he healed the lame and blind and made dead persons live again. Miracles have occasionally been reported since the time when Jesus was on earth.

miracle play, an old form of drama: see MYSTERY PLAY.

mirage

A mirage is a trick that light plays on people's eyes, making them see images of things that are not really there.

Most mirages are made by the peculiar way in which light behaves in hot, dry places such as deserts, or in cold, damp places such as the ocean. In a desert, the air close to the sand is much hotter than the air above it. Sunlight is reflected off the layer of warm air, as shown in the picture on the preceding page.

This reflected light fools people, especially those who are very thirsty, into thinking that the light is coming from water. You may have seen these "pools of water" on a highway when you have been riding in a car on a summer day. In many cases, trees and other objects that are several miles away are reflected in these "pools" in the same way they would be reflected by real water.

On the ocean, mirages of ships are formed in the sky by light passing from a ship through the cold air above the water into the warmer air higher up. The mirage often looks like an upside-down ship sailing in the sky. The bending of light in the air above the ocean also explains why ships often seem to be closer than they really are. This mirage is known as *looming*.

A remarkable mirage known as the *fata morgana* makes it appear that ships, houses, or men are floating in the sky above the water. There usually are two mirages, one right-side up, the other upside down. These mirages were first seen in the Straits of Messina, a body of water separating Italy from Sicily. They gave rise to many legends of ghosts and spirits that were believed to haunt the straits.

Many mirages have been photographed and examined by scientists.

mirror

A mirror is a highly polished surface off which rays of light are bounced or reflected in such a way as to give a picture or image of objects in front of it.

Pools of water were the first mirrors. Later, polished metals were used, and then glass, blackened on one side and coated with silver or tin and mercury.

There are three kinds of mirror: plane (flat); concave (curved inward); and convex (curved outward). Convex and concave mirrors often are called *spherical* mirrors.

Libby-Owens-Ford Glass Co.

The salesman sees only his reflection in the one-way glass. But the housewife can see his face from inside the house (inset). If she does not open the door, he will never know he has been seen.

PLANE MIRRORS

A plane mirror is the one commonly used in the home as a wall mirror or a looking-glass. When you stand in front of such a mirror, your image appears to be coming from behind the mirror. Such

The clown lost his head by hiding it behind two mirrors (M) that reflect the side walls but look like pure air.

an image is called a *virtual* image. The image also appears to be reversed. The right side of your body will appear on the left side of the image. If you put your finger over your right eye, it will appear over the left eye in your image.

A plane mirror will regularly reflect light. That is, a beam of light striking the mirror will be reflected as a beam of light, instead of being broken up or diffused into separate light rays. Light falling straight on the mirror will be reflected straight back. Light falling on the mirror at an angle, called an *angle of incidence*, will be reflected in another direction at the same angle, called an *angle of reflection*.

Plane mirrors often are used in periscopes, devices used in submerged submarines to see what is happening on the surface of the water. A periscope has two mirrors, one at the top and one at the bottom. Light strikes the top mirror, which is set in a tube at an angle, and is reflected down to the bottom mirror, set in the tube at the same angle. A person looking into the periscope through a slit near the bottom can see what is happening several feet above and in front of him.

Plane mirrors also are used in carnivals to create what are called *optical illusions,* or tricks of the eyes. One of the most familiar is the "headless" man or woman.

This optical illusion is created by mirrors placed in front of the head of a man or woman sitting in a chair. The mirrors are placed at an angle to each other and so arranged that they reflect the images of the walls on both sides of them. A person looking at the mirrors does not see them but only what he thinks is a

As convex mirror (M) is bent back on its axis (A), it reflects light from more directions than a plane mirror does, and gives a wider view.

wall behind the shoulders of a headless man or woman.

The one-way glass is a type of mirror that partly reflects and partly lets through light. A person looking at the polished side of the glass can see only his own reflection. A person on the other side can see through the glass without being observed.

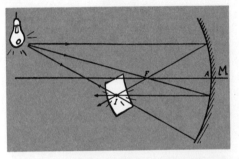

The concave mirror (M) is bent forward on its axis (A). Light from the bulb is brought to a focus at the focal point (F) and is reflected on the paper in the form of a spot of light, or image (I).

SPHERICAL MIRRORS

Spherical mirrors have many important uses, one of the most important being to spread out a beam of light or bring it to a smaller point or focus. A concave mirror brings light to a focus

The spherical mirror (S) brings light to an approximate focus (F), but a parabolic mirror or reflector brings the light to an exact focus (F) and thus gives a more concentrated beam of light.

The headless man is easy to create. All it takes is an arrangement of mirrors so that they reflect opposite walls.

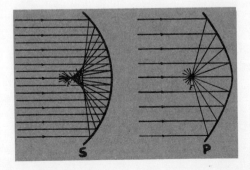

Metropolitan Museum of Art

In ancient times mirrors were made of highly polished metal. The elaborately decorated Etruscan mirror (made of bronze) is between 2,300 and 2,400 years old.

and the spot can be thrown onto a screen. Such a spot is called a *real* image. Concave mirrors also can make virtual images that are larger than those made on a plane mirror. For this reason, a dentist uses a small concave mirror on a long handle placing it behind your teeth to make them appear larger so that he can examine them more closely.

Almost all large telescopes use large concave mirrors to gather the light from near stars so that distant stars can be seen more clearly or photographed.

The largest concave mirror of this kind is in the Mount Wilson Observatory in Palomar, California. It is 200 inches in diameter.

A special kind of concave mirror, made of polished metal and called a *parabolic reflector,* is used in automobile headlights. The mirror is placed behind the light and is shaped in such a way that the light rays come out as a straight beam. Parabolic reflectors are used also in search lights and in photoflash attachments to a camera.

Convex mirrors are used often as rearview mirrors on trucks and automobiles. The image is smaller in a convex than in a plane mirror, making it possible to see more of what is behind you.

Both convex and concave mirrors are used in amusement parks. A person looking into one of them sees himself all out of shape. The reason for this is that light is reflected differently from a curved surface than from a plane surface.

misdemeanor

A misdemeanor is an act that breaks the law but is not considered important enough to call for severe punishment. Examples are parking overtime, littering the streets with trash, or creating a nuisance by making loud noises. A person who commits a misdemeanor usually has to pay a fine but is seldom sent to jail. A more serious crime is called a FELONY, about which there is a separate article.

missal

The missal is a prayer book used by priests in the Roman Catholic Church when they say Mass, and by people who are present at Mass. (There is a separate article about the MASS). All missals are taken from the Roman missal, which is in the Latin language. The missal used by the priest is in Latin, but the missal used by the people usually has a translation of the Mass into the language of their country. It has all the prayers of the Mass and directions telling how the Mass should be said. Some missals give the different Masses for every day of the year. Others are called "Sunday missals" and they have only the Masses for Sundays and holy days when all Catholics have to go to Mass.

missions and missionaries

A missionary is a man who leaves his own home to preach his religion in distant places. He goes where his religion is not yet known or established, and afterwards stays there to help it grow among the people. Most missionaries are Christians, though other religions such as Islam (the religion of Mohammed) have also had missions.

The first Christian missionaries were the Apostles whom Jesus told to go and preach to all nations. The New Testament of the Bible tells about their missionary work in the "Acts of the Apostles" and the Epistles, especially the Epistles of St. Paul. St. PAUL, about whom you may read in a separate article, is often called the greatest of the missionaries. His journeys took him as far away from Palestine as Greece and Rome, where he brought many people into the Christian faith. The missionary work of the early Christians was quite successful. About four hundred years after the birth of Jesus, the Christian faith was spread throughout the known world.

During the Middle Ages, which began about five hundred years after Christ's birth, missionaries moved north to central Europe and northwest to the British Isles. The great missionaries of this period included St. Patrick, who brought the Christian faith to Ireland, St. Augustine of Canterbury, who was an important founder of Christianity in England, and St. Boniface, who is often called the Apostle of Germany.

ROMAN CATHOLIC MISSIONS

During the second part of the Middle Ages, when most of Europe was Christian, missionary activities were not widespread. Then, when the great explorers began to discover new lands, missionaries again began to be numerous. There were several earlier Roman Catholic missionary *orders*. An order is a group of monks, priests, or nuns, who follow certain special rules and live very simply, away from other people. Among the orders were the Dominicans, the Benedictines, the Franciscans, and the Carmelites.

The greatest of the Roman Catholic missionary orders during the period of discovery and settlement was the Jesuits. This order was started in 1534, soon after the voyages of Columbus. They traveled to the New World and to the Far East, the Orient. St. Francis Xavier, the best known of the Jesuit missionaries, preached in Indian and Japan. St. Isaac Jogues was killed by Indians at Auriesville, New York. Many early missionaries explored the rivers of America and were the first to learn Indian languages and to write books about them. There is a Roman Catholic organization called the Society for the Propagation of the Faith. It is in charge of the work of Catholic missionaries all over the world.

PROTESTANT MISSIONARIES

At first, Protestant churches did not have many missionaries. Later, when Protestantism had grown, Protestant missions were started all over the world. The first Protestant missionaries came to the New World in the 16th century, but they could not survive. There were several later missions, both in America and in other newly discovered places.

The great period of Protestant missionary work resulted from the deep faith of the founder of Methodism, John WESLEY, and his good friend Charles WHITEFIELD. (There are separate articles about both men). Societies were formed to send missionaries to India, Africa, and the Orient. During the 19th century every Protestant country had missionary societies. The people gave generously to pay expenses. Missions were founded all over the world. The missionaries helped to educate people and cure them when they were sick.

This work has been continued in the present day. During World War II, in spite of hardships, missionaries helped those who lost their homes or families. Hospitals, orphanages, and churches destroyed in the war were rebuilt.

There are separate articles on two famous Protestant missionaries, David LIVINGSTONE and Albert SCHWEITZER.

Mississippi

Mississippi

Mississippi is a state in the "deep south" of the United States. Its nickname is the "Magnolia State" because of the many beautiful magnolia trees that grow there. Mississippi is one of the leading cotton states and visitors can see large plantations and fine mansions that remind one of the Old South in the days before the Civil War. Mississippi is named for the Mississippi River, which runs along the state's western boundary.

Mississippi ranks 32nd in size among the states, with 47,716 square miles. In population it ranks 28th, with more than two million people living there. It became a state in 1817, and was the 20th state admitted to the United States. The capital is Jackson.

THE PEOPLE OF MISSISSIPPI

The earliest settlers in the Mississippi region were French and Spanish explorers. Later many more English and Scotch-Irish came and started large farms. These families have lived so long in the state that almost all the people of Mississippi are American-born.

Visitors to Mississippi will see almost as many Negroes as white people. The Negroes were brought as slaves from Africa about 150 years ago, to work on the large cotton plantations. Now there

are more than a million Negroes living in the state, and they make up about half the population. Most of the Negroes work on the farms or in factories.

Most of the people of Mississippi are farmers. Cotton is still their most important crop, as it was before the Civil War, but farmers have learned also to grow many other crops, such as peanuts, sugar cane, rice, sweet potatoes, and corn. They also raise dairy cattle and large quantities of fruits and vegetables. In the past fifty years farmers have raised tung trees. The nuts from these trees produce an oil that is used in paints and varnishes. More than half the tung trees in the United States are grown in Mississippi.

Many people also work in the large pine forests in the southern part of the state. They also cut down other valuable timber that is used for lumber products.

A number of people live in the cities and work in factories, making cottonseed oil, textiles, and paints. Some work in natural gas fields and in the recently discovered oil fields in the southern part of the state.

For a long time, the people of Mississippi were very backward, and there were many who could neither read nor write, particularly among the Negroes. This situation has gradually improved.

The churches are very important in the social life of people in Mississippi. Nearly everyone goes to Sunday School and to church. In the smaller towns especially, people have their clubs and give parties and picnics through their churches. The largest religious group in the state is the Baptists. There are also many Methodists.

WHAT MISSISSIPPI IS LIKE

Mississippi is a state of rolling prairies and hills. The most fertile section is the Mississippi Delta in the western part, between the Mississippi River and the Yazoo River. It is one of the greatest cotton-producing areas in the world. This part of the state is very low, and the Mississippi River would flood it constantly if the people had not built a series of strong walls called *levees*. Even so, sometimes there are serious floods that smash the levees and cause great loss of life and property.

In the central part of the state are the North Central Hills, where the farmers grow peanuts and fruit. This region was once more fertile than it is now. It was ruined when the people cut down the

Biloxi Chamber of Commerce

Father Abram Ryan, the Catholic priest who was "poet of the Confederacy" during the Civil War, lived in Mississippi. A palm grew through the steps of his home, built in typical southern style.

forests, letting the rich soil be washed away. This washing-away is called *erosion*. New forests have been planted to remedy this situation.

In the extreme northeast are the Tennessee Hills, the highest point in the state. Farther south is a fertile, grassy section that is excellent for cattle-raising. In the southern part of the state is the Piney Wood region, with fine forests that produce large quantities of lumber, turpentine, and tar.

Along the Gulf of Mexico, the southern boundary, are the sandy Coastal Meadows. This section has inlets and islands that are ideal for fishing. Many vacation resorts have been built along the coast, which includes the longest man-made beach in the world—26 miles of gleaming white sand.

As in other southern states, there are many small fur-bearing animals. Hunters will find raccoon, squirrel, and opossum.

When Jefferson Davis, President of the Confederacy, lived in Biloxi, he was vestryman of the Episcopal Church of the Redeemer, which now has memorials to him.

The magnolia blossom, Mississippi state flower.

The majestic state capitol building in Jackson was built in 1903 in American classic style.

Jackson Chamber of Commerce

The climate of Mississippi is subtropical, with long, hot summers and short, mild winters. Flowers bloom almost all year long in the southern part of the state, though in the northern part it is somewhat colder, and there is occasional snow. The summers are hot and damp, but they are made somewhat more pleasant by the breezes from the Gulf of Mexico. The average temperature in summer is about 81 degrees, and in winter about 47 degrees.

The Mississippi River has always been the most important means of transportation. The important Mississippi River ports are Natchez and Vicksburg. Railroads and highways now reach to almost all parts of the state. There are airports in the important cities.

THE GOVERNMENT OF MISSISSIPPI

Mississippi, like all of the other states,

is governed by a Governor and a Legislature. The Governor is elected for a four-year term. The Legislature is composed of two houses, a Senate and a House of Representatives. The members of both houses are elected for a four-year term. Judges are elected for an eight-year term. The capital is Jackson. There are 82 counties.

Everybody has to go to school between the ages of 7 and 16. There are about 972 public schools, including 496 high schools, and 28 colleges, universities and other schools of higher learning. Among the principal colleges and universities are:

University of Mississippi, at University. Enrollment, 2,259 in 1953 (1,684 men, 575 women).

Mississippi State College, at State College. Enrollment, 2,775 in 1953 (2,480 men, 295 women).

Mississippi Southern College, at Hattiesburg. Enrollment, 3,100 in 1953 (1,990 men, 1,110 women).

Jackson College (for Negroes), at Jackson. Enrollment, 792 in 1953 (282 men, 510 women).

CHIEF CITIES OF MISSISSIPPI

The leading cities of Mississippi, with populations from the 1950 census, are:

Jackson, population 98,271, the state capital and largest city in the state. There is a separate article about JACKSON.

Meridian, population 41,893, the second-largest city, railroad center, in the eastern part of the state.

Biloxi, population 37,425, the third-largest city, fishing resort, on the southern coast of the state.

Greenville, population 29,936, the fourth-largest city, cotton center, in the western part of the state.

Vicksburg, population 27,948, the fifth-largest city. There is a separate article on VICKSBURG.

MISSISSIPPI IN THE PAST

More than four hundred years ago, Hernando De Soto, the Spanish explorer, was the first white man to visit the region of Mississippi. He and his men were searching for gold, and did not settle in the region. More than one hundred years later the French explorer La Salle claimed the entire Mississippi Valley as part of France. The first permanent settlement was made at Old Biloxi by the French in 1699.

The French settlers had trouble with the Indians, and there were several fierce wars with them. The French were not very successful at starting new settlements, and about two hundred years ago part of the region was given to the British. A section of this was later conquered by Spain. After the Revolutionary War, all of it finally became part of the United States. In 1798 the Mississippi Territory was formed. This territory then included part of Alabama. In 1817 Mississippi became a state and the rest of the territory became the Alabama Territory.

The population grew and Mississippi soon became one of the most important cotton-growing states. There were large plantations, whose rich owners lived in large mansions and owned hundreds of slaves, who worked in the fields. When Abraham Lincoln became President in 1860, and it appeared that the slaves would be set free, Mississippi was one of the states to secede from the Union.

The most important battle of the Civil War fought on Mississippi soil was the Battle of Vicksburg in 1863. It was one of the turning points of the war for the Union Army.

When the Civil War was over, Mississippi was very poor and in a state of disorder. "Carpetbaggers," outsiders owning nothing but carpetbags, controlled the state government and robbed it of millions. The people finally got back control of the state and began to rebuild and prosper, but only in the last fifty years has manufacturing become important in Mississippi. Since then, factories have sprung up rapidly, helped by the building of dams and electric-power lines. In World War II, many war plants were built in Mississippi.

PLACES TO SEE IN MISSISSIPPI

Ackia Battlefield National Monument, 49 acres, at Tupelo, in the northeast, on U.S. Route 78. Site of a Chickasaw Indian village, where the Chickasaws, aided by British troops, repulsed an attack of French and their Choctaw allies, in 1736.

Brices Cross Roads National Battlefield Site, 1 acre, at Baldwin, in the northeast, on U.S. Route 45. Scene of a battle in 1864, in which Confederate cavalry was employed with extraordinary skill.

Biloxi Chamber of Commerce

The Mississippi coast along the Gulf of Mexico has many popular resorts. Both beaches and pools are kept open for visitors who go there the year round.

Biloxi Chamber of Commerce

Jackson Chamber of Commerce

Like most southerners, Mississippians are especially proud of their history and their famous men.

1. Flags representing the eight governments that have ruled in the state. The lighthouse is on the Gulf.

2. Jackson's historic City Hall.

3. "Beauvoir," the home of Jefferson Davis, President of the Confederacy.

4. A memorial at Vicksburg, where the Union won an important victory.

5. A colonial church in Natchez.

Nat'l Park Service Photos

Mississippi's chief crops are cotton and corn. But half the land is covered with valuable forests.

1. Logs for a box factory at Natchez.

2. The Back Bay of Biloxi. The city is a shipping and fishing port.

3. Boat-building, an important industry along the Gulf Coast.

4. Mechanical cotton pickers. Each machine picks about six acres a day.

5. But many plantations still use field hands to pick cotton.

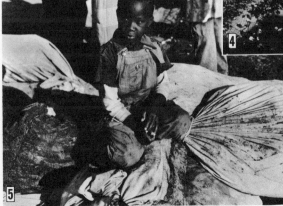

Vicksburg National Military Park, 1,649 acres, at Vicksburg, in the west, on U.S. Route 61. Remarkably preserved fortifications of the 47-day siege of Vicksburg in 1863, during the Civil War.

Delta Plantation, 38,000 acres, five miles east of Scott, in the west, on State Highway 1. The largest cotton plantation in the world.

Natchez, in the southwest, on U.S. Route 61. Has many beautiful, old houses built before the Civil War.

MISSISSIPPI. Area, 47,716 square miles. Population (1957 estimate) 2,185,000. Capital, Jackson. Nickname, the Magnolia State. Motto, *Virtute et Armis* (By Valor and Arms). Flower, magnolia. Bird, mockingbird. Song, "Mississippi." Admitted to Union, December 10, 1817. Official abbreviation, Miss.

Mississippi River

The Mississippi is the most important river in the United States. It is 2,350 miles long. If the Missouri River, which flows into the Mississippi, is considered part of the Mississippi, the combined river would be 3,892 miles long. That would make it the second-longest river in the world. The Nile River in Egypt is thought to be the longest.

The Mississippi flows through the Great Plains of the United States, one of the most fertile farming regions in the world. The Mississippi and its many tributaries (the rivers that flow into it) drain more than one million square miles between the Appalachian Mountains and the Rocky Mountains.

ITS COURSE

The Mississippi rises near Lake Itaska, in Minnesota, as a stream about ten feet wide and less than two feet deep. As it flows south through Minnesota, it is joined by the Minnesota River and becomes deep enough for boats to travel on. The Mississippi continues to widen and deepen as it flows south between high hills. It forms part of the boundary between Minnesota and Wisconsin, and the boundary between Iowa and Illinois. Along this part of the river there are swift rapids. Many dams and locks have been built to let ships through, and the rapids supply useful water power. At Keokuk, Iowa, there is one of the largest power dams in the world and a hydroelectric plant.

Just above St. Louis, Missouri, the Mississippi is joined by the great Missouri River, known as "Old Muddy." For some distance, a person can distinctly see the two rivers as they flow along together. The Mississippi is very clear and the Missouri is a reddish, muddy color. Then the Mississippi becomes muddy.

At Cairo, Illinois, the Mississippi is joined by the Ohio River. Here the river reaches its greatest width, and is almost a mile wide. It winds on past rich and fertile farm land, and forms the boundaries between Arkansas on the west and Tennessee and Mississippi on the east. It then flows into Louisiana and past the city of New Orleans.

Below Baton Rouge is the large Mississippi delta. The river splits into several branches. Between them are deposits of soil brought down by the river over the course of centuries. This lower part of the river winds through swamps and bayous, and finally empties into the Gulf of Mexico. The Mississippi carries more than 600,000 cubic feet of water into the Gulf of Mexico every second.

LEVEES AND FLOOD CONTROL

The Mississippi deposits a great deal of sand, mud and gravel along its banks. This has built up walls, or natural levees, and the river flows between them. In some places the level of the river is higher than the land. These regions are very fertile, but heavy spring rains can make them dangerous. The rushing waters have often burst their banks, flooding cities and farms.

To prevent these terrible floods, men have built high banks of earth and stone, held together with asphalt. These are called levees. The levees usually hold back the waters during flood time, but sometimes the river rises above the levees, and sometimes it breaks through them. The United States government has helped by building canals and channels into which some of the water can go.

NAVIGATION

Most of the year the Mississippi is a peaceful river. Important industrial cities are situated along its banks, and dams on the river provide electric power for many factories. Some of the big cities are: St. Paul and Minneapolis, Minnesota; Dubuque and Davenport, Iowa; St. Louis, Missouri; Memphis, Tennessee; Vicksburg and Natchez, Mississippi; and Baton Rouge and New Orleans, Louisiana.

Tugboats go up and down the river every day, carrying important products. These tugboats can push a long line of barges loaded with cargo. The Mississippi is part of the great waterway system in the United States. It is connected with the Great Lakes in the north by the Illinois Waterway, and ships can sail from Chicago all the way down the Mississippi to New Orleans. The Intracoastal Waterway crosses the Mississippi delta near New Orleans, connecting the river with the Atlantic Ocean.

THE MISSISSIPPI IN THE PAST

Mississippi is an Indian name meaning "Big River." The river is often called the "Father of Waters." More than four hundred years ago, the Spanish explorer Hernando de Soto first discovered the Mississippi near where Memphis, Tennessee, now stands. Later it was partly explored by Marquette and Joliet. Exploring the entire river, from its mouth to its source, was not completed until three hundred years after de Soto by Robert La Salle.

The most important and colorful period of the Mississippi began after 1803, when the United States bought

Massie—Mo. Resources Division

A modern Tom Sawyer and Huck Finn watch a departing stern-wheeler at Hannibal, Missouri, boyhood home of Mark Twain. The great Mississippi River was one of the novelist's favorite themes.

much of the Mississippi Valley in the Louisiana Purchase. Pioneers paddled down the river on rafts and flatboats to settle in the fertile region. A few years later, the first steamboat sailed down to New Orleans, and the Mississippi became one of the most important means of transportation in the country. Large plantations grew up in the south, and huge bales of cotton were carried down the river to the growing port of New Orleans.

Life on the Mississippi a hundred years ago was full of excitement, with its big paddle-wheel steamboats going back and forth. One of the most colorful things to see was the gaily decorated showboats, which would stop at towns along the river and put on plays. Mark Twain wrote several famous books about the river as it was then.

After railroads were built in the West, the Mississippi became less important, but it has continued to be the most important waterway in the United States.

Mark Twain's home in Hannibal, Missouri, is now a museum. It contains objects associated with his work.

Missouri

Missouri is a state in the great midwestern plain of the United States. Its nickname is the "Show Me State" because of an old belief that the people of Missouri have to be shown something before they believe it. When a person says "I'm from Missouri," he means he is doubtful of what has been said, and wants it proven to him. Missouri is famous for its folk tales, told among the people in the Ozark Mountains, and for the river stories that grew up along the Mississippi River, on the state's eastern boundary. Missouri gets its name from an Indian tribe that lived in the same region.

Missouri ranks 19th in size among the

states, with 69,674 square miles. In population it ranks 12th, with more than four million people living there. It became a state in 1821, and was the 24th state to be admitted to the United States. The capital is Jefferson City.

THE PEOPLE OF MISSOURI

Americans from the eastern part of the United States were the first large group to settle in Missouri. Most of them became farmers. Later, people from Germany, Ireland, England, and many other European countries came and worked on the farms and in the growing factories. Most of these families have lived so long in the state that almost all Missourians are American-born.

A large group of people from Tennessee and Kentucky settled in the Ozark Mountains, in the southern part of Missouri. Their ancestors were English and Scottish. They still keep many of their old customs, and they even talk differently from the people in the rest of Missouri. These mountain people live in cabins and love to hunt and to tell stories. They are very suspicious of strangers, but once they accept a new person they are very hospitable.

More than half the people of Missouri live in the big cities and work in large factories. St. Louis is one of the largest manufacturers of shoes in the country. It is also one of the big meat-packing centers. In fact, St. Louis has so many important manufactures that it ranks seventh among the manufacturing cities in the United States. Many people work in the flour and meat-packing plants in Kansas City, which is the second-largest meat-packing center in the country (next to Chicago). The people of Missouri also make more corncob pipes than any other group in the world.

The farmers raise large crops of corn, wheat, oats, and barley. Others raise cattle and produce dairy products. The state is famous for the mules bred there.

There are rich lead mines in the southeastern and southwestern parts of the state. They produce more lead than any other state. Valuable timber is cut in the hardwood forests in the Ozarks.

The people of Missouri belong to many different churches. The largest groups are the Roman Catholic, Baptist, and Methodist. There are more than 200,000 Negroes in the state.

WHAT MISSOURI IS LIKE

The northern and southern parts of Missouri look very different. In the northern half of the state is a large rolling prairie, with many rivers. Here farmers raise corn, fruits and vegetables, and cattle.

In the southern half of Missouri are the rugged and beautiful Ozark Mountains, a favorite vacation area. Thousands come every year to enjoy the fine scenery and to fish in the lakes and streams. Between the high hills are deep valleys where there are flourishing apple orchards and vineyards. The important lead, coal and iron mines are in this part of the state. Hunters will find rabbits, foxes, opossums and other small fur-bearing animals in the woods.

The southeastern corner of Missouri, on the Mississippi River, is one of the most fertile regions. The land is very low and was once covered with thick forests. Now it is a rich farming and dairy section.

The climate of Missouri is quite varied. In the northern part of the state it is fairly cold, but the southeast has a warm climate like that of the "deep South." The Ozarks have mild summers and winters. The average temperature in Missouri in the summer is about 78 degrees; in winter it is about 31 degrees.

Massie—Mo. Res. Div. Photos

The Missouri state capitol (*left*) in Jefferson City is the seat of state government. It also contains many beautiful works of art. Though the hawthorn is the state flower, most people know the famous Missouri mule (*right*) better. But this does not mean that a person is stubborn as a mule when he says, "I'm from Missouri." Missourians are no more stubborn than people elsewhere. They simply take pride in not believing anything until it has been proven to their satisfaction.

St. Louis Chamber of Commerce

St. Louis, the largest city in Missouri, is an important Mississippi River port and rail center.

University of Missouri

The Ionic columns are a feature of the lovely, tree-lined campus of the University of Missouri.

Kansas City Chamber of Commerce

The University of Kansas City, founded in 1932, is another of Missouri's many fine schools.

Massie—Mo. Resources Div.

Above: Missouri was one of the first states to build industry west of the Mississippi. The iron forge that still stands near St. James was operated during the Civil War.

Below: Many of the people who live in the Ozarks have little contact with the outside world. They still practice the handcrafts that were a necessity in pioneer days.

Massie—Mo. Resources Div.

Above: From Graniteville in southwest Missouri comes a lovely pink-colored granite that is often used in statues. The quarry itself is quite beautiful.

No place in the world manufactures as many corncob pipes as Missouri does. In fact, among pipe fanciers the inexpensive corncob is known as a "Missouri meerschaum."

Limestone is Missouri's chief quarry product, but top-quality marble is also found there.

Missouri is not noted as a truck-garden state, but many vegetables and fruits are grown there.

The first lumber mills in the Ozarks were water-powered. Modern mills are a bit more sturdy.

Am. Hereford Assn.

Missouri's $300,000,000-a-year cattle business is centered in the southeast and south central regions of the state.

The people of Missouri use their many rivers for transportation. The Mississippi and Missouri rivers are most important. Railroads and highways reach almost all parts of the state, and there are airports in the important cities.

THE GOVERNMENT OF MISSOURI

Missouri, like most other states, is governed by a Governor and a Legislature. The Governor is elected for a four-year term. The Legislature is called the General Assembly, and is composed of two houses, a Senate and a House of Representatives. The members of the Senate are elected for a four-year term. Members of the House of Representatives are elected for a two-year term. Judges are elected for a ten-year term. The capital is Jefferson City. There are 114 counties.

Everyone has to go to school between the ages of 7 and 16. There are about 4,200 public schools, including 665 high schools, and 55 colleges and universities. Among the principal colleges and universities are:

University of Missouri, at Columbia. Enrollment, 8,340 in 1953 (6,516 men, 1,824 women).

University of Kansas City, at Kansas City. Enrollment, 2,534 in 1953 (1,805 men, 729 women).

St. Louis University, at St. Louis. Enrollment, 8,386 in 1953 (5,078 men, 3,308 women).

Washington University, at St. Louis. Enrollment, 10,534 in 1953 (7,452 men, 3,082 women).

CHIEF CITIES OF MISSOURI

The leading cities of Missouri, with populations from the 1950 census, are:

St. Louis, population 856,796, the largest city in the state. There is a separate article about ST. LOUIS.

Jefferson City, population 25,099, the state capital and ninth-largest city. There is a separate article about JEFFERSON CITY.

Kansas City, population 456,622, the second-largest city. There is a separate article about KANSAS CITY.

St. Joseph, population 78,588, the third-largest city, railroad and industrial center, in the northwestern part of the state.

MISSOURI IN THE PAST

The French explorer La Salle claimed the entire Mississippi River Valley for France almost three hundred years ago. His claim included the region of Missouri. The first permanent settlement in

Missouri leads all the states in mining lead. The industry is centered in the southeastern and southwestern regions.

Missouri was not made until 1735, at Ste. Genevieve. Some years later the French gave their land west of the Mississippi River to the Spanish. The settlers in Missouri were ruled by Spain until 1800, when Spain gave the territory back to France. The region came under the control of the United States three years later as part of the Louisiana Purchase.

In 1812, the Territory of Missouri was formed. Many settlers from the East poured into the region and towns and farms quickly grew. The Indians did not like all these white settlers coming to their land, and they frequently attacked the settlements and killed the people. Finally peace treaties were signed with the Indian tribes and the territory grew even larger. Many southerners came to Missouri with their slaves and started large farms.

When Missouri asked to be admitted to the United States as a state, there was a question of whether it should be admitted as a slave state or as a free state. Northerners and southerners all over the country argued bitterly about Missouri, and finally it was settled by the Missouri Compromise in 1820, and Missouri came into the Union as a slave state. (There is a separate article about the MISSOURI COMPROMISE.)

Although many people were for slavery, many were opposed to it. When the

The Current River in southern Missouri, which is formed by a tremendous spring, is one of America's best fishing streams.

Massie—Mo. Resources Div.

The beautiful Ozarks have made southwestern Missouri a popular vacation spot.

Civil War broke out, Missouri decided to remain with the Union, but many Missourians joined the Confederate Army, and the state was very divided in its loyalty. After the Civil War the big plantations were broken up, and tenant farmers began to work the land instead of slaves.

Cities like St. Louis and Kansas City grew into important manufacturing and transportation centers, and mining developed and attracted workers from other countries. In both World War I and II, Missouri's prosperous farms and factories contributed greatly to the war effort. Today, the Missouri Valley Development is building many dams and reservoirs for flood control, and large power plants to supply electric power.

PLACES TO SEE IN MISSOURI

George Washington Carver National Monument, 210 acres, ten miles south of Joplin, in the southwest, on U.S. Route 71. Site of the birthplace and childhood home of the famous scientist.

Jefferson National Expansion Memorial, 82 acres, in St. Louis, in the east, on

U.S. Routes 61 and 67. To commemorate the territorial expansion of the United States.

Mark Twain Home, in Hannibal, in the northeast on U.S. Route 36. The home where the author of *Tom Sawyer* and *Huckleberry Finn* grew up; now a museum.

Pony Express Monument, at St. Joseph, in the northwest, on U.S. Route 36. A statue to honor the riders who carried mail through dangerous Indian territory between St. Joseph, Missouri, and Sacramento, California, in 1860.

Lake of the Ozarks, 16,500 acres, north of Camdenton, in the central part of the state, on U.S. Route 54. Beautiful scenery and an excellent vacation spot for fishing, boating, and swimming.

Ste. Genevieve, in the east, on State Highway 25. The oldest town in Missouri; many historic buildings and a museum containing old relics.

MISSOURI. Area, 69,674 square miles. Population (1957 estimate) 4,255,000. Capital, Jefferson City. Nickname, the Show Me State. Motto, *Salus Populi Suprema Lex Esto* (Let the Welfare of the People Be the Supreme Law). Flower, hawthorn. Bird, bluebird. Song, "Missouri Waltz." Admitted to Union, August 10, 1821. Official abbreviation, Mo.

Missouri Compromise

In the early years of the United States, Negroes were slaves in the southern states but not in the northern states. The rich southerners, whose wealth came from cotton and other crops raised by their slaves, constantly worried for fear the northern states would try to pass laws to do away with slavery. Whenever a new state was admitted to the United States, there was an argument over whether it should be a "free" state or a "slave" state.

That was the situation in 1819, when Missouri asked Congress to admit it as a state. Missouri had been settled by southerners, and it wanted to enter as a slave state. The northern members of Congress were against admitting another slave state; but at the same time they wanted to admit Maine, and of course Maine, the most northern of the states, would be a free state. The southerners did not want to admit Maine unless at the same time Missouri came in as a slave state.

In 1820 and 1821 the problem was solved by the "Missouri Compromise." In a compromise, each side gives up part of what it has been asking for. Maine was admitted as a free state. Missouri was admitted as a slave state, but it was agreed that from that time on no other state as far north as Missouri could be admitted as a slave state. Henry Clay, the statesman from Kentucky who came to be known as "the great compromiser," was given most of the credit for the Missouri Compromise. He did not propose it, but he supported it in Congress.

The Missouri Compromise was the first of many arguments that arose over the admission of states, and in the end all the compromises failed and the question of slavery was settled by the CIVIL WAR, about which there is a separate article.

Missouri River

The Missouri River is the longest river in the United States. It is 2,714 miles long and is the chief tributary of the Mississippi River. It is called the "Big Muddy" because of the muddy waters along much of its course. The Missouri River rises in Montana and flows southeast through North and South Dakota. As it continues southward, it forms parts of the boundaries between South Dakota and Nebraska, Nebraska and Iowa, Nebraska and Missouri, and Kansas and Missouri. It then winds across the state of Missouri and joins the Mississippi River, which flows down to the Gulf of Mexico. As the Missouri River flows along its long course it gathers a great deal of sand, gravel, and very fine earth, called silt. Every year it carries millions of tons of silt into the Mississippi River. Much of the Missouri is navigable for large boats.

The Missouri River is an important waterway, but the river and its many branches have often overflowed their banks and caused millions of dollars' worth of damage. Sometimes the vast Missouri Basin has also had severe droughts (dry spells) that killed the cattle and crops. This is because the upper part of the valley usually gets too little water, while the lower part of the valley gets too much. In 1944, the United States government started the Missouri River Basin Project. Its purpose was to provide a system of flood control and to build many new dams and reservoirs that would store up water in flood time and use it to provide irrigation in dry periods. Fort Peck Dam in Montana was built as part of the project. It is one of the largest earth dams in the world.

It is not known who were the first white men to explore the Missouri River, almost three hundred years ago. French fur traders followed them, and explored the river farther north. About 1804, Lewis and Clark explored the river up to its course. In 1819, the first steamboat sailed up the river. River traffic grew, and many pioneers going west traveled on the Missouri. After the railroads were built the Missouri became less important, but it may still become one of the chief sources of transportation and water power.

mistletoe

The mistletoe is a plant that grows in many parts of the world where the climate is not too cold. The mistletoe is a parasite, which means that it lives by getting its food from other plants. There are many kinds of mistletoe and many of them live on trees that are deciduous, which means they lose their leaves in the fall. The mistletoe itself is an evergreen plant; it does not lose its thick yellowish-green leaves in the fall. The common American mistletoe has small white berries. It is an attractive plant that is popular for decorating homes during the Christmas season. There is a custom in many countries that anyone who stands under a piece of mistletoe can be kissed. The Druids (ancient Celtic people in England) believed that the mistletoe was sacred. Mistletoe is the flower of the state of Oklahoma.

Mitchell, Margaret

Margaret Mitchell was an American writer. Her novel, *Gone with the Wind,* was the most successful book of this century and the most successful of all motion pictures was made from it. Margaret Mitchell was born in Atlanta, Georgia, in 1900. As a young woman she wrote for newspapers there. She married John R. Marsh, an Atlanta business executive, when she was 25. She worked for years on her long novel, which was a story of the South at the time of the Civil War. Margaret Mitchell received many honors and could have sold another novel for a tremendous price, but refused. In 1949 she was killed in an automobile accident.

Mitchell, Maria

Maria Mitchell was an American astronomer, or scientist who studies heavenly bodies. She lived more than a hundred years ago. She was born in Nantucket, Massachusetts, in 1818, and later taught school there. She became interested in astronomy, and in 1847 she discovered a comet, for which she was rewarded by the king of Denmark with a gold medal. Maria Mitchell then became a professor of astronomy at Vassar College, where she remained until her death in 1889. She was the first woman to be elected to the American Academy of Arts and Sciences, and in 1905 she was elected to the Hall of Fame.

mite

The mite is a tiny animal resembling a spider that lives in almost every part of the world.

The mite has an egg-shaped body and four pairs of legs. It has sharp pincers that it uses to pierce its prey. Many mites are parasites (they live on other plants or animals). Some mites are useful because they feed on insects that are pests to man. Other mites feed on cattle, horses, and dogs and also on human beings. The mites that live on people are hard to find because they are so small, and they are a whitish color. When a human being or an animal is bitten by a mite it causes an unpleasant itch. Some mites feed on plants, such as fruit trees and evergreens. Farmers have poisonous sprays that they use to kill mites. Some mites infest cheese and other foods.

Mites are usually thought of as insects, but to scientists they are a different kind of animal. Mites are *arachnids,* as are spiders.

moa

The moa was a strange bird that lived in New Zealand long ago. There are no moas in existence now, but men have discovered traces of them in rocks that make it possible to tell what they looked like. The moa was a huge bird that weighed about five hundred pounds and was about nine feet high. With its long, thin legs, it probably looked somewhat like an ostrich. The moa could not fly.

Am. Mus. of Nat. Hist.

The New Zealand moa was a strange and interesting bird. Unfortunately, it became extinct in the 17th century because tribesmen killed it for food.

Scientists believe that the early people who lived in New Zealand hunted the moa, and it was such a fat and lazy bird that it could not protect itself, so gradually it died out.

Mobile

Mobile is the second-largest city in Alabama and its only seaport. About 130,000 people live there. The port is on Mobile Bay, part of the Gulf of Mexico. Four rivers flow through the city and empty into the bay.

Many of the people of Mobile work in shipyards. Others work in factories that manufacture railroad equipment, aluminum, concrete, and chemicals. Many ships sail from Mobile to South America. They carry cotton, metals, metal equipment, and corn and other grains, and bring back rubber, bauxite (aluminum ore), manganese, bananas, and other South American products.

The area around Mobile was first settled by the French, more than 250 years ago. Later, Mobile belonged to the British and after that to the Spanish. In 1813, it was taken over by the United States. During the Civil War, Mobile was an important Confederate harbor, and was blockaded by Union ships. The Battle of Mobile Bay, in which the Confederate fleet was defeated, is described in the article on Admiral David FARRAGUT. For pictures of Mobile see the article on ALABAMA.

MOBILE, ALABAMA. Population (1950) 129,009. On Mobile Bay, on Gulf of Mexico.

moccasin

The moccasin is a poisonous snake that lives in swamps and along the banks of streams in the warm parts of the United States. The moccasin often reaches a length of 5 feet. The young snake is light brown or olive green in color, with clear black bands that circle its body. As the snake grows older, these bands fade. The fully grown moccasin snake is a grayish black color.

MOTHS AND BUTTERFLIES

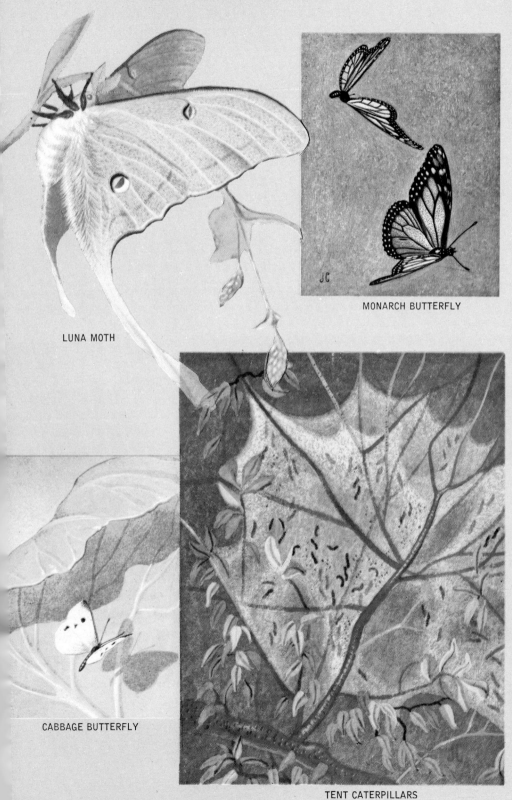

LUNA MOTH

MONARCH BUTTERFLY

CABBAGE BUTTERFLY

TENT CATERPILLARS

MOTHS AND BUTTERFLIES

BUCKEYE BUTTERFLY

CECROPIA MOTH

ISABELLA MOTH

MOURNING CLOAK BUTTERFLY

BANDED PURPLE BUTTERFLY

TIGER SWALLOWTAIL

WOOLLY BEAR CATERPILLAR

The thick-bodied moccasin is often six feet long. It is vicious and its poisonous bite is dangerous to man.

The moccasin is a greedy eater. It will devour birds, fish, frogs, eggs, and almost anything else it can find. When it is angry the moccasin will shake its tail and open its mouth very wide. The inside of the moccasin's mouth is white. For this reason people in the southern part of the United States sometimes call the moccasin by the nickname "cotton-mouth." The bite of a moccasin is very dangerous.

mocking bird

The mocking bird lives in the southern part of the United States, where it is a great favorite because of its beautiful song. The mocking bird is very skillful at imitating the songs of other birds and it can also imitate the sound of a hen or frog. It is about the size of a robin, and is quite plain in appearance. It is a slender bird with short wings, and its feathers are dull gray and white.

The mocking bird builds its nest in a low tree. The female lays pretty green eggs with reddish brown spots. The male is a brave defender of the nest and will fight any enemies that come near. The mocking bird eats insects and sometimes it eats fruit.

mock orange

The mock orange is a shrub that grows in Europe and the United States and in some parts of Asia where the climate is not too warm. The mock orange is sometimes known as syringa. It is a deciduous plant, which means that it loses its leaves every fall. It is a hardy plant that can grow well even in places where there is very little sunlight. There are several different kinds of mock orange, most of them growing to be more than six feet high. The mock orange is a very attractive shrub. It has shiny green leaves and beautiful sprays of white sweet-smelling blossoms that appear in early summer. People often grow mock orange shrubs in their gardens and in parks. It gets its name from the fact that its blossoms resemble the blossoms of the real orange.

models and model-making

A model is a small-scale likeness or copy of something. The models most frequently made are those of airplanes,

Am. Mus. of Nat. Hist.

The mockingbird is able to imitate the calls of as many as thirty other birds.

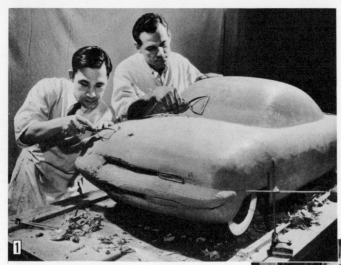

Model-making is a fine hobby because it is good training in the use of the fingers and hands for delicate work. But it is serious business for manufacturers who make models of their products.

X-acto, Inc., Photos

Ford Motor Co.

1. Engineers and design stylists make clay, and later plastic, models of new car designs to be tested for safety, efficiency, and appearance.

2. Tomorrow's pilots learn much about airplanes by making model planes.

3 and 4. Making models of old sailing ships is popular with many. A fully rigged three- or four-master takes infinite patience to build.

5. Special modeling tools make cutting easier.

Canadian Pacific Railway

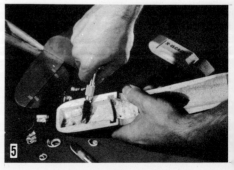

ships, trains, houses, and people. Models are made both for study and for enjoyment. Engineers and architects first make models (or "mock-ups") of ships, planes, and buildings they have designed. They check these for weaknesses in proportion and construction, improvements in design.

Youngsters and grownups of all ages make model airplanes and ships, many of which actually work, for the pleasure of building and operating them. Many inventions are developed through the use of models of devices thought up by their inventors.

Clay modeling by hand is very popular. It is a form of sculpture in which models of people and things are made from clay. The clay is then baked, to harden it. It may be painted and decorated in all sorts of ways to make it as lifelike as its original.

MODEL AIRPLANES

The most popular form of model-making is the building of model airplanes. Millions of dollars each year are spent by model-airplane enthusiasts on balsa wood, tissue paper, razor blades, glue, waterproofing material, and other items necessary in building model planes. Special kits containing blueprints and all the necessary material are sold.

Model planes may contain a small gas, jet, or rocket engine or a rubber band to drive the propeller and enable the models to fly. Each year contests or meets are held throughout the United States to determine the best model. Some model planes have flown as high as 2 miles for a distance of 50 miles.

MODEL SHIPS

Of interest too is the building of model ships inside narrow-necked bottles or jars. Such work takes patience and extreme care. Most of the construction is done outside the bottle. Holes are made in the hull (bottom of the ship) so that pieces of wood can be placed in them once the

materials are inside the bottle. The sails and other movable parts are collapsed and held together by thread before the ship is inserted through the neck. When the ship is placed entirely inside the bottle, the threads are pulled tight and the ship is drawn up to its full size. A great deal of the work is done with long tweezers that are inserted in the bottle to put the various parts of the ship in place.

mohair

Mohair is a fine cloth that is made from the hair of the Angora goat that lives in Asia, South Africa, and Australia. Some Angora goats are now raised in the United States, in Texas. The goat has long silky hair, usually pure white. In the spring its hair is clipped. It is woven into a cloth that is strong and smooth. Mohair cloth does not collect dust and it lasts a long time. It is used to cover couches and chairs, and to make drapes. Mohair has also been used for making wigs and switches.

Mohammed

Mohammed was the founder of the great religion called Islam, or Mohammedanism. His name was formerly spelled Mahomet. He lived about 1,300 years ago. The followers of Mohammed are called Mohammedans or Moslems, and they live in many parts of the world, particularly in Arabia, North Africa, Pakistan, and other parts of Asia. Although Mohammed never learned to read and write, he is considered one of the greatest religious leaders of the world. He brought the idea of one God and of right conduct to many people who before his time had worshiped many gods.

Mohammed was born in Mecca, a city in Arabia, in the year 570. His father died before he was born, and his mother died when he was a young child. He was brought up by his grandfather and his uncle. His uncle had many children of his own and was very poor. Mohammed had no schooling and as a young boy tended sheep. Later he became a camel driver and a caravan leader for a rich widow named Khadijah. When Mohammed was 25 years old he married Khadijah. They were married for many years and she helped him with his religious work.

At the time Mohammed was born, religions such as Christianity, Judaism, Hinduism, and Buddhism had become strong in other parts of the world. But in Arabia, people of different tribes and cities had their own private gods. They did have a word, *Allah,* that stood for any god. Mohammed later used this word to stand for the one and only God that he told his followers to worship.

Several years after Mohammed married, he became very interested in religion. He joined a group of people who called themselves *Hanifs,* or "penitents." He went often to a cave on Mount Hira, where he fasted and prayed. Here, he reported, the Angel Gabriel appeared to him in a vision, holding a scroll on which was written a message that Mohammed understood clearly as coming from Allah, even though Mohammed could not read. At first, Mohammed said, he could not believe that Allah had chosen him to lead the people, but when two years later he had another vision he was convinced, and from that time Mohammed never doubted that he had been chosen to bring the law of Allah to the people. The messages from Allah that Mohammed taught are recorded in the KORAN, the holy book of the Moslems, about which there is a separate article.

At first Mohammed's followers were few. They were mostly his own relatives and friends. Mohammed did not think he was starting a new religion, but reminding the people of an old one that had been forgotten. When Mohammed began to criticize the lesser gods of the people, saying that Allah would punish anyone who believed in them, many people became angry. Finally, after his wife had died, Mohammed had to flee from Mecca north to Medina. This flight, which took place in 622, is called the Hegira. The year 622 marks the beginning of the Mohammedan era in the Moslem calendar. The people of Medina listened to Mohammed's message, and many joined his religion.

Mohammed lived only ten years after he went to Medina. He died in the year 632, when he was 62 years old. During that time he gained more and more people to his religion and trained many of the prophets who spread his faith after he died. There is a separate article on ISLAM that tells more about the religion Mohammed preached.

Mohican, another spelling of the name of the Mahican Indians. James Fenimore Cooper wrote a famous book called *The Last of the Mohicans.* See the article on MAHICAN.

Mojave Desert

The Mojave Desert is part of the Great American Desert. It is in California, south of Death Valley. The Mojave Desert is a hot, dry region of mountains and plains, about 15,000 square miles in size. Few plants can grow there because of the dryness, but there are important deposits of borax, salt, gold, and tungsten. Farmers can grow crops in only a few places where there is irrigation. There are some cattle ranches. The Mojave River is the only river in this region. It flows mostly underground.

mold, a plant that feeds on other plants: see the article on FUNGUS.

mole

The mole is a small animal that lives in many parts of Europe, Asia, and the United States, where the climate is neither too hot nor too cold. Very few people have ever seen a mole because it spends almost all of its time underground. The mole is about seven inches long. It has powerful front claws and a long snout. The mole is so blind that it can hardly tell the difference between day and night, but its very sensitive snout partly makes up for its poor eyesight. The mole is a very hard worker. It spends all of its time digging long tunnels several feet beneath the surface of the earth. As it digs the mole eats the insects and worms that it finds in the ground. It makes a nest in its underground tunnel, and the female mole has five or six babies. The baby moles are almost completely helpless when they are born, but two months later they are fully grown and ready to join in the work.

The mole is useful to man. It has a thick, soft, gray or black fur that is made into fine fur coats. It eats harmful insects, and as it plows the earth to build tunnels it helps the farmers to keep the soil soft and rich.

molecule

A molecule is the smallest particle into which a substance can be divided without being changed into a different substance. Molecules are so small that they cannot be seen by the naked eye. Molecules are smaller than the finest grain of sand. In fact, a grain of sand contains millions of molecules. The air that you breathe is made up of molecules. In one breath of air you breathe in more than a million, million, million molecules.

All matter that is found in nature is made up of molecules. The basic substances of the earth, called *elements,* are made up of molecules. The combinations of these elements, called *compounds,* also are made up of molecules.

WHAT IS IN A MOLECULE

A molecule is not the smallest particle of matter. Molecules are made up of even smaller particles called *atoms.* The atoms in a molecule are arranged in a special way. If this arrangement is changed, the molecules will change into molecules of a different kind, and the substance made up of these molecules will also be changed.

Most molecules contain two or more atoms. A molecule of oxygen contains two atoms of oxygen. A molecule of hydrogen contains two atoms of hydrogen. Molecules that contain two atoms are called *diatomic* molecules. There are some molecules that have only one atom each. A helium molecule contains only one helium atom. Such a molecule is called a *monatomic* molecule. Some molecules contain more than fifty atoms. Such molecules are called *giant molecules,* or *macro-molecules.* The molecules of many viruses that cause sicknesses such as colds, influenza, and pneumonia are giant molecules. So are the molecules of substances such as sugars and starches, called carbohydrates.

All molecules of a particular element or compound have the same size, shape, and weight. All the molecules of an element are made up of the same kind of atoms, and the same number of atoms. Every oxygen molecule contains two oxygen atoms.

The molecules of a compound are made up of two or more different kinds of atoms. They all have the same number and arrangement of atoms. A molecule of water, which is a combination of hydrogen and oxygen, contains two atoms of hydrogen and one atom of oxygen.

CHANGES IN MOLECULES

When two or more elements combine to form a compound, the atoms of their molecules break away from each other and regroup themselves to form new and different molecules. This is known as a *chemical change.*

When one form of matter, such as a solid, changes into a different form of matter, such as a liquid (for example, ice into water), the molecules are unchanged. This is known as a *physical change*. The molecules of water are the same as the molecules of ice. The grouping of the atoms in these molecules is also the same.

SPACES BETWEEN MOLECULES

The molecules that make up all matter are separated by very tiny spaces. The smaller the spaces between the molecules, the more the molecules pull on each other. The pull between molecules of the same substance is called *cohesion*. The pull between molecules of different substances is called *adhesion*.

The spaces between molecules are smallest in solids, where cohesion is therefore greatest. In liquids the spaces are larger, and in gases they are still larger. The cohesion of molecules of a gas is much less than the cohesion of molecules in a liquid or solid.

It is hard to believe that a solid substance such as gold or iron really has spaces between its molecules. However, if a piece of iron is placed in a dish of mercury, the mercury will go in between these spaces and be absorbed by the iron.

BROWNIAN MOVEMENT

Because there are spaces separating the molecules, the molecules can move about. Molecules of matter are constantly moving. The molecules of a gas move about more than the molecules of a liquid or solid. Gas molecules move about in different directions, striking one another and bouncing away. Such motion is called Brownian movement, because a Scottish scientist named Robert Brown discovered it, more than a hundred years ago. The smaller the molecule the faster it moves about.

MOLECULAR WEIGHT

The weight of a molecule is given by a number that compares it to the weight of an atom of oxygen. The weight of an oxygen atom is represented by the number 16. Therefore, the weight of a molecule of oxygen, which contains two atoms of oxygen, is 16 plus 16, or 32. A molecule of carbon dioxide, a gas that is in the air you breathe out, contains one carbon atom (weight 12) and two oxygen atoms (16 each). The weight of a carbon dioxide molecule is therefore 12 plus 16 plus 16, or 44.

Molecular weight is also expressed in grams. For this purpose scientists use a quantity called a gram-molecule, or *mole*. A mole of oxygen weighs 32 grams or a little more than an ounce. A mole of carbon dioxide weighs 44 grams. The number of molecules in a mole of a substance is the same for all substances. The number of molecules in 32 grams of oxygen is the same as the number of molecules in 44 grams of carbon dioxide. The number, 603,000,000,000,000,000,000,000 molecules (six hundred and three thousand million, million, million), is called Avogadro's number, named after an Italian scientist who first discovered this law almost 150 years ago.

Molière

Molière was a great French writer of plays who lived three hundred years ago. He has been called the Shakespeare of France.

His real name was Jean Baptiste Poquelin, and he was born in Paris in 1622. His father and grandfather were servants of King Louis XIII, and young Jean Baptiste at first expected to follow in their footsteps but soon he developed a powerful interest in the theater.

After attending school he became the leader of a small band of traveling actors, and took the name of Molière. He was actor, company manager, and writer while he was traveling with this group. During this time he wrote many short plays and sketches that he afterward expanded into full-length plays.

He published his first play in 1653 and quickly became famous as a writer of comedy. One critic has said that though Shakespeare was a greater genius, Molière was better than Shakespeare at writing comedy. Molière's plays were witty and made fun of the small shortcomings and habits of people in general. They often expressed his scorn and contempt for the foolishness, snobbery and hypocrisy of the social and political life of the time. *Le Tartuffe, le Misanthrope,* and *le Bourgeois Gentilhomme* are among his most famous plays. In 1673, while acting in one of his own plays, he had a stroke and died an hour later.

mollusc or mollusk

A mollusc is an animal that has a soft body and no bones. There are more than seventy thousand different kinds of mollusc and they live in almost every part of the world. Most molluscs live in the water. A few make their homes on land. A mollusc usually has a hard shell that covers its soft body, but there are some molluscs, such as the octopus, that do not have shells. Many kinds of mollusc have a long thin foot that sticks out from the shell. The mollusc finds this foot helpful when it digs and crawls and swims.

The largest mollusc is the giant squid, which has a body about 19 feet long. This squid lives in the sea and few people ever have a chance to see it, although sometimes a dead giant squid is washed up on the beach, especially in Newfoundland. Some molluscs, such as the snail, are very small. Clams, oysters and scallops are molluscs that are good to eat. There is more about molluscs in the article on ANIMALS.

Molotov, Vyacheslav

Vyacheslav Mikhailovich Molotov, once premier and at other times foreign minister of the Soviet Union, became prominent there soon after the Communists gained control in 1917 and was the only Soviet statesman who remained prominent in the government throughout the periods in which first Lenin, then Stalin, had power. Soft-spoken but firm, Molotov more than any other Soviet statesman has resembled the leading statesmen of the Western European and American countries.

Molotov was born in 1890. His real name was Skriabin, and he was the son of a shopkeeper. As a boy of 12 he joined a Communist group. In those days it was dangerous to be a Communist and young Skriabin changed his name to Molotov (which means "hammer" in Russian) to escape arrest. After the Communists began to rule Russia, Molotov rose rapidly in the government. In 1930, when he was 40 years old, he became premier. This was the highest office in the government, but actually Russia was controlled by Josef Stalin. However, from 1930 on Molotov was one of the chief spokesmen of Russian policy toward other nations. When Stalin died in 1953, Molotov was appointed again to be foreign minister, which he had been from 1939 to 1949. Then Molotov joined with some other leading officials in an attempt to prevent Nikita Khrushchev from becoming a dictator as Stalin had been. Khrushchev won, and in July 1957 Molotov lost his high position and was sent as an unimportant diplomat to Outer Mongolia.

molting

When a living creature loses its skin, hair, feathers, or other outside covering, and replaces this covering with a new growth, it is said to *molt.* Many animals molt. Birds lose their feathers and grow new ones after their young birds are born. Some birds grow feathers that are particularly bright and beautiful before the mating season. Young birds often molt several times before they finally develop the feathers they will have during their adult lives.

Some birds, such as the pelican and the puffin, have bills with an outer covering and they molt these outer coverings. Grouse molt their long, sharp claws in the spring.

Animals molt their fur. Deer shed their antlers in the spring or the fall. Shellfish, such as lobsters and crayfish, shed their shells and develop new ones. Lizards and snakes lose their skins and grow new ones.

Many insects molt. The caterpillar changes its skin five times before it becomes a chrysalis. Scientists have discovered that insects that live longest seem to molt most often.

molybdenum

Molybdenum is a hard metal with a bright silvery luster. It has a very high melting point. It is a chemical element, which means that it is one of the hundred basic substances that make up the world. Molybdenum added to steel makes the steel very hard. Molybdenum steel tools are used to cut other metals. Cutting tools move at very high speeds and become very hot, but because of the high melting point of molybdenum they do not melt and lose their sharp edges. The turbine blades of turbo-jet airplane engines are made of molybdenum because it will not melt from the extremely hot gases that turn the turbine. Molybdenum is used in radio, television and X-ray tubes, and in the tips of the wires across which the sparks jump in spark plugs.

By combining molybdenum with other chemical elements, dyes can be made for coloring wool, leather, and silk. When molybdenum is combined with lead, it makes a bright orange-red dye that is used to color paints.

Molybdenum comes from the ore named *molybdite*. This ore is found in many parts of the world, but there is not very much of it. The United States mines more molybdenum ore than any other country. Utah leads in molybdite production, followed by Colorado, New Mexico, Arizona, Nevada, and California. These states mine about 44,000,000 pounds of molybdite a year. Molybdite is also mined in Canada, Chile, Finland, Norway, Yugoslavia, and other countries. A less important molybdenum ore is called wulfenite.

momentum

Momentum is the ability of a moving thing to overcome resistance. The momentum depends on the mass, or weight, of the thing, and on the velocity, or speed, with which the thing is moving.

You find out the momentum by multiplying the mass by the velocity. If a rock that weighs ten pounds falls off a ledge and hits the ground at ten miles an hour, its momentum is 10 times 10, which is 100. If a rock that weighs only two pounds falls off a higher ledge and hits the ground at fifty miles an hour, its momentum is also 100, because that is the result of multiplying 2 times 50.

You can feel the effect of momentum when any moving thing strikes against you. Suppose you stretch your arm out and someone lays a baseball in your hand.

The heavy car will strike the fence with a momentum more than a thousand times as great as that with which the ball hits the fence—even though the ball is traveling much faster than the car.

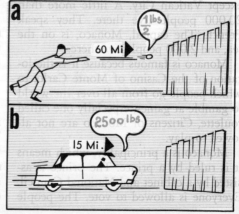

This will not cause your hand to move downward. But suppose the baseball were dropped into your hand from high above. It would be moving so fast that its momentum would cause your hand to move downward several inches. If a fifty-pound weight were laid in your hand, no matter how gently, it would cause your hand to move so far down that you would drop it.

Very heavy objects need not move at high speed to have a large momentum. An automobile that bumps into a wooden fence will smash the fence even though the automobile is moving slowly. A baseball thrown against the fence with the same speed will do hardly any damage. A bullet, weighing only an ounce or so, will go all the way through the wood because of its great speed.

The momentum of an object can be transferred to another object. This is the basis of the game of billiards. If a billiard ball that is moving strikes squarely against a billiard ball that is not moving, the first ball will slow down or stop and the second will roll along with the momentum not used up by the first.

Monaco

Monaco is a tiny country in Europe on the Mediterranean Sea. It is nine miles from Nice, in France, near the border between France and Italy. It has an area of only 370 acres, which is smaller than the area of any other independent country except Vatican City. A little more than 20,000 people live there. They speak French. The capital, Monaco, is on the sea, and 2,000 people live there.

Monaco is famous because it is the location of the Casino of Monte Carlo, to which people go from all over the world to gamble at games, especially one called roulette. Citizens of Monaco are not allowed to play.

Monaco is a principality, which means it is ruled by a prince. The prince is assisted by a cabinet and National Council. Everyone is allowed to vote. The people

French Gov't Tourist Office

This picture shows nearly all of Monaco.

are not taxed because the tax on gambling and the tourist trade pay the government's expenses. The French government controls Monaco's foreign affairs.

In 1956 the American people were thrilled when Grace Kelly, a beautiful Philadelphia girl who had become a famous motion-picture star, married Prince Rainier, the reigning prince of Monaco, and became a princess.

Monaco is a very popular winter resort. The capital has a museum and an Institute of Oceanography, at which scientists study the ocean and ocean life.

MONACO. Area, 370 acres. Population, 20,202. Language, French. Religion, Roman Catholic. Government, principality. Monetary unit, French franc. Flag, two horizontal bands, red and white. Capital, Monaco.

monarchy

Monarchy is a form of government in which a king is the head of the country. The king is said to be the *sovereign,* which means that he has the power to rule. There are other titles that mean about the same thing as king: monarch, emperor, prince, and many others. A country ruled by any one of these, or by a queen, may be called a kingdom, an empire, or by other names, but in any case it is a monarchy.

In a monarchy, when the king dies his oldest son or closest relative (if he has no son) becomes the next king. This is *hereditary monarchy.* In early times, kings were often elected, but for hundreds of years all monarchies have been hereditary. There are two ideas behind hereditary monarchy. One is the *divine right of kings.* It was once believed by many people that God had appointed the kings, and that disobedience to the king would be defiance of God. The other idea was that *royal blood* was different and better than the blood of all other people and that no one could become a king unless he was descended from kings. In modern times, almost no one believes this.

In an *absolute monarchy,* the king has power to make laws, and to put people in prison or have them executed. The king owns everything in the country, and can take it whenever he wants to. In ancient times there were many absolute monarchies, but for several hundred years there have been few. Some countries have been called absolute monarchies, but actually the king had to keep on good terms with the most powerful noblemen or they would kill him and get a new king. A *limited monarchy* is one in which the king has some powers and the people or their representatives have other powers. The people in a limited monarchy have the most important powers, which include the right to make the laws and decide what the taxes will be. One kind of limited monarchy is called a *constitutional monarchy.* This means that there is a written constitution to say what powers the king has and what powers the people have.

The first kings, many thousands of years ago, were either war leaders or high priests who became so powerful that they were able to make their sons kings after them. This created *dynasties,* which are

long lines of kings in which the *succession* (passing on of the king's power) is from father to son. In ancient Egypt and Rome, and until recently in modern Japan, kings taught the people to worship them as gods, to increase their power.

Most European countries have followed the *Salic law.* Under this law, a woman cannot become the ruler and the succession cannot pass through a woman. In England, which does not follow the Salic law, if a king has no son but does have a daughter she becomes the *queen regnant,* which means that she reigns (has a king's powers). There have been several reigning queens in England, beginning with Mary I, more than four hundred years ago. Elizabeth II is a *queen regnant.* In a Salic-law country, the former king's closest male relative would become the king.

A king's wife also is a queen but is a *queen consort.* The king or queen is addressed as "Your Majesty." Sons of a king are *princes* and daughters of a king are *princesses.* They are addressed as "Your Highness." The oldest son of a king is the *heir apparent.* Unless he dies, he is sure to become the next king. He is usually called the *crown prince,* but in England he is called the Prince of Wales and when France was a monarchy he was called the *dauphin.* When the king has no son, his closest relative is called the *heir presumptive.* An heir presumptive loses his place whenever the king has a son.

When a king is officially using his powers, he sits on a big chair called a *throne* in a room called his *court.* He wears a *crown* on his head, and may hold a gold, jeweled rod called a *scepter.* The throne, crown and scepter are said to be symbols of the king's rights and powers, so a new king is often said to inherit the throne, or the crown, or the scepter. A person is officially recognized as king or queen by having the crown placed on his head for the first time. This ceremony is called a *coronation.* When a king or reigning queen signs an official paper, the

Latin word *rex* (meaning "king") or *regina* (meaning "queen") is used, so that George VI of England signed his name "George R." to stand for George Rex, and Elizabeth II signs her name "Elizabeth R." to stand for Elizabeth Regina.

When a king is too young or too sick to reign, one or more other persons are usually appointed to act for him. These persons are called *regents,* and the government is called a *regency.* It is still a monarchy, but its monarch is not reigning in person. England last had a regency from 1811 to 1820, when King George III was insane and the Prince of Wales was regent.

See also the article EMPIRE.

monastery

A monastery is a place where religious men live strictly regulated lives dedicated to their religion. Most monasteries are Christian, but the Buddhist and Moslem religions also have monasteries. Most Christian monasteries are Catholic. Among Protestant churches, only the Church of England has many monasteries.

Men who live in monasteries are called *monks.* They may be priests, or laymen (ordinary men) who have taken vows to remain poor, not to marry, and to be obedient to the man who is in charge of the monastery. The article on ABBEY describes one kind of monastery. Another kind is the *priory.* Sometimes a priory is ruled by an abbey. Convents, in which nuns live, are also called monasteries.

Many early Christians became hermits. They lived alone and spent most of their time praying. About 1,700 years ago, when many hermits lived in the deserts of Egypt, other religious men began to build their huts or "cells" near them. They would try to find a hermit who was very holy and then ask him to instruct them. That is how monasteries began.

Monasteries grew rapidly. In the Middle Ages, many monasteries were like small towns. They had their own farms

Royal Greek Embassy

Monasteries are often built in secluded spots, where the pious monks will be able to pray apart from the world.

and businesses. Some became famous for one product, such as a wine. For example, the Carthusian monks still have a secret formula for making a liqueur, or sweet alcoholic drink, called *chartreuse.*

Monasteries were also important as places of learning, for the monks would spend much time copying manuscripts. This was before the printing press had been invented, so books had to be copied by hand. The learning of the monks and the care with which they copied books preserved many great works that might otherwise have been lost forever. The monks also drew pictures to illustrate the books. Illustrations in a manuscript are called *illuminations.* Many of these are very beautiful. The monks often used gold ink, and even now, many centuries later, the illuminations are bright and attractive. One of the most famous of these is the *Book of Kells,* which is kept in Ireland.

During the Reformation, when the Protestant Christian churches were formed, many monasteries were taken over by kings and other nobles. Their great holdings in land and buildings were used for the state.

The Benedictines and Trappists are two of the best-known Catholic religious orders that have monasteries. Many people of every faith visit the Trappist monastery at Gethsemane, Kentucky.

Monday

Monday is the second day of the week. Its name comes from a word meaning "moon's day," or the day sacred to the goddess of the moon. Monday is the first day of the working week in most Christian countries, coming after Sunday, the day of rest. In the United States, most national holidays that fall on Sunday are celebrated on Monday so that working people will have the additional day of leisure.

Labor Day is always observed on the first Monday in September.

Monet, Claude

Claude Monet was a French painter who lived about a hundred years ago. He was a leader of the Impressionist school of art, which took its name from a critic's comment on one of his paintings, *Morning, Rising Sun.* Monet was born in 1840. As a young man he studied the classical style of painting, but he soon felt he could not express himself in the formal traditions and he began to paint things as he saw them. He paid little attention to the details of his subject, but tried to picture the effects of light and air. His works were laughed at for many years, but gradually they won recognition and Monet became prosperous and well known. Among his famous paintings are *Rouen Cathedral, Water Lilies,* and *Fontainebleau Forest.* Monet was nearly blind for the last ten years of his life, and he died in 1926.

money

Money is anything that people will accept in payment for goods or services, and that can *circulate*—pass from one person to another many times without losing its value. We think of money as being coins or paper money, but actually people have used many different things for money. Fish, stones, corn, skins, cattle and sheep have all been used as money. The American Indians of New England used beads called *wampum* as money. An American farmer of today would not sell his coin for wampum, but neither would an Indian farmer have sold his corn for a printed piece of paper. What makes a particular article money is the fact that the people living in a community are willing to accept it as payment.

BARTER

At one time, long ago, there was no need for money. If a fisherman wanted some vegetables, he found a farmer and exchanged a certain number of fish for a certain number of vegetables. This method of trading one product for another is called *barter.* Barter still exists among certain peoples.

The difficulty with barter was that it was not always convenient. Suppose the fisherman could not find a farmer who happened to want fish at the moment. He would have to do without vegetables. Besides, if the fisherman wanted to exchange his fish for many different products, he would have to make many individual visits and perhaps have little time left for fishing.

HOW MONEY IS USED

Sooner or later, all groups of men found barter very inconvenient. Suppose the fisherman wants corn, but the farmer does not want fish. The fisherman must find someone who wants fish and who is willing to trade something that the farmer wants. He may have to trade several times before he can get his corn. When there is one thing that everyone wants—money—no one has to trade more than once.

Money also makes possible *savings.* A fisherman cannot wait to trade his fish, even if there is nothing he wants at the moment. The fish would spoil. Money, which does not spoil, can be saved until there is use for it.

In order for a certain material to be used as money, it must have certain qualities. It must be durable so that it does not wear out. It must be able to be carried without too much trouble. It must be able to be divided into smaller units in case goods of different values are traded. It must have a steady value so that people will know from one day or month to the next just what their goods are worth in terms of the money.

Not all things that have been used as money had all of these qualities, which is why some of them were abandoned. Stone was too heavy to carry about. Beads tended to get broken. Cattle and sheep might die. In time it was found that the best material for money was metal. In the beginning many metals were used as money, but gradually gold and silver became the most used metals, although some small coins are made of copper, nickel, tin, and other metals.

Curriculum Films, Inc.

Trade brought about the use of money, which in turn made trade easier. Earlier, men used the inefficient barter system.

PAPER MONEY

About three hundred years ago another advance in money was made. People found that while gold and silver coins were convenient for exchanges of small and medium values, when it came to large exchanges it was very cumbersome to carry about many heavy coins to make payment. So paper money came into use. Paper money differs from other money because it has little or no value in itself. The paper of a hundred-dollar bill is not worth a penny. What gives the hundred-dollar bill its value is the fact that the government agrees to pay to the owner a hundred dollars' worth of gold or silver, or something of equal value. People accept a small slip of paper as money because they have confidence in the government.

Another name for paper money is *legal tender*. This means that when anyone tenders (offers) paper money in payment of a debt, the law requires that it be accepted. Coins such as fifty-cent pieces, quarters, nickels, and pennies are also legal tender, because the value of the metal they contain is not as great as the amount stamped on the face of the coins.

UNITS AND STANDARDS OF MONEY

The money of a country is made and controlled by its government. It decides which metals, and how much of the metals, are to be used for money. The United States uses silver in coins worth ten cents or more, nickel and copper in five-cent pieces (nickels), and bronze in pennies (cents). Before 1933 the United States also had gold coins in various values, or denominations, from one dollar up to one hundred thousand dollars. Coins are made in government mints. The United States government has mints in Philadelphia, Denver, and San Francisco. Its paper money is made by the Bureau of Engraving and Printing, in Washington, D.C.

A government also decides what the unit of money should be. In the United States and Canada it is the dollar; in England, the pound sterling; in France, the franc; in Italy, the lira; in Mexico and other Latin-American countries, the peso.

But deciding on a monetary unit means more than giving it a name. More important it means deciding how much the unit is worth. A monetary unit is fixed by law as being a certain quantity of a certain metal. In the United States a dollar is worth $15 \frac{5}{21}$ grains of a kind of gold that consists of nine parts of gold and one part of copper. Until 1933, anyone who wanted to could exchange his money, coins or paper, for gold and get

Unless you are a weight-lifter, shopping with the stone money of Yap is difficult.

Silver money used in Laos is designed to look like the tongue of a native tiger.

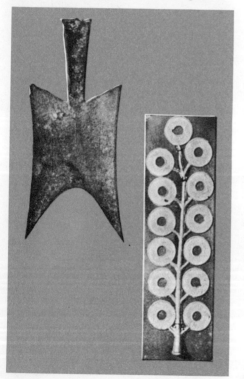

Chase Nat'l Bank Money Museum

The spade coin of China is the earliest known metal money. It was probably used in 2000 B.C. Below it is a tin tree coin of Malacca. It was cast in this form, and the "leaves" were broken off for use.

15 $\frac{5}{21}$ grains of gold for each dollar. When a country's money is exchangeable for gold in this way, it is said to be on the *gold standard*. Some countries have based their monetary units on silver of a certain quantity and these countries are said to be on a *silver standard*.

In the past, some countries, including the United States, have used two metals for their standard. Until 1873 a person in the United States could get either silver or gold for his money. He could exchange a dollar either for a certain amount of gold or for about fifteen times as much silver as gold. This system is called *bimetallism*. Bimetallism did not work out very well and was abandoned by the United States and the other countries that used it.

When a country has silver or gold, or both, as its money standard, it makes coins of these metals and must keep on hand a supply of the metals for people who wish to exchange their money for the standard metals. Until the early 1930s, most countries of the world were on the gold standard and had reserves of gold. But those were depression years and the governments had to use much of their gold reserves. In order to keep as much of the gold as possible, they called in all their gold coins and declared that their money could no longer be exchanged for gold. This act is known as going off the gold standard. In 1933 the United States joined the other countries of the world and went off the gold standard. Even though the world got over the depression and built up the gold reserves again, the countries have not gone back to the gold standard.

At the present time, there are no gold

Wampum made from mollusc-shell beads was used as money and jewelry by Indians.

coins in circulation in the United States. The dollar cannot be exchanged for gold, and anyone who has gold must sell it to the government (unless it is used in manufacturing, as in jewelry, or in dentistry). Nevertheless, the dollar still has a value of a certain amount of gold. The United States government maintains a large supply of gold at Fort Knox, Kentucky, which it uses to settle foreign trade balances with other countries. (See the article on FOREIGN TRADE.)

During the Civil War the Confederate government of Missouri issued war scrip.

money order

A money order is a paper issued by the Post Office Department. It is like a check on a bank, and makes it possible for people to send money safely through the mail. It is not safe to put bills or coins in a letter that is to be mailed, because the letter may be lost or stolen. A money order guarantees that only the person or business to whom the money is sent will be able to get the money.

An application for a money order must be made on a blank provided in all post offices. When the application has been filled out, giving the name of the sender of the money order, the name of the person who will receive the money, and the amount of money that person is to receive, a post-office official makes out a money order that includes all this information. The person sending the money order gives the official the money he wishes to send, plus an additional small charge, and he receives a receipt for his money. Then he encloses the money order in an envelope and mails it. When the person for whom the money is intended receives the money order, he can exchange it for money at any post office.

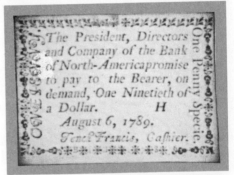
The first United States chartered bank issued paper money worth 1.1 cents.

The pine-tree shilling minted in Boston by John Hull is a noted Colonial coin.

Bronze currency in the form of knives was used as money in ancient China.

The *assignat* of the French Revolution had lands taken by the state as security.

Money orders can be for any amount up to a hundred dollars, and charges for sending them depend upon their amount.

For many years the Post Office Department also sold postal notes, which were somewhat like money orders. Postal notes were discontinued in 1951.

Mongolia

Mongolia is a large region of east central Asia, between China and Soviet Russia. It includes the great GOBI DESERT, about which there is a separate article. It is about one million square miles in area, which is almost four times the size of Texas, and about 3,500,000 people live there, less than half the population of Texas.

Mongolia is divided into two main parts. *Inner Mongolia* is a region of Communist China, 230,000 square miles in size, with a population of about two million. Outer Mongolia, also called the *Mongolian People's Republic,* is supposed to be an independent country but is controlled by Soviet Russia. It is 625,495 square miles in size, with a population of 885,000. Other parts of Mongolia extend into other political divisions of China, such as Manchuria.

THE MONGOL PEOPLE

The people of Mongolia are called

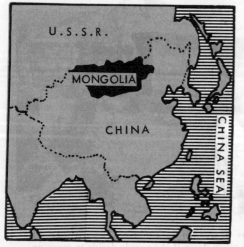

Mongols. They have yellowish skin, straight black hair, and rather square faces with prominent cheekbones and wide noses. Many Mongols are nomads. That is, they seldom stay in one place for long, but constantly move to new homes with their families and flocks. Most of them raise livestock, and a man's wealth is judged according to the number of sheep, cattle and goats that he owns. Most of the people are Lamaists. Lamaism is a form of the Buddhist religion.

Mongols are famous camel-drivers. Marco Polo and other early European travelers to China crossed the Gobi Desert and the rest of Mongolia under their guidance. For hundreds of years, large camel caravans driven by Mongols took goods from north China to Russia and Europe. Roads in Mongolia still follow the routes of the ancient caravans.

In recent times the Mongols have become less nomadic. Their farms produce millet, barley, and wheat. They work at mining iron, coal, gold, lead, zinc, and copper. The Chinese Communist government has built steel mills at Paotow, an important city of Mongolia.

WHAT IT IS LIKE THERE

Mongolia is a high, level region, more than a mile high and bordered on the east, north and northwest by very high mountains. These include the ALTAI MOUNTAINS, about which there is a separate article. The Gobi Desert in the center separates Inner from Outer Mongolia. Mongolia runs as far south as the ancient Great Wall of China.

Most of Mongolia is a very flat country, though it is high above sea level and rises to mountains as high as 12,300 feet in the central part. The region is very dry, and in most spots the only plant is short, tough grass. In many parts, the only buildings are the monasteries belonging to the Buddhist monks. Many of the people live in tents that they can take with them when they move. Only in the

A member of Mongol royalty, wearing high boots, enjoys playing chess with a friend.

Ewing Galloway

Ewing Galloway

Many Mongols are shepherds. They move from one place to another as their sheep and cattle require new grazing land.

Ewing Galloway

A Mongol family has little furniture in its home. The circular grill in the center is used to heat the entire house.

In a typical Mongolian village, the people live in wooden huts that are covered with felt made from sheep wool. The huts can easily be taken down if the people decide to move on.

north, near Soviet Russia, are there any large rivers. Mongolia is very cold in winter and hot in summer.

MONGOLIA IN THE PAST

People have lived in Mongolia for many thousands of years, but the Mongols did not arrive until about six hundred years ago, when GENGHIS KHAN (about whom there is a separate article) established the heart of his great empire in Mongolia. His sons and grandsons increased the empire he founded. In the year 1240 the Mongol empire reached from the Pacific coast of China all the way to the frontiers of Poland and Germany, and included parts of Russia and Hungary, and much of Asia. This empire broke up, but about a hundred years later another Mongol warrior, Tamerlane, or Timur, again established a vast Mongol empire. After Tamerlane's death the Mongol empire declined. There is a separate article about TAMERLANE.

Mongolia never regained importance. The Soviet-style Republic of Outer Mongolia was formed in 1924, with its capital at Ulan Bator, a city of about 70,000. Inner Mongolia fell to the Chinese Communists during the years 1947–1949. The capital is Kalgan, a city of about 150,000.

MONGOLIA. Area, 1,000,000 square miles. Population 3,500,000. Vast, flat region in east central Asia.

mongoose

The mongoose is a fierce little animal that lives in Asia, Africa, and in Spain, where the climate is warm. The mongoose is about 2 feet long. It has a sharp, pointed face with bright eyes. The fur of the mongoose is brown or black, and it has a long, bushy tail. The mongoose is a skillful fighter and it can kill a snake many times its size. Most often the mongoose is the winner in these savage battles, and then it settles down to eat the snake. The mongoose also eats rats, mice, birds, and many other small animals.

The mongoose has great curiosity, and if it spies some interesting object it will go right into a person's house to have a better look. People took the mongoose to Hawaii in order to kill rats. But they discovered that it is fond of killing chickens, and it has become a great nuisance to the farmers. The great English writer, Rudyard Kipling, wrote a popular story about a mongoose named Rikki-tikki-tavi.

Monitor and Merrimac

The *Monitor* and the *Merrimac* were both American warships. During the Civil War they fought against each other in a battle that is famous in naval history. It was the first battle ever fought between ironclad ships; that is, ships covered with iron. The *Merrimac* had belonged to the United States Navy, but it had been scuttled when the Union forces had to leave their naval yard at Portsmouth, Virginia, at the beginning of the Civil War. The Confederates raised the

Am. Museum of Nat. Hist.

The mongoose is small, but it is one of nature's fiercest fighters. It is so fast that it can dodge the poisonous thrusts of a cobra, then seize the snake with its sharp teeth and kill it.

"There's more people than monkeys," complains Bobo, a male macaque, who resents not being listed in the telephone book under "B." (Actually, he chews paper.)

Chicago Park District

sunken ship, changed it into an ironclad, and renamed it the *Virginia.* The rebuilt *Merrimac* defeated several Union ships before it finally met the *Monitor* at Hampton Roads, Virginia, on March 9, 1862. The *Monitor* was a heavy iron ship just built by the Union navy. It was much smaller than the *Merrimac* and had a very peculiar shape. The Confederates made fun of it and called it a "cheesebox on a raft." It looked like a platform with a round tower as it floated in the water. Actually it was so well protected that the *Merrimac* could not hurt it. The battle between the two ships lasted for four hours. Neither ship won a decisive victory, but the *Merrimac* fled to Norfolk and never fought the *Monitor* again. Later the navy made many more ships like the *Monitor.*

monk, a member of a religious order who lives apart from the world. See MONASTERY.

monkey

The monkey is one of the most lively and interesting of all animals. The monkey looks somewhat like man, but not so much as apes do. There are many different kinds of monkey. Usually they are divided into two groups, according to where they live. The monkeys that live in the jungles of Central and South America and Mexico are called the New World monkeys. The monkeys that live in Asia and Africa are called Old World monkeys. There are some important differences between these two groups.

The New World monkeys have more teeth. Their noses are flat, and the nostrils are much farther apart. Almost all of the New World monkeys have tails (called prehensile) with which they can grasp things. This tail is very handy when a monkey wants to travel quickly through the forest. It can use its tail as another arm to swing from one tree to the next.

The monkeys of the Old World have four fewer teeth than the New World monkeys. (The Old World monkey and man both have thirty-two teeth.) The nostrils of the Old World monkey are closer together. None of the Old World monkeys can grasp things with their tails. Many of these monkeys have pouches in their cheeks. They use these pouches to store the fruit, nuts, small birds, and eggs that they eat. Some Old World monkeys eat leaves, and they have no cheek pouches.

Monkeys usually like to sleep at night and are wide awake when the sun comes

Chicago Park District

The capuchin monkey is a well-known American monkey. When excited, it chatters loudly and hops around with great agility.

The Barbary ape, which is really a monkey, peeks at the photographer who is disturbing his meditations on life in the jungle.

N.Y. Zoological Society

Am. Museum of Nat. Hist.

The colobus monkey from Africa seems to think that its white beard requires it to act in a quiet and dignified manner.

"That umpire must be blind! Where's my pop bottle?" Like many monkeys, the howler often looks like a human being.

Chicago Park District

up. Most monkeys live in trees, although some monkeys, such as the Old World baboon, make their homes on the ground. There are tiny monkeys, like the capuchin of South America, which are about as large as a cat. There are large monkeys, like the Old World baboon, which is as tall as a Great Dane dog and very heavy and powerful. Some monkeys are dull brown in color and others are bright yellow. There are monkeys that are covered with hair and monkeys that have no hair. There are friendly, sociable monkeys, such as the rhesus of the Old World, and angry, mean monkeys such as the New World howler.

Monkeys have long been one of man's favorite animals because they are usually full of tricks and have hundreds of funny expressions. Monkeys are intelligent and can be taught to do many tricks. The stunts of monkeys in the circus and in zoos are amusing, and many people have been pleased by the little monkey that the organ grinder has. Some people keep monkeys for pets. You can read about the RHESUS, the CAPUCHIN, and the HOWLER monkeys in separate articles. See also the article on the BARBARY APE.

Monmouth, Duke of

James, Duke of Monmouth, was an Englishman who insisted that he was the son of King Charles II of England and who claimed the right to be king after Charles II died. Monmouth was born about three hundred years ago, in the year 1659. Most of the influential Englishmen did not believe Monmouth was the son of Charles, and when Charles died in 1685, James II, the brother of Charles, was made king. Monmouth found enough supporters to raise a small army in Holland. He landed in England, where he hoped the people would support him and add to his army. He did not get enough support and was defeated by the king's forces. Monmouth was captured and put to death in July, 1685, only six months after the death of the man he said was his father.

monopoly

When different companies are struggling against one another for customers, it is called *free competition,* and it is very good for the public. If one company tries to charge too much, people can buy from another company. But if a single company controls the entire supply of something, it can charge what it pleases and people have to pay the price

or do without. This is called a *monopoly.*

In the years after the Civil War in the United States, companies in the same business began to get together and make secret agreements that they would all charge the same high prices. This was a new kind of monopoly, and was called a *trust.* A "Board of Trustees," representing all the companies, would decide what the prices should be. If some small company outside the trust would try to charge fair, low prices, the trust would set its own prices very low and drive the small company out of business. Then the trust would raise prices again.

The American people became frightened because so many trusts were springing up and were growing very rich and powerful. To prevent this, Congress in 1890 passed a law, called the Sherman Anti-Trust Act because it was introduced by Senator John Sherman of Ohio, to break up these trusts. A newer and stronger law introduced by Henry Clayton, a Congressman from Alabama, and called the Clayton Anti-Trust Act, was passed by Congress in 1914. Today, if a company becomes so big that it can control prices, or if several companies get together to do that, the Department of Justice will use the Anti-Trust laws to stop them.

When big companies in different countries (such as Great Britain, France, Germany, and the United States) make an agreement to control markets, they are called a *cartel.* There is a separate article about CARTELS.

When one person owns or controls the entire supply of something, he is said to *corner the market.* There are many stories about men who have tried to corner the wheat market; that is, to own or to have the only right to buy all the wheat in a country. Since everyone eats bread, a person who could control the price of wheat could make the world's biggest fortune. No one ever succeeded in cornering the wheat market, and today a person would be prevented by law from doing so.

JAMES MONROE

James Monroe was the fifth President of the United States. He served for two terms, from March, 1817, until March, 1825. His administration was known as the "era of good feeling," because there was almost no major political disagreement or financial distress during these years. Monroe became famous for the Monroe Doctrine, the statement in which the United States said it did not want European countries to interfere in the affairs of any country of North, Central, or South America.

Monroe was so popular that he was re-elected without opposition. One member of the electoral college cast his vote against Monroe, although he too wanted Monroe to be elected. He voted against him because he believed that the honor of a unanimous election should be reserved to Washington, who had been re-elected unanimously.

HIS EARLY YEARS

James Monroe was born in Westmoreland County, Virginia, on April 28, 1758. His father was a planter and the family had been in America since 1652. Young James first attended a private school in the county. At the age of 16 he entered William and Mary College. Two years later the Revolutionary War started and he enlisted in the Continental Army. He rose from private to major during the war.

After the fighting was over, he became a member of the Virginia State Legislature, and from 1783 to 1786 he was a

member of the Congress of the Confederation (of American states). This was before the formation of the permanent Congress of the United States, which first met in 1789. Monroe was elected to the United States Senate in 1790.

After his term as Senator, he represented the United States in France, Spain, and England. During his time in France he displeased the government of the United States by showing great friendship toward France. This was considered unwise, because at the same time another representative, John Jay, was in England attempting to negotiate a treaty with Great Britain. At that time, Britain and France were not on friendly terms. It was feared by some Americans at home that Monroe's extreme friendliness toward French officials might cause the British to distrust the intentions of the United States. The United States was trying to keep on equal terms with both, without showing any favor in either direction.

Three years later, in 1799, Monroe was elected governor of Virginia. It was at this time that he proposed settling freed Negro slaves in Africa. Later these freed slaves formed a new country, Liberia, and its capital was named Monrovia in his honor.

Thomas Jefferson was President of the United States in 1803 and wanted to buy the vast territory, then called the Louisiana Territory, which is now the central part of the United States. Jefferson sent

Monroe to buy it from Napoleon, the French emperor. Monroe succeeded, as you can read in the article on the LOUISIANA PURCHASE. Monroe himself said that he was more proud of his contribution to this purchase than of any other thing he had done in his entire public life.

HOW HE BECAME PRESIDENT

James Madison was the next President after Jefferson. At that time England and France were quarreling and in the course of their warfare American ships were captured and American sailors kidnapped by the British. Madison was elected in 1808, and in 1811 he made Monroe his Secretary of State, which is the most important position in the President's cabinet. Therefore Monroe was in charge of the country's foreign affairs during the War of 1812, and after the capture of Washington by the British, in 1813, Monroe took over the office of Secretary of War.

Monroe found both these departments of the government badly disorganized. With great energy and vigor he set to work and made them orderly and efficient in a short space of time. He used his own money to support the city of New Orleans so that it could set up a defense against the British, who were preparing to attack. The Americans won the Battle of New Orleans in 1815.

Monroe had served so well that he was nominated for the Presidency, and elected in the fall of 1816. During his administration he did much to develop the resources of the United States. Florida was bought from Spain, the Missouri Compromise was reached, and the famous MONROE DOCTRINE was stated. (There are separate articles about these events in American history.)

The Monroe Doctrine was part of Monroe's annual message to Congress in the year 1823. It outlined the policy of "neither entangling ourselves in the broils of Europe, nor suffering the powers of the Old World to interfere with the affairs of the New." Monroe added that any attempt on the part of the European powers to "extend their system to any portion of this hemisphere" would be regarded by the United States as "dangerous to our peace and safety," and would accordingly be opposed. The Monroe Doctrine has been an important part of the foreign policy of the United States ever since.

HIS LATER YEARS

After the end of his second term as President, Monroe retired to his estate in Oak Hill, Virginia. There he served as a justice of the peace and presided over the county court. He also served as a member of the board of the University of Virginia, and later took part in the revision of the Virginia State Constitution. Ill health compelled him to resign from this position, and he retired again to his estate at Oak Hill. Soon afterward he moved to his daughter's home in New York, where he spent the rest of his life.

Like John Adams and Thomas Jefferson, Monroe died on the anniversary of the signing of the Declaration of Independence. He died on July 4, 1831, at the age of 73. His body is buried in Hollywood Cemetery, Richmond, Virginia.

MRS. JAMES MONROE

Mrs. Eliza Kortwright Monroe was born in New York, in 1768. Her father was a former British army officer. Eliza Kortwright and James Monroe were married in 1786. They had two daughters. Mrs. Monroe was responsible for the pardon and release from prison of Madame de Lafayette, who had been sentenced to the guillotine during the French Revolution.

Mrs. James Monroe died in 1830, at Oak Hill, Virginia.

Montaigne, Michel de

Michel, Seigneur de Montaigne, was a French writer whose essays are still read throughout the world. He was born in France, in 1533, of a noble family. His education was remarkable. He spoke nothing but Latin until he was 6 years old and had completed a college course at the age of 13.

Montaigne was a brilliant student, but once he had learned a subject he seldom troubled to remember it. He was famous for his bad memory. He could not remember the names of his own servants, often read books he had read before, under the impression that they were new, and forgot the purpose of an errand before it was done. He was also famous for his laziness. His one important work was the writing of the *Essays*. A translation of Montaigne's essays is believed to have been the only book possessed by William Shakespeare. Montaigne died in 1589, at the age of 56, in the chateau in which he was born.

Montana

Montana

Montana is a state in the United States. It is in the northern part of the Rocky Mountains and its nickname is the "Treasure State" because of its rich mineral deposits, especially its vast copper mines. The largest copper mines in the country are in Montana. The state is also famous for its great herds of cattle and sheep and its magnificent mountain scenery. Montana gets its name from a Spanish word meaning "mountainous country."

Montana ranks 4th in size among the states, with 147,138 square miles. In population it ranks 41st, with almost 700,000 people living there. Although Montana is three times as large as New York State, its population is only one-twelfth as large as New York City's. Montana became a state in 1889, and was the 41st state admitted to the United States. The capital is Helena.

THE PEOPLE OF MONTANA

The first settlers in the Montana region, more than two hundred years ago, were French fur-trappers and traders. Later, when gold and silver were discovered, American settlers came in large numbers. They were joined by people from Germany, Ireland, and other European countries. Scandinavians came and settled on farms, and Russians, Italians and English were among the many immigrants who came to work in the growing cities. Today most of the people of Montana are American-born. Thousands of Indians live on large reservations.

More than half the people of Montana live on farms or ranches and raise some of the finest beef cattle and sheep in the country, and large crops of wheat, corn, and other grains. The soil in Montana is so dry that most of the farmers have to use irrigation. Large dams have been built for this purpose on the Missouri and Madison rivers. The Fort Peck Dam on the Missouri River is the largest earth-filled dam in the country and has the third-largest reservoir.

Many people work in the rich mines in the mountains of western Montana. They mine not only copper but also coal, zinc, gold, and silver. Montana leads all other states in the production of manganese, an important mineral in the making of steel. Some of the people work in the large oil and natural gas fields that have been discovered in the past fifty years. In the cities people work at smelting and refining metals, in fruit- and vegetable-canning plants, in flour mills, and in factories that make lumber products. The forests of Montana supply these factories with much yellow pine and Douglas fir.

The largest religious group in Montana is the Roman Catholic, but there are also many Methodists, Lutherans, and Episcopalians.

WHAT MONTANA IS LIKE

Montana is divided into two regions. The eastern two-thirds of the state is part of the Great Plains. It is a farming region that is excellent for the grazing of cattle and sheep. There are wide river valleys and high hills called *buttes* that have been worn down by the wind into strange and beautiful shapes. In the southeastern part of the state are the Montana *badlands* that many people come to see for their remarkable rock formations. In these rocks scientists have found fossils (old skeletons) of animals that lived millions of years ago.

The western part of Montana is rugged and mountainous. These high ranges of the Rocky Mountains are part of the Continental Divide, sometimes called the "Great Divide." The mountains are very beautiful, and people go there on their vacations to enjoy fishing, hunting, and mountain-climbing. Between the high mountain ranges lie fertile valleys where the farmers grow fruits and vegetables. Many of these valleys contain lakes.

The great mining region of Montana is in this western section. In its center is the important city of Butte, which has been described as "a mile high and a mile deep" because there are more than two thousand miles of tunnels, made by miners, under the city. More than two and a half billion dollars worth of copper and silver have been mined in this region since 1864. Butte is said to be built over "the richest hill in the world."

The climate of Montana is dry and healthful. West of the Continental Divide the winters are milder and the summers cooler than east of the Divide. In the eastern part the summers are often very hot and the winters very cold, with blizzards and heavy snowfalls. Montana has been known to have hailstorms in which the hailstones were big enough to kill barnyard animals. The average temperature in winter is about 18 degrees and in summer about 68 degrees.

Many wild animals live in the dense forests of Montana. Hunters have found deer, moose, grizzly bears and many small fur-bearing animals such as the muskrat, beaver, mink, and fox.

For many years the people used the Missouri and Clark Fork rivers, with their many tributaries, as the chief means of transportation. It took the people a long time to build good roads because of the great size of the state and because it was so difficult to get through the mountains. Today there are thousands of miles of paved roads and railroads to almost all parts of the state. There are airports in the important cities.

THE GOVERNMENT OF MONTANA

Montana, like most other states, has a Governor and a Legislature. The Governor is elected for a four-year term. The Legislature is composed of a Senate and

Montana's Indian wars and booming mining towns gave it a violent history.

1. Graves at Custer Battlefield, site of his famous "last stand."

2. An actual photograph of Custer and a group of his Indian scouts.

3. A reconstruction of the express station at Virginia City in 1860.

4. A photograph of Last Chance Gulch, the boom town that became Helena.

Nat'l Park Service

Northern Pacific Railway

Montana Chamber of Commerce

Northern Pacific Railway

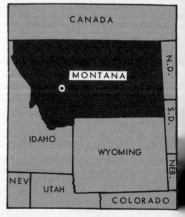

Montana Chamber of Commerce

Above: The Montana state capitol in Helena is the headquarters of the state government. It also houses many historical paintings of the old West. *Left:* The bitterroot, state flower.

Montana Chamber of Commerce Photos

Because of Montana's many snow-covered peaks, the Indians called it "land of the shining mountains." Today the fabulous mountain scenery is relieved by the vast farms of the low-lying regions.

1. Bear grass in bloom. Live glaciers are in the background.

2. Wastelands along the Yellowstone, with startling rock formations.

3. Lewis and Clark Cavern, largest limestone cave in the Northwest.

4. Livestock in Flathead Valley.

5. Salish Indians performing an old tribal dance.

Montana Highway Photos

There are more natural resources in Montana to each member of the population than in any other state. Wheat and livestock are the basis of agriculture. Mining, food processing and lumbering are important industries. The many sparsely populated areas are the home of wild animals. The streams and lakes yield many fish.

Glasgow Chamber of Commerce

Mont. Ch. of Com.   Victor Chem. Co.   U.S. Forest Serv.   Mont. Ch. of Com.

Fish and Wildlife Service

1. Fort Peck Dam on Milk River provides for, and irrigates, a large farm region.

2. Harvesting Montana wheat.

3. Logs cut in the northwest.

4. A chemical plant. This industry is growing in Butte.

5. Branding time on the ranch.

6. Breaking a beaver dam that bottled up a good trout stream.

a House of Representatives. The members of the Senate are elected for a four-year term. The members of the House of Representatives are elected for a two-year term. Judges are elected for a six-year term. The capital is Helena. There are 56 counties.

Everybody has to go to school between the ages of 8 and 16. There are about 1,199 public schools, including 175 high schools, and 11 colleges, universities, and other schools of higher learning. Among the principal colleges and universities are:

Montana State University, at Missoula. Enrollment, 2,202 in 1953 (1,514 men, 688 women).

Montana State College, at Bozeman. Enrollment, 2,000 in 1953 (1,343 men, 657 women).

Montana School of Mines, at Butte. Enrollment, 298 in 1953 (286 men, 12 women).

CHIEF CITIES OF MONTANA

The leading cities of Montana, with populations from the 1950 census, are:

Great Falls, population 39,214, the largest city in the state. There is a separate article about GREAT FALLS.

Helena, population 17,581, the state capital and fifth-largest city. There is a separate aritcle about HELENA.

Butte, population 33,251, the second-largest city. There is a separate article about BUTTE.

Billings, population 31,834, the third-largest city, trading and shipping center for livestock, in the south central part of the state.

MONTANA IN THE PAST

The first white men to enter the Montana region, more than two hundred years ago, were French fur-trappers and traders. They found many Indian tribes living in the plains and the mountains. In 1805, Lewis and Clark crossed Montana. In the next few years fur-trading posts were established but the region re-

Montana Chamber of Commerce

Glacier National Park in Montana offers beautiful scenery and fine boating, fishing, and hiking. In the background is Going-to-the-Sun Mountain.

mained mostly uninhabited for a long time. In 1852 gold was discovered, and miners began coming from all over the United States. Other rich mines were discovered, and the population grew rapidly.

For a time Montana was part of the Idaho Territory, but in 1864 it became a separate territory and in 1889 it became a state.

During these early years the people had many bitter encounters with the Indians. One of the historic battles was in 1876, at Little Bighorn, where General George Custer of the United States Army and his 226 men were wiped out by Sioux Indians.

Since World War II, Montana has built new electric power plants and has continued to expand its program for more irrigation and water conservation.

PLACES TO SEE IN MONTANA

Glacier National Park, 1,013,129 acres, in the northwest, on the Canadian border, on U.S. Route 2. Superb Rocky Mountain scenery forms part of the Waterton-Glacier International Peace Park.

Yellowstone National Park, 151,624 acres, in the southwest, on the Wyoming border, on U.S. Route 89. Most of this park is in Wyoming. Spectacular falls and canyons made by the Yellowstone River.

Big Hole Battlefield National Monument, 200 acres, about 60 miles west of Butte, in the southwest, on State Highway 43. Site of an important battle along the route of the famous retreat of Chief Joseph and his Nez Percé Indians, in 1877.

Custer Battlefield National Monument, 765 acres, about 55 miles east of Billings, in the southeast, on U.S. Route 87. Site of the famous Battle of the Little Big Horn.

Granite Peak, 12,850 feet high, 30 miles west of Red Lodge, in the south, west of U.S. Route 12. The highest point in Montana, with a beautiful view for hundreds of miles around.

Fort Peck Recreational Area, 18 miles south of Glasgow, in the northeast, south of U.S. Route 2. A beautiful vacation spot, with boating, fishing, and swimming.

The great Yellowstone National Park, visited by thousands of tourists from all over the nation every year, has some of Montana's most dramatic scenery.

Montana Chamber of Commerce

MONTANA. Area, 147,138 square miles. Population (1957 estimate) 666,000. Capital, Helena. Nickname, the Treasure State. Motto, *Oro y Plata* (Gold and Silver). Flower, bitterroot. Bird, meadowlark. Song, "Montana." Admitted to Union, November 8, 1889. Official abbreviation, Mont.

Montcalm, Louis Joseph de

Louis Joseph de Montcalm was the commander of the French forces during the French and Indian Wars. In these wars, the French, who had many possessions in the northern United States and in Canada, joined with the Indians to drive the English out of this territory. The French lost the wars and lost most of their territories. Montcalm was killed during the most important battle of the war, the battle of Quebec in 1759. Wolfe, the head of the English armies, was also killed during this battle.

Montcalm was born in France in 1712. He was a marquis, a nobleman. He was only 14 years old when he entered the French army. He had become well known as a soldier before he was appointed the commander of all the troops in Canada in 1756. He was skillful and courageous in the three campaigns at Fort Ontario and Fort William Henry before he was finally defeated at the battle of Quebec.

Monte Cassino

Monte Cassino is a hill, or low mountain, in southern Italy. It is the site of a famous monastery, also called Monte Cassino, that was built more than 1,500 years ago (in the year 529) by St. Benedict. The hill overlooks the town of Cassino, which has a population of about 9,000.

Monte Cassino and the town of Cassino were very important and much talked about in World War II, during the ITALIAN CAMPAIGN (about which there is a separate article). Allied forces had landed in Italy and were trying to move north. German forces were oppos ing them. The Germans established themselves on the hill, which gave them such an advantage that the Allies could not get past. The Allies wanted the Germans to stop using the monastery as a defense post, so that the historic building could be spared, but the Germans would not leave it. The Allies then drove the Germans from the hill with bombs and artillery, but in doing this they damaged the monastery severely.

Montenegro

Montenegro is a small state, called a constituent republic, in southern Yugoslavia. It has many mountains. Its area is 5,343 square miles, which is a little larger than Connecticut. More than 375,000 people live there, but this is less than one-fifth the population of Connecticut. The capital of Montenegro is Titograd, a city of about 12,000. Formerly this city was called Podgoritsa. Its name was changed in honor of Tito, the Yugoslavian dictator.

The people of Montenegro have to work very hard to make a living. In most parts it is difficult to grow crops. Nevertheless farmers there grow wheat and corn in the plains and some barley and rye in the mountains. Most of the people raise sheep and goats, which they let graze in the mountains. There are hardly any factories, but the industrious people make many things at home. In the large forests of eastern Montenegro many people work as lumberjacks.

From 1910 to 1918 Montenegro was an independent kingdom. After World War I it became part of Yugoslavia. Italian soldiers occupied it during World War II.

MONTENEGRO. Area, 5,343 square miles. Population, 376,573. Capital, Titograd. In southern Yugoslavia.

Montessori, Maria

Maria Montessori was an Italian teacher and doctor who devised a system for teaching small children. She believed

Moore-McCormack Lines

Montevideo, capital of Uruguay, is a modern city. It has many public parks, as well as a fine beach on Horseshoe Bay.

that children from 1 to 5 years of age could be best taught by giving them freedom of action and through games and exercises designed to develop their senses of touch, sight, and hearing. The teacher in her system acts mostly as a guide, and the children learn through trial and error. The Montessori method is widely used in European and American nursery schools or kindergartens. Maria Montessori was born in 1870. She founded a school for mentally retarded children, and her success with them led to her ideas on the training of normally intelligent children. The first Montessori nursery school was founded in Rome in 1907. Maria Montessori died in 1952.

Montevideo

Montevideo is the capital and biggest city of Uruguay. It is on the La Plata River, and is the most important port in the country. The busy docks handle most of Uruguay's trade with other nations. More than 700,000 people live in Montevideo. Most of the people work in the large slaughterhouses and meat-processing plants. Farmers ship their cattle, sheep, and hogs from the plains of Uruguay to Montevideo. The meat, wool, and many by-products that are prepared in Montevideo are then shipped to countries all over the world. About one-third of the people of Montevideo are French, Spanish, or Italian.

Montevideo is one of the most beautiful and modern cities in South America. It has many fine boulevards, parks, and buildings, and it is well-known for its clean appearance and excellent methods of sanitation. Montevideo is sometimes called the "City of Roses" because of the hundreds of varieties of beautiful roses that bloom late in autumn. The city also has many fine beach resorts, and it is one of the most popular vacation places in South America.

Montevideo was settled by the Spanish in 1726. When Uruguay won its independence in 1828, Montevideo was made the capital.

MONTEVIDEO, URUGUAY. Population (1943 census) 708,233. Capital of Uruguay. Capital, department of Montevideo. On the La Plata River.

Montezuma

Montezuma was the name of rulers of the Aztec people, a group of American Indians who lived in ancient Mexico. Montezuma I was born about the year 1390, and became emperor about 1437, when he was nearly 50 years old. During his reign he waged many wars on neighboring tribes and succeeded in making the Aztec Empire large and powerful. It extended throughout the central and southern part of Mexico, from the Gulf of Mexico to the Pacific Ocean. (There is a separate article on the AZTECS.) Montezuma I reigned for about 35 years, dying about the year 1470.

Montezuma II was born about 1480 and became the Aztec emperor in 1502. Under him the Aztec Empire reached its greatest size. His campaigns extended as far as Nicaragua and Honduras. In 1519 there were about five million people in his empire.

At that time Spaniards, commanded by Hernando Cortez, began an invasion of Mexico. Montezuma decided to greet the Spanish invaders as friends. At first Cortez treated him with respect, but later there was a battle between Spaniards and Mexicans and Cortez arrested Montezuma and put him in prison. After his release, Montezuma was humble and beaten. He tried to make an address to his people and tell them they should try to get along with the Spaniards, but an angry Mexican threw a rock at him. It struck him in the temple and a few days later he died, in 1520, the last of the Aztec emperors.

Montfort, Simon de

Simon de Montfort was an English statesman who lived about seven hundred years ago. He is given credit for having originated the idea of the House of Commons in the British Parliament. Montfort was born about the year 1208 in France.

Montfort inherited an English title and when he was about 20 years old he went to England and was recognized as Earl of Leicester by King Henry III. Montfort married the king's sister Eleanor and became one of the king's advisers. Later he lost favor with the king and was dismissed.

At this time Henry was being very harsh with the barons and nobles of England. Montfort led them in a protest to the king and forced Henry to turn the government over to a committee of fifteen noblemen. Several years later, the king went back on his agreement and the barons took up arms against him. In a great battle at the town of Lewes, Montfort captured the king and thus became so powerful that he was really the ruler of England.

Montfort called together a Parliament that for the first time included not only representatives of the nobles but also knights and citizens from counties and towns. The Great Parliament has been called the first House of Commons. The fighting went on, however, and in 1265 Montfort was killed in a battle against forces that were trying to restore the king to the throne.

Montgomery

Montgomery is the capital and third-largest city of the state of Alabama. It is on the Alabama River in the "Black Belt" section, which is one of the most fertile regions in the United States. Montgomery is an important manufacturing center, and one of the biggest cotton and cattle markets in the South. More than 100,000 people live in Montgomery. Many of them work in factories that make canned goods, cottonseed oil, candy, and lumber products.

Many people of Montgomery are proud that they are Southerners and that their city played an important part in the Civil War. The state capitol building was the first capitol of the Confederate States of America. Jefferson Davis, the President of the Confederacy, lived in a house in Montgomery that is called the "First White House of the Confederacy." It is now a museum that people may visit.

Montgomery was settled in 1817, and was first called New Philadelphia. Two years later it was given its present name. In 1846, Montgomery was made the capital of Alabama. Today Montgomery is the most important railroad center in the state. Maxwell and Gunter United States Air Force bases are there.

MONTGOMERY, ALABAMA. Population (1950 census) 106,525. Capital, Alabama. County seat, Montgomery County. On the Alabama River. Settled, 1817.

Montgomery, Bernard

Bernard Law Montgomery became famous during World War II when he led the British Eighth Army to victory in North Africa. Later he was for a time commander of all the ground forces in the campaign that began with the invasion at Normandy, France, and ended with the surrender of Germany to the Allied armies. Montgomery was born  in Ireland in 1887. He was a captain in the British army during World War I. Early in World War II he was in command of a division of the British army fighting in France. In 1944 he was given the rank of field marshal, the highest military rank possible. In 1946 he was given the title of Viscount Montgomery of Alamein, which made him a member of the nobility and of the House of Lords in the British Parliament. After the war Montgomery became the commander of the British zone of Germany and then the head of the staff of the British army. He also wrote several accounts of his campaigns during World War II.

month

A month is one of the twelve parts of a year. The twelve months, in order, are JANUARY, FEBRUARY, MARCH, APRIL, MAY, JUNE, JULY, AUGUST, SEPTEMBER, OCTOBER, NOVEMBER, and DECEMBER, about all of which there are separate articles. These names were used by the Romans two thousand years ago, but the length and order of the months have been changed several times since then.

A month originally was the time it takes the moon to make one complete turn around the earth. This is 27 days and almost 8 hours, called a *sidereal* month. Later, a month was the period of time from one new moon to another. This is called a *synodic month*. This time is about 29½ days and is closer to the length of the *calendar,* or *civil,* month fixed by law.

January, March, May, July, August, October and December each has 31 days. April, June, September and November each has 30 days. February usually has only 28 days, but every leap year it is given an additional day, making it 29 days long.

The following verse is the usual way of remembering the number of days in the months:

Thirty days has September,
April, June, and November.
All the rest have thirty-one,
Save February, which alone
Has twenty-eight, except the time
When leap year gives it twenty-nine.

Montpelier

Montpelier is the capital city of the state of Vermont. It is in the valley of the Green Mountains in the center of the state, on the Winooski River. Almost nine thousand people live in Montpelier. Many of them are in the insurance business. Some of them make granite memorials and others work in factories where they manufacture machinery, plastics, and wood products. There are several railroads that go to Montpelier, and there is an airport. Vermont Junior College is at Montpelier.

The capitol is a fine-looking granite building with a dome-shaped top. It was rebuilt about a hundred years ago after the old capitol was destroyed by fire. In the capitol building there is a museum showing things that have to do with the history of the people of Vermont.

Montpelier was settled in 1787. It was named after a city in France. Montpelier was the birthplace of George Dewey, a great admiral in the United States Navy.

MONTPELIER, VERMONT. Population (1950 census) 8,585. Capital, Vermont. County seat, Washington County. On the Winooski River. Settled 1787.

Montreal

Montreal, in the province of Quebec, is the largest city in Canada. It is on Montreal Island in the St. Lawrence River. Nearly a million and a half people live in Montreal. Most of them are of

Montreal, Canada's largest city, is an important business and transportation center. It is a busy but friendly city visited by vacationists from the United States and Canada.

Canadian Pacific Railway

French descent and speak Canadian French as well as English. This large French population makes Montreal the world's largest French city outside of France.

Montreal is the leading business city of Canada. Railroads from all over Canada and steamers that come down the St. Lawrence from the Great Lakes take goods to Montreal. Many of these goods are then put into ocean-going vessels bound for other major ports of the world. Montreal is farther inland than any other major ocean port in the world.

Many of the people of Montreal work in factories, where they make railroad cars, chemicals, paper, electrical equipment, aircraft, clothing, and other products. There are large food-processing plants. The Montreal Stock Exchange is important throughout the world, and the Bank of Montreal, which opened in 1817, is one of the largest in the world.

Montreal is an interesting place to visit. Though most of the city is very modern, there are some old sections that resemble a French city of a hundred years ago. Mount Royal, 869 feet high, overlooks the city. There is a lookout station near the top where visitors can go and look down over the entire city to the St. Lawrence beyond. Horse-drawn carriages carry people to the top of the hill. Montreal has several large parks, including one with a "flower" clock. The hands, numerals and face of the clock are planted with different-colored flowers, and when they are in bloom the clock is very beautiful.

In Montreal there are a fine art gallery and a museum of Canadian history, and also McGill University and the University of Montreal (where courses are given in French). There are many churches, including St. James Cathedral, which is built to look like St. Peter's in Rome. Many pilgrims visit St. Joseph's Oratory, which is one of the best-known Catholic shrines in America.

The French explorer Jacques Cartier visited the site of modern Montreal in the year 1535, when it was an Indian village. The first settlers came about a hundred years later. Most of them were fur traders, and the settlement grew as trade with the Indians expanded. Montreal remained a French possession until 1760, when it surrendered to the British. During the Revolutionary War, American forces occupied Montreal for a short time. In 1832, it became a city.

MONTREAL, QUEBEC. Population (in 1952) 1,320,232. In Hochelaga County. Founded, 1642.

moon

A moon is any heavenly body that revolves around a planet. A moon is also called a satellite. The most familiar moon is the one that revolves around the earth. Many other planets have moons. The planet Jupiter has twelve moons. Mars has two, Uranus, five, Saturn nine (and millions more in its surrounding rings), and Neptune two.

The earth has only the one moon. It is about 2,100 miles wide, and about eighty times lighter than the earth. For that reason, the moon's force of gravity is much less than the earth's. A person who weighs 100 pounds on the earth would weigh only 17 pounds on the moon.

The moon makes a wonderful subject for the astronomer's telescope. On most nights it can be seen very clearly with the naked eye. One reason is that it is the heavenly body nearest to the earth, about 240,000 miles away. Another reason is that the moon has no atmosphere. There are no gases surrounding it to block out the light from the sun. It is this light that causes the moon to shine. The moon has no light of its own.

At certain times of the month, spots can be seen on the moon. Occasionally these spots seem to form the face of a smiling "man in the moon." In spite of many stories written about the strange people on the moon, there is no life on the moon. There is no air, water or soil to support life if it somehow did get on the moon. During the day, the temperature on the moon reaches as high as 212 degrees on the Fahrenheit thermometer, and during the night, it drops to 150 degrees below zero. If there were no other reason, the extreme temperatures on the moon would be enough to make life unbearable.

THE CRATERS

The spots seen on the moon are really large chains of mountains, deep holes or craters, and long stretches of flat plains. There are about 30,000 craters. Many of them have been named after famous men such as Copernicus, Plato, and Galileo. The craters are huge pits, some a hundred miles across. The sides rise straight up like walls many miles high. On the outside of the holes the ground usually drops away sharply.

Scientists have many theories about how these craters were made. One theory is that the craters were made by bubbles bursting in the hot melted rock of the moon when it was first created. Another theory is that after the moon cooled, huge pieces of rock, traveling at great

The diagram shows how the sun's rays hit the moon as it travels around the earth (E). The outer circle shows the eight phases of the moon as seen from the earth.

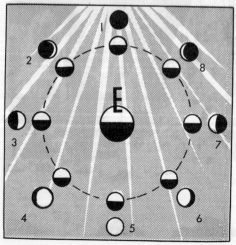

speed through space, may have hit the moon so hard that they left holes, just as a stone does when it is thrown into the sand.

The moon turns on its axis in the same way as the earth turns on its axis. It takes the moon about the same time to make one complete turn on its axis as it does to make one complete turn about the earth. For this reason, the moon keeps the same face toward the earth at all times. We always see the face of the man in the moon but never the back of his head.

PHASES OF THE MOON

Always one half of the moon is lighted by the sun, but we do not always see this lighted half, because the moon is moving around the earth at about 2,300 miles an hour and changing its position. It takes the moon about 27 days and 8 hours to go once around the earth. This is called the *sidereal period*.

Sometimes we can see all of the lighted half of the moon. Then we have a full moon. When we seen no moon at all, the moon is almost between the earth and the sun. We cannot see the moon then because its dark side is turned to us. The sun's light is so bright that the unlighted moon is lost in its brightness. We call this the new moon. The time between new moons is called the *synodic period* and is about 29½ days. This is the basis for the month.

When we see only a thin moon, then we are looking at it from away off on one side. This thin part is called a *crescent,* which means "increasing." When we see only a half moon, the moon is on one side of the earth. When we see the moon full-faced, it is almost behind the earth and the sun is in front of the earth. The different positions of the moon are called its phases.

ECLIPSES

Sometimes the earth gets between the sun and the moon, and the sunlight can-

Yerkes Observatory Photos

The moon is of great interest to astronomers because it is so close to the earth that it can easily be studied.

1. The old moon in the arms of the new. The slender crescent seems to embrace the earth-lit night portion.

2. An eclipse of the sun. The moon is encircled by a corona, or crown, of sunlight.

3. The still, dead surface of the moon. Some craters are almost 150 miles across.

4. An artist's idea of the moon's landscape. Mountains rise to 20,000 feet.

not shine on the moon. So the moon's light gets very dull, until we can scarcely see it. This is an eclipse of the moon. An eclipse means that something is shutting off the light from something else. The earth keeps the sun from shining on the moon for about two hours during an eclipse of the moon.

There can be an eclipse of the sun, too. This happens when the moon gets between the earth and the sun. Then the sunlight is shut off from part of the earth.

THE HARVEST MOON

At a certain time of the year the full moon rises at nearly the same time for several nights and keeps shining for many hours. This happens in autumn, or harvest time, when the farmers take in their crops. At this time many farmers work late at night by the light of the moon. That is why the early autumn full moon is called the harvest moon.

TIDES

There is a much more important thing the moon does for the earth. It keeps the waters of the earth moving all the time, in the rising and falling movements that are called tides. The moon makes the tides. As it goes around the earth, it pulls on the earth by its force of gravity. This pulls the waters back and forth.

Mooney, Cardinal

Edward Francis Mooney was a priest of the Roman Catholic Church who was made a cardinal. Cardinals are called princes of the Church. Edward Mooney was born in Mount Savage, Maryland, in 1882. He went to school at St. Mary's Seminary in Baltimore, Maryland, and then in Rome, Italy. When he was 26 years old he became a priest. In 1933 he was made Bishop of Rochester, and in 1937 he was made the first Archbishop of Detroit. Nine years later he was appointed a cardinal. Cardinal Mooney did much important work in promoting the welfare of people in Detroit and was a great friend of labor unions. He was a gracious and gentle man with a good sense of humor. He died in 1958.

moonflower

The moonflower is a climbing plant that is a member of the morning glory family. It grows in the tropical parts of America, where the climate is very warm. In the United States, the moonflower grows in Florida and elsewhere in the South. It is a perennial, which means that it grows from the same roots every year. The moonflower vine grows to be almost twenty feet high. It can be trained to grow very well on fences, porches, and trellises. It will also grow over a low tree or bush. The moonflower is a beautiful plant with many large heart-shaped leaves. The kind that is most often seen has white flowers that are about six inches across. Another kind of moonflower has smaller, purple blossoms. The moonflower gets its name because the flowers open at night and close during the day. Moonflowers have a very sweet smell.

moonstone

A moonstone is a kind of gem. It has a bright, milky, bluish color much like the full moon's. When you look at a moonstone, you see glowing beneath its surface a milky white line of light. Ever since ancient times, superstitious people have believed that this glow grows brighter as the moon becomes fuller and dies out as the moon wanes. Of course, this is really not true. In ancient India, people believed that if a man put a moonstone in his mouth he would speak beautiful words to the woman he loved.

Scientists tell us that moonstone is a rare kind of a very common rock called feldspar. The best moonstones are found in Ceylon, Burma, and Madagascar.

A kind of rock called satin spar looks very much like moonstone. It is much softer than real moonstone, and soon loses its polish. An ancient Roman naturalist named Pliny complained that dishonest jewelers sold satin spar for real moonstone.

Moore, Thomas

Thomas Moore was an Irish poet who lived more than 150 years ago. He was the most popular of all poets of his period, with the possible exception of Lord Byron. Moore was born in Dublin in 1779, and attended Trinity College in that city. He started to study law, but at the age of 21 he published a volume of poems entitled *Anacreon,* and thereafter earned his living as a writer. His best-known works include a long romantic poem called *Lalla Rookh,* and shorter poems called *Irish Melodies,* many of which were written to fit Irish tunes that he knew. One of the most famous is known and sung today as *Believe Me If All Those Endearing Young Charms.*

Moore was a fine singer, and often entertained his friends with his own songs.

Moore died in 1852, at the age of 72.

Moors

The Moors are a people who now live along the Mediterranean coast of North Africa, chiefly in Morocco. They are of Arab and Berber ancestry, speak the Arabic language, and follow the religion of Mohammed. Othello, the hero of Shakespeare's famous tragedy, is a Moor. From this play, many people get the idea that the Moors are Negroes. Actually they are not.

The religion of the Moors is very important in their history. They first became followers of Mohammed about 1,200 years ago. Soon they were the fiercest fighters in the holy wars against the Christians, whom they called infidels (non-believers in Mohammedanism). In the year 711, the Arabs and Moors invaded Spain, and soon they occupied most of the country. At the same time the Moors also became more and more powerful in North Africa, until finally they ruled both Spain and Morocco.

Spanish Tourist Inform. Office

There are many examples of Moorish architecture in Spain. The Alcazar at Seville is one of the finest.

In Spain, the Moors founded a great civilization. The most powerful Moorish state was at Cordoba. They built beautiful buildings and opened fine universities. Other Moorish cities were Toledo and Seville. Then, gradually, the Moors began to lose power. The Caliphate (state) of Cordoba fell to Spanish forces in 1031. In 1212, the Spanish broke the Moorish hold on Spain and only the Moorish kingdom at Granada remained. About 280 years passed before King Ferdinand was able to defeat the Moors completely. This took place in 1492, the same year that Columbus discovered America.

The Moors were given the choice of either being driven out of Spain or of becoming Christians. Many of them became Christians, and were called Moriscos. The Spanish government never trusted them, and they were often persecuted. In the late 16th century the Moriscos revolted and most of them were forced to leave Spain.

Anyone who visits Spain is impressed with the great influence of the Moors on that country. Many of the most beautiful buildings are of Moorish origin and have a very distinctive style. Just as important was the learning that the Moors brought to Spain, and therefore to Europe. They knew a great deal about science, and this helped modern Europe to develop.

moose

The moose is a large member of the deer family. It makes its home in Europe, the United States, and parts of Canada. The moose is a strange-looking animal with great hunching shoulders, a short neck, and long skinny legs. It has long, shaggy, brown hair and a grayish face and stomach. Its antlers are flat and very large, sometimes spreading six feet across. Hanging from its throat is a loose fold of skin covered with long hair; this is called a *bell*. It has a large underlip that sticks out. The moose is about six feet high at the shoulder and weighs more than a thousand pounds. The moose eats grass and leaves and tender branches. It cannot bend its short neck down low enough to eat grass or drink water, but must get down on its knees to eat. Usually the moose prefers to reach up and eat the leaves that grow on small trees. It is fond

Copyright Curriculum Films, Inc.

A moose's short neck and long legs make grazing difficult. Often, to reach the tender top leaves, a moose presses a sapling toward the ground with its body.

of water lilies and in the summer will wade out into ponds to get them.

The moose is usually a timid animal, but in the autumn, during the mating season, the males become fierce and fight savage battles for the females. The female moose most often has one calf in the spring, although sometimes two or three are born. There were once thousands of moose but so many of them have been killed that there are very few now, and they are protected by law.

Moose, Loyal Order of

The Loyal Order of Moose is a fraternal organization, or a kind of club, for men. Members join to enjoy one another's company, but also to take part in the charitable work of the organization. Members over 65 who have been members for a certain length of time may wish to live at the old folks' home called Moosehaven in Orange Park, Florida. The Moose also supports the orphaned children of its former members at a childrens "city" in Mooseheart, Illinois. The Loyal Order of Moose has about one million members, who are organized in about 1,700 individual lodges throughout the United States. Wives and daughters of members may join the women's auxiliary, known as the Women of the Moose, which has about 250,000 members. Headquarters of both organizations is in Mooseheart. The head of the Moose is known as the director general. At meetings of the lodges the officers wear special collars, with a moosehead insignia, to designate their office, and there are special passwords.

Moravia

Moravia is a province in Czechoslovakia. Its area is about 8,000 square miles, almost the same as the state of Massachusetts, and more than two million people live there. Moravia is a beautiful and fertile region, surrounded by mountains. Most of the people follow the Roman Catholic religion, and there are also many Lutherans. Many of them are farmers who raise grain, flax, and sugar beets. Others work in cities manufacturing cotton and woolen goods, leather goods, and machinery. The main city is Brno. (There is a separate article about BRNO.)

Moravia was given its name by Slavs who settled there more than a thousand years ago. More than four hundred years ago Moravia, then connected with Bohemia, became part of the Austrian Empire. In 1918 it became part of the newly formed Republic of Czechoslovakia. During World War II Moravia was a protectorate of Germany, but after the war it was restored to Czechoslovakia.

MORAVIA. Area, 8,219 square miles. Population (in 1948) 2,293,773. Province in central Czechoslovakia.

Moravians

Moravians are members of a Christian church, called the Moravian Church, or the Renewed Church of the Brethren. Moravians recognize Jesus as the source of all truth, and imitate the forms of worshiping God used by the Apostles, as told in the New Testament. The first Moravians were followers of John Huss, about whom there is a separate article. They lived in Moravia and Bohemia, in what is now Czechoslovakia. This was five hundred years ago. They were persecuted for a long time. After the Thirty Years' War, few Moravians were left. They were called the "hidden seed" and secretly kept the Moravian Church alive. As their numbers grew, the Moravians sent missionaries all over the world. Many Moravians came to colonial America, and settled in Pennsylvania. There they founded many cities, including Bethlehem and Nazareth in Pennsylvania. Many people visit Moravian churches to hear the singing. Moravian hymns are popular with people of all religions.

More, Sir Thomas

Sir Thomas More was an English statesman and writer. He is best known

for having invented the word "Utopia" as a term for an ideal country. He used the word as the title of one of the books he wrote. More was born in London in 1480 and attended Oxford University. He became a lawyer and was a very successful one. His skill as an orator won him many political positions, and eventually he became a Member of Parliament.

At one time, More was a friend of King Henry VIII, but he disapproved when Henry divorced his first wife, Catherine of Aragon, and married Anne Boleyn. Because he refused to acknowledge this second marriage, More was charged with treason, and in 1535 he was condemned to death. He was beheaded on July 6, 1535. His last act was to move aside his beard before the executioner struck, saying: "Pity that should be cut; that has not committed treason."

Sir Thomas More was a very pious man, and in 1935 the Roman Catholic Church proclaimed him a saint, so he is also St. Thomas More. His feast day is July 9.

Morgan, Henry

Henry Morgan was a pirate who lived about three hundred years ago. Later he became a respectable and important man, and eventually was made lieutenant governor of Jamaica. He was born on a farm in Wales about the year 1635. He was of an adventurous nature, and farm life was too quiet for him. He went to sea, and for many years he was a professional pirate. The island of St. Catherine in the West Indies was his headquarters for some time, and much of his piracy was done around the Caribbean Sea. He had a large crew of pirates, adventurers from all parts of Europe. He made a fortune over a period of years, and was finally satisfied that he had treasure enough to live in luxury the rest of his life. He settled in Jamaica, and King Charles II of England appointed him lieutenant governor of the island and gave him a knighthood, which made him Sir Henry Morgan. He died in 1688.

Morgan, House of

One of the most famous banking firms in the world is called the "House of Morgan." The first member of the Morgan family to become a banker was Junius Spenser Morgan, who was born in Springfield, Massachusetts, in 1813. He went into the dry-goods business in Hartford, Connecticut, and later in Boston, and made large profits. When he was about 40 years old he became a banker and was even more successful. At his death in 1890 he was worth about ten million dollars.

John Pierpont Morgan, the son of Junius, was the most famous member of the Morgan family. He is usually called Pierpont Morgan. He did not enter his father's banking firm but formed a different one, whose chief office came to be in New York City. He was born in 1837 and became active in the banking business during the period following the Civil War, when great industrial and railroad firms were being formed. J. Pierpont Morgan persuaded rich men in England and European countries to invest in these firms, and he made big commissions. He found the investors needed to supply the money to found the United States Steel Corporation, which for many years was the biggest company in the world. He died in 1913.

The son of J. Pierpont Morgan, who had the same name but was always called J. P. Morgan, carried on the work of his father's banking house, which was called J. P. Morgan and Company. He was born in 1867 and died in 1943.

Both J. Pierpont Morgan and his son J. P. Morgan were interested in art and literature. They had famous collections of paintings and they supported a fine library in New York City.

Mormon

A Mormon is a person who belongs to the Church of Jesus Christ of Latter-Day Saints. This Church, a Christian sect, was founded about 125 years ago by Joseph Smith, in Palmyra, New York. In 1827, he reported that an angel had appeared to him and had given him a mission to found a Church; and had led him to gold plates on which was written the Book of Mormon, or Golden Bible. Smith said the book was written by the prophet Mormon, who lived in New York 1,550 years ago, and that Mormon had hidden the Golden Bible so that it was unknown until Joseph Smith found it.

By 1831, Joseph Smith had many followers. He moved to Kirtland, Ohio, and soon new believers joined him from all over the United States. These people had very deep faith, but their beliefs were different from those of their neighbors and the Mormons were often attacked and made the butt of jokes. Other Mormon settlements were opened in Missouri. People there were also unfriendly, and Joseph Smith and many others were put in jail. Finally, the Mormons left Missouri and moved to Illinois. There they founded a city called Nauvoo. Though they were admired for the way they built the city, their customs made many people angry. The governor of Illinois put Joseph Smith and his brother in jail. A lawless mob broke into the jail on June 27, 1846, and shot and killed both of them.

Brigham Young was chosen to be the new leader. He decided to move beyond the already settled parts of the United States and chose what is now Utah as a place where the Mormons could live in peace and not be troubled by neighbors. The Mormons made the long journey and settled in what is now Salt Lake City. They used the name Deseret, or "land of the honeybee," for their new territory.

Under the leadership of Brigham Young the Mormons were very successful, but many people still disliked them and the Mormons in turn did not trust outsiders, whom they called "Gentiles." Much of the early trouble came from "forty-niners" going to California for gold. Later there were fights between the Mormons and the judges and troops sent to Utah by the Federal government. These conflicts did not stop until after Utah became a state in 1896.

MORMON BELIEFS

Mormons believe that God has an invisible body, and that He was once a man, but became perfect in both mind and body. There are two kinds of priest in the Mormon Church. Church business is under the priests of Aaron, while spiritual matters are under the priests of Melchizedek. The Council of the Twelve Apostles rules the church and is important in the business as well as the religious life of Mormons.

One Mormon teaching was that one man may have many wives at the same time. Such a practice is called *polygamy*.

Chicago Historical Soc.

The Mormons built a handsome temple in Nauvoo, Illinois, in 1846. But they were forced to leave the state in the same year and the temple was completely destroyed by fire a few years later.

Today, though polygamy is not forbidden on religious grounds, the Mormon marriage ceremony states that the bride and groom will follow the laws of the nation. Since polygamy is against the law, a Mormon may no longer have more than one wife.

Most Mormons still live in Utah, and people are no longer hostile to their religion. Many Mormons have moved to other places in the United States and many are missionaries in other lands.

morning glory

The morning glory is a climbing plant that grows in the warm parts of South America and United States. Morning glories also grow in Japan. Some morning glories are perennial, which means they grow up from the same roots every year. Others are annual and have to be planted each year. Many people grow morning glory plants in their gardens. It is a hardy plant that grows quickly and reaches a height of about fifteen feet. It climbs over porches and fences and garden trellises. It has trumpet-shaped, purple, blue, and white flowers. Most morning glory flowers close during the day.

Some morning glory plants are dwarf, that is, they grow only about one foot high. The dwarf kinds are popular for planting in hanging baskets. They produce many blossoms that do not close during the day.

Morocco

Morocco is a kingdom in northwest Africa, across the Strait of Gibraltar from Spain. Because of its location, which is important in wartime, many countries have sought control of Morocco and for many years it was controlled mostly by France and partly by Spain. In 1957 Morocco became an independent country. Morocco is about 190,000 square miles in size, which is about the size of California, and about ten million people live there, about as many as there are in

California. During World War II, many American soldiers landed in Morocco.

The capital of Morocco is Rabat, but Fez, where the king makes his headquarters, is also considered a capital.

THE PEOPLE OF MOROCCO

Most of the people in Morocco are Berbers. They have lived there longer than any other race of people. They speak their own language, which is very old and which has in it many words taken from the languages of other peoples who settled in Morocco. One of these peoples were the Arabs, who speak Arabic. Many Arabs are nomads, or wanderers, who have no permanent homes but live in tents. Moroccans are often called Moors, a name used chiefly for people of mixed Arab and Berber descent.

About 400,000 Europeans, mostly French and Spanish, live in the cities of Morocco. There are also about 190,000 Jews. Most of the people of Morocco, except the Europeans, are Moslems (follow the Mohammedan religion).

Morocco

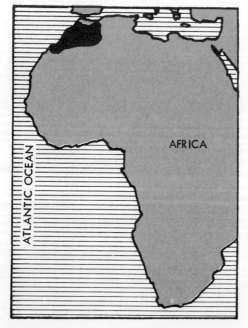

French Gov't Tourist Office

Dressed for the desert, an Arab carries his skis up a mountain near Fez. There are several fine ski resorts open in Morocco during the winter season.

Most Moroccans are farmers. They raise wheat, barley, olives, and citrus fruits. City people work in factories that make building materials, textiles, shoes, and soap. They also weave carpets. Some Moroccans live and dress like city dwellers in the United States and Canada, but many of them still wear their native dress, with the Mohammedan women wearing veils over the lower part of their faces. Most of the poorer people lead simple lives and few can read or write.

WHAT KIND OF A PLACE IT IS

Morocco is a country of mountains, fertile plains, and deserts. The Atlas Mountains stretch across the country from southwest to northeast, and in some places rise more than 13,000 feet. Along the Mediterranean are the Riff Hills. Between these hills and the Atlas Mountains are fertile plains for farming. South of the Atlas Mountains is the Sahara Desert. Morocco has a number of small rivers that flow into the Sahara and dry up. The Moulouya, the most important river, flows north into the Mediterranean. The climate of Morocco along the coast is warm but is made comfortable by the breezes from the sea. In the interior of the country, especially in the desert, the summers are extremely hot.

The principal cities of Morocco are:

Casablanca, the largest city, an important seaport, population (1954) 742,000. (See CASABLANCA.)

Marrakesh, an inland city, population (1952) 215,312.

Fez, one of the capitals, an inland city, population (1952) 179,372. Seat of a large Moslem university.

Rabat, the official capital, a seaport on the Atlantic, population (1954) 171,000.

Tangier, on the Strait of Gibraltar, a historic city in international affairs, population (1956) 162,000. (See TANGIER.)

Meknes, an inland city near Fez, population (1952) 140,380.

HOW THE PEOPLE ARE GOVERNED

In 1958 Morocco was ruled by the king (formerly called the sultan) in national affairs and by the heads of the many tribes and communities in local affairs. The people had little voice in their government. But the king, Mohammed V, and his advisors were preparing a constitution to give Morocco a more democratic style of government, based on the governments of France and other European democracies.

MOROCCO IN THE PAST

Morocco was settled more than two thousand years ago as a province of the Roman Empire, and later was conquered by the Arabs. More than two hundred years ago, the coast of Morocco on the Mediterranean was part of the famous Barbary Coast. Fierce Mohammedan pirates used to attack ships and capture Christians to be held for ransom or sold as slaves. European countries became interested in Morocco about a hundred years ago, and several countries tried to get control of it for political reasons. Several times the struggle for Morocco almost brought about a war. In 1912, the French were given control of part of

French Gov't Tourist Office

A young Arab girl of Morocco wears hand-wrought jewelry that jingles as she walks.

Morocco and Spain was given smaller parts.

After World War II, the people of Morocco rebelled against foreign rule and independence was granted to them by France in 1956 and Spain in 1957. Tangier was made an international zone in 1923.

MOROCCO. Area, 171,031 square miles. Population (1956 estimate) 9,823,000. Capital, Rabat. Languages, French, Spanish, Arabic, Berber, and others. Religion, chiefly Mohammedan. Government, kingdom. Monetary units, the French franc and Spanish peseta. Flag: Green, with red Seal of Solomon.

Morris, Gouverneur

Gouverneur Morris was one of the men who helped write the Constitution of the United States. He was a great lawyer and statesman and helped with many of the problems that the new United States faced. He was the American minister to France from 1792 until 1794, and in 1800 he became a member of the United States Senate. Gouverneur Morris was born in Morrisania, New York, in 1752, and died there in 1816. His family had been among the earliest settlers in New York and were rich and aristocratic. His brother, Lewis, was a signer of the Declaration of Independence.

Morris, Robert

Robert Morris was a signer of the Declaration of Independence. He has been called the "financier of the Revolution" because he managed the financial affairs of the colonies during their fight for independence. Morris not only borrowed money for the colonies, but he also gave money of his own for the support of their armies. He and other citizens founded a bank in Philadelphia that paid the expenses of the armies, and in 1781 Morris supplied almost all of the money necessary to carry on the campaign against Cornwallis, the leader of the British forces. Robert Morris served as secretary of finance and secretary of the treasury under the Confederation, the government used in the colonies before the present Constitution was adopted. Later he helped write the Constitution and was a senator from Pennsylvania in the first Congress of the United States. Robert Morris was born in England in 1734, and came to the United States when he was 13 years old. He settled in Philadelphia, where he became a wealthy businessman. In his old age, Morris lost his fortune. He died a poor man in 1806.

Morris, William

William Morris was an English poet and artist who lived about a hundred years ago. He was born near London in 1834 and attended Oxford University, where he studied architecture and painting. He was interested in the design of furniture, wallpaper, art fabrics, and stained glass. He invented the Morris chair, a kind of big armchair that was popular for many years.

Morris is best remembered as a poet. His most popular poems are based on myths and legends, such as *Sigurd the Volsing, Defense of Guinevere,* and *The Life and Death of Jason.* Morris died in 1896, at the age of 62.

Morse, Samuel F. B.

Samuel Finley Breese Morse was an American artist and inventor. His portraits were among the best that were painted by American artists of his time, but he is remembered chiefly because he invented the telegraph.

Morse was born in Charlestown, Massachusetts, in 1791. His father was Jedidiah Morse, who wrote the first geography ever published in the United States. Samuel F. B. Morse was graduated from Yale in 1810 and the next year went to England to study art with the American painter, Washington Allston. Morse became well known as an artist in the United States and was the first president of the National Academy of Design.

In 1829 he went back to Europe and stayed for three years, traveling and painting. It was aboard ship on his way home that he conceived his idea for the telegraph. He heard  a discussion of how someone had produced a spark from an electromagnet, and this gave the idea for the telegraph. Several years later, in 1835, he ran half a mile of wire around a room and proved to his own satisfaction that his invention worked. Two years later he gave a public demonstration of the telegraph.

Morse persuaded Congress to run a telegraph line between Baltimore and Washington. Many people then sued him, claiming that he had stolen their inventions, but he finally won full credit. In his later years, nearly every country in the world bestowed honors on him. He was 91 when he died, in 1872.

See also the Morse Code, in the article on the TELEGRAPH.

mortgage

A mortgage is a kind of contract by which a person borrows money and gives some kind of property (usually real estate) as security. This means that if he does not pay back the money, the person who lends it may take his property instead.

The person who borrows the money is called the *mortgagor*. The person who lends the money is called the *mortgagee*. The contract itself is a *mortgage deed* or *bond*.

Usually a person puts a mortgage on a new house that he is buying, because he does not have enough cash to pay for the house in full. This kind of mortgage is called a *purchase-money mortgage*. Mortgage loans are usually made by banks, and they will usually lend one-half to two-thirds of what they consider to be the full value of the property. The mortgagor pays interest on the money lent by the bank, and also makes regular *amortization* payments. For example, a person owns a house worth $10,000. He borrows $5,000 on a mortgage. The first year he pays $250 in interest (which is at the rate of five per cent) and also pays $500 as amortization. At the beginning of the second year he owes only $4,500 on the mortgage. During this year he will pay only $225 in interest, and again he will pay $500 to amortize or reduce the loan. At the beginning of the third year he will owe only $4,000, and so on.

Most mortgages on new houses in the United States are repaid in monthly payments, which are about the same as would be paid in rent for the same house. The monthly payments go on for fifteen or seventeen years. Each payment includes part for interest and part for amortization, but it is worked out in advance so that the same amount is always paid each month. The loan is usually made by a bank but guaranteed by the Federal Housing Administration (FHA) or another branch of the United States government. In return for this guarantee, the bank pays a small part of the interest to the FHA.

When a mortgagor fails to make his payments, the mortgagee can *foreclose*. This means that he takes the property. Every state and country has very strict laws to control mortgages and foreclosures.

If a person owns a house that can be sold for $20,000, and cannot pay a $5,000 mortgage, the mortgagee cannot foreclose and own the house. He must put the house up at auction to be sold. Suppose the house is sold for $20,000 at the auction. The mortgagee can take the $5,000 he lent, plus all interest that is due to him, plus whatever it cost him to foreclose the mortgage. Everything else goes back to the mortgagor. This amount is said to be the mortgagor's *equity* in the property.

Morton, William

William Thomas Green Morton was an American dentist who lived about a hundred years ago. He was one of the first men to use anesthesia successfully. During his time, most people had to undergo operations while they were awake, and they suffered great pain. William Morton began to practice dentistry in Boston, Massachusetts, in 1842. One of his friends, a chemist named Charles T. Jackson, interested him in using a gas called sulfuric ether as an anesthetic. A patient inhaling sulfuric ether would fall into a deep sleep and would feel no pain during the operation. Morton first tried this gas on animals, then on himself, and finally on a patient. He was so successful that many other dentists and doctors began to use anesthetics. Morton was born in 1819 and died in 1868. Read also the article ANESTHESIA.

mosaic

Mosaic is a decoration made by fitting together pieces of colored stone,

Left: Moscow's Kremlin was the seat of the Soviet government until 1954, when the government decided to make it a museum.
Below: Red Square, Moscow's oldest section after the Kremlin, where citizens gather for public affairs.

Ewing Galloway

glass, tile, or other material, into a design or picture. The making of mosaic is ranked as a fine art because a *cartoon,* or colored design, must first be made and this requires the skill of an artist. In making mosaic, the area to be decorated is covered with a special cement. When this has hardened slightly, the colored pieces, or *tesserae,* are set in place according to the prepared design. Since the pieces are never perfectly flat, they reflect light differently and this adds greatly to the effect of the mosaic.

Mosaic is one of the most ancient arts. Mosaic designs on ivory were made in Egypt and Mesopotamia thousands of years ago. Mosaic was adopted by the Greeks, and later by the Romans, who used it not only for pavements but also for pictures such as landscapes, battle scenes, and portraits of great men. In the early days of Christianity, mosaic came to be used for the inside walls and ceilings of churches.

Ravenna, a city in Italy, became the world's center of mosaic work, and some examples of the art found there have never been surpassed. Oil paintings by such artists as Raphael have been copied in mosaic, the work sometimes taking as long as twenty years and requiring fifteen thousand different colors of stone and glass. Some mosaic has been made of precious stones.

Ewing Galloway

Moscow

Moscow is the capital of the Soviet Union, or the Union of Soviet Socialist Republics (Russia). It is on the Moscow (Moskva) River. Moscow is the largest city in the Soviet Union and one of the world's largest cities. More than four million people lived there in 1939, and the population has since been estimated as high as six million. Its people work in factories that make textiles, machinery, foodstuffs, leather, and many other things. Most of the people live in apartment houses, but many live in the suburbs and travel to work in Moscow every day. Moscow is very overcrowded, even though many new apartment buildings have been built since 1935. The government even had to build new stories on top of old buildings to give the people more space to live in.

The people in Moscow love music, ballet, and plays. The Moscow Art Theater is widely known. Moscow also has many theaters. Few of the people in Moscow have automobiles. They travel on buses, on streetcars, and on a big subway that was built about twenty years ago. The subway stations have marble walls with murals painted on them. The shops, factories, and office buildings are all owned by the government. There are many libraries, museums, youth clubs, stadiums, and schools, which are also run by the government.

THE KREMLIN AND RED SQUARE

Moscow has very old churches and palaces with high domes, but it also has big modern buildings and parks. In the center of Moscow stands the Kremlin, the most important structure in the city. It has walls of pink brick. The Russian czar (emperor) and his court once lived there. For thirty years it was the headquarters of the Communist government of Russia. Beginning in 1954 it was turned into a huge public museum. There is a separate article on the KREMLIN.

The Kremlin faces Red Square. This huge square is more than a half-mile long, and the people hold national parades and important celebrations there. In Red Square is the Lenin Mausoleum, built of many different colored granites. In this tomb lie the bodies of Nikolai Lenin and Josef Stalin in glass-covered coffins.

Moscow was founded more than eight hundred years ago. About four hundred years ago, Czar Ivan the Terrible made Moscow the capital of Russia. Moscow was the scene of much fighting through the centuries. In 1703, Peter the Great moved the capital to St. Petersburg (now Leningrad, but Moscow remained an important city. In 1812, Napoleon captured Moscow with his French army. Much of the city was destroyed, but the Russians finally won the war. In the Russian Revolution in 1917 there was much fighting in Moscow. The Soviet government moved to Moscow in 1918,

and it again became the capital of Russia. During World War II, the Germans tried to capture the capital, but the Russian Army drove them back. Since the war, the city has been partly rebuilt.

MOSCOW, U.S.S.R. Population 4,847,000 (1956 estimate). Capital of U.S.S.R. On the Moscow River.

Moses

Moses is called the "liberator of the Jews," for the Bible tells us that he led them from slavery in Egypt to the Promised Land in Palestine. He was a great law-giver who gave his people the rules (the Ten Commandments) that have guided them and millions of other people for the last 3,100 years. It is believed that Moses wrote the first five books of the Old Testament, which are also called the *Pentateuch* and the *Books of Moses.*

The Book of Exodus, the second in the Bible, tells the story of Moses. He was born in Egypt at a time when the Egyptians were treating the Jews very cruelly. The pharaoh (king) of Egypt was afraid there were getting to be too many Jews, so he passed a law saying that all Jewish male children were to be killed. At this time Moses was only three months old. His mother, whose name was Jochebed, put him in a basket woven of bulrushes and put the basket in the Nile River, hoping he would not be found and killed. Moses was found by an Egyptian princess. She pitied him and took him home. By chance, she asked Jochebed, Moses' own mother, to care for him.

When Moses grew up to be a young man, he heard a voice coming from a burning bush. He recognized it as the voice of God, and it told Moses that he would free his people from slavery. Moses could not talk without stammering, and he thought this would prevent him from being a forceful leader. But God appointed Aaron, Moses' brother, to be Moses' helper. He would speak for Moses, whose stammering made talking before an audience difficult. They went to

Michelangelo portrays Moses as a man of
great strength and dignity. In his right hand
are the tablets of the Ten Commandments,
the foundation of moral law.

MOUNT SINAI

Moses and his people stopped at
Mount Sinai. Moses went alone up the
mountain. God appeared to him there.
To Moses God renewed the covenant, or
promise, that He had made to Abraham
and the Jewish people. Then the Lord
gave Moses the Ten Commandments.
They were written on stone tablets.

When Moses went down from Sinai,
he found the people worshiping an idol,
a golden calf. In anger, he broke the tablets containing the commandments. But
then he made a great sacrifice, and offered himself to the Lord to make up for
the sins of the people. The Lord spared
Moses. After a year at Sinai, Moses commanded the people to follow him again.

THE FORTY YEARS

The next part of the journey took forty years. The Jews set out. Moses sent
spies into Canaan, a country to the north,
to find out about it. When the Jews
reached the River Jordan, they were
afraid of the people who lived on the
other side. Even Aaron and Moses lost
courage. The Lord punished the people
for their lack of faith by sending fiery
serpents that killed many of the people.

Finally, the country across the Jordan
was divided among the tribes of the Jewish people. In the Book of Deuteronomy,
the fifth book of the Bible, Moses again
told about the laws that were first described in the books of Numbers and Le-
viticus. He was permitted by God to look
down from Mount Nebo at the Promised
Land, the goal of his hopes. But he died
without entering the land. After his
death, the people mourned him for thirty days, because he had delivered them
from slavery. Through Moses, God had
established His law for the Jewish people. They reached the Promised Land
and the forty years of wandering were
over.

Pharaoh and demanded in the name of
the Lord that the Jewish people be set
free. Pharaoh refused.

Then God sent nine plagues, or misfortunes, to Egypt, but still Pharaoh refused to let the Jews go. Then, in the
tenth plague, God killed the oldest male
child in every Egyptian house but he
passed over (spared) the houses of the
Jews, and this is told about in the article
PASSOVER, in another volume of this encyclopedia.

Now Pharaoh was very much afraid,
and he let the Jews leave Egypt. Moses
led them out of the hated country. Then
Pharaoh was sorry that he had been so
frightened and sent Egyptian soldiers out
after their former slaves. Moses guided
his people across the Red Sea, whose waters rolled aside to let them through.
When the Egyptians followed, the waters
rolled back, and the Egyptians were
drowned.

Moses was the great law-giver. Before
him there were many systems of law, but
none lasted very long. The Mosaic law

has never been weakened since the time of Moses. It has been the foundation on which the laws of all great religions of the Western world have been built. Christians and Mohammedans, as well as Jews, still honor its principles.

Moses, Grandma

Grandma Moses is the popular name of an American farm woman who began to paint when she was 78 years old and became famous throughout the world for her pictures. Her full name is Anna Mary Robertson Moses, and she was born in New York State in 1860. As a child she loved to draw, but she grew up like any farm girl, married, and had ten children. She worked on the farm, and after the death of her husband in 1927 she ran the farm herself.

When Grandma Moses was in her seventies, the farm work became too hard for her. One of her daughters suggested that she embroider pictures in wool to amuse herself. Then her fingers became too stiff to hold a needle, and Grandma Moses began to paint in oils. Her fame began in 1939, when an art collector saw some of her paintings and bought all he could get. Since that time she has painted about 800 pictures. Mostly she paints landscapes in a style called *primitive*. Primitive art is done by persons who need not have training but who have natural talent. Grandma Moses' pictures are full of tiny details that make a farm scene look alive and familiar. Her colors are sharp and bright, and all of her paintings are cheerful and happy in mood. Among the best of them are *From My Window, The Old Oaken Bucket,* and *Catching the Thanksgiving Turkey.*

Moslem, a follower of Islam, the religion of Mohammed: see ISLAM and MOHAMMED.

mosque

A mosque is a Moslem house of prayer. (Moslems follow the religion of Mohammed.) From the outside, a mosque is most easily recognized by the four *minarets,* which are towers at each corner of an open courtyard. The call to prayer is given from the top of the minarets. The courtyard has walls on three sides. The fourth is open and usually has several pillars.

The main building is the prayer hall. There are no chairs or benches in the prayer hall. Rugs, on which the Moslems kneel to pray, cover the floor. On one wall there is a prayer niche, which shows the direction of Mecca. This is necessary because Moslems, when they are praying, always face Mecca, the city where Mohammed was born. Next to the prayer niche is the *mimbar,* or pulpit, and near the mimbar is the *cikka,* a raised platform from which the prayers and services are read.

Many mosques, especially those in Persia, have bulb-shaped domes on top of the minarets and the main building. These are often very beautiful, but are not a necessary part of a mosque. There are famous mosques in Mecca and Medina. One of the most famous in Istanbul, Turkey, was formerly the famous Christian church of St. Sophia.

mosquito

The mosquito is an insect that lives in many parts of the world. It grows best in places where the climate is warm and moist. Mosquitoes are also found in cold parts of the world, such as Alaska. The mosquito is a great pest to man and animals.

The bite of a mosquito itches and is very annoying. Some mosquitoes carry very tiny organisms called viruses, which cause dangerous diseases. The *aedes mosquito* carries the virus that causes yellow fever, and the *anopheles mosquito* carries the virus that causes malaria. There are separate articles on MALARIA and YELLOW FEVER.

Although the mosquito can be dangerous and is a nuisance, it is a beautiful

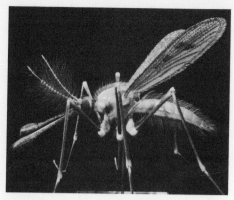

An old joke maintains that mosquitoes this large grow in New Jersey. Actually the malaria-bearing anopheles from the tropics does not need to be enlarged in order to do harm to human beings.

insect. The female has a long delicate beak that it uses to pierce the skin and suck the blood of its prey. Only the female mosquito bites. The female lays its eggs in ponds and still water that collects in swamps or drainpipes or even in buckets. The eggs hatch quickly. Some mosquito eggs hatch in only a few hours. When the eggs hatch they are *larvae* (often called "wigglers"). They feed on water plants. After a while the larvae turn into mosquitoes. Mosquitoes do not fly long distances but often they are carried for miles by the wind. Man has developed many poisons and other ways to get rid of mosquitoes.

moss

Moss is an important group of plants that grow in almost every part of the world. There are thousands of different kinds of moss, and some of them are very beautiful. Most moss grows best in places where the climate is moist and warm and the soil is damp. In places where the climate is cold and dry, moss shrivels up and looks as if it were dead. When the weather grows warmer and there is rain, the moss comes to life again. Moss is found on tree trunks, on logs, on rocks, and on objects in rivers. Some moss is pale green, some is dark green, and there is moss that is almost black.

Moss has a soft stem and many tiny green leaves. It does not have regular roots, but clings to the ground or the trunk of a tree or a rock by tiny threads on its underside. Instead of seeds, moss has spores, tiny powdery structures that make it possible for new moss to grow. (You can read about spores in the article on PLANTS.) Moss does not have any flowers.

Moss is useful to other plants because it keeps their roots warm. People who grow flowers often use moss for this purpose. Moss also provides a home for many different kinds of insects. Reindeer and cattle eat some kinds of moss.

moth, a kind of insect: see BUTTERFLIES AND MOTHS.

Mother Goose, an imaginary author of nursery rhymes: see the article NURSERY RHYMES.

mother-of-pearl

Mother-of-pearl is the smooth inside layer of the shells of certain shellfish, especially oysters, mussels, and abalones. It is usually whitish or grayish and seems to have the colors of the rainbow just below its surface. Cameos are cut from mother-of-pearl, and brooches, buttons, letter openers and knife handles are made from it. It is also used for inlaying musical instruments and furniture. It is an important by-product of pearl fisheries.

Mother-of-pearl is made of the substances called *aragonite* and *chonchiolin,* which are manufactured by the body of the shellfish. These are the same substances that pearls are made of. Mother-of-pearl is sometimes called *nacre.*

Mother's Day

Mother's Day is a holiday that has been observed in the United States since 1914. Before that it had been observed in certain cities for several years. It was first observed in Philadelphia in 1910. Mother's Day is the second Sunday in May. Unlike most holidays, which are proclaimed by the governors of the separate states, Mother's Day is declared by a proclamation of the President of the United States.

On Mother's Day all mothers are honored, whether living or dead. There are special services held in most churches to do honor to the mother and to the home. Many people buy their mothers presents on this day. In some parts of the United States it has become the custom to wear a red carnation if one's mother is living, and a white carnation if she has died.

motion

Motion is the act of going from one place to another. The famous English scientist, Sir Isaac Newton, who lived about three hundred years ago, explained motion in terms of three laws, known as Newton's laws of motion.

The first law of motion states that an object will move only if there are forces on it that do not balance each other (are not equal and opposite in direction). Thus we say that motion can take place only if an unbalanced force acts on a body.

A book will remain motionless (at rest) on a table top unless it is pushed or pulled. The book is at rest because its downward force (weight) on the table is balanced by the upward force of the table top. The two forces are equal and opposite.

When objects are acted on by an unbalanced force, their motion may be one of two kinds: *rectilinear* (motion in a straight line), and *rotational* (motion in a curved line). Newton's first law also says that a body set in motion will move in a straight line unless acted on by an unbalanced force. When a ball rolled along the floor moves in a curved line, it is because the force of friction between the floor and the ball moves it off its normally straight path. Friction is the unbal-

anced force. (There is a separate article on FRICTION.)

Newton's second law states that if an object is acted on by an unbalanced force, its speed will continue to increase (called *acceleration*) as long as the force continues to act on it and remains unbalanced. The direction of motion will always be in the direction in which the force is acting. The greater the force, the greater the acceleration.

The third law of motion states that for every action there is an equal and opposite reaction. This law is the explanation of jet propulsion. Gases leave a jet engine with great force. This causes an equal and opposite force in the engine, which drives the jet plane forward. See the articles on JET ENGINE, FORCE, and INERTIA.

motion pictures

Motion pictures, usually called "the movies," are the most popular form of entertainment that has ever been invented. Millions of people the world over see motion pictures every week in theaters, and in their homes many people show family movies that they have made themselves. In recent years television has taken many people away from movie theaters, but television is another form of motion pictures and many of the programs shown on television are produced on film.

HOW THE MOVIES DEVELOPED

For hundreds of years men tried to invent a way of recording action in permanent form, but no practical way was found until Thomas Edison invented a motion-picture camera, about 1893. The Lumière brothers, two Frenchmen, may have invented the first movie camera some years earlier, but Edison's was the first practical one. The pictures taken with Edison's camera were shown in penny arcades, in a machine that the viewer turned with a crank. Later, movies began to be shown on screens in stores and halls where seats had been installed. The ad-

Motion Picture Assn. of America

One of the first movie studios was built on a Philadelphia rooftop in 1900. In the early days of movies, all scenes had to be shot outdoors in the sunlight.

mission price to these places was a nickel, so they were called *nickelodeons.*

The movies shown at this time were very short and had almost no stories. They just showed some kind of interesting action, and people went to see them because of their novelty. Some wise movie men believed that people would be interested in movies that told stories. They wrote simple stories to be acted out and photographed. Their studios were in open lots and even on the roofs of buildings. In those days all scenes, even those supposedly taking place indoors, had to be shot in full sunlight. No artificial light was bright enough.

It was not long before people began to go to the movies regularly. As the producers (the men who were in charge of making the pictures) saw that they could make a great deal of money from the movies, they made longer and more elaborate pictures. Regular theaters that had live stage performers added movies to their shows and found their business improving. Many theaters gave up the stage shows and showed only movies.

In a short time audiences began to find favorites among the actors and actresses who appeared on the screen. At first, the names of the players were not even mentioned, but when the producers realized that audiences were interested in the movie actors, they began to feature their names. Actors and actresses who were particular favorites were given bigger parts, and their names were advertised more than the pictures they played in. They became known as movie stars, and the star system has continued to this day. Some of the early movie stars were Mary Pickford, Douglas Fairbanks, Charlie Chaplin, Francis X. Bushman, Maurice Costello, and William S. Hart. Movie stars are probably the best-known people in the world today, and audiences know more about them than they do about presidents and kings.

The first motion picture to tell a complete story was *The Great Train Robbery,* made in 1903. It was one of the first movies in which the camera photographed scenes from different positions instead of remaining fixed in one spot. An equally important movie was *The Birth of a Nation,* a story of the Civil War, made by D. W. Griffith in 1915. This was the first long, expensive movie of the kind made today. In one part of this story, Griffith put the camera on a truck and, as a group of soldiers rode their horses at breakneck speed, the camera kept pace with them, making a very exciting effect that people had never seen before. Griffith also introduced other uses of the camera that we see in almost every movie today. One of them was the *close-up,* which is a picture of a person or an object taken from so close that you can see every detail of it.

By the time of World War I, movies were being made in large studios especially built for the purpose. Most of the studios, which had been in New York, moved to Hollywood, California, where there was plenty of sunshine. Hollywood was also near many different kinds of natural settings that could be used for pictures — mountains, deserts, seashores, farm country, or almost any other scene. The movies by this time were a big business, and stars and producers made enormous amounts of money.

20th Century-Fox

There are many kinds of motion picture, from the short animated cartoon to the multi-million-dollar musical extravaganza.

20th Century-Fox

20th Century-Fox

20th Century-Fox

Swiss Nat'l Railway

1. A historical movie, set in ancient Egypt, requires research into clothing styles.
2. A drama of family life is not filmed on such a grand and expensive scale.
3. The Western, with its fast action and outdoor shots, is favored by young audiences.
4. The musical is full of bounce and gaiety and is usually filmed in color.
5. Drawings come to life in the animated cartoon, loved by young and old alike.

Until 1927 the movies were "silent." Conversation appeared in printed form, called *subtitles,* that appeared on the screen between scenes. In 1927 the first talking picture was introduced. Al Jolson sang and the actors talked in *The Jazz Singer.* The next year the first all-talking picture was made, and within a very short time all movies were being made with sound.

Not long after the introduction of sound, a good way of making movies in natural color was found. The most effective method was called *Technicolor.* The use of color has increased gradually ever since, but it is expensive and most movies are still made in black and white.

Up to the end of World War II, movies drew enormous audiences. As many as ninety million people went to the movies in the United States every week. After the war, a great new rival came into being. This was television. Instead of going to the movies, people sat at home and watched television. Desperately, the motion-picture industry tried to find a way to get people back into the theaters. They found a partial answer in making longer, more expensive and more spectacular pictures than ever before and by using a wider screen than before, to make the actors appear more lifelike. They also made plans to show the new films on home television sets, through a system by which viewers can pay to see them.

HOW MOVIES ARE MADE

The motion-picture camera is very much like a still camera, which is described in the article on PHOTOGRAPHY; but, unlike the still camera, the movie camera rapidly photographs many individual pictures, or *frames,* on a strip of film. For sound pictures, the camera photographs twenty-four frames each second. Each frame is a photograph of a part of the action. The strip of film is then run through a projector, which casts one frame at a time onto a screen. A *shutter* passes in front of the projector's lens and

blocks out the picture between each two frames. It does this so fast that the audience is not aware of it. The audience sees the frames, one after the other, so fast that the people and things in them seem to move as they do in real life.

Motion-picture film used for professional movies is 35 mm. (millimeters) wide (about 1⅜ inches). Home movie film is 16 mm. or 8 mm. wide.

The sound portion of a movie is recorded on a separate strip of film, which runs at the same speed as the photographic film (and is said to be synchronized with it). Sound is picked up by a microphone and then changed by an electronic system into light that is printed on the film in the form of different patterns or lines. Usually more than one sound strip, or sound track, is used in the making of a film: one for the dialogue (the actors' words), one for the sound effects (noises and other natural sounds), and one for the musical background. When the picture is finally assembled, all the different tracks are made into one and are printed at one side of the picture strip. Until recently it was very difficult for home movie makers to add sound to their pictures, but a new process, magnetic sound recording, makes it easy to do this.

A professional motion picture is the work of many skilled persons. Writers produce a *shooting script* that details all of the film's action and dialogue. A picture may be made of hundreds of different scenes or shots, and each one is described and numbered in the script. When the script is approved by the *producer,* who is in complete charge of the picture, actors are chosen, a *director* is selected to give instructions to the actors, and the shooting begins. This may be in a studio or *on location.* A location is a place outside the studio that has been chosen because it provides a good background for the story.

When you enter a studio where a movie is being made, all may seem to be confusion, but actually everyone is busy

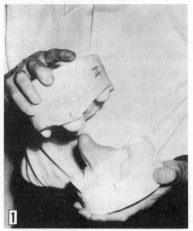

United Artists Corp. Photos

One of the most important jobs in a motion-picture studio is that of the makeup man. It is his task to make over the face of an actor so that it fits the part he is playing. For example, when José Ferrer played the part of Cyrano de Bergerac he had to be given the long, ugly nose for which Cyrano was most famous.

1. After a cast had been made of Ferrer's face, a nose was modeled to fit his features.

2. Holding the plaster cast, the actor looks over his new nose before trying it on.

3. When it is put in place, it is almost impossible to tell that the fake is not the real thing.

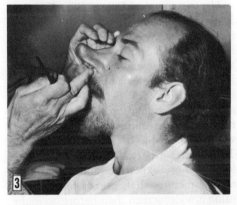

Left: The makeup man travels with the cast when a motion picture is made "on location" (outdoors, in actual scenery, not in a studio). Here, on location in Africa, actor Humphrey Bogart is made up while his wife, Lauren Bacall, watches.

Right: The same motion picture is being made in two forms at once, one for English-speaking countries, the other for German-speaking. The English leading lady is being made up at the left, the German one at the right.

The movie screen shows the audience only a small part of the work that goes into making a movie. The men and women behind the scenes are necessary to a good movie.

20th Century-Fox

20th Century-Fox

20th Century-Fox

20th Century-Fox

Metro-Goldwyn-Mayer

1. The director supervises the work of all the people who work on a motion picture.
2. He watches as a writer and script girl go over a script to decide on needed changes.
3. The color card helps the camera man judge the colors he will get in a color movie.
4. "Actors" include animals trained not to spoil a scene by doing the wrong thing.
5. Members of the cast "line up" for instructions before a brief scene is shot.

Movie sets create a world of make-believe. *Left:* From the tiny model of a village, stagehands build the "real" thing. *Below:* It's raining on the fire escape, which looks as if it is several stories above the ground, but the director is completely dry.

United Artists Corp.

at his job. In preparation for shooting, the cameraman is telling a group of electricians high up on a scaffold just how he wants the many lights placed. In a corner, the stars are rehearsing their dialogue as the director listens. The sound man, seated at a control panel, is testing his equipment. An assistant director is placing chalk marks on the floor of the set to guide the actors in their movements before the camera so that they will remain in focus and within the picture frame. A cameraman's assistant is putting film in the camera and placing the camera in a "blimp." A blimp is a covering for the camera that deadens the noise of its mechanism so that it will not be picked up by the sound recorder. If the camera is to be moved during the scene, it will be placed on a truck called a *dolly.* Or it may be placed on a *boom* that can carry the camera high into the air or move it about wherever the director wishes.

United Artists Corp.

"TAKING" A SCENE

When all is ready, the director calls for a rehearsal of the scene. The scene may last only a minute or less on film, but he goes over it many times. He must make sure that the actors do their parts properly, that the camera is photographing

it exactly as he wishes, and that the microphone, which usually is hung on a boom or arm just out of view of the camera, is picking up the sound clearly. When the rehearsal is completed, the director orders a "take." This means that the scene will be recorded by the camera and sound apparatus. Often several takes are made before the director is satisfied. When the scene is finished, the technicians prepare for the next one.

The scene that is taken next may or may not be one that follows in order in the shooting script. Very often scenes from the beginning and end of the picture are shot together. The reason is that

Metro-Goldwyn-Mayer

The prop room at a motion-picture studio can furnish anything, from the palace of a French king to a shack in the far North.

they may take place in the same setting, and it is cheaper for the company to shoot all the scenes that take place there at the same time than to leave the set standing until it is needed again.

When the day's shooting is finished, the film is developed and looked at by the producer and director to make sure that the scenes are just right. The developed scenes of a day's work are called *rushes* or *dailies.*

When all the shooting is completed the film passes into the hands of the *editor.* His job is to fit together all the individual shots, trim bits of the scenes if they are not good or are too long, and arrange

A film editor, or "cutter," watches a scene that is about to be "cut" into a finished picture. He uses a "movieola," a miniature motion-picture theater.

Metro-Goldwyn-Mayer

to have certain special effects made. These special effects include fade-ins, fade-outs, dissolves, and wipes. In a *fade-in,* a scene gradually appears on the screen. A *fade-out* is the reverse; it makes one scene disappear. A *dissolve* makes a scene gradually melt into another. A *wipe* removes one scene from the screen, meanwhile replacing it with another.

When all the scenes of a picture are assembled, the background music is recorded. Then a *print* of the picture (a film that can be put through a projector) is made and shown to a preview audience at some out-of-the-way theater. The audience is asked to write its reaction to the picture. Sometimes changes are made as a result. Then more prints are made, sent out to theaters, and *released* (shown to the public).

From the start of shooting to the end may take twelve weeks or even longer. It is not unusual for a motion picture to cost a million dollars, and some cost several million.

WIDE-SCREEN MOTION PICTURES

Most important movies today are made by one of the wide-screen systems. They are called wide-screen systems because the picture they show is wider than the one for a regular screen. One of these systems, CINERAMA, is described in a separate article.

A regular screen is about $1\frac{1}{3}$ times wider than it is high. (This relation, called the *aspect ratio,* is written 1.33 to 1.) Other systems use aspect ratios of 2 to 1, 1.85 to 1, or 2.66 to 1.

Wide-screen movies have become popular because their scenes have almost a three-dimensional effect. Actually three-dimensional ("3-D") pictures have been popular from time to time, but they require the audience to wear special glasses and their popularity has never lasted long.

In the wide-screen system known as CinemaScope, a special camera lens, called an *anamorphic lens,* is used in front of the regular lens. This squeezes onto a regular 35-mm. film frame a picture that is twice as wide as usual. Then, when the picture is projected, another anamorphic lens is placed on the projector, and this spreads the image out again, to fill a screen that is 2.66 to 1 instead of 1.33 to 1. A slightly curved screen is used.

Another wide-screen system is Vista-Vision. This uses a regular lens, but it runs the film through the camera sideways and photographs two frames at once. This makes each picture almost twice as wide as the regular 1.33 to 1.

Home movies can also be made in wide-screen proportions by using a Vistascope attachment in front of the camera and projector. The Vistascope attachment is available for both 16-mm. and 8-mm. cameras.

The Todd A-O process, introduced in 1955, uses a curved screen that extends for 128 degrees (about one-third of a full circle, and more than three-quarters of what the eye normally sees). Cinerama also uses a curved screen, but while Cinerama uses three cameras, Todd A-O uses only one camera, which has several lenses. The Todd A-O camera uses 65-mm. film, almost twice as wide as regular film. The screen is 50 feet wide and 25 feet high.

Motley, John Lothrop

John Lothrop Motley was an American historian and statesman who lived more than a hundred years ago. He was born in 1814. After his graduation from Harvard, in 1831, he went on a long tour of Europe and became very interested in the history of the Netherlands. He wrote several important books about the Netherlands, the most famous being *The Rise of the Dutch Republic.* In 1841 Motley was made secretary of a United States legation in the capital of Russia. Twenty years later he served for six years as United States minister to Austria, and shortly afterward President Grant appointed him minister to Great Britain. However, Motley quarreled with other United States

statesmen, particularly with the Secretary of State, Hamilton Fish, and Grant had him recalled. Motley died in 1877.

motorboat (see BOATING)

A motorboat is a boat driven by an INTERNAL COMBUSTION ENGINE, about which there is a separate article. The engine is connected to a propeller by means of a shaft. The turning of the propeller in the water at the rear drives the boat.

The size of a motorboat ranges from 15 to 50 feet, from a small speedboat carrying one or two people to the large motor yacht, driven by twin engines and carrying as many as 15 people, with kitchen and sleeping space. Motorboats of various constructions and sizes are used for racing, fishing, or cruising, and even as a temporary summer home.

Most motorboats are equipped with an engine located inside the boat, near the middle. Such boats are classified as *inboard* motorboats.

The bottom of a motorboat may have various shapes, depending on what the boat is used for. *Speedboats* usually have a V-shaped bottom to allow them to move through the water more easily. A *hydroplane,* or highspeed racing boat, has less of a V-shape. It is so constructed that the front of the boat rises up from the water when the boat is moving at high speed. This enables the boat to move along on top rather than through the water, reducing the friction between the water and the boat and bringing it to speeds as great as 160 miles an hour. Large boats, which are not designed for high speeds, have rounded bottoms.

Motorboats usually are made of hardwood such as oak, pine, and teak wood. Steel is too heavy. Many boats are made of an alloy of aluminum.

A small boat can use a portable engine, weighing twenty pounds or more, that can be carried and attached to the stern of the boat. Such boats are classified as *outboard* motor boats. Although usually used on boats that do not require

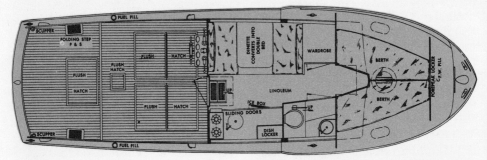

A good motorboat can be used for fishing, cruising, or racing. The diagram above shows the various parts of the trim 32-foot cruiser pictured at the right.

speeds greater than 35 miles an hour, some outboard motors can develop speeds as great as 70 miles an hour.

motorcycle

A motorcycle is a kind of bicycle that is driven by an INTERNAL COMBUSTION ENGINE, about which there is a separate article. The engine is located under the driver's seat. On some motorcycles, a chain from the engine drives the rear wheel. On others, the engine turns a shaft that serves as the rear wheel's axle.

Motorcycles are used for police patrol, pleasure riding, and racing. They can travel at speeds as great as 150 miles an hour, using about one gallon of gasoline for every 60 miles. The American Motorcycle Association conducts races every year, including hill-climbing, cross-country racing, and track racing.

A motorcycle is fast, maneuverable, and inexpensive to operate. Many motorcyclists form clubs and go on trips together.

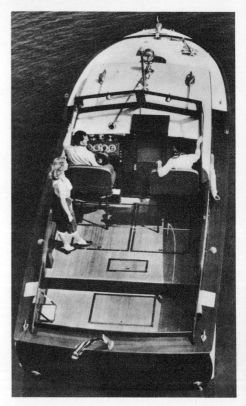

The speed of a motorcycle is controlled by turning one of the grips on the end of the handle bars. It works like the accelerator pedal of an automobile. Transmission gears enable the driver to run the motorcycle at different speeds.

A motorcycle is heavier and longer than a bicycle. The seat is lower, giving the driver greater control. There are footstands on both sides for the driver's feet. Often there is a seat in back of the driver for another passenger. A motorcycle may be equipped with a sidecar, supported by an extra wheel and attached to the side of the motorcycle, in which a passenger sits.

A *motorbike* is a regular bicycle with a small engine attached to the rear wheel. When the engine is running, it turns the wheel. When the engine is off, the rider can pedal as on a regular bicycle.

A *motor scooter* has only two wheels, as a motorcycle or bicycle has, but between them it has a board on which the driver can place his feet while he rides. The rear wheel is driven by a small engine under the driver's seat. A motor scooter can go as fast as 40 miles an hour.

motor vehicles

Automobiles, trucks, buses, and certain tractors are called motor vehicles. They carry their own engines and go wherever they are steered instead of being confined to tracks as streetcars and trains are. There are literally thousands of ways in which one motor vehicle can be different from another, yet there are other ways in which all motor vehicles are alike.

The vehicle begins with a steel frame, two long pieces of steel that run the length of the vehicle and two crosspieces at the front and rear. These are securely fastened together in the shape of a rectangle. At each corner there is a wheel. Each pair of wheels, front and rear, is fastened together on a crosspiece called an *axle* and are attached to the frame by springs. When a wheel passes over a rough place it moves the spring rather than the frame, which reduces jolting of the frame. Each wheel is also attached to a device called a *shock absorber*. This is a hydraulic device similar to the one that closes doors automatically and keeps them from slamming. The shock absorber helps the springs to prevent jolting.

In the front of the vehicle the frame supports an engine. This is almost always an INTERNAL COMBUSTION ENGINE, de-

scribed in a separate article. The engine turns a long rod called a *driveshaft* that leads to the rear axle. The driveshaft is attached to a gear that turns the rear axle. The turning of the rear axle turns the rear wheels and this makes the vehicle move. Nearly every motor vehicle is driven by its rear wheels. The machinery where the driveshaft meets the rear axle is called the "rear end."

There is always a universal joint on the shaft. This keeps it from bending if bumps in the road cause the rear axle to move up and down.

One of the gears is in the rear end and is called a *differential*. It permits either rear wheel to turn over more slowly than the other. If the vehicle goes around a corner, the inside wheel must turn more slowly than the outside wheel, because it has a shorter distance to go.

FRONT-WHEEL AND FOUR-WHEEL DRIVES

When a vehicle is driven by its rear wheels, the front wheels are used only for steering. Each front wheel is hung on a sort of pivot so that it can move from left to right. Bars attached to these pivot devices lead to a steering wheel above the frame. The driver of the vehicle sits behind the steering wheel. By turning the steering wheel he guides the vehicle.

There are certain advantages to having a vehicle driven by its front wheels instead of by its rear wheels. Some of the power is lost in turning the long driveshaft. (Some automobiles have their engines in the rear for this reason.) The vehicle is less likely to skid on the road if the driving wheels are always pointed in the direction in which it is going. With rear-wheel drive, the driving wheels are always pointed forward. Some automobiles have used front-wheel drive. The difficulty has always been that it requires more complicated machinery to drive wheels that can constantly change direction.

Automobile Manufacturers Assn.

A 1908 automobile would look strange to-day but the basic design has not changed: A metal frame with a wheel at each corner; a gasoline-burning engine at the front; a driveshaft carrying the power to the rear wheels.

Automobiles that must run in heavy sand and mud are sometimes built with four-wheel drive. This means that the power from the engine goes to the front wheels as well as to the rear wheels. The same kind of driveshaft and "rear" axle is used. The jeep used by the United States armed forces has four-wheel drive.

Heavy buses and trucks often have a "gas-electric" or "diesel-electric" drive. The engine does not turn a driveshaft. It turns an electric generator. This produces electricity, and the wheels are driven by electric motors run by this electricity.

TORQUE

Torque is twisting action. As the rear wheels turn, they try to turn the rear axle along with them. Therefore the rear axle must be held so that it cannot move. This is done by a torque tube, a tube fastened from the rear axle to a crossbar in the center of the frame, and also by rods that run from the rear axle to the sides of the frame. The driveshaft runs through the torque tube. The tube protects it against dirt and rocks thrown up from the road.

TRACTORS AND TRAILERS

Tractors are used on farms to pull farm machinery. The kind of truck that pulls a trailer is also called a tractor. The semi-trailer is most used. The front end of the trailer rests on the rear of the tractor (truck); the back on the trailer has its own wheels. The trailer is attached to the tractor by a big disk that is mounted at the back of the tractor. This disk is called a "fifth wheel," but it is nothing like the wheels that motor vehicles ride on. The fifth wheel permits the trailer to turn from side to side as the tractor turns.

In a separate article on the TRACTOR, the crawler-type tractor is described. This kind of tractor is driven by a moving tread, of which the best-known make is called *caterpillar*. Some trucks are driven by similar treads. They have wheels in the front, for steering, and the tread in the back. They are called *half-tracks*.

CONTROLS AND BODIES

Behind the engine of nearly any motor vehicle there is a seat for the driver, where he can use the steering wheel and other controls such as the brakes and can see an instrument panel that shows how the engine is operating, how much fuel he has, and so on. The frame, wheels, and driver's equipment are called the *chassis*. There is almost no limit to the number of different bodies or types of equipment that can be mounted (put on top of) the chassis. See the articles on AUTOMOBILE, BUS, and TRUCK.

THE BEST OF GOOD READING

LITERARY TREASURES

The novels, plays, poems, and other works of the most celebrated and historic writers of the English language in all lands and times

VOLUME

14

Manon Lescaut—Moonstone

Edited by

ALBERT H. MOREHEAD

Executive Editor, HAROLD J. BLUM

Drawings by RAFAELLO BUSONI

Design by DONALD D. WOLF *and* MARGOT L. WOLF

BOBLEY PUBLISHING CORP.

ACKNOWLEDGMENTS

Outlines in this volume were written by Elizabeth MacLean, James Wilhelm, Janet Wilson, Dina Dellalé, Hanz Holzer, Martin Keen, Robert Condon, Bruce Brown, Grace Egan, Grace Shaw, Christopher Lazare, Sylvia Plapinger, Marion Segal, Jeanne Rosenthal, Anne Tjomsland, and the Editors.

Manon Lescaut

Novel by Abbé Prévost (Antoine François Prévost d'Exiles, 1697–1763). Published 1731.

THE CLAIM TO FAME of this 18th-century French book is that the great composers Massenet and Puccini both elected to write operas based on it. The principal feature of the novel is that it presents a woman irresistible because of her beauty—the same kind of woman that has appeared in some millions of pages of literature but that apparently is quite rare in life because so few men have met her or her sister. At least in this novel she succeeds in ruining her men, which seems to be the mission in life of such women.

Chaps. 1–4. The 17-year-old Chevalier DES GRIEUX is finishing his studies at Amiens. With his friend TIBERGE he watches the arrival of the coach from Arras. One of the passengers is a beautiful girl, MANON LESCAUT, about to enter a nearby convent. Des Grieux falls in love with her at sight, approaches her, and persuades her to meet him that night, when he declares his passion. Eager to escape the convent, Manon goes with him to Paris, where the two live together for three weeks in bliss. Then, since Manon continues affluent while his own money is running out, des Grieux suspects her of infidelity.

Under orders from des Grieux' father, three servants kidnap the young man and take him to his father's house. The father tells him that Manon is a harlot, having sold her favors to M. DE B—F. The grief-stricken son wishes to return to Manon, but his father keeps him locked up for six months. Tiberge visits him often, confirms that Manon is a harlot, and urges des Grieux to take holy orders. The Chevalier is persuaded to enroll at the Seminary of Saint-Supplice. He plunges into study to banish Manon from his mind. In two years he is ready for his public examination.

The outstanding ability of the candidate carries his name throughout Paris. Manon comes to hear him and is carried away by his fervor. She seeks him out after the ceremonies and des Grieux is again infatuated. He abandons his calling to go with Manon to Chaillot. Here they live happily but extravagantly on Manon's money. They also take quarters in Paris, where they are visited by Manon's brother, who presently moves in. LESCAUT is in the Royal Guards but is a gambler and a scoundrel. When the Chaillot house burns to the ground, Lescaut advises des Grieux to let Manon practice her profession to recoup their fortunes. Des Grieux refuses but accepts the alternative suggestion of becoming a professional gambler. His luck is good and he obtains money from Tiberge under pretense of reform. The new period of extravagant luxury ends when a maid and a valet abscond with their money and jewelry. Manon then becomes the mistress of a wealthy eccentric, M. DE G—— M——. Des Grieux joins the household under pretense that he is a younger brother from whom Manon cannot bear to be separated.

Chaps. 5–7. The Chevalier is deeply depressed when Manon enters the house of her patron. Manon declares that she will remain true to des Grieux, and they plot to flee together after Manon has obtained money from old M. de G—— M—— that night. But their flight is quickly discovered. Police arrest the couple, return the booty to its owner, imprison Manon in the Magdalen, the Common Hospital for prostitutes, and send des Grieux to Saint-Lazare prison.

Des Grieux hopes to escape, and succeeds in ingratiating himself with the prison officers. Hearing of his good conduct, M. de G— M— visits him in the prison. The Chevalier hears for the first time that Manon has been committed to the Magdalen; incensed, he attacks the old man, and thus ruins his chance for a reprieve. He forms new plans of escape for both himself and Manon. Tiberge helps by smuggling a letter to Manon. Lescaut furnishes transportation and a pistol, and the Chevalier succeeds in escaping. Then Manon gets out by disguising herself in men's clothing. The lovers first take refuge in Lescaut's house, then leave for fear of detection. Lescaut is killed by a fellow gambler with a grudge, and the couple continue alone to the inn at Chaillot.

Chaps. 8–10. Financed again by the faithful Tiberge, the couple enjoy another idyllic period. Then young M. DE G—— M——, son of the old man, falls under Manon's spell, and presses her to become his mistress. Manon recounts this to des Grieux, and the two plan to dupe the son as they had duped the father. For greater safety, Manon demands money and jewels in advance, and the gullible young man gives them to her. On his way to claim his reward, young M. de G— M— is waylaid by ruffians hired by des Grieux, but his servant escapes and hurries to the father. The old man calls the police, who again arrest the plotters and return them to their former prisons. The Chevalier soon obtains his freedom through intervention of his father. He then plans to obtain freedom for Manon by use of his meager inheritance.

Chaps. 11–13. Des Grieux learns from a prison guard that Manon has been sentenced to exile and will be sent to America on the next boat. Desperate for time, des Grieux tells the entire story of his love for Manon to his father, but his appeal for help is refused. Next he tries to arrange an attack on the guards who will accompany the convicts to the point of embarkation, but is frustrated. Finally he obtains passage to accompany Manon by posing as her husband.

In New Orleans the couple begin an exemplary life. The GOVERNOR befriends des Grieux with a minor appointment. Wishing to legalize their union, the Chevalier asks the Governor's permission to marry Manon, but is refused, because the Governor's nephew, M. SYNNELET, has fallen in love with her. Synnelet and des Grieux fight a duel. Des Grieux thinks he has killed his opponent; he and Manon flee, but fatigue combined with ill health overcome Manon and she dies in his arms. Des Grieux buries her and falls on the grave in a coma. He is found and brought back to New Orleans, where Synnelet is recovering. Tiberge arrives from France and escorts des Grieux back to his country and his family.

Manon, overcome with fatigue, dies in the arms of Des Grieux

The Man Without a Country

Story by Edward Everett Hale, 1822–1909.
Published 1863.

THIS IS ONE OF THE MOST famous and one of the best known of American short stories. (Today we might call it a novelette.) When it was written, patriotism was a far more active and personal emotion than it is today; but even by today's cynical standards the reader will probably find himself in sympathy with the idea of a man who in losing his identification with his country lost all he had.

FRED INGHAM, an American naval officer, reads of the death of PHILIP NOLAN aboard the U.S. Corvette *Levant*. Ingham then tells the story of "the man without a country," as Philip Nolan was known. (Official papers relating the case were probably destroyed when Washington was burned in the War of 1812, so that Ingham's reminiscences are probably the only remaining record.)

When Nolan was a young officer in the "Legion of the West" stationed near New Orleans, he met and was fascinated by AARON BURR. He was drawn into Burr's conspiracy to found a Western Empire. When Burr was exposed, Nolan also was brought to trial and was convicted of conspiracy. Asked if he wished to say anything before sentence was pronounced, Nolan cried out "Damn the United States! I wish I may never hear of the United States again."

The presiding judge, Colonel MORGAN, soon rendered the verdict, "The Court decides, subject to the approval of the President, that you may never hear the name of the United States again."

Nolan was taken to New Orleans and put aboard a government vessel bound on a long cruise. For the rest of his life he remained on ships at sea, being transferred to an outbound ship whenever necessary to keep him from entering an American port. He was not permitted to talk with the sailors unless an officer was present, and all personnel were instructed never to mention anything pertaining to the United States in his presence. He was allowed to read foreign newspapers, but only after all items mentioning the U.S. had been clipped out. He was also allowed books, and the most poignant of many incidents aggravating the hardship of his self-chosen lot grew out of a book.

With a group of officers, Nolan was reading aloud (Scott's) "The Lay of the Last Minstrel" when he came to the lines

Breathes there the man with soul so dead,
Who never to himself hath said—
This is my own, my native land!
Whose heart hath ne'er within him burned,
As home his footsteps he hath turned
From wandering on a foreign strand?—
If such there breathe, go, mark him well.
For him no minstrel raptures swell;
High though his titles, power, and pelf,
The wretch, concentred all in self . . .

At this juncture, Nolan stumbled to his feet and threw the book into the sea.

Ingham, the narrator, had many conversations with Nolan, and was hard put to conceal from Nolan that his native Texas had been taken into the Union. A letter to Ingham from his friend DANFORTH narrates Nolan's last illness and death. Nolan had made a shrine of his stateroom, draping it with American flags and patriotic symbols. He had drawn from memory a map of the United States, with the quaint old names—Indiana Territory, Mississippi Territory, and so on. He had even guessed that Texas was a state.

At Nolan's pleading, Danforth tells him much of what has happened in the United States during his exile of nearly 50 years. Nolan dies happy with his father's badge of the Society of the Cincinnati pressed to his lips. His will requests that he be buried at sea and that a monument be erected at Fort Adams bearing the legend "In memory of Philip Nolan, Lieutenant in the Army of the United States."

Man's Fate

Novel by André Malraux, 1895–
Published 1933. Translated from the
French by Haakon M. Chevalier; ©
1934 by Harrison Smith and Robert
Haas, Inc. (ML, 33)

THERE WAS A TIME when André
Malraux was the darling of international Communists and this novel had
much to do with it. Despite its propa-
gandistic aspects, *Man's Fate* is worth
reading because Malraux knew his
China, having lived there, and was a
great writer who could interpret the
sensations of a person drawn into such
circumstances as afflicted his Chinese
characters. *Man's Fate* won the Prix
Goncourt despite the fact that it
was undisguised propaganda. Malraux
changed politics and when he did so
he changed very radically, becoming a
Gaullist.

Part I. 1. CH'EN TA ERH, a Chinese terrorist, is anguished at the thought of committing a murder for the sake of the revolutionary forces. Clutching a dagger and a
razor, Ch'en approaches the sleeping victim.
Convulsively, Ch'en stabs himself in the arm
as if to prove that the resistance of the flesh
is no obstacle. Finally, he draws the dagger
and plunges it into his victim, then he
steals the important paper for which he has
committed the murder. The dead man had
negotiated the sale of guns to the government. By obtaining the paper authorizing
the sale, the Chinese insurrectionists will be
able to commandeer the guns and thereby
be in a better position to capture Shanghai.
Ch'en feels his anguish subsiding as he
leaves the murder scene. Hastening to the
phonograph record shop of HEMMELREICH
and his partner, LU YU HSUAN, Ch'en
hands over the paper authorizing the delivery of the arms to KYO GISORS, one of the
organizers of the Shanghai insurrection.
Kyo reads that the arms have not yet been
paid for, but he assures the others that he

will be able to obtain them anyway.
KATOV, a Russian organizer, questions
Ch'en about the crime, but Ch'en cannot
express in words the familiarity with death
that has established itself in his being. Kyo
advises Ch'en that the revolutionary troops
will probably arrive in Shanghai the following day to touch off the insurrection.
Making plans to take the arms from the
ship *Shantung,* Kyo plots to have the ship's
anchorage changed to thwart interference.
After the failure of the February uprising,
Kyo was authorized by the Chinese Communist Party to coördinate the insurrectionist forces. Kyo heads for a night club,
the Black Cat, in search of the Baron de
CLAPPIQUE, a Frenchman who deals in
antiques, opium and smuggled wares. Clappique agrees to help Kyo's forces by using
his influence to have the ship's anchorage
moved. Meanwhile, Katov goes out to enlist
volunteers to get the rifles.
2. Ch'en visits old GISORS, Kyo's father, a
former professor of sociology at the University of Peking. Though dismissed because of
his revolutionary teachings, old Gisors is not
an active participant in the movement.
Ch'en feels an attachment to the old man,
who was once his teacher and like a father to
him. Ch'en reveals that his victim of the previous evening was the first person he has
ever killed. Gisors instinctively sees that ter-
rorism is beginning to fascinate the young
man. Ch'en states that he will soon die, and
Gisors surmises that this is what Ch'en
wishes above all things. Aspiring to no
glory or happiness, Ch'en wants to give to
death the meaning that others give to life
by dying on what is for him the highest
plane possible. Gisors perceive that Ch'en
is a person incapable of living by an ideol-
ogy that cannot immediately become trans-
formed into action. After Ch'en's departure,
Gisors thinks of his son Kyo, whose life is
dedicated to helping the Chinese masses.
For Kyo, this can be achieved only by Communism. **3.** Katov and Kyo, accompanied
by forces dressed as government soldiers,
board the *Shantung,* where they overpower
the ship's officers and succeed in unloading

the firearms. A truck awaits them at the wharf, and the firearms are distributed to the various insurrectionist posts.

Part II. 1. FERRAL, president of the French Chamber of Commerce and head of the Franco-Asiatic Consortium, is distressed because of the general strikes that have idled thousands of Chinese workers. The Consortium is a network of business enterprises throughout Asia. Ferral visits MARTIAL, head of the Shanghai police, who informs him that the government's last chance against the revolutionary forces approaching Shanghai is an armored train carrying White officers. Ferral surmises that once Shanghai falls to the revolutionary army the Kuomintang will have to choose between democracy and Communism. For Ferral, it is essential that democracy win, for if Communism takes a strong hold, the Consortium and all French trade in Shanghai will be destroyed. Ferral hopes to prevent the taking of the city before the army arrives. Martial discusses Gen. CHIANG KAI-SHEK'S relations with the Communists. He tells Ferral of a rumor that Moscow has given orders to the political commissars to let their own troops be beaten before Shanghai; thus discredited, Chiang Kai-shek might be replaced by a Communist general.

2. Ch'en and his fellow insurgents overpower the police officers in the local precincts, stealing their firearms. Amid the gunfire, Ch'en's attention is drawn to an enemy whose leg has been torn off, his hands tied behind his back. Although there is danger of a grenade exploding in his face, Ch'en is overcome by a feeling much stronger than pity, a feeling that he himself is the man bound hand and foot. Ch'en cuts the cords; he then questions his own action, but decides that he could not have done otherwise. Nonetheless, he feels he has been foolish to suffer anguish over the man he murdered the night before.

3. The insurrection is seriously undermining Ferral's economic interests. He meets with Martial and an envoy sent by Chiang Kai-shek to question the police chief's intentions, should Chiang break with the Communists. The envoy asks Martial to guard Chiang, as there have been rumors of an assassination attempt. Ferral later confers with LIU TI YU, chief of the Shanghai Bankers' Association, to discuss Chiang's plans to break with the Communists, a step which he feels will benefit their economic interests. Ferral stresses the necessity of helping Chiang. The Communists are organizing the peasant unions in the rural districts; these organizations will attempt to nationalize the land and declare credits illegal, two measures that would strike a death blow to Ferral's economic interests. Ferral urges the necessity of an immediate decision, because all the governmental cantonments have fallen to the insurgents and the revolutionary army will be in Shanghai the following day. The chief danger lies in Hankow, where the Red Army was being formed. **4.** The army of the Kuomintang is to reach Shanghai in a few hours. The assembly of delegates secretly united by the Kuomintang party before the insurrection has elected a central committee, the majority of whom are Communists. Kyo is disturbed to learn, however, that the Executive Committee formed to organize a new municipal government in Shanghai is not Communist-controlled. Kyo tells one of his soldiers that workers' militias will be organized in

Ch'en cuts the cords

Shanghai and that a new Red Army is being organized in Hankow to suppress the power of Chiang's Kuomintang. Upon learning later that the newly elected Shanghai Prefect is not a Communist, Kyo is angered and unable to understand why the Communist International seems to be following a line of leaving the power in Shanghai in the hands of the bourgeoisie. He resolves to visit Hankow to see the Communist leaders.

Part III. Kyo arrives in Hankow and tells VOLOGIN, a Communist official, that he believes the wrong policy is being pursued in Shanghai. Vologin disagrees, saying that by working within the framework of the Kuomintang, the Communists can undermine Chiang Kai-shek and ultimately gain power for the Party. Ch'en announces his plan to assassinate Chiang Kai-shek, but Vologin expresses firm disapproval of such a terrorist activity. He stresses obedience to the Party above all personal opinions and beliefs.

Part IV. 1. Clappique meets Count SHPILEVSKI in a bar. Because Clappique once saved the life of KÖNIG, the German who heads Chiang's police, König has sent Shpilevski with a warning that Chiang's police are planning to close in on the Communists and that Clappique is known to have aided them in getting arms from the *Shantung*. However, he is to be given a day of grace to escape. Clappique decides he must warn Kyo. 2. Ch'en is ready to carry out his plan to assassinate Chiang Kai-shek. Holding a bomb in his briefcase, he encounters Pastor SMITHSON, his first teacher, who asks Ch'en what he has found in place of the Christian faith he has abandoned. Ch'en replies that he has found another faith in Communism. Ch'en is to throw the bomb as Chiang's car passes on the street. Ch'en enters an antique shop to get a good vantage point. When Chiang's car appears, Ch'en rushes out in the street but the shopkeeper, following him to discuss a purchase, stands in his way and prevents him from throwing the bomb. Three thwarted assassins go to Hemmelreich's shop but Hemmelreich refuses to shelter them, fearing he might risk his child's safety. After their departure, Hemmelreich reproaches himself. Still anxious to murder Chiang, Ch'en decides that the assassins must throw themselves under the car with

a bomb. This idea brings him a feeling of exaltation, but the others refuse to risk their lives in this manner. Meanwhile Clappique tells Kyo of Shpilevski's warning. Kyo refuses to leave Shanghai, but he offers Clappique money to escape and agrees to meet him at the Black Cat that night. Since his return from Hankow, Kyo has been secretly trying to organize combat groups against Chiang, but the Chinese Communist Party's propaganda of union with the Kuomintang has paralyzed his efforts. 3. Katov visits Hemmelreich and tells him that if one believes in nothing, one is forced to believe in the virtues of the heart, which is what Hemmelreich has done in refusing shelter to Ch'en for the sake of his child. 4. The political situation has made great trouble for Ferral. His American credits are about to be cut off and the industrial enterprises of the Consortium show a large deficit. Communism must be crushed in China if he is to win help from the French government. Ferral discusses fanaticism with Gisors. 5. Ch'en, clutching the bomb, rushes with ecstatic joy at Chiang Kai-shek's car. An explosion follows, and Ch'en is killed.

Part V. 1. Clappique has learned that Chiang's special troops are planning to move in at 11 o'clock that night. He must warn Kyo to stay away from any meetings. Clappique decides to gamble what little money he has left in order to win enough to finance his department from Shanghai, in the event that Kyo is unable to help him. Intoxicated by the excitement of gambling, Clappique remains at the gambling tables long past the appointed hour of his meeting with Kyo, but loses all of his money. 2. Kyo and his wife MAY wait at the Black Cat. Word comes that a bomb has been thrown at Chiang's car, but Chiang was not in the auto. Kyo realizes that if the Communists have to fight Chiang's forces tonight, they will be beaten for lack of firearms. When Clappique fails to appear, Kyo and May head for the committee headquarters. As they reach the street, May is knocked unconscious and left on the ground, while Kyo is knocked on the head and hauled away in a waiting automobile. 3. Hemmelreich returns to his shop that evening to find that Chiang's soldiers have invaded it and have killed his wife and

The bomb explodes, killing Ch'en

child. Although he feels grief, he also feels the profound joy of liberation, for now he too can kill. He rushes to Communist headquarters and joins those preparing to fight despite the shortage of firearms. **4.** Clappique, remorseful at his failure to warn Kyo in time, promises Gisors that he will try to influence König to have Kyo released from prison—or at least to prevent the young man's being shot. However, König feels he has already repaid his obligation to Clappique, and refuses to release Kyo. **5.** After a vain struggle, the Communists are overpowered by the members of Chiang's Kuomintang.

Part VI. 1. Kyo is placed in a prison cell. In the next cell, he hears a guard whipping another prisoner, a senseless idiot. Kyo offers the guard money to stop beating the wretch. König offers to spare Kyo's life if Kyo will work for him. Kyo refuses to enter the service of his enemies. **2.** Clappique, in disguise, boards a ship leaving Shanghai. Another passenger is Ferral, who is returning to France to seek financial support for the failing Consortium. **3.** In prison, Katov and Kyo have kept a vial of cyanide on their persons in order to kill themselves and thereby escape the executioner. From time to time prisoners are called out to be tortured to death. Kyo takes the poison and dies. In committing this act, he feels a sense of peace despite the present circumstances. During his life he has fought for something that had deep meaning for him. What, he asks himself before he dies, would have been the value of a life for which he would not have been willing to die? Kativ, feeling even more alone after Kyo dies, offers his cyanide to Suan, who takes it and dies, leaving Katov to a death by torture. **4.** Kyo's body is returned to his family for burial. For old Gisors the world no longer has any meaning.

Part VII. 1. In Paris Ferral confers with the Minister of Finance and important French financiers but is unable to gain support for the Consortium, which is thus doomed to disintegrate. **2.** Gisors is now living in Kobe with a Japanese friend, an artist named KAMA. Gisors tells May, Kyo's widow, that he has decided to refuse a professorship in Moscow and plans to remain in Kobe. May, however, heads for Moscow to work in the Communist movement.

The Marble Faun

Novel by Nathaniel Hawthorne, 1804–1864.

Published 1860. (PB, PL59)

THIS NOVEL IS THE WORK of a great novelist in his later years. Hawthorne wrote The Marble Faun ten years after he had written the two works that are considered his masterpieces, The Scarlet Letter and The House of the Seven Gables. When he was appointed a United States consul in England he took the opportunity to tour the Continent. His travels in Italy suggested a novel set there and he wrote The Marble Faun. In this novel he turned to the occult but produced a novel quite agreeable to the modern taste.

Chaps. 1–5. The mysterious, dark-eyed painter, MIRIAM SCHAEFER, and her two American friends, HILDA, a painter, and KENYON, a sculptor, note the striking resemblance of their young Italian friend, DONATELLO, to the sculpture of the marble faun by Praxiteles in the Capitol at Rome. Many rumors circulate about the origins of Miriam, who appeared in Rome suddenly without any introduction. While touring the Catacombs, she loses her way and is guided back to her friends by a sepulchral stranger, who thereafter haunts her and is often used by her as a model.

Chaps. 6–11. Miriam visits gentle Hilda and discloses that she is soon going away for the summer. She asks Hilda to deliver a small packet for her after four months, unless she hears otherwise, to the Cenci palace, once the home of Beatrice Cenci, who, in the 16th century, harassed by her father's cruel treatment, arranged his murder. Hilda shows Miriam an exquisite copy she has made of Guido Reni's famed portrait of Beatrice. Miriam keeps a date with the unsophisticated, childish Donatello, who tells her he loves her. She is charmed by his simplicity but warns him she is a dangerous person. "If you follow my footsteps they

will lead you to no good. You ought to be afraid of me." Donatello swears that he will always love her. Miriam decides to be for an hour as he imagines her, and joins him in gay dancing with others in the woods to the music of a vagrant band. Her mood is shattered when she sees her strange model among the dancers. She insists that Donatello leave, though he offers to rid her of the model, whom he hates. Her persecutor tells Miriam she must leave Rome with him, leaving no trace of herself behind. He adds that he has the power to force her compliance. It seems that they have known each other before, as he speaks of the destiny they must fulfill together and of how he has tried to bury the past until their encounter in the Catacombs. He hints at Miriam's association with a dreadful crime in the past.

Chaps. 12–23. Hilda learns from Kenyon that Donatello is the Count DI MONTE BENI, of a noble Tuscan family. The four friends take a moonlight stroll with other artists among the ruins of Rome. Miriam is disturbed by the appearance of her "shadow" and begs Donatello to flee the evil that hangs over her and that threatens him too. He insists on remaining, and when Miriam's dreadful persecutor reappears, Donatello throws him over a precipice. The deed is seen by Hilda, who on the following day does not keep her appointment to join the other three at the Church of the Capuchins. In the church the others see a dead monk in his bier. Donatello and Miriam are aghast to recognize him as the man Donatello killed. Miriam declares she and Donatello must part forever, and her despondent lover accepts her verdict. She calls on Hilda, who, horrified at the scene she witnessed, tells Miriam they can no longer be friends. Hilda confirms Donatello's claim that Miriam's eyes "bade" him do what he did.

Chaps. 24–30. Kenyon, visiting Donatello at his gloomy old castle in Tuscany, finds him living alone with a few old servants, greatly changed from the playful youth his friend had compared with Praxiteles' faun. Kenyon notes that the brooding Donatello bears a horrifying emotional burden and that he has acquired a soul out of the grief and pain he has suffered. Kenyon models a bust of his host, but the work goes badly until by accident he achieves the expression Donatello wore when flinging his victim over the precipice. Still unaware of the murder, Kenyon is shocked. Donatello insists the bust must remain as it is, but the sympathetic sculptor alters it.

Chaps. 31–35. Miriam, wan and in mourning, comes to Monte Beni. Kenyon says he believes that Donatello still loves her, but with a depth attuned to his new maturity. He proposes to take Donatello to Perugia, where she can meet them as if by accident. At Perugia, she senses that the man of intellect who has replaced the faun still loves her. Donatello asks forgiveness for deserting her and declares that their lot lies together. Kenyon leaves them to seek Hilda in Rome.

Chaps. 36–45. In Rome, Hilda, wretched and alone, feels stained by the guilt of her secret. Though of Puritan heritage and unwilling to become a Catholic, she is moved to enter the confessional while in St. Peter's. With the burden of her secret lifted, she is serene when she meets Kenyon. Suddenly remembering Miriam's package, she delivers it to the Cenci palace and disappears.

Chaps. 46–50. Miriam and Donatello assure the worried Kenyon that Hilda is safe. Miriam discloses her own background: She is of strangely mixed parentage and connected with a wealthy, influential family of Southern Italy that was linked a few years back with a horrifying event. She was suspected of complicity but declares her innocence. The spectre of the catacomb was an evil figure that had haunted her life. Later, Hilda reappears, having been imprisoned in a convent because of her entanglement with Miriam and because of her confessor's hope that he might convert her. Donatello gives himself up for imprisonment, and Miriam disappears. Hilda and Kenyon decide to marry and return to their own country.

Marius the Epicurean

Novel by Walter Pater, 1839–1894. Published 1885. (ML, 90)

WALTER PATER WAS KNOWN chiefly as a critic and left only a few works of fiction. *Marius the Epicurean* is his one important novel and is a major work commensurate with the importance of its author. It has in it a great deal of the philosophical depth that had won its author an eminent position in the literary world of England, where in his day there were many other giants. The novel is interesting and quick in tempo.

Part I. Chaps. 1–7. Young MARIUS is a devout lad who takes much satisfaction in participating in the worship of the ancient Roman household gods. He enjoys fulfilling his obligation to the great populace of "little gods," dear to the Roman home, which the pontiffs have placed on the sacred list of the *Indigitamenta,* to be invoked on special occasion: Vatican, who causes the infant to utter the first cry; Fabulinus, who prompts the child's first word; Cuba, who keeps him quiet in his cot; and Marius's favorite, Domiduca, the goddess who watches over one's safe homecoming. Marius lives at the family home, White-Nights, a rural estate much shrunken in size due to the squandering of the family fortune by Marius's grandfather. Marius enjoys the simplicity of the farm life and loves the beauties of nature. He is strongly attached to his widowed mother, whose sorrowing at the loss of her husband seems to be ever fresh. Marius passes a peaceful boyhood, more given to contemplation than to action. He nourished a boyish ideal of priesthood, which has faded but left behind a sense of dedication that remains all through his life. In his teens, he is taken

Marius in the temple

to a temple of Aesculapius, among the hills of Etruria, for the cure of an illness. Marius is pleasantly impressed by the beauty of the temple and he gladly enters into the solemnity of its rites. He returns home from the temple cured. His mother is seriously ill and dies soon afterward. Added to the sorrow of his loss is Marius's remorse at the childish anger he expressed at what was to be her last departure from home. Marius soon leaves White-Nights to live in the house of a guardian at Pisa. Here he attends a school modeled after the Academy of Plato. He becomes friendly with FLAVIAN, son of a freedman, who is a leader among the students. Together they eagerly read all the books they can get. Marius hopes to participate in a new school of literature, with Flavian at its head, which would revive the beauties of Latin; but Flavian dies of the plague brought back from the Danube by the legions of Emperor MARCUS AURELIUS.

Part II. Chaps. 8–14. Heartbroken, Marius finds consolation in the philosophy of Heraclitus, which teaches that everything perceived by the senses is in continual flux and so is impermanent. Seeking further, Marius comes upon the writings of Aristippus, the Cyrenaic, who teaches that our direct sensations, whatever their shortcomings, are the only certain

knowledge we possess. *Life,* he learns, *is the end of life.* Marius is eager to experience the richness of sensations offered by the golden age of Marcus Aurelius. However, he does not seek hedonism, whose excesses would be foreign to his nature. Not pleasure but fullness of life is the goal. *Be perfect in regard to what is here and now* is the precept that inspires him. At this time Marius is summoned to Rome by a friend of his father, who has recommended Marius to the emperor as a private scribe, or amanuensis. The Marius family owns a house on the Caelian hill in Rome and Marius goes there. At an inn he meets CORNELIUS, a young officer in the famed Twelfth Legion. The two young men become friends, and Cornelius undertakes to acquaint Marius with Rome. The city is giving Marcus Aurelius an ovation; Marius is happy at the colorful sights and new sounds, and particularly at the ceremonies. Marius is presented to the emperor. In the imperial chamber are the empress, FAUSTINA, and her children. It is the birthday of one of the children, and the emperor departs to make birthday offerings to the household gods. This act deeply touches Marius. Yet later, at the Coliseum, Marius sees the emperor sit passively through the bloody spectacle below, neither approving nor disapproving. Marius, in his clear disapproval, feels superior.

Part III. Chaps. 15–19. Marius listens to the lectures of the Stoic philosophers and many other views heard in Rome. He finds that he can no longer maintain his Cyrenaic beliefs, yet he is not clear as to what he now believes. A year from the time of his first summons to the imperial palace, he is called again. He is impressed anew by the peace and serenity in the countenance of Marcus Aurelius, as the emperor gives him an armful of scrolls to be edited. Later Marius is present at the death of one of the emperor's small sons, sees Aurelius take the dying boy in his arms, and feels keen sympathy for the ruler.

Part IV. Chaps. 20–28. Marius notices that Cornelius has friends of whom he never speaks; but after each visit with them Cornelius returns refreshed and invigorated. One day Cornelius takes Marius to the home of a matronly widow, CECILIA, whose house is a church of those who called themselves Christians. Marius, true to his Epicurean philosophy, sets about surrendering himself to the new doctrines heard here, in order to make a perfectly liberal inquiry into them. Later, Marius sees a Christian service. He is impressed by the expressions on the faces of the worshippers; he senses in their beliefs a dramatic action with a single appeal to eye and ear, which for him is the most beautiful thing in the world. He is drawn again and again to Cecilia's house, for though he cannot accept the Christian beliefs the poetry of their expression holds him strongly. Moreover, he feels that Cecilia may fulfill a need he has long felt, a desire for a woman to be a sister to him. Marius visits his old home, White-Nights, and finds it deserted and dust-covered. Melancholy induces him to have all family burial urns, which stand around the walls, buried. He looks upon himself sadly as the last of his race. Cornelius visits him at White-Nights. One morning Cornelius goes out of the house. Marius follows, knowing that because the plague is still abroad, the inhabitants of the region will not trust a stranger. Just as Marius finds

his friend, the hills of the district billow crazily in an earthquake. By the time the two friends reach the town, the populace is enraged at the Christians, whom they blame for the earthquake. Marius and Cornelius are arrested, but because of their rank they are able to demand trial in Rome. They begin a march with other captives to the great city. Rumor spreads that one of the captives is not a Christian. Out of love for his friend, and because he believes that Cornelius is to be Cecilia's husband, Marius tells the guards that Cornelius is the one not Christian and bribes them to release him. As the march wears on, day after day, Marius becomes utterly weary of life. The harshness of the march weakens him and he falls ill. Believing him unable to proceed, the guards leave him in care of some country folk, who care for him tenderly. In his last delirium, he thinks that Cornelius has gone on a mission to deliver him from death. As he sinks into death, the people utter Christian prayers over him, place between his lips a wafer, and anoint him with oil. They inter his remains in one of their secret burial places.

Martin Chuzzlewit

Novel by Charles Dickens, 1812–1870. Published 1844.

THE IMPORTANT THING about *Martin Chuzzlewit* is that in it Dickens revealed vicious antagonism toward the United States, an attitude that had not appeared in *The American Notes* that he wrote about his first visit to America in 1842. Except for this special feature, which made *Martin Chuzzlewit* one of the most discussed books of its time, the novel is just a Dickens novel, no better than most and not so good as some. *Martin Chuzzlewit* did introduce one of Dickens' most famous characters, Mr. Pecksniff.

Chaps. 1–2. Mr. PECKSNIFF, an architect and land surveyor, informs his two daugh-

ters, CHARITY and MERCY, that a new student is coming in place of JOHN WESTLOCK, who is leaving.

Chaps. 3–4. An old man lies desperately ill at the Blue Dragon Inn in the village. He is attended only by a girl of 17. The inn's landlady, Mrs. LUPIN, sends for Pecksniff, who recognizes MARTIN CHUZZLEWIT, the elder, a relation of his. Rumors about the old man's wealth keep Pecksniff interested in his health, and he haunts the inn—as do several other villagers. The village seems thickly populated with relatives of Chuzzlewit. They form a group for consultation as to how they may acquire his money. In the midst of their conniving, Chuzzlewit and the girl leave the village for parts unknown.

Chaps. 5–6. TOM PINCH, Pecksniff's student and drudge, is sent to Salisbury to meet the new student, for whom he is instructed to ask as Mr. MARTIN. The new student proves to be another MARTIN CHUZZLEWIT, grandson of the old man. Pinch learns that Martin is in love with old Martin Chuzzlewit's young attendant, but she gives him no encouragement.

Chaps. 7–10. Pecksniff sets young Martin to work designing a grammar school, but they are interrupted by the appearance of MONTAGUE TIGG, on an errand to borrow from Tom Pinch; Tigg and CHEVY SLYME have run up a bill at the Blue Dragon. Martin recognizes Chevy Slyme's name as that of a disreputable kinsman. Mrs. Lupin accepts Tom as security for his friends. MARK TAPLEY, man-of-all-work at the inn, says he is going to leave the Blue Dragon in search of his fortune, after avowing his love for Mrs. Lupin. Pecksniff and his two daughters go to London, and they find that they have companions on their coach journey—ANTHONY CHUZZLEWIT, one of the disappointed kinsmen, and his son, JONAS. Pecksniff and his daughters go to the boarding-house of Mrs. TODGERS. One

Mr. Pecksniff and Martin

day they go out to seek RUTH PINCH, Tom's sister, to whom Pecksniff has a letter. Ruth is a governess with a family in Camberwell, and there they find her. Pecksniff greets the grateful sister of his grateful pupil, and keeps his eye on the daughter of the house. The business that brought Pecksniff to town appears when old Martin Chuzzlewit pays a visit. He is friendly to the Pecksniffs but insists upon the dismissal of his grandson from their house.

Chaps. 11–14. Young BAILEY, a servant at Todgers', announces a visitor for Miss Pecksniff. It is Jonas Chuzzlewit, who proposes to show the girls the town, after which they should dine with him and his father. The invitation is accepted. Jonas devotes himself to Charity, the older, but is really interested in Mercy. At dinner in the bachelor establishment of Anthony Chuzzlewit and his son appears the only other member of the household, an old clerk named CHUFFEY. Tom Pinch has meanwhile been in luck, for young Martin has said he will take care of Tom after coming into his fortune. Also, John Westlock has come into some property, and he invites Tom and Martin to dine with him. The conversation at the dinner shows the innocent character of Tom, the complete selfishness of Martin, and the generosity of John, who has paid Tigg's debt without Tom's knowledge. Next morning Mr. Pecksniff pointedly ignores Martin. When Martin demands an explanation, Pecksniff pretends to have uncovered some misdeed of Martin's, at which the young man scornfully departs, announcing his determination to seek his fortune in America. He has very little capital—a good suit of clothes, a watch, and a half sovereign that Tom Pinch surreptitiously gave him. He seeks in vain for some way of working his passage like a gentleman to the United States. When he is almost hopeless, he receives an envelope containing a £20 note but no message. He meets Mark Tapley, who offers his services as companion-valet and begins his duties by taking a letter to the girl companion of Martin's grandfather. She and Mark meet in the park, and she is instructed to use Tom Pinch as a go-between for letters thereafter. She gives Mark a diamond ring for her lover.

Chaps. 15–17. Martin and Mark set out for the United States and have a miserable steerage passage. The ship is boarded in New York by hordes of youngsters crying the papers—the *New York Sewer, Family Spy, Stabber, Peeper, Rowdy Journal,* and the like. A representative citizen of the new

Martin and Mark find that their Eden property is a swamp

country greets Martin. He is Col. DIVER, editor of the *Rowdy Journal,* and he introduces Martin to the war correspondent of his paper, JEFFERSON BRICK. The two take him to their boarding house, kept by Major PAWKINS, where Martin has an opportunity to learn something of American manners. Martin goes to bed somewhat disheartened.

Chaps. 18–20. In London Jonas Chuzzlewit is enjoying his wealth in anticipation, and one evening he stealthily digs out Anthony's will for a foretaste of pleasure. He is interrupted by Pecksniff and exits in panic. Anthony has sent for Pecksniff, perhaps to discuss Jason's probable intention of marrying Pecksniff's daughter. The next morning Anthony is dead, and Pecksniff calls in a professional nurse, Mrs. SAIREY GAMP, who helps Mr. MOULD, the undertaker. He escorts the late Anthony to his grave, the only real mourner apparently being Chuffey. The funeral over, Jonas goes to the country with Pecksniff. He asks Mercy to marry him, thereby angering Charity. The confusion is worse confounded by the unexpected appearance of old Martin Chuzzlewit and MARY GRAHAM, his attendant.

Chaps. 21–23. In New York, Martin sets out with Mark to Eden, recommended to him as one of the most promising investment spots in America. At the railway terminus they are introduced to the agent of Eden, ZEPHANIAH SCADDER. As a result of his claims, they sink nearly all of their savings into a choice lot in Eden. They reach Eden at last, only to find it a swamp, breeding malaria and miasma, with one solitary inhabitant. It is a bitter end to Martin's hopes.

Chaps. 24–29. Pecksniff is worried over having old Martin Chuzzlewit under the same roof as Jonas, and is surprised when the old man seems amenable. Mercy announces her intention of marrying Jonas; old Martin tries to dissuade her, but she pays no attention to him or the signs of evil that are becoming more and more apparent in Jonas himself. Jonas is often mentioned by a deliriously feverish man whom Sairey Gamp is tending at night, having been hired for the purpose by John Westlock. Daytimes she takes care of Chuffey. This daytime employment ceases, however, when Jonas and his bride come home and Mercy takes over the housekeeping. POLL SWEEDLEPIPE, Mrs. Gamp's landlord, comes to take her home, accompanied by Bailey, who is now working for Tigg Montague. The latter, formerly known as Montague Tigg, has enjoyed a reversal of fortune; he is now chairman of the Anglo-Bengalee Disinterested Loan and Life Insurance Company, in which he is associated with DAVID CRIMPLE, formerly Crimp, the pawnbroker; Dr. JOBLING, who attended Anthony Chuzzlewit and is now the firm's medical officer; also a man named NADGETT, who makes inquiries for the office.

They have considered Jonas as a possible policy buyer, but Tigg decides that he would be most useful in the company, as one of its directors. Jonas is told in some detail how the company operates. Mrs. Gamp's patient, Mr. LEWSOME, tries to tell John Westlock something, but whatever he says gives Westlock the impression that Lewsome is still delirious.

Chaps. 30–32. Charity, still bitterly angry at Jonas, vents her wrath on her father. Finally she leaves to live at Todgers'. Pecksniff is relieved, as he has some deep designs of his own. He has achieved some influence over old Martin and plans to clinch his position by marrying Mary, to whom he proposes. She rejects him flatly. She tells Tom Pinch the whole story, and his erroneous picture of Pecksniff crumbles. Pecksniff has been eavesdropping. In Tom's presence, he tells old Martin that he overheard Tom making love to Mary. Tom does not deny it, for fear the truth will anger Martin at both Mary and his grandson. Pecksniff thereupon discharges Tom, who goes off with the blessings of all the neighborhood. Charity, meanwhile, at Todgers' has succeeded in winning the affections of Mr. MODDLE, who at one time was in love with Mercy.

Chaps. 33–35. Young Martin Chuzzlewit falls in the dismal swamp of Eden. Mark tends him; but no sooner is Martin well than Mark becomes ill. In nursing his friend, Martin gains some idea of his own selfishness as well as Mark's fidelity and Mary's sacrifices. On Mark's recovery, they go back to New York. Mark hires out as cook on a ship and thus pays their passage to England.

Chaps. 36–38. Tom Pinch and his sister Ruth—who has left her unpleasant situation as governess—take lodgings in Islington. John Westlock is as friendly and kind as ever, and is much taken with the pretty Ruth. Tom sees Charity and Mercy and learns of Mercy's dismal marital state. Although Tom does not know it, he passes Nadgett in the street. Nadgett is on his way to tell Tigg Montague something about Jonas that gives Tigg a formidable weapon to hold over Jonas's head.

Chaps. 39–42. As Tom is looking for a job, John Westlock brings the news that a Mr. FIPS has offered—in the name of an anonymous benefactor—a job as secretary and librarian at £100 a year. Tom goes to work, still uninformed as to his employer. Jonas and Mercy attempt to leave town, but a packet from Tigg Montague halts them. Tigg makes it clear that Jonas is in his power. Jonas goes off with Tigg on a trip for the purpose of hooking Pecksniff, but on the way the carriage overturns and young Bailey—who had accompanied the rascals—is left for dead.

Chaps. 43–47. Mark Tapley and young Martin arrive at the Blue Dragon. Martin is unable to see his grandfather alone, for Pecksniff stays in the room. Pecksniff, however, is properly bilked by Jonas and Tigg Montague, who take most of his property from him. It is now revealed that the man who gave Tom the packet for Jonas is none other than Nadgett, a man of mystery all round. At Jonas's house, a dismal gathering of friends and relations breaks up early. That night Tigg Montague is killed.

Chaps. 48–49. Tom goes with Mark and Martin to see John Westlock, who is talking with Lewsome. Lewsome says he supplied Jonas with a drug that doubtless caused Anthony's death. Tom recalls something Chuffey said that tends to confirm this, and they call on Mrs. Gamp to keep her eye on Chuffey. The landlord brings the news that Bailey is dead, Tigg has vanished, Crimple has absconded with the company's money, and Jonas has accused the firm of swindling him.

Chaps. 50–54. Next day Tom is visited in the library by old Martin Chuzzlewit, who is his secret benefactor. Now the old man is ready to expose Pecksniff. Jonas is about to murder Chuffey when he is confronted by old Martin, young Martin, Lewsome, Mark Tapley, Chevy Slyme, and Nadgett. Nadgett has traced the murder of Tigg to Jonas. Handcuffed, Jonas bribes Chevy Slyme to let him step into the next room, where he takes poison rather than face prison. Now old Martin can release his wrath at Pecksniff and his hypocrisy. Martin's fortune is distributed so that Mary and young Martin can marry; Mark marries Mrs. Lupin; John Westlock marries Ruth. Only Charity is still unwed. Mr. Moddle rebels at the last minute and runs away, determined never to be taken alive, as his farewell letter declares.

Medea

Play by Euripides, 480–406 B.C.
Produced 431 B.C. (NAL, MT241; RE,
29).

SCHOLARS CONSIDER the *Medea* of
Euripides the high point in ancient
Greek drama. The story of Medea is a
standard in Greek legend. She helped
Jason and the Argonauts to overcome
her father and she fled with Jason and
married him. In some legends, including the one Euripides follows, she was
a powerful sorceress. After she had
lived with Jason for some years, he put
her aside for a more desirable wife,
and she used her sorcery to avenge the
wrong. The play covers this phase.

The nurse of MEDEA'S children laments
the series of events which have led to her
mistress' cruel fate. She recounts Medea's
despair since her unjust abandonment by
JASON. Knowing Medea's strong will and
dangerous nature, she fears the con-
sequences. Medea is heard crying to the
gods for her own death and for the destruc-
tion of Jason and his new bride. Medea
enters and speaks to the CHORUS about the
unhappiness of women and their unequal
rights among men. CREON tells Medea that,
because of threats she has made, she and her
sons must leave Corinth immediately. He
does not believe her promises of peace and
ignores her pleas, but finally consents to let
her stay one more day so that, for the sake
of her children, she can plan the journey.
He walks away and Medea reveals that before leaving Corinth she will murder the
king, his daughter, and Jason, and she tries
to decide on the best possible method.

Jason approaches and offers Medea any
provisions she might need, saying her exile
has been self-imposed by her angry threats.
In bitter rage she recounts the help she
gave him during his travels, killing his
enemies and forfeiting her family and home.
Now she is unjustly forsaken for a new
bride. He explains that his decision to marry

the king's daughter was made so that their
sons might grow up with royal brothers
and the whole family might live comfortably. He denounces women but renews his
offer of help, which she rejects. AEGEUS,
King of Athens, is passing through Corinth
and Medea tells him of her misfortune.
Ignorant of her evil plotting, he promises
her a home and protection in his land while
he lives. With this accomplished, Medea
makes plans for revenge. She will apologize
to her husband and beg him to allow their
two sons to stay in Corinth. She will then
send the children bearing gifts to the new
bride, but these will be anointed with
poison drugs; and the princess, and anyone
who touches her, will die wretchedly. Before fleeing Corinth Medea will slay her
children, partly to prevent their falling into
enemies' hands but also to pain her husband. The women of the chorus try to dissuade her.

Jason believes Medea's false words and
agrees to intercede for her. The children
are sent with the gifts, and the guardian reports that the two boys may stay in Corinth.
Medea then almost relents in her treacherous plan, thinking of her love for the

Medea rejects Jason's offer

children and her pain in bearing and nurturing them. But hatred overpowers her maternal feelings. With incongruous tenderness she kisses her sons, then unable to look at them any longer, sends them into the house. A messenger brings the news that the princess and the king are dead, describing in detail their ghastly and tortured ending. Medea is satisfied, but knows she must finish her job. She has one final moment of softness, then steels herself for what is ahead. Medea goes into the house, the children's cries are heard, and blood flows out beneath the door. Jason arrives, looking for his sons, afraid the king's kinsmen might try to avenge on them their mother's murder. The women of the chorus tell him, to his horror, what has happened. Just then Medea appears above the palace roof in a chariot drawn by dragons. In a fiery speech, Jason assails her for her treacherous deed. He realizes now the folly of marrying "a tigress" from a barbarian land who was a traitor to her father and home. Jason begs for a chance to touch once more the soft flesh of his children, and to give them proper burial. But Medea refuses, saying she will carry them away and bury them herself so that no one will be able to rifle their tomb. She predicts a horrible death for Jason, and says she will go, safe in the chariot given her by her grandfather, the Sun, to stay in Athens. Jason cries out to Zeus to witness his suffering.

The Merchant of Venice

Play by William Shakespeare, 1564–1616.

Produced about 1596. (PB, PL60)

THIS IS ONE of Shakespeare's most popular comedies. The main plot was apparently intended to be the one based on traditional Oriental stories in which the hero must solve a riddle to win the fair lady. After starting to write a play on this theme, Shakespeare apparently found that the story of Shylock and the pound of flesh was far more suited to his genius and he made it the main theme. The Merchant of Venice has been criticized and there have been many suggestions that it be omitted from school reading and from performance because the villain Shylock is a Jew, but in Shakespeare's times Jews and the entire Jewish people were customarily cast as villains and Shakespeare's play is outstanding because in it he develops an eloquent defense of the Jew's right to just treatment and freedom of worship. He fashioned the ending to suit his audiences' prejudice, but not before he had produced many speeches justifying or at least explaining Shylock's quest of vengeance.

Act I. 1. ANTONIO, a wealthy merchant of Venice, is approached by his friend, BASSANIO for a loan. Bassanio is in love with a rich widow, PORTIA, and needs funds to court her properly. Antonio is short of cash because his ships are at sea, but agrees to raise what money he can for Bassanio. 2. At Belmont, Portia discusses her many suitors with her maid, NERISSA. The maid prefers Bassanio to all others. 3. Bassanio calls on SHYLOCK, a money-lender, for a 3-month loan of 3,000 ducats. Shylock insists that Antonio stand surety for the loan. Shylock hates Antonio, who, he says, has "spit upon my Jewish gabardine." Antonio retorts that Shylock may lend the money as to an enemy, and Shylock agrees to make the loan in return for a bond entitling him to a pound of Antonio's flesh if the loan is not repaid on time. Antonio accepts, confident that his ships will come to port in ample time.

Act II. 1. The Prince of MOROCCO visits Portia and asks her to marry him. 2. LAUNCELOT, a servant who is quitting the service of Shylock, meets his blind father GOBBO, who does not recognize him: "It is a wise father that knows his own child." The son says that henceforth he will serve Bassanio. GRATIANO, known as a playboy, asks and is permitted to go with his friend Bassanio to Belmont. 3. Launcelot takes leave of Shylock's daughter JESSICA, who admits that her father's house is hell. **4.** A masquerade is planned for that evening to celebrate Bassanio's departure to woo Portia. LORENZO, a friend of Bassanio, loves Jessica and plans to elope with her. **5.** Shylock berates Launcelot for leaving him. Having to go out, Shylock turns his keys over to Jessica, warning her to keep the doors locked because of the masquerade revels. **6.** Jessica, disguised as a page, elopes with Lorenzo, taking some of her father's money with her. **7.** Portia explains that in conformance with her father's will she must test her suitors before choosing. The Prince of Morocco fails the test of selecting the proper one of three caskets shown him; Portia is happy to see him go. **8.** Shylock is distraught to find his daughter and his ducats gone. **9.** Another of Portia's suitors, the Prince of ARRAGON, selects the wrong casket and fails the test.

Act III. 1. Most of Antonio's ships have been lost. Shylock gloats; "Hath not a Jew eyes . . . hands . . . affections, passions?" Does he not crave revenge just as a Christian does? Shylock has sent TUBAL to search for Jessica. Tubal cannot find her. **2.** Portia is attracted to Bassanio. She puts him to the test but aids him with a song containing clues to the answer, which he thereupon gives correctly. She gives him a ring and promises to marry him. Meanwhile, Gratiano has won Nerissa. Lorenzo arrives with Jessica. Bassanio receives bad news from Venice: Shylock demands repayment. Portia offers to pay the debt, and arranges a quick marriage so that Bassanio may then hurry to Venice to save Antonio. **3.** Shylock has Antonio imprisoned. Friends assure Antonio that the Duke of Venice will not permit the bond to stand. **4.** Portia bids Nerissa procure mens' clothing for Portia and herself, so that they may go to Venice in disguise of lawyer and law clerk. **5.** Launcelot, in a comedy scene, tells Jessica that her conversion to Christianity is not a blessing because it might raise the price of pork.

Act IV. 1. The trial of Shylock against Antonio begins in Venice, the duke presiding. Bassanio offers Shylock twice the amount borrowed, but Shylock is adamant: he wants Antonio's life. Even the duke's plea cannot move him. Nerissa, in disguise of a law clerk, delivers to the Duke a letter from BELLARIO, a learned lawyer of Padua. Bellario recommends a "young doctor of Rome," who soon arrives—this "BALTHAZAR" is Portia in disguise. As Antonio's counsel, Portia offers three times the sum owed; Shylock refuses. Portia appeals to his mercy, to be freely granted—"The quality of mercy is not strained (forced)." Shylock refuses. Finally Portia grants that the bond entitles him to take a pound of flesh, but asserts that if he sheds a drop of Antonio's blood his property will, under the laws of Venice, be forfeit to the state. Thus checked, Shylock agrees to take instead the triple indemnity. Bassanio is ready to pay, but Portia stops him. Since Shylock has refused this settlement in open court, he cannot have it now. And, since he has plotted against the life of a Venetian citizen, half his goods are forfeit to Antonio and the other half to the state. Antonio refuses to take his half, but requests that Shylock be compelled to will it to his son-in-law Lorenzo and also that Shylock be required to become a Christian immediately. The now abject Shylock agrees. Portia refuses a fee for her services. She requests only the ring Bassanio is wearing; he very reluctantly gives it to "Balthazar." **2.** Nerissa likewise contrives to get her husband's ring away from him. The two women hurry back to Belmont.

Act V. Portia and Nerissa pretend to be incensed that their husbands have given away the rings they swore to cherish forever. Bassanio and Gratiano finally realize that the two women were "Balthazar" and the law clerk. Lorenzo and Jessica are given the signed document in which Shylock acknowledges them as his heirs. As a final cheerful note, word comes that the previous report was erroneous—Antonio's ships have come safely to harbor.

The Merry Wives of Windsor

Play by William Shakespeare, 1564–1616. Produced about 1597.

SIR JOHN FALSTAFF was the most popular comic character Shakespeare created. He was so popular in *Henry VI* that Shakespeare catered to popular demand and wrote an entire play about him. (According to some accounts, he wrote *The Merry Wives* by the direct command of Queen Elizabeth.) Because of its contemporary popularity and its history, the play is one of the best known among Shakespeare's plays, but as a work of art it cannot be given high rank. It is simply a quite competent farce written for money-making purposes.

Act I. 1. SHALLOW, a country judge, and his cousin SLENDER complain to Sir Hugh EVANS, a Welsh parson, of the indignities they have suffered from Sir JOHN FALSTAFF. As they approach the house of Master PAGE, a Windsor gentlemen, Evans advises Slender to court his daughter, ANNE PAGE, for she has a substantial dowry. Page is entertaining Falstaff and his hangers-on, BARDOLPH, NYM, and PISTOL. Page and Evans effect a truce when the two parties met and begin to bicker. 2. Evans sends a letter to Mistress QUICKLY enlisting her influence with Anne Page on behalf of Slender. 3. Falstaff schemes to obtain money by wooing Mistress PAGE and Mistress FORD, both of whom hold their husbands' pursestrings. He writes amorous letters to both and asks Nym and Pistol to deliver the letters. When they refuse, he reviles them and entrusts the message to the boy ROBIN. For revenge, Nym and Pistol resolve to inform Page and Ford of the plot. 4. Dr. CAIUS, a French physician lodging with Mistress Quickly, asks her to intercede on his behalf with Anne Page. When he learns Evans has made the same request for Slender, he writes Evans a challenge to duel.

FENTON, a gentleman, also courts Anne Page.

Act II. 1. Mistress Page and Mistress Ford compare the letters sent them by Falstaff. Indignant, they resolve to trap Falstaff, and enlist the aid of Mistress Quickly. Meanwhile, Nym and Pistol inform Page and Ford. Page is merely amused, but Ford decides to take action. He asks the HOST of the Garter Inn to introduce him to Falstaff under the assumed name "BROOK." 2. Mistress Quickly carries pretended messages of encouragement from both women to Falstaff. Ford is introduced as Brook. He begs Falstaff's aid in procuring Mistress Ford, whom he has long coveted. Falstaff assures him he shall have her before the night is out. 3. Dr. Caius awaits Evans in a field near Windsor. Instead, Shallow appears; as a judge, he forbids the duel. The host persuades Dr. Caius to swallow his wrath and to call upon Anne Page.

Act III. 1. Evans awaits Dr. Caius in another field. The host has averted the duel by sending the two men to different fields. Shallow and Slender reconcile the foes. 2. Ford mets Mistress Page on the way to his house. He thinks she is really going to meet Falstaff, and resolves to catch the guilty pair. 3. Mistress Ford gives orders to have a big laundry basket full of dirty linen taken out of the house and emptied in a ditch. Falstaff arrives with amorous intent, which is interrupted when Mistress Page rushes in with the news that Ford is returning to the house. Falstaff hides in the laundry basket, which is carried out as Ford enters to search the house. 4. Anne Page indicates to Fenton that he is her choice, but her father favors Slender. The latter admits to Anne that he has little heart for the suit urged by Shallow and Page. 5. Falstaff returns to the inn wet and bedraggled. Mistress Quickly apologizes for the fiasco and promises that Falstaff shall have another opportunity to see Mistress Ford alone. "Brook" enters; Falstaff tells the story of his bad luck with Mistress Ford, but holds out the hope that Brook may still meet her.

Act IV. 1. Falstaff is at a second rendez-vous with Mistress Ford while Mistress Page and Mistress Quickly plot his downfall. **2.** Again Mistress Page interrupts the rendezvous to warn that Ford is returning. The two dames dress Falstaff in women's clothes, and also send out the laundry basket as a blind. Ford searches the basket furiously and finds nothing. Mistaking the disguised Falstaff for an old crone he hates, he cudgels "Mother Prat" out of the house. **3.** The host agrees to furnish three horses to the German guests who have hired the Garter Inn for a week. **4.** Mistress Page and Mistress Ford tell their husbands all about their jokes on Falstaff. New sport is plotted: Falstaff is to be induced to meet the ladies in the park, disguised as Herne the Hunter. —Page plans to let Anne elope with Slender, while his wife plans to let her elope with Dr. Caius. **5.** Falstaff has returned to the inn. Mistress Quickly brings him the latest message from the ladies. The German guests have decamped with the horses. Dr. Caius says the duke they pretended to serve does not exist. **6.** Fenton pays the host to help in confounding the other suitors of Anne Page.

Act V. 1. Falstaff tells "Brook" about the second fiasco. He urges Brook to accompany him to Windsor Park. **2.** Page, Shallow and Slender are waiting in the park. **3.** Mistress Page tells Dr. Caius he can find Anne in the park by her green costume. **4.** Evans also is in the park, to aid Slender. **5.** Falstaff is in the park, disguised as Herne the Hunter. The two ladies accost him but then flee on hearing a noise. Falstaff is engulfed by masquerade figures of fairies and hobgoblins, who pinch and beat him. All the friends and children of Page and Ford have joined in this prank. Dr. Caius elopes with a green-clad figure and Slender with another; both turn out to be pages, rather than Anne Page. The real Anne Page has been found by Fenton. They finally obtain her parents' consent to their union. Falstaff is finally told how he has been duped.

Falstaff is pursued by masquerade goblins, who pinch and beat him

Merton of the Movies

Novel by Harry Leon Wilson, 1867–1939.
Published 1922 by Doubleday & Co.
© 1922 by Harry Leon Wilson.

HARRY LEON WILSON was never accorded his just position as a humorous novelist—nor, as a matter of fact, as a serious novelist, in which field he proved himself similarly capable. He is best remembered for one of his minor novels, *Merton of the Movies,* principally because it proved so successful when adapted for the Broadway stage and then for the motion pictures. Wilson wrote nostalgic and sentimental novels of somewhat earlier periods that were still within the recollection of his middleaged readers. *Merton,* however, is an exception; it is based on Wilson's experience when he first went to Hollywood to acquire some of the easy money available to authors. The novel is a satire on Hollywood customs and characters of the 1920s.

Chaps. 1–3. MERTON GILL is a clerk in the emporium of AMOS GASHWILER in Simsbury, Ill. He is ambitious to become a movie actor. He is abetted by his friend TESSIE KEARNS, who wants to write screenplays. Both have taken mail-order courses in their fields. Together they attend the local movie house, where they are revolted by low comedy but enthralled by the screen adventures of the glamorous star BEULAH BAXTER.

Chaps. 4–6. Having saved some money, Merton takes leave of absence from Gashwiler and goes to Hollywood. He rents a furnished room, assumes the stage name of CLIFFORD ARMYTAGE, and tries to get a job at the Holden lot. After a week of pavement-pounding, he catches the eye of the woman in charge of hiring extras. She is amused at his unsophistication and rusticity. She gives him a chance to see the inside of the movie lot, and he is entranced by the bizarre sights and sounds—but the weeks go on without a job. Merton makes the acquaintance of some of the extras, among them the MONTAGUE family—the father and mother, old troupers, and the daughter FLIP. This girl has all the self-assurance that Merton lacks, and he shies away from her. He notices that others do not appear to resent her flippant, almost brazen, manner, and that she gets plenty of work. At last Merton is called for his first job—two days for $15. He appears in a cabaret scene in "The Blight of Broadway," as a diner bored by his pretty companion. Later he gets a second bit, as a Bedouin walking the street of an Arabian town.

Chaps. 7–11. Merton's savings are almost exhausted. Rather than abandon his hopes, he gives up his room and takes lodging at night in the movie lot whenever he can find a set that includes a bed. One night in a huge tank built for an episode in the Beulah Baxter serial, he makes a shocking discovery. His idol is married; her husband is none other than the uncouth director SIG ROSENBLATT. Worst of all, during the filming of the perilous scene Beulah is not even on the lot—her part is played by Flip Montague. His admiration of Beulah and scorn for Flip undergo revulsion. On emerging from the tank, Flip sees Merton and notes the signs of destitution. She proposes to buy him a meal, but he stalks away in offended dignity. Later he wanders back to the deserted set and is surprised by Flip, who has returned to search for a lost pin. This time she succeeds in buying him a meal, lending him money, and persuading him to let her help him get a job. Next day she contacts JEFF BAIRD, the man who makes the low comedies that Merton despises. Baird is interested in her account of Merton as an actor who can play a scene "straight" no matter what absurdities are going on around him, and he agrees to give Merton a trial.

Chaps. 12–15. Flip takes Merton to see Baird. Though reluctant to be associated with slapstick, Merton hands over the stills he has had taken of himself registering various emotions. Baird is secretly convulsed with amusement; he signs Merton at $40 a week. After Merton has made some study of the films of HAROLD PARMALEE, he is considered ready for work. Skillfully guided by the director and writers, Merton plays his rôle with utmost seriousness, unaware that his over-acting is extremely funny on the screen. The ending, set in the old West, has Merton imitating BUCK BENSON, a cowboy hero of Hollywood. Lest Merton become aware of the hoax, Baird delays release of the first picture until a second is almost finished. Even then, difficulties arise. Merton objects to appearing in the same film with a cross-eyed man, one of the warhorses of the Baird productions. Baird persuades Merton that the cross-eyed man supports a large and sickly family and that to throw him out of work would be inhumane. In like manner Merton is reconciled to the circumstance that his film fiancée is a brawny six-foot woman weighing a couple of hundred pounds.

Chaps. 16–20. The new picture is a satire on another Hollywood idol, EDGAR WAYNE, who is always cast as a simple country boy with a heart of gold. Merton. falls easily into the part, but begins to notice things. His own salary has been raised to $75, yet the cross-eyed man gets $1200 a week! Through intervention of Flip, Merton is signed to a 3-year contract at $250. Merton realizes he is falling in love with Flip. He buys her a watch to celebrate the première of his first film, but she tells him to withhold the gift until after the event. She and Baird are now feeling anxiety and remorse at Merton's coming discovery that he has been duped. At the premier, Merton is at first puzzled by the laughter; then he begins to perceive what an absurd figure he cuts. He is outraged, but in the following days he is mollified by the storm of praise for this new-found comic talent and by the handsome offers that pour in. He accepts his fate, marries Flip, and settles down to the life of a famous comedy star.

A Message to García

Novel by Elbert Green Hubbard, 1856–1915.
Published 1899.

THIS SHORT TALE or essay is a piece of straight inspirational writing. It has a place in the history of American literature because of its tremendous popularity when it was published. Millions read it and talked about it and some corporations bought large quantities of copies to distribute free among their executives and friends. The book itself was quite decorative, that being Hubbard's primary business: he had founded the Roycrofters, a printing and publishing establishment dedicated to the making of better-looking books than were being produced by most publishing houses. Most of the Roycrofters' designs would seem corny to modern designers but they made an unquestionable contribution to the improvement of book design in the United States.

During the Spanish-American War, President McKinley wished to get an urgent message to GARCÍA, leader of the insurgents. A man named ROWAN undertook to find García, and set off into the jungles of Cuba. Three weeks later he emerged on the other side of the island, having with great difficulty and perserverance traversed hostile country on foot and delivered the letter.

HUBBARD praises the man who can accept responsibility and, without stopping to ask questions, get the task done. He castigates others as falling short of this ideal, among them clock-watchers, gold-brickers, buck-passers, those whose sympathy is all for the "downtrodden worker" with none for the harassed employer who ages before his time trying to get "ne'er-do-wells to do intelligent work." Among workers, he says, indifferent and slipshod work is the rule. For this reason, socialism is far in the future. If men will not act for themselves, what will they do when they are asked to act for all? The man who never strikes or gets laid off "is wanted in every city, town and village—in every office, shop, store and factory. The world cries out for such: he is needed, and needed badly—the man who can CARRY A MESSAGE TO GARCÍA."

Rowan with great difficulty and perseverance traverses hostile country

Metamorphoses

Poems by Ovid, 43 B.C.–18 A.D. Published about 8 A.D. Translated from the Latin in 1567 by Arthur Golding. Other translations. (Everyman, 955)

OVID'S METAMORPHOSES was not a work intended primarily to recount the stories of the ancient Greek and Roman mythology; he used the mythology principally as illustrations of certain philosophical conclusions. Nevertheless, in the course of the work he managed to include nearly all the classical mythology and as a result the Metamorphoses have been used more than any other source for the standard versions of the stories. Bulfinch relied primarily on Ovid. Since the Metamorphoses is a Latin work, nearly all the gods and goddesses are better known to English readers by their Latin than their Greek names. The title, Metamorphoses, simply means changes or transformations. The work presents the philosophy that nothing is stable in the universe; gods change to men and animals, men to animals and plants, animals to stones and plants.

The poet says he will begin from the earliest times and recount events down to the period in which he lives. Out of primitive Chaos in which all matter was intertwined, some primary god separated the basic elements of fire, earth, air, and water. Out of the mixtures of these elements came primary forms. At last the nameless god desired "a living creature of finer stuff than these, more capable of lofty thought, one who could have dominion over all the rest." And thus man was born. This early time was the Age of Gold, when life was perfect. The prime god SATURN is exiled by his son JUPITER (or JOVE), and the Age of Silver follows, in which the seasons appear. Then, comes the Age of Bronze, filled with evil and violence. Jove calls a council of the Olympian gods and declares his intention to destroy most of mankind. A worldwide flood covers most of the earth. Only one man and woman survive, the chaste DEUCALION and PYRRHA. When the waters subside, Deucalion asks the ocean goddess THEMIS how to repopulate the earth. Themis tells him to throw his mother's bones over his back. Bewildered by this advice, Deucalion at last realizes that this "mother's bones" are the earth itself, mother of all men. He and his sister-wife Pyrrha then toss rocks over their shoulders, and a new race of men is born. Plants arise from various origins. For example, the manly god

APOLLO loves a nymph named DAPHNE, who is too coy to return his passion. One day Apollo chases the girl through the woods and is about to catch her. Daphne prays to Apollo's sister DIANA, goddess of chastity, who changes the girl into a laurel tree. Thereafter Apollo uses the laurel wreath to signify victory in athletic contests.

The greatest of all transformers is Jupiter. Jupiter falls in love with the maiden Io and tries to hide the affair from his jealous wife, JUNO. Juno, however, sees through his protective clouds and watches her husband turn the nymph into a white heifer. Juno sets the many-eyed beast ARGUS to guard the heifer night and day. Taking pity on the girl, Jupiter sends his mischievous messenger son MERCURY to slay the beast. Mercury puts Argus to sleep with his magic cap and wand, freeing Io, who wanders about the world. Juno takes Argus's eyes and sets them in the tail of the peacock, her favorite bird. Eventually Jove changes Io back into a woman again. Jove also falls in love with a nymph, CALLISTO. Again Juno spies this infidelity and changes Callisto into a huge bear. One day this bear wanders in the woods and comes upon her son ARCAS, a hunter. Arcas prepares to shoot his own mother, but Jove intercedes by snatching them both up into the heavens. He makes them the Great and Little Bear.

Narcissus at the river

Juno, enraged by her husband's mercy, complains to FATHER OCEAN. As a result, neither constellation ever dips below the ocean's waters. Jove also becomes enamored of a princess of Sidon named EUROPA. He sends her a dream in which the girl realizes that some great honor awaits her. Then, transforming himself into a beautiful white bull, Jove approaches the princess on the sands of the Mediterranean coast. Europa climbs on his back for a ride, and Jove flies wildly away with her to the secluded island of Crete. Later the continent of Europe is named in her honor. Meanwhile Europa's father sends his son CADMUS to search for the missing girl. Cadmus wanders to Greece, where he decides to found a city. While preparing a sacrifice, his men are frightened by a golden snake that Cadmus later kills. To atone for this sacred snake's murder, Cadmus plants man-producing seed in the fields. An army of soldiers spring up, but they kill one another until only five remain. These five soldiers then aid Cadmus in building the city of Thebes.

One of the saddest victims of Juno is ECHO, a nymph who often helps Jove deceive his wife. In rage, Juno dooms Echo to repeat only the last phrases of words spoken to her. Poor Echo then falls in love with an arrogant young man, NARCISSUS, who refuses to accept any offer of love, preferring to sit on a riverbank and watch his reflection in the water. Slowly Narcissus pines away in fascination with his own image. Echo can do nothing but repeat his mournful words until the young man dies. Even in the underworld Narcissus contemplates himself, while Echo fades away until she is just a voice. Narcissus's memory remains as a beautiful yellow flower.

Another beautiful plant arises from the tragic love of PYRAMUS and THISBE. Great brick walls in the city of Babylon keep the two lovers apart. Still, they manage to communicate through a chink. They agree to meet at a deserted place in the forest. The girl Thisbe arrives early and is frightened away by a ferocious lion. In her flight, she loses her cloak, which the lion mauls and drops. Later Pyramus arrives and spies the torn cloak. Assuming that his beloved is dead, the young man drives his sword through his breast. Thisbe returns to the grove and sees her dead lover. She then commits suicide with the same sword. From that time on, the white-berried mulberry trees that grow in the grove change their color to red in memory of the lovers' unfortunate deaths.

One of the world's most significant changes, the seasons, is attributed to CERES, goddess of grain. Her lovely daughter PROSERPINE is playing on the island of Sicily when she is spied by PLUTO, god of the Underworld. The vengeful VENUS forces her son CUPID to wound the god. He thereby falls in love with Prosperine and carries her away to his dark palace. The grain goddess then begins to search the world for her daughter. Since she no longer cares for the crops, everything withers and becomes barren. At last Ceres comes upon the spring ARETHUSA, who tells her what has happened to her daughter. Ceres complains to Jupiter, who promises to return the girl if she has not eaten in Hell. Unfortunately Proserpine has already tasted Pluto's food. When Ceres refuses to accept this judgment and threatens to destroy fertility forever, Jupiter effects a compromise. Proserpine is allowed to spend half of the year on earth with her mother, and half of the year in Hades as its queen. When Proserpine is on earth, the seasons are spring and summer; when Proserpine is in the underworld, the seasons are fall and winter.

King TEREUS marries PROCNE, the daughter of King PANDION, and takes her to northern Greece. After a time, Tereus remembers Procne's sister, PHILOMELA, and contrives a way in which he can have her too. He begs his wife to allow him to bring the girl to live with them. His wife consents, and Tereus goes back to Pandion to escort the other daughter to his home. On the return journey, Tereus cannot restrain his passion and forces himself on the young girl. When Philomela threatens to reveal everything to his wife, Tereus cuts out her tongue and imprisons her in a tower. Philomela uses her cunning to weave a tapestry of the crime and send it to her sister. When Procne summons her to the palace, the two conspire revenge. Procne's son ITYS comes into the room and the sisters seize and kill the boy. They then boil his body and serve it to Tereus at a banquet. When Tereus demands to see his son, Procne hurls Itys' head at his father and

suddenly Tereus grasps what his wife has done. He pursues the sisters, but Procne changes into a swallow and Philomela into a nightingale. Tereus himself changes into a hawk and he still pursues the two delicate birds throughout the world.

One of the most touching stories concerns the flight of the great artist DAEDALUS. Daedalus is called to Crete to build a great labyrinth to contain the half-bull, half-man MINOTAUR that terrorizes the countryside. After completing the immense edifice, however, he receives very bad treatment from King MINOS, who refuses to allow him to leave the island. Daedalus and his son ICARUS fashion wings of feathers and wax to fly over the ocean. The father cautions his son to strike a middle path. If they fly too high, the sun will melt the wax; if they fly too low, the salt spray will weigh the feathers down. Icarus, however, is exhilarated by the power of this new invention and soars higher and higher. He flies too near the sun and his wings disintegrate and he falls into the ocean and drowns. Daedalus successfully reaches the mainland. [The myth is a parable of the "middle path" or "golden mean" expounded by ancient philosophers.]

Ovid recounts the external aspects of the Trojan War, the Quest of the Golden Fleece and Hercules' Labors. He does not dwell long on any of these events, because they are covered more thoroughly by other poets. At this point Ovid enters human history. He continues to repeat his theme: Nature ever makes up forms from other forms. Nothing perishes in the whole universe. Birth is but the beginning of a new form, and death but cessation of a former one. Then, suddenly reversing his position at the end of the poem, he proclaims that the advent of Augustus Caesar will nullify all change by the stability of the Roman Empire. [This statement is assumed to be ironic.]

A Midsummer Night's Dream

Play by William Shakespeare, 1564–1616.
Produced about 1595. (PB, PL679)

THOUGH THIS PLAY contains some of Shakespeare's most beautiful early poetry (from a period when he was not quite so philosophical as he became in later years) and though Mendelssohn wrote beautiful music for it, the play is overcluttered with complications and is hard to read and hard to perform. It was produced in a spectacular and ambitious production by Max Reinhardt, both as a live performance and as a motion picture with a cast both famous and talented, in 1935. But the motion picture, like most motion-picture productions of Shakespeare, did not make money (there have been exceptions to this, principally the productions of Laurence Olivier, but they have been few).

Act I. 1. THESEUS, Duke of Athens, has decided to marry HIPPOLYTA, the queen of the Amazons, at the next new moon. PHILOSTRATE, the master of revels, is ordered to arrange festivities. EGEUS comes to court with his daughter HERMIA and her two suitors, LYSANDER and DEMETRIUS. Egeus wants her to marry Demetrius but she is in love with Lysander. The Athenian law provides the choice of death or a monastery for a disobedient child. The two lovers decide to escape from Athens rather than submit. Hermia is to meet Lysander in a forest outside of the city. HELENA, a friend of Hermia, is taken into their confidence. Helena is in love with Demetrius. He has spurned her advances but she hopes to change his mind by betraying the plot of Hermia and Lysander to him. **2.** At QUINCE the carpenter's house in Athens, a group of craftsmen meet and decide to put on a play in honor of the Duke's wedding. After some bickering about the rôle each will get,
they decide to meet at the Duke's Oak for their first rehearsal.

Act II. 1. In the forest, PUCK and a FAIRY discuss the recent discord between OBERON, King of the Elves, and his queen TITANIA, over the possession of a little boy. Oberon and Titania accuse each other of love for Hippolyta and Theseus respectively. Oberon instructs Puck to pluck a certain flower, the juice of which makes a person fall in love with the first thing he sees on awaking. Puck is to drop this juice into the eyes of Titania, so that she may fall in love with some creature of the woods. Demetrius, followed by Helena, searches the same woods for Hermia. They quarrel and Demetrius tells her to leave him. Oberon, overhearing, now tells Puck to drop the liquid into the eyes of an Athenian youth who is in the forest and has refused his lady. Oberon himself will drop the liquid into Titania's eyes. **2.** Oberon puts the drops into Titania's eyes but Puck puts his drops, intended for Demetrius, into the eyes of Lysander, the first Athenian youth he encounters. Helena, looking for Demetrius, chances to wake up Lysander and he falls madly in love with her. Lysander pursues Helena into the woods. Hermia goes to look for Lysander.

Act III. 1. The craftsmen meet near the spot where Titania lies asleep. BOTTOM gives stage directions for the play, which is "Pyramus and Thisby." Puck decides to play a prank on them by slipping a donkey's head over the shoulders of Bottom. The other workmen flee in terror, thinking Bottom has been bewitched. Bottom does not understand. He starts to sing to keep his courage up. This awakens Titania, who immediately falls in love with Bottom. Titania tells her Fairies to wait on her new lover and to bring him to her bower. **2.** Puck reports his prank to Oberon. Hermia and Demetrius arrive, quarreling. She accuses him of having killed Lysander and she runs from his attentions. Lysander and Helena enter, while the exhausted Demetrius lies down to rest. Oberon puts the magic flower juice into his eyes. The noise of Helena's rejection of the amorous Lysander awakens the sleeping Demetrius. Since he sees Helena first on opening his eyes, he now falls madly in love with her and the two men compete for her favors. The noise brings back Hermia, who thinks Helena has stolen Lysander's love. The men decide to fight it out. The women run off into the woods. Oberon decides to straighten out the situation. He orders Puck to put the four lovers on the ground side by side and has him remove the spell from Lysander with the juice of another flower.

Act IV. 1. Titania is still under the spell and carries on her love affair with the donkey-headed Bottom. They finally fall asleep in each other's arms. Oberon has in the meantime gotten hold of the child, which was the object of his quarrels with Titania. He orders Puck to remove the donkey head from Bottom. He then awakens the queen, who is now free of the spell. She and Oberon fly away together. As the sun rises, Theseus and Hippolyta, with their followers, arrive in the woods to hunt. With them is Egeus, who sees his daughter asleep on the ground with her companions. Again he demands that Demetrius marry Hermia, but Demetrius tells him he loves Helena. Theseus is so pleased with this solution that he decides on a triple wedding. Bottom is the last one to wake up. He thinks he has had a rare vision. **2.** The craftsmen are unhappy over the loss of Bottom, having no one to play his rôle. Bottom turns up just in time.

Act V. 1. In Theseus's palace, the craftsmen put on their play. Bottom is Pyramus the lover, and FLUTE is Thisby. At midnight the couples retire and leave the palace to Oberon, Titania, and their elves, to celebrate their reunion.

The Mill on the Floss

Novel by George Eliot (Mary Ann Evans Cross, 1819–1880).
Published 1860. (PB, PL509)

IN AMERICA this is one of the best-known of George Eliot's novels, partly because excerpts from Book I were for many years used in "readers" in elementary schools. *The Mill on the Floss* was written in George Eliot's most fruitful period and was one of her best works. The novel (and River Floss) are set in Warwickshire, in central England.

Book I. Boy and Girl. 1–3. Mr. TULLIVER, his wife BESSY, his son TOM, 13, and his daughter MAGGIE, 9, live at Dorlcote Mill near the village of St. Ogg's on the River Floss. Although Mr. Tulliver has made a good living as a miller and farmer, he does not want Tom to follow in his footsteps. He decides to give Tom the best education money can buy. He laments only the fact that Maggie rather than Tom has inherited the brains in the family. Mr. Tulliver sends Tom to a boarding school run by a clergyman named STELLING. **4–5.** Various incidents show how great is Maggie's love for Tom. Whenever she does something to make him angry, and he says he does not love her, she is very hurt. **6.** After a quarrel with Maggie, Tom goes to play with his friend BOB JAKIN. Bob cheats at a game and the boys exchange blows, Tom exhibiting a keen sense of justice. **7.** Mrs. Tulliver's sisters, the former Misses DODSON, Aunt GLEGG, Aunt PULLET and Aunt DEANE, come to visit the Tullivers with their husbands. All three have married well; they believe Bessy has married below herself. They are critical of Mr. Tulliver and mock the Tulliver children, especially Maggie with her dark skin, unruly hair, and madcap ways, comparing her unfavorably with Mrs. Deane's daughter LUCY, who is blond, neat, and well-mannered. The relatives disapprove of the school Mr. Tulliver has chosen for Tom. Mrs. Glegg and Mr. Tulliver have a serious quarrel, as a result of which Mrs. Glegg threatens to call in a £500 note she holds on the Tullivers' property. **8.** Mr. Tulliver decides he must pay Mrs. Glegg. His sister, Mrs. MOSS, who has married badly, owes him £300. He goes to her, but the Mosses are in no position to repay him. **9–11.** Lucy comes to stay with the Tullivers and Tom is kind to her and ignores Maggie because of her pranks. Maggie, in a fit of anger and jealousy, runs away to the gypsies, thinking that life among them will be pleasant; but she is soon disillusioned by their filth and their food and is happy to be returned to her home. Her father, who always takes Maggie's part, scolds his wife and son for mistreating her. **12–13.** Mr. Glegg convinces his wife not to call in her money but Mr. Tulliver writes to her that he will pay her within a month and wants no more favors from her. The family breach grows and Mrs. Glegg does not visit the Tullivers until the night before Tom is to leave for school.

Book II. School Time. 1. Tom is unhappy at Mr. Stelling's; his ambition is to work at the Mill. Maggie visits him, the only bright spot of his first months at school. **2.** When Tom is home for Christmas, his father is having legal troubles. Mr. Tulliver's pet peeve is lawyers—in particular Mr. WAKEM, who is representing the neighbor with whom he is feuding. **3–4.** Tom returns to school and finds that Mr. Stelling has a second pupil, Mr. Wakem's crippled son PHILIP. Tom admires Philip's artistic talents and intelligence but is prejudiced because of his father and his deformity. However, the boys help each other. **5–6.** Maggie, again visiting Tom at school, meets and takes a liking to Philip, especially when he is kind to Tom, who has injured his foot. Maggie and Philip kiss, promise to remember each other, and say they will kiss again whenever next they meet. Maggie goes away to school with Lucy but is called home when Tom is in his fifth and last half-year. She goes to school to get him, bringing the bad news that Mr. Tulliver has lost his legal case and stands to lose everything—his mill and his land. Tom and Maggie go home to their new life of sorrow; their childhood and their happiness are over.

Book III. The Downfall. 1. When Mr. Tulliver realizes he is ruined, he has a stroke. Tom tells Maggie she must never speak to Philip again. **2–4.** Mrs. Tulliver's relatives show no real sympathy for the Tullivers. All the household goods are to be sold and they do not offer to help the family keep their most cherished possessions. Tom gets out his father's will, which states clearly that he wishes the Mosses' note destroyed. Tom insists that his father's will be honored, though this means losing everything. **5.** Tom goes to Uncle Deane, in hope of getting a good position, but Mr. Deane says Tom should have learned bookkeeping rather than Latin. **6.** Bob Jakin comes to see Tom for the first time since the boys fought and generously offers Tom a considerable sum of money. Tom appreciates the offer but feels he cannot accept it, even though all the household furnishings are sold. **7–9.** Mrs. Tulliver begs Mr. Wakem not to buy their mill and their land; Uncle Deane's firm, Guest and Co., seems willing to buy it. But Mr. Wakem decides to buy the mill to humiliate Mr. Tulliver by letting him stay on and work for wages. Mr. Tulliver sadly agrees but has Tom write in the family Bible that he will never forget what Wakem has done and will seek revenge.

Book IV. The Valley of Humiliation. 1–2. The Tullivers are living economically; their creditors have been paid in part, and Mr. Tulliver strives to repay them in full before he dies. **3.** Maggie feels hardest hit by the family misfortune, for she has lost not only her possessions and way of life but seemingly her father's and brother's love. One day she reads a passage by Thomas à Kempis that completely changes her outlook. She decides that her miseries have come from caring only about her own pleasures; from now on she will live only for others. Her life becomes one of self-renunciation.

Book V. Wheat and Tares. 1. In the Red Deeps, a favorite spot of hers near the mill on the River Floss, Maggie sees Philip for the first time in five years. He has followed her there. Philip expresses his love for her but Maggie says they must keep apart; seeing him has made her long once again for the full life she has forsworn. She tells Philip she is not free to love him, but she agrees to meet him again secretly by the river. **2.** Tom, with his integrity, family regrets, pride, and personal ambition, is doing well in his job with Uncle Deane's firm. Still, he and his father are accumulat-

Maggie and Philip meet for the first time in five years

ing money only at a slow rate. Bob Jakin proposes a business partnership to Tom, and Tom and Bob succeed in borrowing money for their venture from the Gleggs, without the knowledge of Tulliver, who disapproves. **3–4.** Maggie and Philip see each other often. Philip tries unsuccessfully to convince Maggie that her resignation is willful and senseless. They declare their love for each other, but Maggie insists that it be kept secret, for she would never do anything to wound her father. **5.** Tom learns of their secret rendezvous and makes Maggie swear on the Bible never to see Philip again. She pleads that she be allowed to see him once more and Tom goes along. Tom is rude, questions Philip's intentions, and mocks his deformity. He drags Maggie away; sister and brother exchange harsh words. **6.** Tom surprises his father with the profits from his private enterprise: The creditors can be fully paid and honor restored to the Tulliver family after four years. **7.** After paying the creditors, Mr. Tulliver encounters Mr. Wakem on his way home. They have a fight, which brings on Mr. Tulliver's second stroke. Maggie asks her father to forgive the Wakems, but he refuses. He dies that night.

Book VI. The Great Temptation. 1. Aunt Deane has also passed away and Mrs. Tulliver has gone to manage her house at St. Ogg's. Lucy is home and expects Maggie to come for a long visit. Lucy and her beau, the very handsome and very wealthy STEPHEN GUEST, hope Maggie will not object to seeing Philip Wakem, for Philip is one of their closest friends; they hope to be a happy foursome. **2–3.** Maggie finds life at the Deanes', with its daily round of boating, music, good food, and good books, a delightful change from her life at the third-rate school in which she had been teaching. Maggie and Stephen like each other from the very start. Maggie tells Lucy the story of her love for Philip. **4.** Maggie goes to see Tom, who is now boarding at the home of Bob Jakin and Bob's new bride, for she had promised never to see Philip again without his consent. Tom is displeased but agrees that she may see Philip as a friend at the Deanes'. **5.** Uncle Deane compliments Tom on seven years of good work. Tom asks his uncle to have the firm buy his father's mill and land from Wakem, to satisfy one of Mr. Tulliver's dying wishes. Mr. Deane says the request will be considered. Even this business-loving man finds it sad that Tom cares only for business. **6.** Maggie is happy for the first time in years. She has been well-received in St. Ogg's society. She and Stephen care a great deal for each other. Lucy, though always with them, does not seem aware of their affection. On the night before Philip is to return, Stephen visits Maggie at a time when he

Stephen showers Maggie with kisses.

knows Lucy will be out. 7. Maggie tells Philip they can at least be friends. Lucy remains blind to the attraction between Maggie and Stephen, to whom she is almost engaged, but Philip perceives the bond at once. 8. Lucy suggests to Philip that he try to persuade his father to sell Dorlcote Mill to Mr. Deane, in the hope that Tom will then forget his hatred of the Wakems. Mr. Wakem is amenable to this idea; he will not agree to have any direct transactions with Tom, but he agrees to accept Maggie for his son's sake. 9. Lucy tells Maggie that the mill and land will soon be Tom's again; she is surprised at Maggie's apparent lack of enthusiasm. Maggie plans to leave the Deanes and take a new situation. Lucy, distressed, asks Maggie if she does not love Philip enough to marry him. Maggie says she does but that to marry Philip would mean giving up Tom, which she cannot do.

10. One night at a dance Stephen and Maggie step outside and he showers her with kisses. She is offended at the liberty he has taken. Later that evening she implies to Philip that she would marry him were it not for Tom. 11. Maggie visits the Mosses and Stephen goes to see her there. He vows his love for her and finally she admits hers for him. 12. Tom and Mrs. Tulliver now live at their old home once again. Lucy tells Tom how Philip persuaded his father to sell the mill to Guest & Co. and to accept Maggie as a daughter-in-law. This only makes Tom dislike the Wakems all the more. 13. Philip, Lucy, Maggie and Stephen are to go on a boat ride but somehow Lucy and Philip have other plans and Maggie and Stephen go alone. The tide carries them farther than they had planned. Stephen wants to take Maggie away and marry her. They spend the night on a Dutch boat. 14. They land at the

town of Mudport the following morning and go to an inn. Though Stephen pleads, Maggie says she will not betray Lucy, who has been so good to her, nor will she hurt Philip. Stephen warns Maggie that she cannot return to St. Ogg's because of all the talk there will be, but Maggie is sure that Lucy will believe her and she leaves Stephen.

Book VII. The Final Rescue. 1. Five days after leaving with Stephen, Maggie returns to Dorlcote Mill. She plans to tell Tom everything but he will not listen. In his mind she has disgraced the family and betrayed her best friend. Mrs. Tulliver decides to go with Maggie. Bob Jakins will take them into his house. **2.** St. Ogg's "society" scorns Maggie although Stephen, now in Holland, has written a truthful letter to his father which completely exonerates her. Maggie now turns to Dr. KENN, the kindly parish priest, for counsel. **3.** Of all people, Aunt Glegg takes Maggie's part and invites her to stay at her house. Maggie receives a fond letter from Philip, who has gone abroad. He expresses his great love for her and trust in her. **4.** Maggie longs only for Lucy's forgiveness. Lucy, who has been ill, is going to the seashore with Stephen's sisters; the night before she leaves, she steals out of the house and goes to see Maggie. She assures Maggie that she believes she never meant to deceive her. **5.** Dr. Kenn,

unable to find Maggie a position in St. Ogg's, has made her his own children's teacher; but he is recently widowed and soon there is gossip about Maggie and himself. He advises her to leave St. Ogg's; he will get her a good position in a nearby community. Maggie gets a letter from Stephen, in which he reproaches her for her perverted notion of right. He begs her to come to him. Maggie feels that for her there can never be love without pain; pain is her cross to bear in life and she hopes that death is not far off. The River Floss has flooded. Maggie must leave Bob's house when the water rises. The current takes her boat past the mill. Her mother is not at home but Tom is stranded there and Maggie rescues him. Their boat capsizes and brother and sister are drowned together, united at last—in death.

Conclusion. Five years later, the flood's damages had been repaired. All the principals were alive but Tom and Maggie, whose bodies, found in close embrace, were buried together. Two men visited their tomb; both felt that their keenest joy and sorrow were forever buried there. One visited the tomb again years later with a sweet face by his side. The other always came alone and spent most of his time in the Red Deeps section by the River Floss, where the buried joy seemed to hover still.

Maggie rescues Tom from the mill where he was stranded

Minna

Novel by Karl Gjellerup, 1857–1919. Published 1889. English translation from the Danish published 1913.

GJELLERUP, a winner of the Nobel Prize for Literature in 1917, was a Dane but lived in Dresden for many years and in this novel the principal setting is Saxony, along the Elbe River south of Dresden, in the resort area near the border of Czechoslovakia. The novel is very emotional. The author, in a note, professes to have received the manuscript from his friend Fenger; explains that Fenger died not long after Minna, of a combination of tuberculosis and a broken heart; and proposes a motto for the story, from Thomas More: "To live with them is far less sweet/than to remember thee."

Book I. Chaps. 1–10. At the end of a busy semester at the Dresden Polytechnic (college), I, HARALD FENGER, a Dane, decided to spend a whole month of my vacation at Rathen, a small village on the Elbe. Aided by a local schoolmaster I finally found a room overlooking hills and the river. Below my pension was a sumptuous villa. The schoolmaster confided that a very attractive governess lived there. I went to Rathen by boat. I observed a pretty young lady (MINNA JAGEMANN) on board and managed to settle myself near her and the two little girls in her care. She wore an adorable little hat with a silver-grey veil. I glanced at her as unobtrusively as possible and decided I could easily fall in love with her type. I was sure she had noticed me, for at times she blushed over her book. I presumed it was a book of poetry, but it proved to be a German-Danish dictionary. When we reached Pirna I looked with some interest at its acropolis, Sonnenstein, earlier a fort and at present a large insane asylum. I had struck up enough acquaintance with the young lady to lend her my steamer rug,

on account of the cold rain, and when the call came to disembark at Rathen we folded it together, our hands touching. "Thank you!" she said, and hurried off. I never expected to see her again.

I was exploring the country around my pension one day when I discovered a small grotto with a bench and small table in front. On the bench lay a small book, a German-Danish dictionary. After a while the owner, the girl I had met on the boat, appeared. She cried out, as she had not expected to see anyone. I asked why she was interested in Danish and she said she had known one of my countrymen. She vanished as soon as she could politely get away. At this second meeting she made a still deeper impression on me; she was the most beautiful girl I had ever seen. I went to see the schoolmaster. He told me the governess had been associated with a Danish painter who had jilted her. I felt very disturbed. Later one fine day I met her outside a cave; "Wotan's Cave" was painted on the rough stone wall. We talked about Wagner, literature, Faust, Marguerite. I went often again to Wotan's Cave, but in vain.

Every day about 1 P.M. I took dinner at the Erbgericht hotel. There I met an old German-Jewish couple whom I knew from Dresden; I had met their son, IMMANUEL HERTZ, at the polytechnic. The father had been a merchant in Königsberg. They had taken a house in Rathen near the river. They told me they had a relative, a girl, they wanted me to meet; she was a governess. I wondered if this was fate.

I met Minna on one of my walks and we agreed to pretend we had not met before. We were presented to each other by the Hertzes and it seemed that they thought we were well matched. I was happy, day after day, falling more and more in love.

Young Hans, the landlord's son, wanted to take us to his father's mine to watch blasting. While waiting for the workmen to arrange things, Minna told me about her home. It was simple but lacked happiness and was not homelike. Her father, until his death a year before, could not bear to have strangers come to the house. With the Hertz family she had found a real home. On our way home we picked blueberries, at first with our fingers, then with our mouths; and our lips met in a heavenly kiss. She said goodbye and hurried home, alone.

Book II. Chaps. 1–10. I walked in a dream along the bank, convincing myself that the story of the Danish painter was just gossip. As I walked along, Hans came running to bring me a letter he thought I had dropped while we watched the blasting, but it was Minna who had dropped it. In the dim light I made out the inscription on the envelope: To Artist Axel Stephensen, Denmark. I felt chills running up and down my spine. I knew the man. From what the schoolmaster had said, it must have been a couple of years since he saw her in Dresden, yet they still wrote to each other! I sent the letter to Minna.

A letter from Minna arrived in the morning. It told me more of her history. Her mother had six sisters. Their mother was busy in the house; the father occasionally beat them. With that sort of upbringing, five of them had babies before they were married. The other, Minna's mother, the youngest sister, did not; but Minna grew up with the idea that the more admirers a girl had, the more she rose in the opinion of others. A young musician moved in with them and she became attached to him in a childlike way. He asked Minna's mother for her hand but her mother said she was too young. The musician left and Stephensen came. He told Minna he had come only on account of her. One day the musician returned. He asked Minna for a kiss when he was leaving and it was given. Stephensen had overheard at the door and from then on he wanted Minna in his own way. A thousand times she wept because she had fallen so low in the opinion of one whom she later came to love, for she was really innocent. Stephenson became more and more demanding, but when Minna spoke of marriage he said an artist must be free. They parted with the understanding that they would correspond and be friends.

Minna also sent me a letter she had written to Stephensen: "I have made the acquaintance of a young student by the name of Fenger, a countryman of yours. I often meet him at the Hertzes'. He is very

tall but stoops a little, and sometimes it seems to me that his chest is not very strong. I would be sorry if that were the case."

The Hertzes made a trip to Prague and invited Minna and me to accompany them part way. We went with them as far as Schandau. When we tried to get back to Rathen we found that there was no boat and there was nothing to do but go to a hotel. At the hotel we were given adjoining rooms (and the clerk leered). We gave each other a long goodnight kiss. Then we rapped another goodnight on the wall between our rooms. I was overcome with the feeling of not only loving, but being loved in return. We had reached an understanding.

The Hertzes returned frm Prague. We went to see them, arm in arm, and our health was drunk in Rhine wine. Hertz was ill from the cold and damp of Prague. Minna asked me to call on her mother in Dresden.

Book III. Chaps. 1–6. As soon as I could, I went to see my future mother-in-law, Minna's mother, in Dresden. If I had kept a diary, I would have written: "At ease—my mother-in-law is harmless." Two days later Minna arrived. She was depressed about something; it was a letter from Stephensen, which she showed me. He still expressed love. She did not understand; for he had urged her "to marry an honest man!" She played the piano for me. We explored Dresden and in the evening looked toward Rathen, our lost paradise. We went to the opera. The glance of love Minna gave me at the end I shall not forget till my dying day. But in the evening, at dinner in a little café, we encountered Stephensen!

Book IV. Chaps. 1–9. Stephensen began at once to remove the glove from his right hand, and Minna began to unfasten hers. She wore my ring. Stephensen stared at it morosely. She introduced me to him as her fiancé. We bowed almost too politely. He said he had come to town to copy Correggio's Magdalene. We left the café, and I took Minna home. I stole a last kiss at the street door. Then on the other side of the street I saw a dark figure. He crossed over to me; it was Stephensen. We went together to have a glass of beer. He touched on my financial position; could I support a family? I resented his acting as though he were

Minna's guardian, but he said, "She will have to choose between us!" I replied, "She has chosen!" "No, she has not. She must be free to choose!"

The next evening I went to see Minna only to learn that it was possible for her to love two men. She said, "Perhaps I really love you best!" I felt as if I had received a blow! Finally I told her that I was the one who had severed the agreement. It was only the day before that we had exchanged rings! I left my purse, telling her to return it if she wanted me.

At home I found two letters. One was from my uncle in England, asking me to come to work for his firm within two weeks. The other was from Immanuel Hertz, congratulating me: He also had loved Minna and had been burnt. The purse was returned, and in a few minutes I was at the Jagemann door. Stephensen was there, talking to Mrs. Jagemann. Stephensen asked to sketch me. He also made a sketch of Minna and gave it to her, for her to give to the one who needed it most. Minna went to see an aunt at Meissen. A couple of evenings later I received a letter in Minna's handwriting.

Book V. Chaps. 1–8. My hand shook violently as I tried to open the letter. The first thing that I saw was the sketch of Minna, which she had sent me. The letter said, "It is all over; I must be his. I feel powerless to break with my first love to start all over with you." At first the loving tone soothed my pain. Then the reaction: Why hadn't I gone to her room at Schandau and made her mine! I could gladly have changed places with old Hertz, who was dying. He died, and at his burial I saw Minna in mourning. I felt it was the burial of our love rather than of old Hertz. I heard from young Hertz that Stephensen had gone to Denmark to arrange matters. A week later I went to England.

Year after year passed in hard work. In the fourth year after I left Dresden I met a German musician who turned out to be the one who had lived with Mrs. Jagemann in Dresden and had been Minna's first half-childish lover. I became homesick, stopped visiting the house of a young lady I was half-courting, and a week later was in Copenhagen. After two weeks without seeing Minna, I heard Stephensen's voice in a café, effaced myself, and watched Minna.

She looked tired. I listened to aesthetic conversation about the future of art. A smiling blonde at their table was near fainting with admiration for Stephensen: She was his model. He flung out clever sentences. A smile of cold disdain played on Minna's face. Then later I heard Minna laugh so loudly that it froze the whole party.

I made a business trip to Sweden and Russia for my uncle, and returning to Dresden made a visit to Rathen. There at the old grotto I met Minna and Stephensen; it seemed like a hallucination. "I saw you at the café," said Minna. I went with them as far as Pirna, then left for Dresden. On the evening train I saw Stephensen's face at a car window. He stepped out alone. He told me Minna was at Sonnenstein. I mumbled as if I did not grasp the meaning. He said Minna was not really insane, merely melancholy and upset. My skepticism gradually changed to fury and I shook my fist in his face. But he pulled away and was lost in the crowd. I went to Pirna, where the chief physician told me there was no immediate fear for Minna's mind but that she had an old heart lesion that might end with sudden death. He did not want me to see her at that time.

She sent me letters; I read them without tears until I came to a strangely crumpled and buckled one from me, which she had carried next to her heart. I pressed it to my lips and sobbed like a child. "Good night, Harald," she wrote, after telling me about Stephensen's infidelities—the blonde woman who posed as a model, and others—going back to the very first year. Her child had died. "I feel I belong to you. I never was his!"

I happened to see a portrait of her in an antique shop, Stephensen's pastel portrait of her. I bought it and let it slide into the river. When I reached my room that day there was a letter from the chief physician stating that Minna had died from coronary thrombosis that morning. I undertook to arrange for the funeral. I was able to obtain space near the resting place of Hertz and his wife, under one of the giant poplars. On the grave I ordered placed a broken column of the most exquisite Saxon Serpentine, without any inscription other than the name

MINNA

The Misanthrope

Play by Molière (Jean Baptiste Poquelin, 1622–1673).
Produced 1666. (ML, T29)

MANY CRITICS HAVE CALLED this the masterpiece of Molière, a playwright acknowledged to be France's greatest. Molière was a satirical dramatist, poking fun at nearly all phases of fashionable society, and *The Misanthrope* falls into this pattern. The title part is that of Alceste. Molière undoubtedly intended through Alceste to express his scorn of the artificiality of French society, yet he made Alceste also a comic character—as evidenced by the fact that Molière originally played the part himself and Molière liked comic parts. The message seems to be that while it is stupid to conform entirely to social conventions, it is just as stupid to reject them entirely and be a rebel in one's own world.

Act I. 1. ALCESTE accuses his friend PHILINTE of bowing to the deceitful practices of the age in flattering everyone indiscriminately, even those unworthy of affection. Philinte replies that a little deception is often necessary to avoid hurting people's feelings. He advises Alceste to pay more attention to winning his lawsuit. The talk turns to CÉLIMÈNE, beloved of Alceste. In Philinte's opinion, she is a far less likely choice for Alceste and his high principles than someone like ÉLIANTE, Célimène's cousin, or even her friend, the prudish ARSINOÉ. Alceste agrees with Philinte but says that in matters of love good sense does not always rule. **2.** ORONTE, also a suitor of Célimène, asks Alceste's opinion of a sonnet he has written. Alceste replies that it is poorly written. Oronte is deeply insulted. Philinte intercedes, praising the sonnet, and averts a quarrel. Philinte chides Alceste for not being more diplomatic, but Alceste refuses to listen.

Act II. 1. Alceste accuses Célimène of bestowing her interest on too many suitors. She replies that she cannot help her attractiveness, but she loves him alone. **2.** The servant announces the arrival of ACASTE, a marquis. **3.** Alceste accuses Célimène of giving her attention to everyone, regardless of worth. She replies that it is important to keep on the good side of such influential persons as Acaste. **4–5.** Alceste warns Célimène that she must choose between her other suitors and him. Acaste and CLITANDRE arrive. Both are in love with Célimène. Célimène makes sarcastic, witty remarks about various persons. The marquises enjoy it; Alceste objects. **6.** A guard, representing the Marshals of France, comes to summon Alceste, to settle the quarrel between him and Oronte over the sonnet.

Act III. 1. Clitandre and Acaste discuss their respective progress in winning Célimène. They agree that should either of them seem to be gaining the advantage, the other will withdraw. **2–3.** Acaste discusses Arsinoé's reputation of being a prude. Célimène says that her prudishness merely hides her desire to have a lover, which her feeble charms have always prevented. **4.** Célimène greets Arsinoé with a great show of fondness. **5.** Arsinoé says she is compelled by friendship to tell Célimène that many people have begun to criticize her conduct. Célimène retorts that Arsinoé should pay less attention to the actions of others and concern herself more with her own. Arsinoé says she is not interested in the attentions of suitors; that such attentions are generally bought at too great a price. **6–7.** Arsinoé tells Alceste that she can prove Célimène is untrue to him.

Act IV. 1. Philinte tells Éliante that Alceste would be far better off if he loved her rather than her fickle cousin. Éliante says she might welcome Alceste's attentions. Philinte declares that should Alceste succeed in his suit with Célimène, he would be happy to win Éliante for himself. **2.** Arsinoé has given Alceste a letter written by Célimène and intended for Oronte. The letter indicates that Alceste is not the only man in Célimène's heart. Incensed, Alceste

offers his love to Éliante. She replies that a
spurned lover often turns to another out of
revenge, but that later the lover's anger
subsides and he returns to his beloved.
Alceste declares that he will never relent.
3. Alceste confronts Célimène with the
proof of her unfaithfulness, but artfully she
makes him doubt its truth. He begs her to
prove her innocence, but she replies that
Alceste should not doubt her love. 4. Alceste
learns that his lawsuit is proceeding badly
and that he is threatened with arrest.

Act V. 1. Alceste has lost his lawsuit and
regards this as proof that the world is cor-
rupt and deceitful. He plans to withdraw
from society and has asked Célimène to go
away with him. 2. Oronte and Alceste tell
Célimène that she must choose between
them. She calls their demand unreasonable.
3–4. Acaste confronts Célimène with a
letter she has written to Clitandre, in which
she makes fun of all her suitors and professes her love for Clitandre. 5. Oronte says
he will be made a fool of no longer, and
tells Alceste he may have Célimène. 6.
Arsinoé tries to console Alceste. Alceste
asserts that he has no intention of seeking
consolation in a new love with Arsinoé,
and she indignantly denies any such intention. 7. Alceste tells Célimène he will forgive her if she will go away with him and
retreat from the world. She expresses ab-
horrence of withdrawing from gay society.

Alceste and Célimène part

Alceste declares that he now loathes her.
8. Alceste tells Éliante that he is unworthy
to pursue her, having only the remainder
of a heart now. He has begun to feel he was
not meant to marry, whereupon Philinte
and Éliante pledge their love for each other.
Alceste gives his good wishes to the union
and announces his intention to seek a secluded spot on earth. Philinte tells Éliante
they must persuade him to abandon this
idea.

Mr. Britling Sees It Through

Novel by Herbert George Wells, 1866–
1946.
Published 1916. © 1916, 1944 by H. G.
Wells.

THIS WAS ONE of the most popular
novels of World War I and perhaps
the most popular that the prolific H. G.
Wells wrote. It is not a war novel;
rather it is a novel about Englishmen
at home during the trying years and
about their relationships with Americans and their attitudes toward Germans. Critics were surprised that Wells
would take for his underlying theme
such difficult topics. With his usual
versatility, Wells did very well with
them.

Book I. Chaps. 1–5. It is Mr. DIRECK's
first trip to England. He is the overpaid
secretary of the Massachusetts Society for
the Study of Contemporary Thought and
has come to persuade Mr. Britling, a famous
writer, to deliver a series of lectures to the

members of his society. Mr. Britling invites him for the week-end at his country home, Matching's Easy, in Essex. Direck finds England more charming than he expected, but Mr. Britling is another matter, not at all what the very American Mr. Direck expects of a Britisher. The casualness of his costume is a disappointment. There is none of the mildness expected of a country gentleman: Mr. Britling bristles with a naturally irritable mind. The two men like each other instantly. Direck looks forward to their drive to the house, but this is only the third time Mr. Britling has driven and it is a harrowing experience for both of them.

Direck is confused at the Britling household, which is thoroughly British. There are EDITH BRITLING, his charming preoccupied hostess, and two small barefooted boys who resemble her husband. There is HUGH, a lad of 17, a son by Britling's first marriage; also an old aunt, a German tutor, and Mr. Britling's secretary, TEDDY. Teddy lives in a cottage on the estate with his wife, LETTY, and her sister, CECILY CONNER. Cecily is a beautiful, lively girl of great intelligence; Direck quickly falls in love with her.

The week-end is a great success. Mr. Britling is inordinately proud of England, though he expresses it chiefly by abuse. Direck joins in all the pastimes and enjoys himself tremendously. He has several serious discussions with his host on the possibility of war with Germany. Mr. Britling believes war will never come. Even while they are talking, events are leading to the assassination of Archduke Francis Ferdinand of Austria.

On his last morning of the week-end, Direck goes for a drive with Mr. Britling. They collide with a motorcycle. Direck is injured, while Britling is only badly shaken. It pleases Direck that he has the monopoly of damage, for Cecily is very sympathetic and helpful. Mr. and Mrs. Britling insist that he must not leave until he is recovered, and he is delighted to prolong his visit.

Very different from the contentment of the bruised Direck is the agitation of Mr. Britling. He is sleepless and physically restless. The smashing of the car has upset certain plans he had for conducting his eighth love affair. Mr. Britling's first marriage was happy and passionate. His second is profoundly incompatible. Edith runs his house and children smoothly, but there is no excitement. This is now being provided by Mrs. HARROWDEAN, an attractive widow. The love affair does not run smoothly, for she is demanding and emotional. And there is OLIVER. Oliver is a staunch, dull admirer who stands ever ready to marry her at a moment's notice. The affair is a series of quarrels, recriminating letters, and joyful reconciliations.

Direck's wounds heal sooner than he wished. Before he leaves on a tour of Europe, he tells Cecily that he loves her and wishes to marry her. She asks for time to think it over, as she is confused in her own mind about the merits of marriage. She promises to give him an answer soon.

The clouds of war begin to gather. The German tutor is recalled to Germany and sadly leaves the Britlings to serve his country. Germany goes on the march. First France and Belgium are invaded, then Russia prepares to invade Germany. Mr. Britling tries to adapt his thinking to the horrible fact that war is here. He knows that Germany will never win, because Germany does not understand the spirit of man. On his way to see Mrs. Harrowdean, he thinks over the state of the world. His mind becomes absorbed with the present events and he decides that Oliver can have Mrs. Harrowdean. He hurries home to commit his thoughts to paper.

Book II. Chaps. 1–4. Upon the invasion of Belgium, Great Britain declares war. The Britling household organizes itself to be of the utmost use. Direck is in Germany; he immediately departs for England, anxious to be with Cecily at such a time. She welcomes him absent-mindedly and turns all her attention to England and the war. Direck feels like an outsider, for the United States stays neutral, but he is determined to stay near the girl he loves.

The members of the Britling household are drawn one by one into active service. Teddy, who laughs and jokes at all serious matters, is the first to join the armed forces. He is followed by Hugh Britling. Mrs. Britling applies her organizing ability in work for the Red Cross. Mr. Britling has difficulty finding his niche, but finally joins the local volunteers and is given the assignment of guarding public buildings and transportation. Matching's Easy is opened to

Belgian refugees, and the unused barn is pressed into service as a billet for soldiers.

To a man of Mr. Britling's nature the war demands a great deal of thought. It is hard for him to realize just why the war happened. The German attitude is do or die with a vengeance, while the Englishman treats the whole affair as an honorable sport. The German campaign of hate is inconsistent, in Mr. Britling's mind, with the good Germans he has known. He realizes that there is good and evil on both sides; he foresees that as time goes on the English will become as embittered and cruel as the enemy. Wars are always the same and so are the people who fight them.

Hugh is sent to the front in Flanders, in the same regiment as Teddy. After a quick skirmish, Teddy is missing; this is the first worry to enter the Britling establishment. Letty grieves silently. Mr. Britling's uneasiness mounts. He finds he can no longer express in writing what he is thinking. Direck, to enhance himself in Cecily's eyes, leaves for Europe to find out what he can about her brother-in-law. While he is gone, Mr. Britling receives news that Hugh was killed in his first battle. Edith tries to comfort him, but loneliness for his son engulfs Britling. War now becomes a matter of revenge.

Book III. Chaps. 1–2. Letty remains firm in her belief that Teddy is alive, though Direck has found substantial evidence that he has been killed. Direck returns and tells Cecily that she must prepare her sister to accept her husband's death. Cecily finally convinces Letty that there is no further hope. Letty asks to be left alone. Everything in the house reminds her of her life with Teddy; she goes for a long walk to adjust herself to life alone. She meets Mr. Britling and recounts what Cecily has said. She is resentful that Teddy died for nothing and that the whole war is a mistake. Spurred by his own grief at the loss of Hugh, Mr. Britling has thought out the aims of the conflict. He tells Letty he does not believe that the war is being fought in vain. He believes that Hugh has died for a cause that is worth his life. The Germans are enforcing a way of life reprehensible to democratic peoples. When the Germans are defeated the world will be a better place to live in. Letty is comforted. She begins to accept Teddy's death, and returns home determined to carry on. She can hardly believe her eyes as she approaches her cottage —Teddy is there waiting for her. He is alive, discharged from service because he had lost a hand. In her joy at her husband's return, Letty does not notice that Cecily is strangely silent. Direck has joined the Canadian Army as a volunteer. Cecily realizes that she loves him.

Through his agent in New York, Mr. Britling learns that the German tutor was killed in the same battle as Hugh. He was a good boy and Mr. Britling realizes that his parents must be grieving for him just as Mr. Britling grieves for Hugh. He tries to write them of his feelings, but after a night of futile effort he destroys the letter. The war has claimed good from each side. Morning and the sunrise sweep across Matching's Easy and with it comes hope—hope for the better world.

The German tutor lies dead on a battlefield in France

Mr. Midshipman Easy

Novel by Frederick Marryat, 1792–1848.
Published 1836.

PERHAPS THE OUTSTANDING feature of Captain Marryat's books is that the man had such a tremendous store of miscellaneous minor knowledge. It is impossible to read a Marryat book without learning a great many items of miscellaneous information that are interesting if nothing else. Among his adventure novels, this is the outstanding one. It is authoritative, for Captain Marryat was a sea captain; his store of miscellaneous information, in fact, came from the fact that he had sailed almost everywhere and had been a keen observer wherever he went. Marryat's books are no longer read, more's the pity.

Chaps. 1–3. NICODEMUS EASY is a wealthy gentleman philosopher. He believes that all men are born to inherit an equal share of the earth, to have equal rights. But no one agrees with him. Mrs. Easy bears a child, to Mr. Easy's delight. After long argument they decide to name him JOHN, or JACK by nickname. Dr. MIDDLETON brings in a wetnurse named SARAH for Jack. Mr. Easy examines her head, for he is interested in craniology. He finds that her bumps of benevolence, veneration, modesty and philoprogenitiveness are amply developed, so he is satisfied. Jack appears not to imbibe these qualities from Sarah's milk, however, for he snatches, scratches, and pulls hair.

Chaps. 4–5. Jack is spoiled by his doting mother. Dr. Middleton perceives this and suggests that the boy be sent away to school. Mr. Easy demurs because boys are flogged at school—inequality! One day in a moment of brattishness Jack spills boiling water on his father's legs, and then is sent off to school. The master, Mr. BONNY-CASTLE, does not flog his pupils—he canes them instead. Jack learns the meaning of discipline.

Chaps. 6–7. Jack becomes imbued with his father's ideas on equality. To test them he one day goes fishing in a private pond. Gamekeepers appear; Jack argues that it is only "might" that has brought about the distinction of property. The gamekeepers agree, and with all their "might" they throw Jack in the pond. Next Jack climbs a tree to steal apples. An outraged farmer sets a bulldog to guard the tree; a bull attacks the dog; Jack scrambles from the tree and is attacked by the bull; leaping over a hedge, he lands in a beehive; while running, he falls down a well. So much for equality! Jack decides to go to sea with Captain WILSON, a friend of the family who has borrowed £1,000 from Mr. Easy. Jack thinks that at sea he will find a state of true equality.

Chaps. 8–12. Purseproud Jack insults the first lieutenant, Mr. SAWBRIDGE—on the grounds of equality. Captain Wilson treats Jack leniently because of his debt to Mr. Easy. He explains to Jack that some of the officers may act as if they are superior, but really it is all "zeal" in carrying out the obligations of His Majesty's navy, which are *equal* for all. Jack is violently seasick for the first few days of the voyage. He asks for some crumpets but gets only slop-soup from the steward, MESTY, a Negro ex-slave who was originally a prince in his own country. Later at the captain's table Jack voices his theories about equality, to the shock and amazement of the listeners. He gains some friends, however, among them the one-eyed Mr. JOLLIFFE, Mesty the Negro, and several of his midshipmen cabinmates after he soundly thrashes the bully of the cabin, named VIGORS. An officer named ASPERS attached himself to Jack because he knows that Jack has plenty of money. One day Jack sees the unpopular boatswain, BIGGS, punishing a sailor for being late for a summons because he was putting his pants on. "Duty before decency" roars Biggs. The next night, while Biggs is sleeping at an inn, Jack swipes his pants. Biggs is obliged to return to the ship pantless, to the great merriment of the crew. In a fit of rage, Jack one day kicks the purser's steward, an ex-pickpocket, EASTHUPP, down a hatchway. In another instance Jack is punished for not obeying a command with alacrity. He begins to learn "non-equality."

Chaps. 13–15. A Spanish merchant convoy is attacked by Jack's ship, the *Harpy*. Jack is given command of one of the small cruisers sent out for the attack. He captures one of the small Spanish boats. Instead of obeying orders to return, he with friend Mesty and the crew of eight, set out to catch something big. They sight a large Spanish gunboat; during the night they board it and overcome all the men aboard. The prisoners, with two gentleman and three lady passengers, are put aboard the smaller vessel and shoved off. Jack and his crew sail away. That night, while Jack sleeps, all the men get drunk and the ship buffets its way about the Mediterranean without a helmsman. Jack locks up the wine, but he is not a trained navigator and the boat is gale-driven upon an uninhabited island. The crewmen go ashore and presently plan a mutiny, but three of them, in trying to swim back to the boat, are eaten by sharks. After two months the crew's wine and provisions are exhausted and they beg Jack to take them aboard. Meanwhile Mesty has told the story of his life to Jack. He was once a prince and great warrior, with many wives, in Africa; he collected the skulls of his enemies; he was captured by slave-traders and taken to America; he escaped to England and shipped aboard the *Harpy*, where he was put into the degrading position of mess-steward.

Chaps. 16–21. Jack and his crew eventually encounter the *Harpy* battling a Spanish gunboat. They help the *Harpy* to win. Everyone is delighted to see the hero and his crew again and the prize they have brought. Mesty is made ship's corporal. Biggs and Easthupp insult Jack, and he challenges them to a duel. They meet on land for the fight; not knowing how three are supposed to duel, they form a triangle and each shoots at the next man. Easthupp is shot in the buttock and Biggs through the cheek, while Jack is unscratched. Jack and his friend GASCOIGNE hire a small boat to take them to Palermo. They shoot four pirates who attempt to board them at night. The boat is wrecked in a gale,

but Jack and Gascoigne escape with their lives. They fall asleep in a hay wagon, which during the night is driven to a farm. They wake in time to stop two young men from killing an elderly man, Don REBIERA DE SILVA. One of the assailants is Don SILVIO, son of the Don's illegitimate half-brother. It is discovered that Don Rebiera's beautiful daughter, AGNES, is the girl who was aboard the Spanish ship captured by Jack. All are delighted, and Jack and Agnes fall in love. Jack and Gascoigne go on to Palermo, where they make friends with Agnes' two brothers. A captain discovers that Jack and Gascoigne are AWOL and claps them in irons. Agnes' brother kills the captain in a duel. Jack and Gascoigne are taken back to the *Harpy*. (Here the author inserts a polemic against the misuse of language by senior naval officers to their junior officers.)

Chaps. 22–24. Jack relates his adventures to the governor of Malta, Sir THOMAS, who is delighted. The *Harpy* goes off on another cruise and captures a large French vessel. The success is due partly to Jack's cleverness and partly to an explosion that kills many men. Next Jack and Gascoigne ship under Captain HOGGS to fetch some bullocks from Tetuan. Captain Hoggs falls in love with JULIA, sister of the Tetuan vice-consul, Mr. HICKS. Gascoigne falls in love with a beautiful Arabic girl, whom he courts in the disguise. Both he and Hoggs want to elope with their ladies. Jack arranges a trick whereby Hicks in disguise pretends to be both women. The boat pulls out, and in the morning all are infuriated, including Hicks, who is obliged to travel all the way to Malta and back in petticoats. Jack goes to a masquerade dressed as a devil. In this guise he scares off some monks from doing an evil deed, and rescues a rich old dowager from bandits, who prostrate themselves at the sight of the devil.

Chaps. 25–28. In pursuit of a frigate, the *Harpy* runs into a tremendous gale and is hit by lightning. A fire on board is smothered with wet blankets, Jack's bright idea. Captain Wilson receives a check for 1,000 gold dubloons from the estate of the dowager rescued by Jack. Jack at the time had given the captain's name as his own. Jack considers leaving the service to marry

The Harpy engages in battle with a Russian frigate

Agnes. Don Silvio appears and is arrested on Jack's identification.

Chaps. 29–33. The *Harpy* encounters a Russian frigate, and a furious broadside battle with guns ensues, which culminates in English victory. Upon return to Malta the *Harpy* sights a wrecked galley boat and takes time out to rescue the galley slaves and put them ashore. Among these men is Don Silvio. Jack is worried for Don Rebiera, and upon reaching Palermo he notifies the army of the prisoners on the loose. With Gascoigne, Mesty, and the Don's two sons, he forms a barricade around Don Rebiera's house in case of attack by Don Silvio and the galley slaves. The attack comes, and the defenders are driven back floor by floor. Don Silvio sets fire to the house but the defenders are saved by the arrival of troops. Jack now wishes to marry Agnes but Father THOMASO, the family priest will not approve. When Jack tries to bribe him through Mesty, the priest gives Mesty some powder with which to poison Jack. Mesty pretends to have done this and then flees with the priest. But en route

Mesty poisons the Father with his own powder. On his return, Mesty is captured by Don Silvio, whom he kills.

Chaps. 34–41. Jack receives news that his mother is dead and his father has gone somewhat out of his mind. Jack quits the service and returns home with Mesty; he finds the household and estate in a mess due to his father's ideas on equality. Jack argues with his father that all men are not equal, and that it is fortunate that society is structured so that each may find his level. A few days later Mr. Easy is found dead in a formidable machine he had built to further the science of phrenology. Jack buys a frigate to fetch Agnes with style. In the Mediterranean the frigate aids a ship that turns out to be captained by Jack's old friend, Sawbridge. Later in the trip the frigate beats off an English warship bent on impressing her crew. Agnes is finally picked up and all return to England, where Jack becomes a happily married and highly respected country gentleman of conservative political outlook and much wealth. Mesty becomes his majordomo.

Moby Dick

Novel by Herman Melville, 1819–1891. Published 1851. (PB, PL28; RE, 6; NAL, D1229; ML, G64 & 119 & T26).

PERHAPS THE ONLY GROUNDS on which critics agree about this book is in placing it among the classics of world literature. In part it answers the classic definition of a novel, for it tells a connected story with a beginning, a middle, and an end; but it follows some 18th-century patterns in digressing frequently for essays and there are some parts that one can class only as poetry. Some critics, perhaps most, have considered *Moby Dick* an allegory in which the white whale represents the abstraction of evil, but could a writer so sensitive as Melville cast as evil an animal that simply defends itself against attack? The variety of the characters is great and Melville's portrayal of them is superb. At least some of the incident and character-casting must be considered allegorical or symbolic, including the name of the vengeful Captain Ahab, who like the Biblical Ahab pursued false gods. Contemporary critics simply did not know what to make of this book and Melville had great trouble getting it published. Now it has surpassed in esteem every other American work of its kind.

Chaps. 1–13. Call me ISHMAEL. Some years ago, having little money and nothing to interest me on shore, I decided to go to sea. Ordinarily when I go to sea, I go as a merchant sailor, but this time I took it into my head to go on a whaling voyage. I set out for Nantucket. I was forced to remain two nights, en route, in New Bedford. I stayed at a waterfront hotel, the Spouter Inn, where I was made to share my bed, very much against my will. Had I seen my bedfellow in advance, I do not think anything could have induced me to sleep with him. He was a huge, bald, tattooed black-skinned harpooner with strange habits of worship and a collection of shrunken heads. The fellow's name was QUEEQUEG. At first I thought he was a cannibal, but he showed himself to be a harmless and most affectionate sort. The next day being Sunday, I attended the whaleman's chapel. The sermon was on the sin of Jonah and his repentence in the belly of the whale. I returned to the Inn. Queequeg made me a present of an embalmed head, divided his $30 with me, swore to be my bosom friend, and invited me to join in the worship of his wooden idol. Then he told me he was a South Sea Islander, son of a native king, and that he ran away to Christendom early in life. As he, too, was anxious to go to sea again, we set out for Nantucket together.

Chaps. 14–27. I signed Queequeg and myself aboard the *Pequod,* a whaling vessel under command of Captain AHAB, who was described to me as a good swearing man, somewhat strange, never jolly, who had lost his leg to a whale on his previous voyage and was desperately moody and savage. Some said that his name, Ahab, that of the wicked king of old whose blood was licked by dogs after he was slain, was somehow prophetic. Queequeg and I were stopped by a strange sailor who hinted that anyone sailing with Captain Ahab was doomed, but we took no account of his veiled warnings. The *Pequod* sailed the following day and we were on board. Captain Ahab remained below deck for the first few days. The steering was left to the chief mate, STARBUCK, a steadfast man of action, courageous but superstitious, and to the second mate, STUBB, a happy-go-lucky fellow. These two, and FLASK, the third mate, were armed with whaling spears; in battle with the whale, they acted as a trio of lancers, just as their harpooners, Queequeg, TASHTEGO, and DAGGOO, were flingers of javelins.

Chaps. 28–46. Several mornings later,

Captain Ahab appeared on the quarterdeck for the first time. His whole high, broad form seemed to be made of solid bronze and shaped in an unalterable mould. A livid white scar threaded its way out from among his gray hairs and continued right down one side of his scorched face until it disappeared in his clothing. No allusion was made to this scar throughout the voyage, except once when it was said that Ahab had lived forty years before he had been branded thus and that he had gotten this mark at sea. In place of his lost limb, he wore a barbaric ivory leg fashioned from the polished bone of a sperm whale's jaw. The ship headed southward, looking for a school of whales. One morning the captain ordered everybody aft. He took out a Spanish gold piece and hammered it to the mainmast, shouting "Whosoever of ye raises me a white-headed whale with a wrinkled brow, a crooked jaw, and three holes punctured in his starboard fluke, shall have this gold ounce." It was this whale, MOBY DICK, that had chewed off Ahab's leg. Ahab vowed to chase him "round perdition's flames." "And this is what ye have shipped for, men," he cried, "to chase that white whale on both sides of land and over all sides of earth till he spouts black blood and rolls fin out." All the sailors cheered Ahab save Starbuck, who declared that he

was game for the whale's jaw and game for the jaws of death, but that he had come to hunt whales and not his master's vengeance, and further, that it seemed madness, blasphemy in fact, to be so vengeful against a dumb brute. Ahab replied that he would strike the sun if it insulted him and that he saw in that white whale outrageous strength with an inscrutable malice sinewing it. With that, Ahab called for liquor and the crew drank a frantic toast to the death of Moby Dick. I, Ishmael, was one of that crew and my shouts went up with the rest, because Ahab's quenchless feud seemed mine. I learned the history of that murderous monster. From time to time, vessels reported they had encountered a Sperm Whale of uncommon magnitude and malignity, which after attacking assailants with great ferocity and cunning had always escaped them. Few hunters were willing to encounter the peril of its jaw. Some of the more superstitious said Moby Dick was both ubiquitous and immortal.

Chaps. 47–65. On a sultry afternoon we sighted our first school of sperm whales. Instantly all was commotion. Five crewmen, natives of Manila, were lowered in one of the three whaleboats. Their leader was FEDALLAH, a white-turbaned old man, who was to remain a muffled mystery to the last. My boat, commanded by Starbuck, was

"Thar she blows!"—The first school of whales is sighted

Stubbs went after the whale

nearly swamped by a whale and we huddled in it, drenched through and shivering from cold, all night before the *Pequod* found us. Weeks later, as we were passing the Cape of Good Hope, we came across a whaler whose men told us that some time previously Moby Dick had killed one of their number.

Chaps. 66–86. Near Java we came upon a sperm whale, and the boats were lowered into the water for the second time. Stubb went after the whale and killed it with Tashtego's aid. Then began the long process of hauling in the prize. When it was finally brought alongside the ship, we turned to the business of stripping it of its blubber, which yields more than 100 barrels of oil, and of beheading it and hanging its head from the side of the ship. The rest of the body was thrown back into the sea. As we were melting the blubber down into oil, we were hailed by another whaler, the *Jereboam,* whose captain told us that his first mate had been killed by Moby Dick.

Chaps. 87–99. As we were crossing the Straits of Sundra, we came upon a huge school of whales headed in the same direction. After a lengthy chase, Queequeg succeeded in harpooning only one of them. The others escaped, to be chased later by

the *Rose-Bud.* Shortly afterward, PIP, the little Negro shipkeeper, was put into Stubb's whaleboat in place of the after-oarsman, who had sprained his hand. As they were paddling upon a whale, Pip leapt overboard and was left behind in the sea for several hours. By the time he was rescued, he had gone mad.

Chaps. 100–109. We met the *Samuel Enderby,* an English ship, and Ahab asked if it had seen the white whale. In answer, the captain held up an arm consisting of whalebone from the elbow down. Ahab boarded the *Samuel Enderby* to hear the story of the captain's encounter with Moby Dick. He was told that Moby Dick was heading East when last seen. In returning to the *Pequod,* Ahab broke his ivory leg and had to have another made.

Chaps. 110–115. Queequeg fell ill of fever. Thinking himself near death, he requested that a coffin-canoe be made to hold his remains. But he suddenly rallied and recovered. Thereafter he used the coffin as a sea-chest.

Chaps. 116–117. One night after we had slain four whales, Fedallah prophesied that before Ahab could die on this voyage, he must see two hearses on the sea, the first not made by mortal hands, and the second made of wood grown in America. Furthermore, Ahab could not die until Fedallah himself was dead, and only hemp could kill him.

Chaps. 118–132. Nearing the equator, Ahab decided he could do without his quadrant, a foolish toy that indicates only where it is not where it will be or where it is going. Thenceforth, Ahab would guide the ship only by compass and dead reckoning. That night we were caught in an electrical storm; lightning struck and set fire to the mast. The crew begged Ahab to change his course, but Ahab vowed again, before the burning pillar, to find and kill Moby Dick. Next day the compasses were awry. When the log was heaved, the line broke and the log slipped away. Next a man fell overboard; the dried-out lifebuoy sent after him sank, whereupon Queequeg offered his canoe-coffin as a substitute. On the following day we met a large ship, the *Rachel,* whose crew had seen Moby Dick only yesterday; the captain's son was lost chasing the white whale. The captain requested the *Pequod* to unite with the *Rachel* in the search for the missing whaleboat, but Ahab refused. Now that he was so close upon his prey, he did not want to lose a minute's time. And so began the chase, with Ahab remaining on the deck at all times.

133–135. At last Moby Dick was sighted by Ahab. The captain ordered the boats away and took the lead in the chase. As he neared Moby Dick, the whale shot his head under the boat and split it to pieces. The men were finally rescued, after the whale had been driven away. On the second day, the men managed to bury three harpoons in the white whale, but the whale turned and twisted so as to tangle the lines. Stubb's and Flask's boats were destroyed, though the men were rescued. Ahab managed to cut his own boat free, but Fedallah was killed. Starbuck tried without success to persuade Ahab to give up the mad pursuit. On the third day, the boats quickly overtook Moby Dick, who this time seemed to be possessed by the devil himself. As Ahab drew near, he saw the remains of Fedallah bound to Moby Dick's back. This, then, was the first hearse. The boats were swamped by the whale; all but Ahab returned to the ship. Ahab still pursued the whale with his iron. In retaliation, Moby Dick bore down on the ship and smote its starboard bow, till men and timbers reeled and water poured through the breach. This was the second hearse—and the *Pequod's* wood was American. As the ship went down, Ahab hurled his harpoon at the whale, but the line ran foul and the hemp rope twisted around his neck, pulling him out of the boat. Everyone perished, except myself. I clung to Queequeg's canoe-coffin for two days before the *Rachel* picked me up.

A Modern Comedy

Trilogy (three novels) by John Galsworthy, 1867–1933.
Published 1928 by Charles Scribner's Sons; © 1928 by John Galsworthy.

THIS SECOND TRILOGY, three full novels, on the Forsyte family, concludes Galsworthy's treatment of the process by which the English upper middle classes (the moneyed, principally the merchant classes) rose to social equality with the nobility and gentry—or near-equality, for among both there remained a slight and submerged consciousness of a difference. (See *Forsyte Saga*.) Galsworthy did not stop writing about the Forsytes here; there is a third trilogy, *End of the Chapter*, which includes the novels *Maid in Waiting, Flowering Wilderness,* and *One More River;* but they were not essential to the message. Nor were they quite such good reading. *A Modern Comedy* compares very favorably with the original Forsyte books.

The White Monkey

Part I. Chaps. 1–3. Sir LAWRENCE MONT meets his son, MICHAEL, and Michael's best friend, WILFRED DESERT, a poet. Together they go to Michael's for tea with his young wife, FLEUR. Wilfred, who is in love with Fleur, asks her if there is any hope for him. She turns him down. That night, as Michael and Fleur prepare to leave a musicale they have attended, Wilfred comes up to Fleur and threatens to go East if she will not encourage him. She arranges to meet him the following Sunday. **4–6.** Michael and Fleur give a dinner party to celebrate their second wedding anniversary. Fleur meets Wilfred in an art gallery on a Sunday morning. She tells him that perhaps he may hope. As she is leaving, she meets her father, SOAMES FORSYTE, and invites him home to dinner. **7–8.** Soames goes to a meeting of the P.P.-R.S. (Providential Premium Reassurance Society), which Sir Lawrence also attends. Soames demands that a full report on the society's foreign commitments be ready within a week. TONY BICKET, one of the

packers in the publishing house of Danby
and Winters (of which Michael Mont is a
junior partner), is caught stealing books.
Michael asks Wilfred to speak to Mr.
DANBY in Bicket's behalf. Wilfred does,
but Danby fires Bicket. 9–11. Michael and
Fleur attend a party at her Aunt ALLISON'S.
Wilfred tells Michael that he is in love with
Fleur. Michael tells Fleur, who does not
know what to say. Soames' cousin GEORGE
FORSYTE is seriously ill and asks Soames
to add a codicil to his will. Soames is
especially taken with a picture of a strange
white monkey hanging in George's bedroom. George dies. Bicket has not been able
to find another job and is selling balloons
on the street. Soames passes by and buys
several balloons, tipping Bicket generously.
12–13. The P.P.R.S. meets again and to
Soames' gratification a full report of foreign
interests is made. At Soames' club VAL
DARTIE, his sister WINIFRED'S son, asks if
he can refuse the three horses left him by
George, since Val cannot afford to pay the
legacy tax on them. Soames advises him not
to accept them. Soames goes to Fleur's for
dinner and prods her about having a family.
Soames blows up the balloons he bought
from Bicket, and floats them out the
window. Michael, who has been to the
Labour candidates' meeting, catches the balloons and takes them to Fleur.

Part II. Chaps. 1–3. Soames is visited by a
young Mr. BUTTERFIELD, from the P.P.R.S.
office, who tells him that Mr. ELDERSON of
the Board of Directors has been given great
discretionary powers. VICTORINE BICKET,
Tony's wife, asks Michael to get Tony's job
back. Michael cannot but he gives her a
note to his friend, the artist AUBREY
GREENE, asking him to use Victorine as a
model. Greene consents to use her. 4–6.
Fleur visits Wilfred in his apartment. They
see Michael in the street below. Frightened,
Fleur departs and visits an art gallery across
the street. Soames buys the picture of the
white monkey from the estate of George
Forsyte. Fleur is visited by HOLLY DARTIE,
sister of Fleur's American cousin and old
love, JON FORSYTE. Jon is not married and
is raising peaches in South Carolina. JUNE
FORSYTE, Fleur's cousin, tells Michael she
saw Fleur entering Wilfred's apartment.
Michael is heartsick. Soames tells Michael
of Fleur's love affair with Jon Forsyte,

Victorine poses in the nude

emphasizing that it was over months before
she married Michael. 7–9. Victorine goes
to Aubrey Greene's studio. She consents to
pose for him in the nude, since she wants
to earn money quickly for passage to Australia for herself and Tony. Soames confers
with Sir Lawrence on the information given
him by Butterfield. Together they visit
Elderson, whose response is to dismiss Butterfield. Soames asks Michael to try to place
Butterfield at Danby and Winters. 10–12.
Fleur is heartsick, lying on her rug. Hearing
a slight noise, she goes to the window, and
finds Wilfred's face staring in at her.
Michael, returning home, sees Wilfred
coming from his house. He asks Fleur if
Wilfred has been with her. She tells Michael
of seeing Wilfred's face at the window.
Michael dashes over to Wilfred's apartment,
jubilant with the news that Fleur is to become a mother, but Wilfred has left "for the
East." Michael arives at Paddington Station
in time to say farewell to Wilfred.

Part III. Chaps. 1–6. Tony sees a newspaper reproduction of Greene's painting of
Victorine. He comments on the resemblance. Butterfield has made quite a success
of his salesman's job at Danby and Winter's.
Victorine asks Michael and Greene not to
tell Tony that she was the model for
Greene's picture. Soames is interested in

buying the picture. But Tony does find out that Victorine was the model. He goes to Michael to find out more. Michael threatens to tell Victorine of Tony's theft of books if he makes any trouble for her about modeling. Tony returns home and is reconciled with Victorine. **7–9.** Soames confronts Elderson with a demand that the stockholders be told of the loss of German insurance. Elderson is cool and calm. Later Soames receives a note from Elderson confessing his transgression and implying that he is going abroad. **10–14.** Soames makes a post-nuptial settlement of £50,000 on Fleur. Soames advises the removal of the picture of the white monkey until after Fleur's baby arrives. Soames and Sir Lawrence attend the shareholders' meeting and Soames explains the Elderson affair but the stockholders are critical and Sir Lawrence and Soames resign. Soames then stops at his office and directs GRADMAN, his long-time chief clerk, to notify the family, with the exception of his sister, Winifred Dartie, that he will no longer handle their legal affairs. Fleur has a son and Fleur and Michael decide to make Aunt Allison and Wilfred Desert their son's godparents. Soames and Michael rehang the picture of the white monkey.

INTERLUDE: A SILENT WOOING

Jon Forsyte is recovering from a bout of flu at a hotel in South Carolina. He meets FRANCIS WILMOT and his sister ANNE. Anne and Jon go horseback riding together. Later, when Jon visits Anne at her home, they fall in love.

The Silver Spoon

Part I. Chaps. 1–5. FRANCIS WILMOT calls on Fleur, when he visits London, and is invited to be a house guest. Michael has given up publishing and is a member of Parliament. Soames has taken up golf. **6–7.** Soames is disturbed over a bit of gossip in the newspaper about Fleur's "salon." He attends Fleur's "salon" and overhears MARJORIE FERRAR refer to Fleur as a "snob." He makes a scene and orders her out of Fleur's house. Fleur cries herself to sleep over the scene. Francis is fascinated

with Marjorie and steals out in the middle of the night to locate her apartment. **8–9.** Marjorie's father, Lord CHARLES FERRAR, demands that Soames write letters of apology to those who heard him call Marjorie a traitress. Soames refuses. He tells Sir Lawrence of the affair and Sir Lawrence goes to see the Marquess of SHROPSHIRE, Marjorie's grandfather. The Marquess informs Sir Lawrence that he has not spoken to his son, Lord Charles, in six years but if Marjorie comes by he will speak to her. Soames and Michael return home to find that Francis is leaving. Fleur is very angry with her father for his outburst. Francis meets Marjorie accidentally at a tea dance at his hotel. She invites him to her apartment for tea next afternoon. After the visit, Francis goes to Fleur and tries to smooth over the affair, but Fleur is not at all interested. **11–14.** Soames visits the newspaper that commented on Fleur's "salon." The editor gives him no satisfaction. Michael has embraced the political philosophy called Foggartism, which advocates a balance between city and farm workers; it recommends sending youths to farms in various parts of the Empire. Marjorie Ferrar brings action against Fleur for letters Fleur has written to her friends, calling Marjorie a "snake of the first water," and sues Soames for ordering her to leave Fleur's home. Soames, Michael and Fleur make plans for an out-of-court attack on Marjorie Ferrar.

Part II. Chaps. 1–2. Michael delivers his maiden speech, on Foggartism, in Parliament. Sir ALEXANDER MACGOWN, Marjorie Ferrar's fiancé, intimates that as a former publisher Michael has an interest in the sale of Sir JAMES FOGGART'S book, and the next day, MacGown and Michael exchange blows. **3–7.** Marjorie is painting a portrait of Francis and MacGown is enraged. Michael visits Sir James Foggart, finding him to be an 84-year-old dreamer, out of touch with present-day reality. Michael is very depressed. Soames evolves a plan to trap Marjorie into defending an immoral book by writing a defense of it to a newspaper column. He enlists young Butterfield's help. Michael starts a small poultry farm on an unused portion of his father's land, in an effort to rehabilitate three down-and-out city workers he has met. He and Fleur go to a dinner where the ROYAL

PRINCESS comments favorably on Michael's speech in Parliament. 8–9. Soames visits the offices of Marjorie's solicitor and offers £1,500 and a mutual apology to settle out of court. After a delay, he receives a letter saying that Marjorie will settle only for a full apology from Fleur. In the meantime, Soames has continued gathering evidence of Marjorie's lack of moral sense. Marjorie, carried away, promises to marry Francis, and MacGown warns Francis not to trespass. 10–12. Michael's agricultural experiment is temporarily halted by the suicide of one of his workers. Fleur sees Wilfred, just back from the East. A telegram summons her to Francis, who is ill at his hotel with pneumonia. She sees a note Marjorie has written him, asking him not to see her any more. In the evening paper, Fleur reads of Marjorie's engagement to MacGown. Marjorie goes to visit Francis at his hotel and Fleur lets her in, but Francis refuses to see her. He recovers from his pneumonia.

Part III. Chaps. 1–4. Soames and Michael confer with Sir JAMES FOSKISSON, their trial lawyer, after being rebuffed by Mac-Gown on an offer to settle out of court. The Marquess of Shropshire promises Michael and Sir Lawrence that he will discuss the libel trial with Marjorie. Marjorie has breakfast with her grandfather and he advises her to settle out of court, but Mac-Gown refuses to consider the idea. 5–8. At the trial, Foskisson questions Marjorie closely regarding her morals. When she refuses to answer his question as to whether she has ever had a liaison, her attorney stops the trial and settles out of court. Francis Wilmot stops in to say goodbye to Fleur and Michael. 9–12. Fleur and Michael go to a party, at which Marjorie is present. Everything is strained. When they return home, Fleur asks Michael to take her on a trip around the world. Marjorie is despondent about her debts. Her grandfather agrees to pay them all if she will promise to reform. She agrees. Michael decides he cannot take Fleur on the round-the-world trip until Parliament closes in August. Soames offers to acompany Fleur on the trip, meeting Michael en route.

INTERLUDE: PASSERS BY

Soames is in Washington with Michael and Fleur. He catches a glimpse of Jon Forsyte and his young wife, Anne, and finds they are all staying at the same hotel. He goes to great lengths to make sure that Fleur does not meet Jon. That night he watches silently as IRENE FORSYTE, Jon's mother and Soames' first wife and only love, plays the piano in the hotel salon.

Swan Song

Part I. Chaps. 1–2. The General Strike of 1926 is on. Michael and Fleur organize a canteen to feed the volunteer railroad workers. They enlist NORAH CURFEW to help them. Winifred Dartie, Soames' sister, hears that her son Val, his wife Holly, and Holly's brother Jon Forsyte, are coming up to London to help in the strike. Winifred asks Fleur to let Holly help in the canteen. Soames plans to come up from Mapledurham, his country place. 3–6. Jon stays with Val and Holly. He has sold his Carolina peach farm and plans to buy a fruit farm in England. His wife, Anne, remains in Paris with Jon's mother, Irene. As Soames is being driven to London, a young chorus girl asks him for a ride. Soames is appalled at her nerve but gives her a ride. Val goes to work as a stoker during the strike. He eats at a canteen and discovers that his cousin, Fleur Mont, is running it. A college friend of Val's visits him to borrow money. After he leaves, Val's mother misses a valuable snuffbox. Soames tracks the man to his club and questions him about the snuffbox. He denies any knowledge of it. Then Soames tracks the man back to Winifred's door. Confronting him, he offers to buy the snuffbox back for £10. 7–10. The strike is over. Michael meets his uncle HILARY, a vicar, who has a slum-clearance project. Fleur is introduced to Anne, who has just come from Paris. All the while, she is planning an "accidental" meeting with Jon. Fleur goes early to Holly's. Only Jon is up. They chat, and she invites Anne and him to lunch the next day. Fleur's little boy, KIT, is introduced to Anne and Jon. 11–13. Soames, learning that Fleur has been talking to Jon alone, worries for fear Fleur and Jon will resume their love affair. Michael wonders about Jon and Fleur's old affair, and why they had parted. June Forsyte, Fleur's

cousin and Jon's half-sister, tells him how
Irene, Soames' first wife, left Soames and
married JOLYON FORSYTE, Soames' cousin.
Jon is the child of the Jolyon-Irene marriage.

Part II. Chaps. 1–6. Val decides to race
his colt, RONDAVEL, at Ascot. Soames is
determined to prevent Fleur from meeting
Jon, but he is unsuccessful and during the
races Fleur and Jon briefly disappear together. Val's horse wins his maiden race.
Kit contracts measles and Fleur spends the
days of his illness and convalescence dream-
ing of Jon. Michael and his father visit the
Marquess of Shropshire and several other
gentlemen to organize a committee for
Uncle Hilary's slum-conversion project.
7–9. June Forsyte tries to persuade Fleur to
have her portrait painted by June's newest
protegé, HAROLD BLADE. Fleur arranges to
take Kit to a summer cottage in a village
not far from where Jon and Anne will be.
She meets Jon on the train going down. Jon
goes down to Wansdon, thinking of Fleur
and Anne—double-hearted, he calls himself. 10–11. Val Dartie's college friend
STAINFORD, the man who stole the snuffbox, brings Val information that SINNET,
whom Val considers his best stable boy, is
making the colt Rondavel ill. Reluctantly,
Val pays Stainford £50 for the information.
12–13. Fleur is restless when she has been
at the summer cottage a week and has not
seen Jon and Anne. Impulsively, she returns to London and goes to June's, where
Blade is painting Anne. Fleur watches Anne
and Jon, as Anne is being painted. Soames

goes down to take Fleur and Kit home.
Arriving the night before, he goes to a
hotel at which a costume party is being
held. He sees Fleur and Jon dancing together, seeming lost in another world, as
Anne watches them.

Part III. Chaps. 1–2. Soames and Michael
talk of Fleur. Michael has noticed her pre-
occupation. Soames advises him not to do
anything rash—merely wait. Michael tries
to interest Fleur in the slum-conversion
project. She decides to start a rest home for
city girls. She asks her father for financial
aid, buys an old house located an hour's
drive away from Jon, furnishes and staffs
the house, learns to drive a car—all with a
view to being near Jon. Soames and Fleur
arrange to have her portrait painted by
Blade. 3–6. Fleur starts her sittings. Jon is
also having his portrait painted by Blade.
Fleur schemes to meet Jon. She forgets her
purse after a sitting. Returning to June's to
retrieve it, she meets Jon and drives him
part of the way home. Later she again meets
Jon and drives him out to see her rest home.
Stainford forges a check in Val's name for
£100. Soames exacts from Stainford a
promise not to bilk Val again. Soames hires
Butterfield as Gradman's assistant. 7–9.
Fleur and Jon meet and go to Robin Hill,

Val has decided to race his colt at Ascot

his boyhood home, the scene of their young romance. They walk to the coppice, their former trysting place. Fleur asks Jon to claim her, and he does. Afterwards, Fleur asks Jon when they will meet again. He rushes off. She drives home, disconsolate. Jon writes a note to Fleur saying that it is all over. That evening Anne tells him that she is to have a child. Looking at him, she guesses what has happened between him and Fleur. He promises never to see Fleur again. **10–12.** Fleur goes to meet Jon at Green Hills Farm, but he is not there. He has left a note telling her that Anne has guessed the situation, and that they must never see each other again. Soames drives to Sussex and spends a happy day tracking down his Forsyte ancestors and their lands. He stops at Fleur's rest home to take her to Mapledurham for the weekend. He is most distressed over her appearance. **13–16.** Fire breaks out in Soames' picture gallery. He rushes in to save the paintings and is severely injured. Fleur had been in the gallery smoking, shortly before, but she is so distraught she hardly remembers. She is at Soames' bedside as he dies and promises him that she will be "good." Michael is told by Holly that the affair is all over. Michael is much relieved.

Moll Flanders

Novel by Daniel Defoe, 1661–1731. Published 1722. (PB, C44; ML, 122 & T8; RE, 25).

THE FULL TITLE is *The Fortunes and Misfortunes of the Famous Moll Flanders.* A striking feature of the book is that the novelist Defoe obviously liked his heroine and condoned her immoralities and her crimes. The picture of the late 17th and early 18th centuries is justly famous and there is no moralizing to spoil the effect. Defoe's best-known book is *Robinson Crusoe* but it should be *Moll Flanders.*

The narrator does not divulge her true name, since she is too well known to the authorities at Newgate Prison and Old Bailey.

MOLL FLANDERS is the daughter of a convicted felon, who gave birth to her in Newgate prison while awaiting sentence. The mother was afterward transported to a plantation in America and was forced to leave the child in the hands of gypsies. Moll escapes from the gypsies at Colchester and is put in the charge of a good woman who runs a little children's school. Moll learns to read and write and to keep herself clean and neat. She becomes an excellent needlewoman as well. When she is 12 years old, she is asked to live with a gentleman's family nearby. But her nurse cannot spare her for more than a month, so she returns to the school for the next two years. She becomes an assistant to the teacher and is very happy. When Moll is 14, the nurse dies and the school is disbanded.

Moll goes to live with the family she had visited two years before. She receives all the advantages of wealth—French, music, dancing, and vocal lessons—and she is treated as a member of the family. Her ripening beauty soon attracts the attention of the two young gentlemen of the house. The elder brother secretly courts her and plies her with golden coins, and she, truly in love for the first time, succumbs to his advances. He tells her he considers them married in each other's eyes and promises he will legally marry her when he receives his estate. In the meantime, the younger brother, ROBIN, falls in love with "Mrs. BETTY," as Moll refers to herself, and tells the family that he means to marry her. The elder brother, having tired of Mrs. Betty, tries to persuade her to marry his brother. Upset by the elder brother's infidelity, and not loving the younger brother, Moll falls into a decline. Eventually she recovers, and resolves to leave the family. But they are too fond of her, and she and Robin are married. They are happy enough for five years, but Robin dies, leaving her with two small children. At his death, she leaves the children with his parents. Moll marries a draper and they embark on an extravagant way of life. She has a child, but it dies. To escape prison for his debts, he is forced to flee to France. As he is leaving, he tells her where he has hidden his liquid assets and absolves her from the marriage. She never sees him again.

Next Moll marries a man who has a plantation in Virginia. They sail to America, where they meet the husband's mother. Moll gets along so well with her new mother-in-law that she asks her husband if his mother can live with them. The mother-in-law amuses Moll with the backgrounds of the leading citizens of the infant colony. Moll and her husband are very happy together and they have three children, two of whom die. One day, the mother-in-law tells Moll the background of her own life. She was a former Newgate prisoner, convicted of a felony, and branded on the palm of her hand. Moll questions her more closely and learns, to her horror, that her mother-in-law is, in reality, her true mother. This means that her husband is her brother! Moll does not know which way to turn. Finally, she tells her mother of their predicament. To-

gether, they tell the brother. He is so shocked he offers to commit suicide as a way out. Moll dissuades him and leaves for England.

At the seaside resort of Bath, Moll becomes friendly with a gentleman whose wife has become mentally unbalanced. After several years' acquaintance, during which time Moll nurses him during a serious illness, they begin to live together as man and wife. She has three children by him, only one of which lives. After another serious illness, he repents of his sins and tells her he can see her no more. He offers to provide for her and their child. She asks for £50 more than he offers, knowing that this is the last money she will get from him. He takes the child, and she leaves for London.

Moll is now 42, and hardly wealthy. She meets a woman who is going to visit a sister and brother in Lancashire, near Liverpool. Moll is invited to accompany her on the trip and accepts. Before she leaves London, Moll goes to her bank for advice on how to handle her financial affairs. The banker, after a short acquaintance, becomes enamored of Moll and promises to marry her as soon as he is divorced from his erring wife. Moll puts him off gently, but not finally. Moll and her friend proceed to Lancashire

Moll discovers that her supposed mother-in-law is actually her mother

where the brother, JAMES ("JEMMY"), and his sister meet them. After a short courtship Jemmy and Moll are married. They prepare to depart for his estate in Ireland. When Jemmy discovers that Moll is not the wealthy woman he had supposed, he confesses that he has no estate in Ireland. Though really in love, Moll and Jemmy part; Moll goes back to London, where she bears a baby boy. She writes to her old friend, the banker, who has now divorced his wife, and is most anxious to marry her. They met at Brickhill and are married.

Moll lives for 5 years with her banker-husband, during which time she has two more children. He dies, and she spends the next 2 years in idleness, watching what money she has dwindle away. One day in an apothecary shop she steals a bundle left by a customer. This is the beginning of Moll's life as a thief in London.

Early in her career as a thief, she befriends a child on its way home from dancing school, and steals its gold necklace. Another time, she breaks a store window and steals two diamond rings. She does not know how to dispose of her ill-gotten goods. She resolves to return to her old "governess," the woman who took care of her when she bore Jemmy's child. The governess has turned pawnbroker. She disposes of Moll's stolen goods and Moll moves in with her. As Moll becomes well-known among the thieves, her governess advises her to try a few robberies dressed as a man. Moll follows her advice but gives up the plan after a narrow escape, during which she is encumbered by her disguise.

One evening at Bartholomew Fair, Moll meets a gentleman who is smitten with her. Under the influence of wine, he takes her to a hotel, where she yields to him. Afterwards, he takes her for a ride in his hired coach. When he falls asleep, Moll steals his gold watch and other valuables, and decamps. On hearing of Moll's adventure, the governess goes to the gentleman, returns his gold watch to him, and tells him that she is only acting for a good woman, who is overcome with remorse. The gentleman rewards the governess handsomely and asks to meet the charming thief. Moll and the gentleman are reconciled and enter into a liaison. He visits her once a month, providing for her handsomely, but his visits become less frequent, and Moll returns to stealing. This time she is caught, but she obtains a shrewd attorney, who proves her case to be one of mistaken identity. The accuser has to pay Moll £200 and provide her with a new suit of black silk.

Moll then takes on another pursuit—that of "guiding" gentlemen at the gaming tables, pocketing some of their winnings for herself. She even travels to Harwich and relieves travelers of their luggage. Shortly after her return to London, she attempts to steal some brocade. Two maid-servants catch her. Moll is thrown into Newgate prison, miserable and remorseful. Her governess sends a minister to her and she repents of the sins of her past life. In the meantime, the governess is trying to obtain Moll's freedom. One day, a new prisoner is brought in, her Lancashire husband, Jemmy. The governess eventually obtains an excellent attorney for Moll and Jemmy. He succeeds in having their sentences transmuted from the death penalty to transportation to the colonies.

Moll and Jemmy find they have almost £500 with which to start their life in America. Moll also has £300 that the governess is to use to send them articles that may be scarce in America. In Virginia, Moll learns that her mother has died and that her husband-brother, who is now senile, is living with their son, HUMPHREY, on the plantation. Moll's mother has left her a part-interest in the plantation, which Humphrey is managing. Humphrey is generous to his mother. Jemmy and Moll settle on a Maryland plantation they have bought and become successful farmers. For eight years their plantation thrives. Then they sell it at a nice profit, return to England, and settle down to a quiet life, repenting the wicked lives they once led.

Monsieur Beaucaire

Novelette by Booth Tarkington, 1869–1946.
Published 1900.

FOR ONE WHO WISHES to read something for sheer pleasure, not have to think too hard, and enjoy high romantic adventure, and who does not have too much time available at the moment, there is no story better worth recommending than *Monsieur Beaucaire*. Tarkington was a fine writer and he handled his romantic story very well. Anyone in a passing sentimental mood can be defied not to love it.

Chap. 1. VICTOR, quondam barber-hairdresser of the French Ambassador to the Court of St. James, has recently undergone a transformation into M. BEAUCAIRE, one of Bath's elusive and ambiguous "gentlemen of parts." Beaucaire has had occasion to observe the shady practices of the impoverished Duke of WINTERSET at the gaming tables, and he traps the duke in the act of cheating. Now Winterset must either face exposure or mollify this "greasy barber." Beaucaire demands merely that the duke present him to the beautiful and aloof Lady MARY CARLISLE at Lady MALBOURNE'S ball that evening. The duke agrees to take Beaucaire to the ball, under still another assumed identity, that of an improvised Duc de CHATEAURIEN. Winterset has a personal interest in Lady Mary, since his best chance to recoup the family fortunes is by marrying an heiress. Beaucaire laughingly warns him to give up all hope of such an alliance once the Duc de Chateaurien is on the scene.

Chaps. 2–4. At Lady Malbourne's ball the Duke of Chateaurien, resplendent in white satin court dress, has taken precedence over all of Lady Mary's other beaux and he is seeing her now to her sedan chair. He pleads for a rose from her corsage; she refuses. Mysteriously, just before her chair is carried off, a blood-red rose drops at his feet. Winterset warns him that roses last only till morning, and that this rose is an unlucky color. In the season that follows, Chateaurien becomes the pampered hero of fashionable Bath society. The only fault one can find with him is that he is a poor hand at gambling. Captain ROHRER, known for his skill as a duelist, provokes a quarrel with the French duke; Chateaurien ignores him until Rohrer makes insulting remarks about a member of the French Royal house, the Princess of BOURBON-CONTI. Then Chateaurien challenges the captain and, after casually running him through the left shoulder, sends a basket of blood-red roses to the Duke of Winterset. Another captain denounces the Duke of Chateaurien as an impostor and is wounded lightly by Chateaurien in a second duel. Chateaurien explains that he has fought the duel not in defense of his own honor, which is unassailable, but because he connot overlook the reflection upon his sponsor, the Duke of Winterset. By this time Lady Mary holds Chateaurien in special favor. One night he escorts her return to Bath from a country mansion, riding horseback alongside the window of her carriage. Although the formidable Lady Rellerton shares the vehicle, Lady Mary is able to enjoy privacy with her admirer by putting her head out the carriage window. She has begun to commit herself romantically when a band of horsemen charges down the highway, scattering her outriders and storming her carriage. Masked, but with bared swords, they descend upon Chateaurien shouting "Kill the barber!" Chateaurien fights a losing battle against overwhelming odds; the Bath gentlemen in Lady Mary's escort stand by idly. The masked horsemen truss up Chateaurien and prepare to administer a lashing. But the wind finally carries the Frenchman's voice around the bend of the road, where his retainers have been posted. They make short work of their master's assailants, whose ringleader turns out to be the Duke of Winterset. Winterset explains to Lady Mary how he has been blackmailed by this M. Beaucaire, former barber to the

Beaucaire attempts to reason with Lady Mary but she scorns him

French Ambassador. Beaucaire admits to Lady Mary that he originally came to London as a barber in the ambassador's suite. Winterset gives him 24 hours to leave Bath forever. Beaucaire jauntily replies that Winterset and his horsemen will find him in the Bath Assembly Room in exactly one week at 9 o'clock in the evening. Lady Mary drives off, scornful of the self-confessed barber.

Chaps. 5–6. The evening of Beaucaire's promised return to Bath finds BEAU NASH, the "King of Bath," promenading his crowded Assembly Room. The turnout is the celebrated mixture of wit, beauty, fashion and high aristocracy that characterizes his personal following. An added note of brilliance is the expected attendance of the Comte de BEAUJOLAIS, a young French Prince of the blood who just arrived from Paris that afternoon, accompanied by the Ambassador of Louis XV, the Marquis de MIREPOIX. Nash has taken the precaution of having the house and grounds surrounded by an armed guard, ready to seize Beaucaire should he show his face. The last Nash had heard of his whereabouts was that he disappeared a day ago from a neighboring farmhouse where he had been recovering from his highway "accident." The account

of Winterset's encounter with the Frenchman has made the rounds of the Bath drawing-rooms and Winterset has become a hero. He has returned to Lady Mary's favor, too. As 9 o'clock strikes, Nash sends a footman out to see if the guards have caught Beaucaire on the grounds. There is a buzz of excitement and anticipation as the French Royal Prince and Ambassador are announced. The crowd rushes forward to catch a glimpse of the distinguished foreigners, and Lady Mary is caught in the crush. Winterset extricates her and goes to fetch her a glass of negus [hot wine punch]. Looking about her for a chair, she notices a small side salon and gratefully discovers that it is empty except for two men playing cards. The cardplayers turn out to be MOLYNEUX, a Bath dandy of her own set, and M. Beaucaire. She reviles Molyneux for keeping such low company, but offers him the opportunity to clear out before she spreads the alarm that Beaucaire is present. Beaucaire attempts to reason with her, but the Beauty of Bath is deaf to his plea. Winterset enters, accompanied by six friends. He has just been informed that Beaucaire entered the Assembly through a side door, accompanied by Molyneux. He has come now to eject the barber forcibly.

He offers to conduct Lady Mary to the door, but she prefers to wait. Winterset now notices that Beaucaire's chest is adorned with royal orders and decorations. He sneers at these as the fruits of robbery and commands his henchmen to rip them off Beaucaire's coat. Molyneux withdraws into the ballroom and returns with the young Count of Beaujolais and the French Ambassador. Beaujolais throws his arms around Beaucaire and addresses him as "Philippe" and "brother." The truth comes out: "M. Beaucaire" is indeed his older brother; Beaujolais has been sent to Bath to put an end to Beaucaire's masquerade and fetch him back to France. The man who slipped out of France disguised as M. de Mirepoix's hairdresser, Victor—the whilom gambler, Beaucaire—the self-styled Duke of Castlenothing (Chateaurien)—is in reality His Royal Highness, Prince Louis-Philippe de Valois, the Duke of Chartres, Duke of Orleans, etc., etc., cousin to his most Christian Majesty Louis XV, King of France. He has been sulking in Bath to avoid making a marriage of the King's choice. Now that the King has relented and sent word that he is free to marry whom he pleases, Louis-Philippe has decided to return to his designated fiancée in France. He has discovered that he wants to marry her. She is loving and sweet, and what is more, he informs a contrite and humbled Lady Mary, she is the kind of woman who would go right on being loving and sweet to him even if he suddenly turned out to be a lackey.

The Moon and Sixpence

Novel by W. Somerset Maugham, 1874– Published 1919. © 1919 by W. S. Maugham & Doubleday & Co.

THOUGH THIS NOVEL is granted to be based on the life of Paul Gauguin, the French post-impressionist painter, it is a novel and not historical fiction. By common consent, Maugham's greatest novel is Of Human Bondage, but nearly everyone places The Moon and Sixpence second among his works. For convenience' sake Maugham made his fictional representation of Gauguin an Englishman, but Maugham was born in France and lived and studied much there and was quite capable of interpreting the French Gauguin as well as he could the English Charles Strickland.

1. The author of the book, SOMERSET MAUGHAM, reveals that when he first met CHARLES STRICKLAND he did not perceive anything extraordinary about him. However, time has proved the artist's greatness, and even those who do not like his art cannot help but be arrested by it. Much has been written about Strickland since he was acclaimed a great artist, not all of it true. Strickland lived in obscurity and was inclined to make enemies rather than friends. Strickland's son, glossing over his father's transgressions, described him as an excellent father and husband, whereas Dr. WEITBRECHT-ROTHOLZ, an art historian, went into detail about all the bizarre experiences in Strickland's life. 2–3. A trip to Tahiti led Maugham to write this book. As a young author who had achieved some success with his first book, Maugham lived in London and attended many literary teas. 4. At a tea at the home of ROSE WATERFORD, Maugham is introduced to Mrs. CHARLES STRICKLAND, a well-known hostess to all the literary figures in London. Rose Waterford tells Maugham that Mr. Strickland is just a dull stockbroker who never attends his wife's literary fêtes and is not interested in the arts. 5–6. Mrs. Strickland invites Maugham to dinner but warns him that Charles, although she loves him, will probably bore him to death. The party is indeed tedious. 8. Maugham is astonished to learn from Rose Waterford that Strickland has run away from his wife. A long-standing appointment forces Maugham to visit Mrs. Strickland that day. Mrs. Strickland, in the

company of her brother-in-law, Colonel MACANDREW, reveals her distress and says that Charles has run off to Paris with a woman, after 17 years of married life. **9.** The colonel tells Maugham that the family never suspected anything. There had been no quarrels; Strickland simply sent a note to his wife that he was going to Paris and would never return to her. **10.** Mrs. Strickland asks Maugham to go to Paris to see Charles. She will not give her husband a divorce and sends the message that she is waiting for him to return.

11–14. Maugham finds Strickland in a shabby hotel in Paris. He is unshaven and wearing old clothes, but seems more at ease than when he was a well-dressed broker in London. Maugham is astonished by the extraordinary callousness with which Strickland tells him that he never intends to see his wife again and does not care what happens to her. Neither does it matter to him what people think of him. At mention of another woman, Strickland laughs scornfully, saying he would never have done what he has for a woman. He reveals, to Maugham's increasing astonishment, that he wishes to paint and plans to learn even though he is in his forties. **15–16.** Surprisingly, Mrs. Strickland is more enraged than if Charles had fallen in love with someone. She feels sure he will never return but she no longer cares because now she hates him. Left to make her own way, Mrs. Strickland establishes a shorthand and typing business.

17. Five years later, Maugham goes to Paris to live. Before he leaves London he stops to see Mrs. Strickland; her business is doing well. **18–19.** In Paris, Maugham meets an old friend, an artist named DIRK STROEVE. Although a bad painter, Stroeve has a great love of art. He is quick to discover talent and most generous to his fellow artists who, unfortunately, are inclined to take advantage of his good nature. Stroeve introduces Maugham to his wife, BLANCHE, with whom he is deeply in love. She is a tall, reserved woman and Maugham wonders why she married Stroeve. Maugham asks Dirk if he knows Strickland and Dirk does, adding that Strickland is a great painter. Blanche interjects that she dislikes him as he is rude. Dirk takes Maugham to see Strickland. **20–21.** Strickland is more ragged in appearance and much thinner,

yet he gives an impression of great strength. For five years he has worked tirelessly at his art but has sold no pictures. He has refused to accept help from anyone and so has lost much time in solving technical problems. Strickland seems to be aiming at something he does not perceive clearly, for he is never satisfied with his work. **22–23.** During that winter, Maugham sees Strickland from time to time, but his pleasantest hours are spent in the company of Dirk Stroeve and his wife. **24–26.** Dirk learns that Strickland is ill. Against Blanche's will Dirk takes Strickland to their apartment to care for him. Strickland is an extremely difficult patient, and behaves abominably. Blanche proves a capable nurse, and gives no evidence of the dismay she showed earlier. **27–31.** After regaining his health, Strickland ejects Dirk from his own studio, saying he cannot work in the same room with him. A week later, Blanche leaves Dirk for Strickland. Maugham is sure Strickland does not love Blanche, as he seems incapable of love. **32–33.** Dirk sends Blanche a note through Maugham, saying that if she is ever in trouble he will help her and bears her no ill feeling. **34–35.** Strickland deserts Blanche and Blanche is in critical condition in the hospital, having taken poison. Dirk and Maugham visit the hospital, but Blanche refuses to see her husband. **36–38.** Dirk; too tired to weep, tells Maugham that Blanche has died and that he is planning to return to his native Holland. **39.** After Blanche's funeral, attended only by Maugham and himself, Dirk returns to the studio where they once lived. He finds a picture of Blanche painted by Strickland. In a fit of rage he is about to slash it to pieces, when something stops him. He realizes the painting is a work of art, and he is afraid to destroy it. To Maugham's astonishment, Dirk invites Strickland to Holland because they had both loved Blanche. Strickland refuses harshly, and Dirk leaves for Amsterdam. **40–42.** Strickland invites Maugham to his studio to see his work. Although Maugham has a genuine horror of Strickland, he is also curious to discover the artist's motives. With inhuman callousness, Strickland reveals that he feels no remorse at Blanche's death. He tells Maugham that Blanche married Dirk after she had been seduced and

The paintings are disappointing

become pregnant by the son of a wealthy Roman family in whose household she served as governess. Dirk found and married her after she attempted suicide. Strickland considers love a weakness and wants no woman's desires to dominate him. Maugham is disappointed in Strickland's paintings. However, he sees that here is a real power trying to express itself. A week afterward, Strickland goes to Marseilles, and Maugham never sees him again. **43–44.** Discussing Strickland's character, Maugham calls him an odious man but a great one, who cared nothing for fame or money and asked only of his fellow men that they leave him alone.

45–46. Visiting Tahiti many years later, Maugham meets Captain NICHOLS, who knew Strickland many years before in Marseilles and was the person who first suggested that Strickland go to Tahiti. **48–49.** Maugham meets several people who knew Strickland, including a merchant, COHEN, and Mrs. TIARE JOHNSON, the proprietress of a hotel in Tahiti. **50.** Maugham believes that some men, like Strickland, are born out of their proper surroundings and always long for a home they know not. He tells a story that illustrates this belief. **51–52.** Mrs. Johnson tells Maugham that she found a wife for Strickland because she felt sorry for him. The wife was a young Tahitian girl named ATA, who owned some property on the island. Strickland and Ata went to live in seclusion on her property, and Maugham believes these were probably the happiest years in the artist's life. They had two children. **53–54.** Maugham meets Captain BRUNOT, who also knew Strickland. Brunot says that what held Strickland was a passion to create beauty, which gave him no peace. **55–57.** Doctor COUTRAS, physician on the island, tells Maugham that he treated Strickland during his last illness—leprosy. Although the natives are horrified by this disease, Ata refused to leave him. When Doctor Coutras reached the hut in which they lived, he found Ata sobbing on the floor and Strickland dead. On the walls of the hut Strickland had painted a wonderful and elaborate composition, breathtaking in its magnificence. But Strickland had extracted a promise from Ata that she would set fire to the house, so this last mighty work was destroyed. **58.** Upon returning to London, Maugham visits the first wife of Strickland, who is now living in modest comfort, having inherited some money from her sister. Maugham tells her what he learned about Strickland in Tahiti, omitting mention of Ata. With great ingenuity, she insinuates that her relations with Strickland had always been perfect. Maugham meets her son, ROBERT, now a grown man, and cannot help thinking of Strickland's Tahitian son.

The Moonstone

Novel by Wilkie Collins, 1824–1889. Published 1868. (ML, 27).

THIS IS CONSIDERED the first detective novel of the modern pattern written in the English language, although the other famous Collins mystery novel, *A Woman in White,* preceded it. *The Moonstone* so impressed Collins' friend Charles Dickens that Dickens began a mystery novel of his own, *The Mystery of Edwin Drood,* but unfortunately had not completed it at the time of his death.

Prologue. The Moonstone, a fabled yellow diamond of India, is acquired by JOHN HERNCASTLE at the storming of Seringapatam, 1799. The dying Indian from whom he takes it prophesies that the gem, once glowing in the forehead of an idol and now in a dagger, will have its vengeance on him and his people.

First Period. Chaps. 1–7. GABRIEL BETTEREDGE, the trusted house-steward of Lady (JULIA) VERINDER, tells how the diamond was brought to Lady Julia's Yorkshire home in 1848 by her nephew, FRANKLIN BLAKE. Franklin informs Gabriel that the gem has been left to John Herncastle's niece, Lady Verinder's daughter, RACHEL, on her 18th birthday. The conditions of the bequest are that Lady Verinder must be alive on that date and that Franklin's father serve as executor. The men speculate on whether Herncastle's motive is revenge on his sister, Lady Verinder, because she joined others in shunning him when there were rumors that he had gained the diamond by evil means.

Chaps. 8–11. During the four weeks before Rachel's birthday, Franklin falls in love with his cousin. No one can fathom Rachel's feelings. The housemaid, ROSANNA SPEARMAN, a rehabilitated convict, seems madly in love with Franklin. On Rachel's birthday, Franklin gives her the Moonstone. The famed gem casts a blight on the festivities, because of the recent appearance of three mysterious Indian jugglers in the vicinity. A guest, the celebrated traveler in India, Mr. MURTHWAITE, tells Betteredge and Franklin that the so-called jugglers are actually high-caste Brahmins in disguise and undoubtedly wish to steal the diamond to replace it in the idol's forehead. Next morning the diamond is gone from the unlocked drawer where Rachel put it. The police suspect the Indians but discover they were in town at the time of the theft. Rachel is distraught and refuses to coöperate with the investigation. Rosanna Spearman appears to know more about the jewel than she should.

Chaps. 12–13. Sergeant CUFF, a London police detective imported by Franklin, suspects that Rachel has stolen her own diamond with the aim of pawning it to pay debts, and has made Rosanna her confidante. His suspicions are raised by Rachel's insistence on departing to visit her aunt. Franklin is pained by her extreme hostility to him and arranges to go away. Rosanna disappears and is traced to the nearby quicksand, where it is obvious she committed suicide. Rachel, questioned by her mother, asserts she never spoke privately with Rosanna and never had the diamond after she put it away on her birthday. Lady Verinder takes Rachel to London to distract her.

Second Period. I. 1–6. As told by Miss DRUSILLA CLACK, a spinster cousin of the family, GODFREY ABLEWHITE, a handsome young barrister, philanthropist, and also a cousin, is set upon and searched. It is believed the Indians suspect him of having the diamond, since he was a guest in the Verinder home during the birthday events. The same day Mr. LUKER, a dealer in old gems and a money-lender, has a similar experience and is robbed of a receipt for a valuable jewel he has just deposited in his bank. Godfrey presses Rachel to marry him. She confesses her love for another man, a "wretch," but accepts. At this time Lady Verinder is found dead. **7–8.** Rachel, by her mother's will, is left under the guardianship of Godfrey's father. After a visit from her family attorney, MATHEW BRUFF, she breaks the engagement. Godfrey remains calm, but his insulted father refuses to remain as her guardian.

II. 1–3. Mr. Bruff recalls that under Lady Verinder's will Rachel is no heiress but has merely a life interest in her parent's property. It was Bruff's statement to Rachel that Godfrey was interested in her money that caused Rachel to jilt Godfrey.

III. Chaps. 1–10. Franklin tells of his return from traveling in the East because of his father's death and his own inheritance of a large fortune. He loves Rachel, though he has tried to forget her. Rachel is now living with a widowed aunt. Her new guardian refuses to see him. Resolved to unravel the mystery, he goes to Yorkshire, where Gabriel reveals that Rosanna left a letter addressed to him. Franklin reads her message, which directs him to go to the quicksand and pull out a certain chain. He does so and discovers a nightgown marked with his name and bearing paint smears from Rachel's bedroom door. The thief thus appears to be himself. An accompanying note from Rosanna explains that she discovered his paint-stained nightgown and hid it, fearing he would be revealed as the culprit. Her suicide resulted from despair at his departure. Returning to London, he reports this news to Bruff, who realizes that Rachel's coldness toward Franklin comes from her belief that he is the thief. When Franklin finally sees Rachel she scorns him, saying she herself saw him take the diamond. Seeking new clues, Franklin makes a fruitless visit to Mr. CANDY, the Verinder family doctor, who was a guest at the birthday party and has since been seriously ill, with a resulting loss of memory. Confiding in the doctor's assistant, EZRA JENNINGS, Franklin learns that Candy in delirium spoke of Franklin. Jennings displays his notes on the doctor's wanderings. They reveal that at the birthday dinner, in pique at Franklin's scorn of medicine for his sleeplessness, the doctor arranged to give him an opiate, intending to come by next day and explain his little trick. The doctor's illness and his loss of memory prevented the explanation. Jennings believes Franklin took the diamond in a trance induced by the drug and seeks to vindicate him by reproducing the event with a similar dose.

IV. Jenning's diary tells of the reopening of the Yorkshire house for the experiment. Rachel, who has returned, unknown to Franklin, places a crystal in the drawer where she had put the diamond. Franklin takes the opiate and soon rises from his bed in a trance, expressing worry that the Indians may still be in the house and will steal the diamond. He goes to Rachel's room and repeats his action by taking the crystal. He lets it fall to the floor, then falls into a deep sleep.

V. Franklin recalls awakening next day with no memory of these events. A quick reconciliation with Rachel, now aware of

In a trance, he goes to Rachel's room and takes the crystal

his innocence, follows. In London, Mr. Luker takes the diamond from the bank and gives it to a mysterious sailor, who next day is found murdered with an empty jewel box beside him. Sergeant Cuff discovers the sailor to be Godfrey Ablewhite in disguise.

VI. Epilogue. Sergeant Cuff writes to Franklin that evidence shows that the Indians murdered Godfrey. He reveals that Godfrey had lived a lavish existence, unknown to his family and friends, on wealth stolen from a trust fund of which he was a trustee. The money was due the heir soon after Rachel's birthday. Entrusted by Candy with putting the drug in Franklin's drink,

Godfrey later saw his cousin take the diamond. He himself received the diamond from the dazed Franklin, who asked him to place it in the bank for safety. Seeing an answer to his financial needs, Godfrey kept the gem. He received a small loan on it from Luker to tide him over and later arranged to have it cut up into separate stones when he could redeem it.

Sergeant Cuff has the Indians traced to a ship bound for Bombay, from which they disappeared. In 1850 Mr. Bruff gets a letter from the traveler, Murthwaite, reporting that he has been in India and has seen the Moonstone once more in the forehead of the idol.

The Mother

Novel by Grazia Deledda, 1875–1936. Published 1923 by the Macmillan Co., New York. © 1920 by Grazia Deledda.

THE ITALIAN Nobel Prize winner Grazia Deledda (in private life Signora Madesani) was one of many upperclass women who elected to write about the peasantry. The Mother is a distinguished study of the conflict between the flesh and the spirit. It has been her most popular book in English translation.

Chaps. 1–2. In the little village of Aar, in Sardinia, a young priest, PAUL, has come to assume the parish, which has been without a pastor for several years. His mother, MARIA MADDELENA, keeps house for him. She has been aware for some months that he has more than a priestly interest in AGNES, a young woman living with only her servants in a large house not far from the presbytery. Paul goes to see the woman at night. His mother watches him go down the path to the orchard gate, and sees the gate open to receive him. The mother's heart is anguished, for this is the way to the darkest of sins. She yearns to be able

to save him before he is lost—and her heart goes out also to the woman. The woman needs to be saved as well as Paul, for her sin also would be great.

Chaps. 3–4. Paul's mother speaks to him, tells him she knows where he has been, and begs him to stop before it is too late. Paul is angry and says he has been visiting with one who is ill. The mother is not deceived, and once again begs him not to do anything wrong. He angrily insists that he knows what is right and what is wrong for him. He goes to bed, and reviews his life—and his feelings for Agnes. He admits to himself that he loves her and he knows she loves him. He reflects on his life as a seminarist, when his mother worked as a kitchen drudge so that he might attend. During these years he met the prostitute, MARIA PASKA, and visited her several times. However, after he took his vows of chastity he never even entertained a thought of violating them—until he felt the mysterious, wonderful attraction of Agnes.

Chaps. 5–6. Paul's mother awakens him for morning mass. With grim determination he writes a note of farewell to Agnes, giving it to his mother to deliver. He goes to the Church, where his sacristan, ANTIOCHUS, awaits him. Antiochus wants to become a priest also. A message comes that an old hunter of the hills, NICODEMUS, is dying, and the priest is needed. Antiochus returns to the presbytery with the priest's mother. Thinking of Agnes's wealth and her property, the mother almost unconsciously asks aloud why priests are not allowed to marry. Paul and Antiochus set out but when they reach the hunter's cabin he has disappeared.

Chaps. 7–8. Nicodemus has fled to his hut, halfway up the mountain. Before Paul sets out for there, a young widow comes in with her daughter, NINA MASIA. She says the girl is possessed by a demon and begs the priest to exorcize it. Paul does not believe in demons that inhabit human bodies, but he reads a passage that deals with the exorcizing of devils and the child calms quickly. He reflects that the only demon is the one in himself. He goes with Antiochus to the old hunter's hut and administers the final sacrament. Then Paul asks to be taken to see Antiochus's mother and Antiochus is excited at the thought of the honor Paul will do his mother's little wineshop by visiting it. Paul actually wants to ask Antiochus's parents if they are very sure he wants to become a priest. On the way back to the village, Paul notes signs of festivity. The villagers are celebrating his defeat of the devils in Nina Masia's body, which they consider a true miracle. There are fireworks and feasting, and the wine shop of Antiochus's mother does a fine business. Paul decides to ask some of the revelers home with him, so that he may be sure of keeping away from Agnes that night. He feels that he is saved if he can get through the night without seeing her.

Chaps. 9–10. The men who go back with the priest to his house leave early. Antiochus has waited because the priest wanted to see his mother, and together they go out. Maria Maddelena goes to bed, praying that her son will not go to the woman this night. She is filled with a premonition that he will, however. At the wine shop, Paul tries to tell Antiochus's mother how momentous a decision it is to set out for the priesthood. She speaks with some acerbity, and says that Antiochus can do as he wishes. Antiochus declares that he wants to be a priest, and thus his fate is decided. On leaving the shop, Paul sees one of Agnes's servants, who tells him that her mistress is ill. She fell, and they found her lying unconscious and

bleeding from the nose. Will the priest not come and see her? Paul is tempted to go, but at length says that he will not. He bids the servant go home, and return if a serious need arises.

Agnes and Paul

Chaps. 11–12. Paul tells his mother that Agnes is ill. He exaggerates her illness, because he so desperately wants to see his beloved again. His mother tells him to do as his conscience dictates, and he goes to Agnes. She asks him almost angrily why he has come, and refuses to believe that he has forsworn her because of his fear of God. It is his fear of man, and public opinion. And he has come back, not because she is presumably ill, but because he loves her, as she loves him. Desperately, passionately, he falls into her arms and kisses her. She thinks that they will go away together, and the world will forgive them. Paul tries to explain that he offers her eternal spiritual love, but that they must not think of anything else. When she is convinced that he is in earnest, she tells him that he must then get out of the village that very night. He protests that he has to say mass the next morning, and cannot possibly go so soon. She then declares that if he does not, she will denounce him publicly in the church as a seducer of women. She is deadly serious, and he knows that she is. His only hope of appeasing her is to accede to her demand, or to enter into a life of darkest sin. He goes home.

Chaps. 13–14. Paul tells himself that Agnes will not carry out her threat, but by the time he wakes in the morning his conviction has reversed itself and he feels certain that Agnes will do as she threatened. He is tempted to feign illness, but this will only postpone the inevitable. He sets out for the church, but before he leaves he tells his mother of Agnes's threat. She too is terrified, but slowly she gathers her cloak and scarf about her and proceeds to the church. Paul hears the confessions of women who wish to take communion, and the scent of lavender on their clothing brings Agnes terribly near to him. He begins the Mass. His mother is there, stiff and pallid, suffering with him. Mother and son both look toward Agnes, waiting for the moment when she will rise and approach the altar rail to utter her denunciation. The suspense mounts, and with it the inner tensions of both mother and son. The communion is served, and Agnes thinks of what she is about to do. She is denouncing herself no less than the priest, and she knows that the people of this village have always respected her family—the nobles of the region. As she meditates, and as the mass drones on to its conclusion, she knows that she cannot do what she has planned, regardless of how bitter she may feel. The priest turns his eye in her direction frequently. Finally the mass is over and Agnes gets to her feet. The priest believes that she is about to utter her denunciation, and so does his mother. Both are transfixed. Agnes kneels, crosses herself, arises, and turns to leave the church. She has said nothing. A woman shrieks; Maria Maddelena is dead. Her son rushes to her side; he knows she has died of the suspense. In his misery and guilt, his eyes meet the eyes of Agnes, across the width of the church. There is nothing to say.

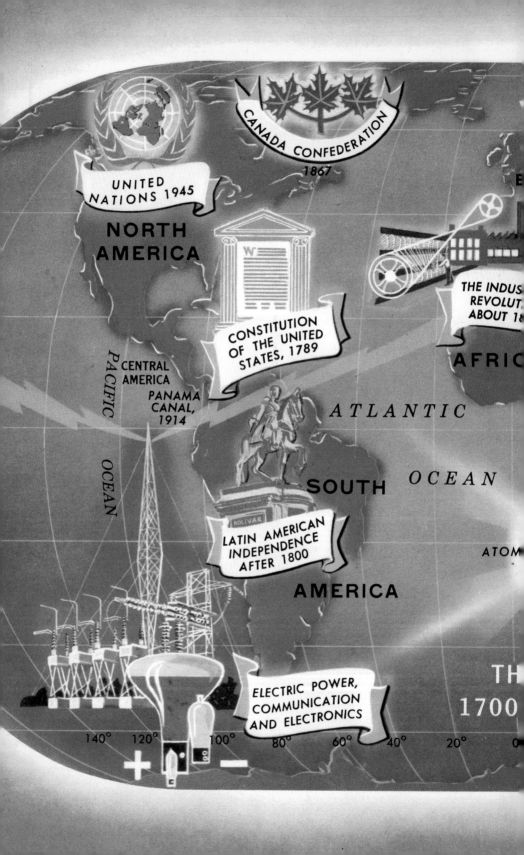

CANADA CONFEDERATION
1867

UNITED
NATIONS 1945

NORTH
AMERICA

THE INDUS
REVOLUT
ABOUT 18

W

CONSTITUTION
OF THE UNITED
STATES, 1789

AFRIC

PACIFIC

CENTRAL
AMERICA

PANAMA
CANAL,
1914

ATLANTIC

OCEAN

OCEAN

BOLIVAR

LATIN AMERICAN
INDEPENDENCE
AFTER 1800

SOUTH

ATOM

AMERICA

TH
1700

ELECTRIC POWER,
COMMUNICATION
AND ELECTRONICS

140°   120°   100°   80°   60°   40°   20°   0